Bill Crozier
Minnesota City
Minnesota 55959

D1495236

The Asians

The Asians
Their Heritage and Their Destiny

Fifth Edition

Paul Thomas Welty

J. B. Lippincott Company

Philadelphia

New York / San Jose / Toronto

Fifth Edition

Copyright © 1976, 1973, 1970, 1966, 1963 by J. B. Lippincott Company.

Paperbound: ISBN 0-397-47359-1
Clothbound: ISBN 0-397-47358-3

Library of Congress Catalog Card Number 76-27357

Printed in the United States of America

135798642

Library of Congress Cataloging in Publication Data

Welty, Paul Thomas.
  The Asians.

  Bibliography: p.
  Includes index.
  1. Asia. 2. Asia—Social life and customs. I. Title.
DS5.W44 1976   309.1'5   76-27357
ISBN 0-397-47358-3
ISBN 0-397-47359-1 pbk.

contents

Foreword *vii*

Prologue *1*

1 The Humanity of Asia *7*

2 Asians Look at Americans *13*

3 The Physical and Economic Setting *21*

4 The Asian Village *39*

5 Ideology, Society, and Politics *49*

6 South Asia *58*

7 The Ideology of India *65*

8 Hinduism *68*

9 Buddhism *78*

10 Social Life in India *86*

11 Caste in India *89*

12 The Family in India *101*

13 The Woman of India *108*

14 Politics in India *117*

v

15 Pakistan and Bangladesh   131

16 Islam   138

17 East Asia   152   *12-10*

18 Chinese Ideology   158

19 Confucianism   163

20 Taoism   176

21 Legalism   183

22 Buddhism in China   190

23 Chinese Social Life   195

24 Gentry and Peasantry in China   198

25 The Clan in China   209

26 The Family in China   217

27 Politics in China   228

28 Korea   250

29 Japan   255

30 Japanese Ideology   257

31 Shinto   261

32 Buddhism in Japan   270

33 The Japanese Family   274

34 The Japanese Woman   286

35 Politics in Japan   296

36 Southeast Asia   313

37 Religion in Southeast Asia   320

38 Social Life in Southeast Asia   330

39 Politics in Southeast Asia   337

40 Asians Are People with a Destiny   354

Selected References   361

Index   377

foreword

A number of American universities have for
some time been the leading centers in the world
for the study of Asian societies. Work on Asia at
the graduate or more advanced undergraduate
level has been sufficiently widespread to produce a considerable demand for suitable textbooks and has been going on long enough to
produce a number of highly competent scholars
to write them.

Interest in the study of Asia at less advanced
levels is more recent. People have come increasingly to feel that Asia is so important in the
modern world that a good general education
should give some knowledge of Asian societies
as well as of Western societies. Consequently,

courses on Asia are being started at high school and beginning college levels. For this it is much harder to find suitable textbooks, partly because the demand has existed for a shorter time and, more important, because a textbook at this level is harder to write. A suitable book needs to discuss some rather profound issues briefly and in simple language. It has to convey to a student brought up in a highly industrialized society the very different conditions of life which prevail over most of Asia, and it has to deal with some fundamental problems of cultural differences in order to overcome widespread misconceptions among people who have not thought clearly about these problems—a category which has included men in responsible positions as well as high school and college students.

The failure to understand cultural differences leads to a pair of fallacious beliefs. On the one hand, people start with the correct assumption of a common humanity and jump to the false conclusion that the differences between Western culture and the various Asian cultures are superficial, that the social sciences as worked out for Western societies can be applied with comparatively little change to Asian societies or that their political problems can be discussed in terms of comparatively simple analogies with the West. On the other hand, people start with the correct assumption that there are quite profound differences between Asian and Western societies and jump to the false conclusion that Asians are fundamentally different in nature from people of European descent.

In fact, the wide differences between the ways in which people behave in different societies can be explained by differences in their institutions and forms of organization and by the differences in their traditional systems of belief. There may be real differences in predominant temperament between different races, but a large part of the differences in patterns of behavior between different societies can be explained in terms of a common human nature influenced by different social institutions and different ideologies.

It follows that the most important task of a book introducing Asia to the American student is to give some understanding of the social and economic environment in which most Asians live and of the various systems of thought which influence their approach to present-day problems, just as the thinking of people in a Western culture is influenced by their environment and traditions. (It is, of course, important to keep clear the distinction between saying that certain factors influence people's thinking and saying that these factors determine their thinking. In many Asian societies the educated elite has taken the lead in rejecting important parts of the traditional system, but, even so, the form of the reaction has been influenced by the tradition it was reacting against.)

A book which has succeeded in this task will have given students a foundation on which they can build an increasing understanding of Asia as they acquire more detailed information. A book which has not provided this foundation may impart a lot of miscellaneous knowledge about Asia but will not have given any real understanding.

It is the great merit of *The Asians* that it puts its main emphasis on this most important and most difficult task, while also giving the main outlines of geography, history, politics and government, for the main areas of Asia from Pakistan round to Japan. It is, perhaps, not too difficult to give an American student some understanding of the daily life of a typical Asian in various areas, but it is extremely difficult to give in clear and simple language a short account of a complex system of religion of social philosophy. However, the reader will find such accounts of Islam, Hinduism, Buddhism, traditional Chinese social philosophy, and Japanese Bushido and Shinto. Though such short accounts can obviously only give the outlines of their subjects, they give these outlines clearly and correctly. (I checked the section on Buddhism by asking a friend from a Theravada Buddhist family to read it and he reported that it was a good summary of basic Buddhist beliefs as held and practiced in his part of Southeast Asia.)

Thus, students who use this book to start their study of Asia can obtain not only an outline knowledge of history, geography and politics, but also the basis of a background knowledge of Asian ways of life and ways of thought which can make it possible for them to turn their knowledge about Asia into a real understanding of Asia.

Lindsay of Birker
Professor of Far Eastern Studies
The American University
Washington, D.C.

Prologue

This book has been written to introduce the
people of Asia. It is not possible to tell the complete story about a people so numerous, so diverse, and so ancient, in one relatively short
encounter, but perhaps this introductory survey
will stimulate those unfamiliar with the non-
Western world to want to know the people of
Asia more intimately and more fully. I have
tried in the following pages to give some insight
into the forces that have made the Asians what
they are today. I have broadly sketched the
landscape where they live and work, discussed
their ideologies and ideals, emphasized certain
aspects of their social and political life, and conveyed, I hope, some appreciation of their aspirations and destiny.

To counter any preconceptions which might prevent the Western reader from responding to what follows with a sympathetic and receptive mind, I have first called attention to the Asian people. I have then commented on some of their attitudes toward Americans which, I believe, will reveal something of the high barrier of stereotype and misconception separating the two peoples. Too frequently, when we first meet others of another race and culture, many of us become preoccupied with the differences which distinguish us from them and tend to ignore the fundamental humanness that we share with them. I have long believed that many Western minds have been closed to an understanding of the Asians by the feeling, conscious or unconscious, that they are too alien to be comprehended and too strange ever to become familiar. It is a natural human reaction to exclude the unfamiliar and incomprehensible. If there is anything I want to underscore most heavily in my presentation, it is that I am writing about people, people who are seeking in their own special way for that better life we all desire here and hereafter. I would not want my words on their dissimilar approaches to truth and happiness to obstruct the perception of their questing humanity.

Engaged in a mighty effort to find alternative patterns of life, the Asians of this century are not a static people. New ideas and institutions from elsewhere have been introduced into Asian life and are compelling them to uproot, review, and change treasured conceptions deeply rooted in the past. This process is necessary but torturing, and change and conflict are often found together on the Asian scene today. Sometimes the Asians are able to resolve these conflicts through compromise and adaptation. At other times they protest fiercely in an attempt to preserve the integrity of their own revered traditions. I have tried to show the dynamic character of a people in transition.

I have stressed those qualities of the Asians which in my opinion best illuminate them on an introductory level. For example, I have pictured the external unity which links the Asians together with physical and spiritual bonds, but I have also shown the diversity which distinguishes Asians from one another and is apparent even among those living within the same areas. The Pakistanis and the Indians both live in South Asia and were closely associated for centuries upon a common land, but there are radical differences in their religious viewpoints and in their approaches to life on earth. The Japanese of East Asia borrowed extensively from their Chinese neighbors, but it will become evident in what follows that there are characteristics of the Japanese social and political life which sharply differentiate them from the Chinese of yesterday and today.

I have presented the Asians on a regional and topical basis. Since it has become customary to group the Asian people into the three regions of South Asia, East Asia, and Southeast Asia, I too will introduce them in this order. But there are more cogent reasons for presenting them in this order. The great religions of Hinduism, Buddhism, and Islam went forth from South Asia and ·shaped the minds and cultural landscape in many Asian lands. The human, earthly philosophies of Confucianism and Taoism, originating in China in East Asia, have sometimes played a major role in molding the cultural, social, and political systems of other Asian countries. Culturally and ethnically, the people of Southeast Asia continue to reflect the deep and pervasive influences of the South and East Asians upon their way of life. By knowing something about these people we can better understand the Southeast Asians. In terms of international politics, it is also desirable to meet the people of South and East Asia first, for the largest and most powerful nations are found in these two areas. Their political and military activities affect the lives of all Asians and, for that matter, all mankind.

Within these Asian regions I have focused on topics which I feel are important for an understanding of most of the people in these three areas. Thus, because the vast majority of South Asians live on the Indo-Pakistan subcontinent and there developed conceptions and practices which have influenced multitudes of Asians, I have treated in some detail the ideologies and the social and political life of these people. I have chosen, for example, to underline the development of Pakistan into an independent state and to elaborate on the ideology of Islam which gives meaning and purpose to the life of the Pakistanis and many other Asians. In the case of Sri Lanka (Ceylon), on the other hand, I have elected to point out briefly some of its more important problems and the significance of its location, for most of the Ceylonese are of Indian origin, hold the religions of Buddhism or Hinduism, and are related to the Indians by many social similarities.

In considering East Asia, I have commented in some depth on the ideologies and social and political life of the Chinese and Japanese who are the largest groups in this region. The civilization of the Koreans, though possessing its own distinguishing features, was substantially shaped by the Chinese and, to a certain extent, by the Japanese. I have, therefore, confined my remarks about the Koreans to their unhappy history of invasions and to the economic and political problems they have had to face.

The region of Southeast Asia is partitioned into a variety of countries whose citizens share numerous ethnic, social, and economic characteristics with other Asians but also differ from South and East Asians and from each other. Their concentration on the good earth near the life-giving waters of the river and the sea, and their deep involvement in raising food are typical of the entire Asian scene. But most of them are not driven by the specter of starvation which is the feared comrade of so many of their fellow Asians elsewhere. Millions of them share with other Asians the name of Buddhist, but their interpretation of Buddhism demands more of them than does the interpretation accepted by their neighbors. They, like other Asians, stir restlessly when the cry of colonialism resounds among them, but the emotional appeal of nationalism has widened the cleavages which keep them apart.

I have surveyed Southeast Asia on a regional basis rather than country by country. There are too many countries to introduce individually and with justice within the restricted space of this introduction. Consequently, I have dared to attempt a brief regional synthesis of their religious, social, and political life. This method of treatment will necessarily result in a number of generalizations, but I will be more than satisfied if it stimulates a search for a more detailed knowledge of these people among the interesting and informative books that have been written especially about them.

I have made every effort to achieve the great value of simplicity in this introduction. I am primarily concerned with the presentation of a general picture. In the light of my purpose, it is impractical and most difficult to document adequately every statement or to include everything pertaining to the complexity of the Asian scene. My observations flow from the personal and priceless experience of living, working, and sharing pleasures and sorrows, successes and failures, with the Asians over a long period of time. Although complete knowledge of them can never be mine, I have related what I think is significant in their way of life, in their thoughts, and in their yearnings. My words are intended to be preliminary rather than final, and I trustfully write with the expectation that those seeking a deeper and greater knowledge of the Asian people will find in this beginning a helpful introduction to more detailed commentators.

It is my strong conviction that all of us should have some fundamental knowledge of the Asians. It is important because of our common humanity. It is frequently profitable and always stimulating to contemplate and savor alternative approaches to happiness. But more immediate and compelling is the goading fact that their fate is inextricably involved with ours. Their ideas, their feelings, their tensions, their struggles, in one way or another impinge upon our daily lives with a vigor and impact undreamed of only a relatively short time ago. I call upon the Japanese, Chinese, Koreans, Laotians, Vietnamese, and other Asians to witness the truth of this statement.

For more than a hundred years the nations of the West influenced the policies of most Asian nations, and their fate was to a large degree dependent upon the Westerner. In earlier times Asian powers had been at least as strong as those of the West. The Mongol invasions reached the Adriatic in the thirteenth century, the Turks besieged Vienna in 1683, and Chinese naval expeditions reached East Africa in the fifteenth century. But from the sixteenth century on, Western society started to change and by the end of the eighteenth century had gained vastly greater power. During the period beginning in the sixteenth century with the sea journeys of the adventurous Portuguese and ending with World War II, the nations of the West struggled to dominate Asia. Portugal, Spain, Holland, France, England, Germany, Russia, and America vied with one another on that continent. By the end of the nineteenth century the great mass of Asia was under their guardianship. It was only natural, then, that Western interests should prevail, overriding the desires of the governed Asians. Their destinies lay in other hands.

The conclusion of World War II brought radical changes for them and for us. One by one Asian nations became independent and Asian statesmen became exclusively occupied with advancing Asian interests. Policies formulated on the basis of Asian interests do not always harmonize with Western conceptions of a good Asian policy, and many of us are often left confused, groping, and upset, by the outcomes of these policies. Our reaction stems in large measure from a lack of knowledge of the feelings, needs, and desires of the Asian people and from a misunderstanding of reality in Asia. Ignorance of Asian realities can lead only to continued antagonisms and possible bloodshed; a comprehension of these realities is essential if conflicts of interest are to be minimized.

These thoughts have spurred me to record something of the heritage and destiny of the Asian peoples. I have sought to write with clarity and simplicity, for my task is to inform, not to confuse or to mystify. I have divided the total picture into manageable parts which lend themselves to careful scrutiny. I have also endeavored to present a synthesis by reuniting the parts and giving meaning to the total scene.

1

The Humanity of Asia

The need today is for philosophers and scholars—
whether in Asia or Europe or Africa or the Americas—
who will address themselves to the human situation.
The need now is to talk not about geographic destiny
but about human destiny.

Norman Cousins

Asia is people. People till Asia's earth, write
Asia's poetry, make Asia's laws, fight Asia's wars,
and dream Asia's dreams. Asians are people with
a destiny. Few Westerners grasp the meaning of
this destiny because few outside Asia fully comprehend the humanity of Asians. They think of
them first as inhabitants of a region called Asia,
and only second as fellow human beings.

The humanity which Asians share with the
rest of mankind is overlooked by most foreigners
in their preoccupation with cultural differences
which distinguish Asians from themselves. This
preoccupation with eye-catching differences
blinds them to the basic human needs, human

7

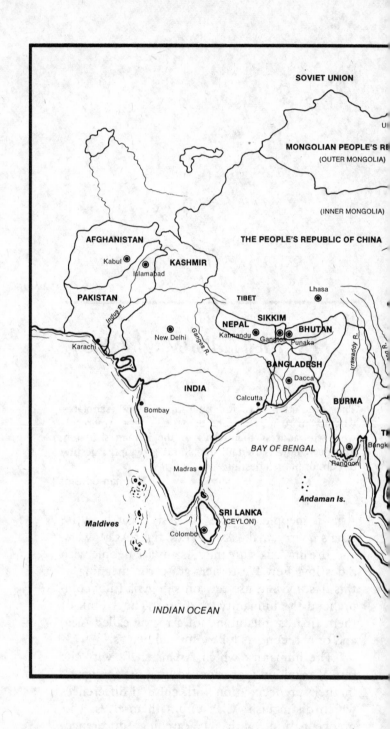

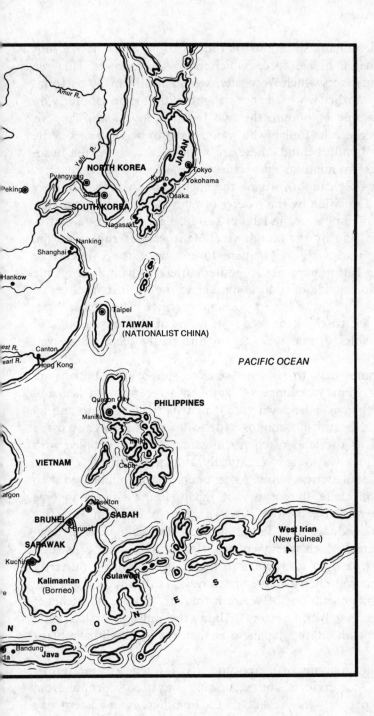

drives, and human aspirations of the Asian people. They do not see the dynamic human forces which move Asians to act. They see only the acts—acts which Westerners would not normally perform. The Asian mother who sells her daughter, the Asian laborer who smokes his pipe of opium, the two Japanese lovers who commit suicide together, the Indian who wanders off to become an ascetic, leaving his family behind—these are some of the acts often head-lined in Western minds as the peculiar substance of Asian humanity.

Most people cannot imagine the anguish of this Asian mother pushed to a decision by the specter of famine. They do not under-stand the harshness of the laborer's life relieved only by a better world given him by the opium pipe. Many cannot appreciate the despair that grips those Japanese lovers when they find every avenue of a future happiness together closed to them. Few people in the world outside of India comprehend the spirit that moves an Indian ascetic to live a life of constant sacrifice. Thus, most West-erners are led to think of Asians in terms of the mysterious and the inscrutable. People who act so differently seem alien, even frightening.

It becomes easy to reduce Asians to stereotypes. Indians are "mystical," "cow-worshippers," and, until recently, "a peaceful people." Japan is a land where all men have buck teeth and all women wear beautiful kimonos. Not so long ago it was also often thought of as the land of cherry blossom festivals, peopled with soldiers who always fight fanatically and make suicide charges. Two prominent writers about Asian people have commented with insight upon these stereotypes of Japan. Frank Gibney in *Five Gentlemen of Japan* writes: "It is hard to pour them [the five Japanese individuals he is describing] into the rigid casts of 'Japa-nese character' which foreigners at different times have construct-ed. . . . It is hard to fit them into the land of Madame Butterfly and neverending cherry blossom festivals, faithfully and gullibly described by generations of Western tourists." James A. Michener in *The Floating World* states: "About the only generalization I could accept about the Japanese is that they will all have black hair."

Thinking in terms of stereotypes has influenced Americans—and others—to draw a line separating "Eastern" people from "Western" people. On one side of the line there is an Eastern way of life—alien, quaint, and mysterious. On the other side, there is a Western way of life—human, normal, and understandable. This belief is classically expressed in Kipling's statement: "East is East, and West is West, and never the twain shall meet."

Kipling, like many today, was unfamiliar with the process known as cultural diffusion. Both Easterners and Westerners have borrowed material products, as well as ideas, mores, and other intangibles, from each other and adapted them to their own cultures. Many non-Asians have learned to taste and like the many spices that come from Asia, enjoy the coolness of silk pajamas upon the skin, and delight in the green depths of their jade rings. Pajamas are a cultural import from India, while silk and jade rings originated in China and Southeast Asia. The carved teakwood chest, the patterned handwoven rug, the small, exquisitely carved ivory statue have been familiar Asian objects in American homes for generations—so familiar that they often go unnoticed now. The clean functional lines of contemporary homes and furniture are distinct influences from Japan. Chinese ideas about education and government have influenced both French and American scholars, and Buddhist philosophy has found a home in many Western countries.

Eastern products and Eastern ideas have become an integral part of the Western way of life. This is because they are products made by *human* hands to meet *human* needs and *human* wants, and humanity knows no geographical boundaries. They are ideas formulated by *human* minds to satisfy *human* aspirations, and Easterners and Westerners share a common humanity.

Products and ideas fashioned by Western hands and Western minds have been welcomed and adopted in all the countries of Asia. There is nothing incongruous about Buddhist monks chanting thousand-year-old scriptures in new air-conditioned buildings. Do not Christian monks chant thousand-year-old scriptures in new air-conditioned buildings? There is nothing unreasonable about Asian soldiers fighting with modern weapons. Do not modern soldiers elsewhere fight with modern weapons? There is nothing unusual about the modern Asian agricultural agent urging the peasant to adopt more efficient farming practices. American farmers, too, had to be prodded to adopt modern practices. In the East today, a steel mill stands beside a field in which a man is pulling a plough; trucks share the streets with men and women bent under heavy burdens; modern air-conditioned apartment buildings shade small stifling huts crowded with people and vermin; jet planes swish over an Asian farmer pushing a squealing wheelbarrow in which sit a man and a pig, and the farmer looks up. wonders, and accepts this latest creation of humanity. In each instance the goal and function is the same, only the method differs.

There is no longer, if there ever was, an Eastern or Western destiny—there is only a human destiny. The destiny of the Asian people can be comprehended only by those who know that Asians are moved by the dynamic forces of human needs, human wants, and human ideals, that they are conscious of the shape and magnitude of their destiny and are determined to mold this destiny to meet their needs.

2

Asians Look at Americans

Why do Americans know so little about India, when we Indians really understand the United States?
Indian Member of Parliament

Many Asians are convinced that they can recognize an American anywhere, that they understand the American mind, and that their conception—and, sometimes, abhorrence—of many American practices and principles is correct.

Asians often have a feeling of affection for Americans. In the recent past they thought of America not only as a vigorous, youthful country but as a country where a new and shining way of life was practiced. They considered the United

States their friend among the great Western powers and the only great nation where Asians could find a sympathetic understanding of their revolutionary ideals. Was not America born of revolution? Was it not a colony that had successfully cast off the greatest colonizing power of that time? Did it not live by a Constitution that guaranteed freedom and the opportunity to pursue happiness in one's own way? Was this not the land of Washington, Lincoln, Jefferson, and Wilson—American statesmen still venerated by Asians as great, living supporters of their dreams of freedom? Educated Asians know American history well. It has inspired many Asian statesmen to strike out against colonial chains. No American awakened the latent nationalism of the Asian people more than Woodrow Wilson when he promulgated his famous fourteen points and proclaimed the right of all peoples to self-determination. Probably the greatest modern friend of Asians, in Asian eyes, was Franklin D. Roosevelt. They felt that he embodied the revolutionary traditions of early America, and some Asian students wept in their rooms and on the streets when they heard of his death. It was as through they had lost a kind and warmhearted friend.

Many Asians believed that they drew with Americans on common sources of strength. Thus, Madame Pandit, the sister of Jawaharlal Nehru, quoted the words of Lincoln to describe the source of India's strength: "What constitutes the bulwark of our own liberty and independence? It is not our frowning battlements, our bristling seacoast, our army and our navy. These are not our reliance against tyranny. All of these may be turned against us without making us weaker for the struggle. Our reliance is in the love of liberty which God has planted in us. Our defense is in the spirit which prizes liberty as the heritage of all men, in all lands everywhere." An official Pakistan document, *The Constitution, A Study,* began: "Democracy, in the classic phrase of Abraham Lincoln, is 'government of the people, by the people and for the people.'"

Prior to World War II Asians did not associate America with the resented nations of Europe. America was a former colony. What did she have in common with the empire-inspired countries of Western Europe? America was not given to colonizing, at least in Asia—the Philippines were acquired as a result of war with a colonizing power and more in the way of an accident than an intentional grab of Asian land—and American statesmen had stated over and over again that they were utterly opposed to the imperialistic practices of the Western powers in Asia. America stood like a giant in the West, the embodiment of all that was good and fine in the Western hemisphere.

"The Great American Tragedy in Asia"

Only since World War II have Americans come to be regarded with wary eyes by many Asians. American strength has become suspect. American technology has become a symbol of materialism, and American economic help has been interpreted to mean the entrance of a new exploiter into Asian fields. Some view Americans as a possible threat to their national independence and dignity, whereas once America was the one country most Asians counted on to help them in their climb to national greatness.

These Asians have begun to think of America and the nations of Western Europe in the same terms. They state that, during World War II, America showed itself ready to sacrifice Asia, provided that Europe could be saved, and that America reserved the atom bomb for use on Japan rather than on Germany. After the war they felt themselves forgotten on their war-ravaged lands, while American billions were poured out to bolster the tottering economies of Western Europe. NATO was formed, and American troops and treaties guaranteed the borders and independence of Western European nations, and even of Greece and Turkey, from outside attack. Some Asians felt that Americans guaranteed nothing in Asia except occupied Japan, South Korea, the Philippine Islands, and the vast seas that washed their coasts.

Thus, in a number of Asian minds, America gradually became associated with Western Europe. When this happened, America came to be regarded with all the old hatreds, antagonisms, suspicions, and fears with which Asians had long viewed the nations of Europe. Also, since America was the greatest Western power, she became to some Asians the leader and main supporter of those whom they resented as the old exploiters of Asia. Thus, slowly, inexorably, almost unnoticed, at least in the United States, America took over the "European Imperialist's" role as the whipping boy for all the ills of Asia. By a tragic historical irony, a great segment of the world's people, who had never really experienced any American imperialism, cast the United States in the role of cohort and champion of Asia's former Western governors. This changing role from one of friend to enemy in the minds of many Asians might be called "The Great American Tragedy in Asia." The aftermath of this tragedy will be with Americans for a long time; it is so easy to destroy, and so difficult to restore.

Publications and the recent American involvement in the war in Vietnam have managed to convince an amazing number of Asians that Americans are too ready to embark upon military adventures. Asians are, for the most part, extremely desirous of maintaining the peace of the world. They realize that any war must inevitably involve them sooner or later, and they prefer it as late as possible. Asians need generations of peace to solve their enormous economic, political, and social problems. To have the greatest power in the world poised on the brink of war, as they picture America, frightens and angers them. Of course, Americans do not want war either, but too few Asians believe this.

To the peasant, laborer, teacher, intellectual, and housewife in Asia, the word "American" conveys the idea of money, vast sums of money. Not so many years ago some Asians believed the story that American streets were paved with gold. The Chinese had received fabulous reports of the gold strikes in California, and they called this state the "Golden Mountain." They still do. This conception of the abundance of gold in California came gradually to be applied to all of the United States. Most Asians still believe that Americans are very, very rich. In many areas of Asia there is a special price reserved for Americans who want to buy Asian goods. Asians reason that it is only fair that those who have so much should pay more and share a part of their great abundance with them. Movies, books, and even official propaganda put out by the United States have helped to reinforce this attitude of the Asian people. What American is not staggered at times by the lavish display of living he or she sees in some movies? The mink, the sable, the wonderful, comfortable house, the magnificent furnishings, the great spread of food, the long gleaming cars arouse the yearning and envy of Americans as well as Asians. The difference is that Americans know that only a very few of the people in this country live in great luxury, while the Asians believe that most Americans live this way. All over Asia the male definition of paradise runs something like this—"a Japanese wife, Chinese food, and an American home." Communist propaganda describing the "poor American worker" has failed to make an impression. Western propaganda which tries to connect a well-fed look and luxurious appearance with a democratic way of life merely compounds the Asian's misconception of Americans: the blood, the labors, the self-denials that are inevitable in the birth and growth of any real democracy are not a part of the Asian's American image. They believe that, for Americans, making money is the most important occupation and that their main goal is to become wealthy. Frank Moraes, editor of India's largest newspaper, *The Times of India*, reported that "In many Eastern eyes America mistakes the means for the end. By exalting private enterprise and the individual it makes the acquisition of wealth for wealth's sake an end in itself."

Some Asians have transferred this conception of Americans to the Asian scene. Disregarding the number of schools, orphanages, and hospitals Americans have established overseas, they think that Americans look upon Asians primarily as objects which may or may not contribute to their materialistic advancement, as a source of labor, and as pawns in the game of war and politics who are less important than the strategic areas they occupy. In other words, these Asians believe that the materialistic bias of the American people blinds them to the humanity of Asians. Americans are accused of seeing only a dollar bill when regarding the Asian scene; they do not see the human being paying the bill. It is ironic that the same dollar bill obscures the richness of America's humanity from these Asian viewers of the American scene.

Asian intellectuals consider the history of the Westerner in Asia marked only by economic exploitation and by political maneuvering with no thought to Asian interests. They describe it as a chronicle of wars fought with and without Asians, but never for Asians. They indignantly accuse Western entrepreneurs of having bulled into their lands accompanied by soldiers and gunboats and lured by Asian products and raw materials. They buttress their case by referring to the manner in which their magnificent cultures were ignored. That foreigners would overlook a culture built with such tremendous effort over the centuries was to have been expected of men obsessed by greed; but some foreigners went further and condemned, reviled, and rejected it with violence, and this was barbarous, uncivilized, and inexcusable. Asians point to the growth of large merchant-sponsored cities on Asian soil which became the gathering places for foreigners and the centers of Western political and economic power in Asia. The handicraft industry of Asia was almost ruined by the flood of cheap machine-made products from the West, and English arms even protected the smuggling of opium into China in order to produce a favorable balance of trade. Asians were convinced then that the only morality the Westerners possessed was a profit morality. This conviction is still stubbornly maintained.

In recent decades too many Asians have tended to associate Americans with the economic exploitation which was fashioned by Europeans, not Americans, in the seventeenth, eighteenth, nineteenth, and twentieth centuries. In the eyes of many Asians, America has become the great modern symbol of a materialistic people with imperialistic goals and ideals.

American materialism is contrasted in Asian minds with Asian "spirituality." Despite the prominent part played in their history and economy by the wealthy literati of China, the samurai of Japan, and the rajahs of India, Asians feel that they possess a more elevated spirit than the Americans. The Indians point to their religious practices and their teaching that all earthly things are ephemeral and transitory as evidence of their basic attitude toward material objects. They cite their saintly men who have given up all worldly possessions in order to bring themselves closer to the goal of spiritual freedom. The Chinese refer to their emphasis upon social relations and upon the necessity for individuals to play their appointed roles in society. The group, the family, the society, is most important; the individual is secondary, and so is any profit he or she makes. The profit is for the family and, more recently, the state. The Japanese call attention to their divine ancestors, their Shinto shrines, their beauty-laden country, as reflecting the essence of their lives. Those who practice Zen Buddhism prefer frugality to abundance, simplicity to ostentation, and quiet meditation to the ceaseless search for material gain. During World War II the Japanese believed they would win "a victory of spirit over matter." American reliance upon material things was inferior to the Japanese reliance upon the spirit. Perhaps a war was started and lost because the American spirit was too well hidden from Asian eyes.

Other Conceptions of Americans

Some Asians have neatly catalogued Americans as "impulsive," "uncultured," "lacking in judgment," and "vigorous." They contend that Americans are overly quick to respond to actions which affect their individual or national interests. Sometimes such quickness creates a feeling of admiration and joy in Asian hearts, as when American generosity comes rapidly and lavishly to the aid of victims of a natural catastrophe. At other times such impulsive responses cause uneasiness, as when Americans seem too eager to offer military solutions to Asian disputes. They feel that this "impulsive" characteristic is associated with a "lack of judgment," and they caution Americans to wait and meditate awhile before taking action. They frequently feel called upon to advise Americans to study carefully all the pros and cons of a statement or a policy before publicizing it to the world, lest anything said by this powerful nation disturb the peace of the world.

They look upon Americans as citizens of a very young country which has not yet had time to build an enduring culture, and they contrast American youth with Asian age. Asia is an old land of settled people. For them age denotes maturity and wisdom in both the individual and the nation. They prize the gift of time which gave them so many centuries to think, to err, to suffer, to experience, to change, to reject, to reform, to change again, and finally to piece together a civilization which worked and withstood the restlessness of humanity. They feel that this accomplishment—the creation of a host of years—has left them with a maturity of judgment and the perspective of age. They sorrow that Americans have not had this advantage, especially since they hold such economic and political power. It is interesting to note that one of the major criticisms often levied by Americans against Asians is that they are slow to act and to make decisions. It appears that too much time or too little time can also contribute to misunderstanding among people.

Asian newspapers generally play up incidents of discrimination against minority groups in the United States, and they resent the sense of racial superiority which this discrimination implies. The Indians were and are the victims of white supremacy laws in South Africa. Under the British they were discriminated against in clubs, employment opportunities, and promotions. The Japanese and Chinese have both experienced American exclusion laws, and, during World War II, the removal of Japanese Americans from the west coast was well-publicized in Asia. Most Asians privately concede that discrimination is a universal human issue, for most Asian countries are also plagued by minority problems.

It is a characteristic of stereotypes that they do not convey a true picture of all individuals. Asians also find Americans baffling because they are continually meeting Americans who are religious, idealistic, and dedicated to humanitarian goals; interested in money as a means to an end; not given to using any means to reach a desired goal, but only those means which in their eyes are right; cultured, sophisticated, and courteous; tactful, forbearing, patient, devoted to working for peace.

For both Americans and Asians, the important and fruitful task of this time is to understand their common humanity and their common goals and aspirations. In the pages that follow an attempt has been made to advance this understanding by showing where and how the Asian people live and what they believe and by discussing selected aspects of their economic, social, and political ways of life.

3

The Physical and Economic Setting

Asia is not just the biggest and most continental or highest or wettest or most diverse of continents. It is interesting because it is the most human.

George B. Cressey

The region called Asia in this book stretches from Pakistan on the west to Japan on the east and from the northern borders of China to the southernmost boundaries of Indonesia. Within these borders are included the countries and territories of India, Pakistan, Bangladesh, Sri Lanka (Ceylon), the People's Republic of China (Mainland), The Republic of China (Taiwan),

George B. Cressey, *The Patterns of Asia,* edited by Norton Ginsburg (Englewood Cliffs, New Jersey: Prentice-Hall, 1958).

Population of Asian Countries

Country	Population	Area Sq. Mi.
BANGLADESH	75,000,000	55,126
BHUTAN	1,050,000	19,305
BRUNEI	150,000	2,226
BURMA	30,000,000	261,789
CAMBODIA	8,000,000	69,898
CHINA (MAINLAND)	850,000,000	3,691,502
TAIWAN	16,000,000	13,592
HONG KONG	4,300,000	398
INDIA	600,000,000	1,229,919
INDONESIA	136,000,000	735,268
JAPAN	110,500,000	143,574
LAOS	3,500,000	91,428
MACAO	300,000	6
MALAYSIA	12,000,000	128,328
MALDIVES	123,000	115
MAURITIUS	900,000	787
MONGOLIA (PEOPLE'S REPUBLIC)	1,500,000	604,247
NEPAL	12,500,000	54,362
NORTH KOREA	15,500,000	46,768
PAKISTAN	70,000,000	342,700
PHILIPPINES	42,500,000	115,707
SINGAPORE	2,300,000	226
SOUTH KOREA	35,000,000	38,023
SRI LANKA (CEYLON)	14,000,000	25,332
THAILAND	41,500,000	198,455
VIETNAM	44,000,000	126,436

Population Distribution per Square Mile

over 250   over 100   over 50

INDIAN OCEA

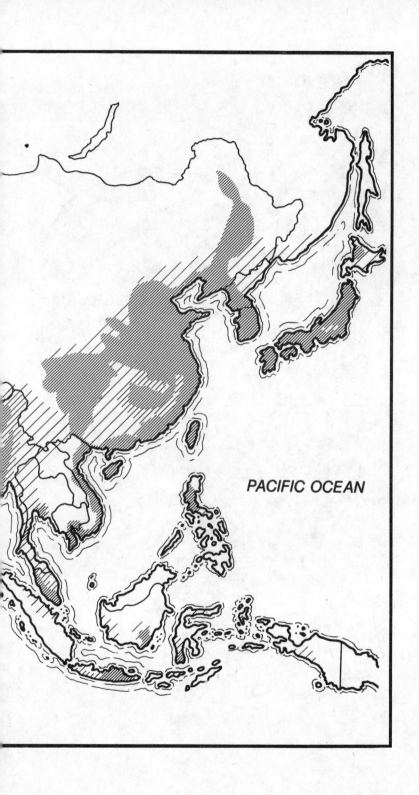

PACIFIC OCEAN

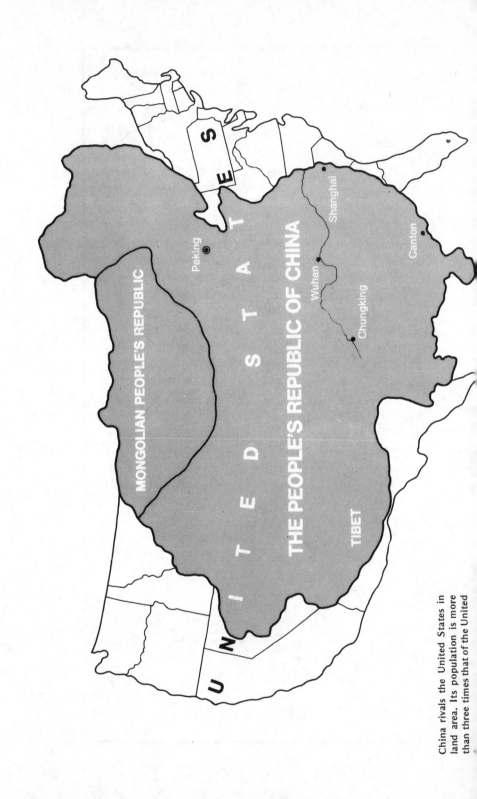

China rivals the United States in land area. Its population is more than three times that of the United

North Korea, South Korea, Japan, The Mongolian People's Republic, Burma, Thailand, Cambodia, Laos, Vietnam, Malaysia, Philippines, Indonesia, Nepal, Bhutan, Brunei, Singapore, Hong Kong, Macao, and the Maldive Islands.

This region has a total area of almost eight million square miles. Some of the individual countries within it are larger than many American and European nations. The People's Republic of China rivals the United States in size. India is larger than any European country except Russia. Indonesia is more than three times the size of France and extends east and west approximately the same distance as that separating the east and west coasts of the United States.

From the western boundaries of Pakistan to the disputed eastern borders of Indonesia, the distance is about fifty-two hundred miles. From the northern borders of mainland China to the southern boundaries of Indonesia, the distance is slightly over four thousand miles. The shortest route from New Delhi, the capital of India, to Peking, the capital of China, is around twenty-five hundred miles. The distance from Karachi, in Pakistan, to Tokyo, is approximately forty-three hundred miles. It is about thirty-two hundred miles from Jakarta, the capital of Indonesia, to Seoul, the capital of South Korea.

Almost two billion persons live in Asia. Of these about a billion and a half live in China and India. This means that approximately every fourth person in the world is Chinese; more than one out of every three persons is either Indian or Chinese.

Generally speaking, wherever there is arable land in Asia, the land is also crowded. Population density in many areas exceeds two thousand persons per square mile of arable land. The greatest concentrations of people are found near the rivers and the coasts. The Chinese live for the most part around the Yangtze, Yellow, and West rivers and along the eastern and southern coasts. The Indians group themselves along the Ganges and Brahmaputra river systems of northern India, and along the rivers and coasts of peninsular India. The deltas of these rivers also support great numbers of people in Bangladesh. In Japan, the densely settled areas are in the central and southern half of the island of Honshu and on the islands of Shikoku and Kyushu. Much of Burma's population is located in the Irrawaddy River delta, and the Mekong River nourishes great groups of Cambodians and Vietnamese. In Indonesia, the islands of Java, Madura, and Bali contain most of the

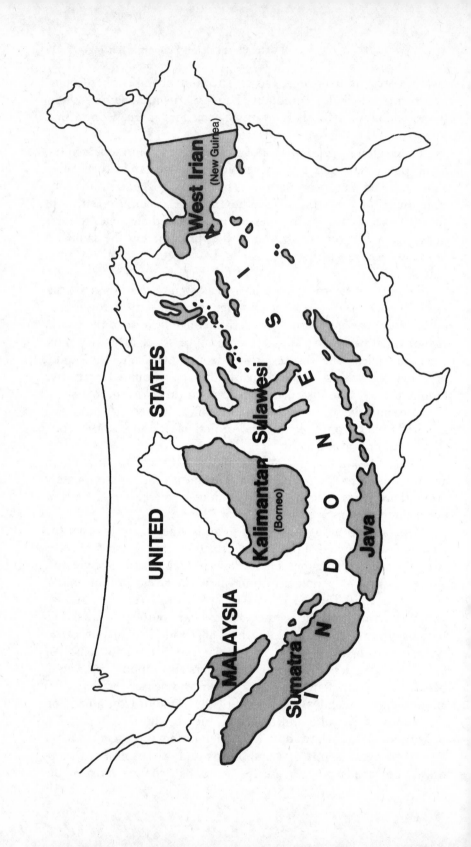

people. Most Asians are concentrated in small sections of their total land area.

In many Asian countries the birth rate is quite high. In Burma, India, Indonesia, Pakistan, the Philippines, Bangladesh, and Nepal the birth rate ranges from forty to fifty per thousand population. But eighteen per thousand in Japan compares favorably to the birth rate in the United States and other Western countries. It has been estimated, however, that the annual average birth rate in Asia is around thirty per thousand, as compared with less than twenty per thousand in Europe. These figures are approximations and subject to change.

The problem of overpopulation plagues every nation except rice-surplus areas like Thailand and Upper Burma. Elsewhere in Asia there is not enough arable land to feed the fast increasing population. With China showing an approximate net increase of twelve to fifteen million per year, and India an increase of almost thirteen million per year, to quote but two figures, it is obvious that the necessity to provide for these extra mouths harasses the people concerned with feeding them. Many observers believe that overpopulation is the paramount problem of Asia.

The Quest for Food

For most Asians the quest for food is continuous and demanding. The unending search for food is the familiar and traditional aspect of Asian life, and agriculture has been the main occupation of Asians for thousands of years. They are primarily interested in obtaining a food supply for themselves and only secondarily in producing crops for a commercial market. Because their fields are generally small and subdivided into scattered parcels and there are many mouths to feed, they are forced to demand much of the land, and this intensive cultivation has encouraged a higher concentration of population in Asia than in other agricultural areas of the world. This system of cultivation required a greater population in order to produce more, which in turn required a greater amount of crops to feed the growing numbers of people. The arable land of Asia has filled up, and for many there is only the

The three-thousand-mile sweep of Indonesia approximates the distance across the United States from east to west. Over half of Indonesia's population lives on the island of Java.

Much of western Europe can be placed within the South Asian subcontinent. This subcontinent has more than twice the number of people who live in western Europe.

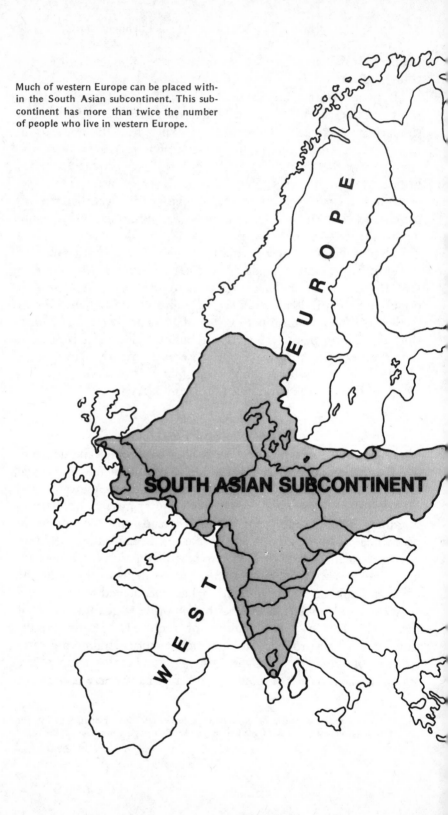

desert, the jungle, and the wastelands left to cultivate. But the system persists in much of Asia, and families continue to multiply, and the quest to feed them becomes even more exacting and arduous.

The Asians' pursuit of food is made harder by physical and social forces which are beyond their power to control. The rains might be delayed or come in too little quantity. Rivers sometimes overflow and destroy the crops of millions of peasants. Locusts, pests of one kind or another, fire, banditry, feuds, wild animals, war, any of a hundred calamities might afflict peasants and destroy their food. Moreover, sickness and the social requirements of funerals, weddings, and other occasions may require an outlay of money so that if a crop is harvested, they must use it for the payment of debts they have incurred because of extraordinary expenses. They live in constant fear that their food may give out before the next harvest, and the threat of starvation is an everpresent reality for millions of Asians.

Many Asians live on the ugly edge of famine. No words can convey the scope and impact of the tragedy of famine. Perhaps it is better this way. Few people can stand the overwhelming shock, the unforgettable memories, and the revulsion that famine leaves with those who witness it. The author can only give the reader some impressions. Row upon row of bodies lying on sidewalks and in gutters, bodies that were once recognizable individuals but now have lost their identity as persons and are merely the common face of hunger. Hopeless eyes and skull-like heads. A village at dusk and a child protesting with wrenching, breaking cries as it tries to suck milk from a dead mother's breast. Weak hands clawing at a few clumps of weeds. A dying man cursing heaven and his fate in a voice almost inaudible. A mother bargaining with one who has rice over the price of one small daughter—she has four other hungry children. She wants four and one-half pounds of rice; he wants to give only four. She receives four pounds of rice for one five-year-old daughter.

These pressures which spring from the physical and social environment cause the Asians to concentrate on the production of grains and cereal crops. Grains are eaten directly, rather than indirectly through the raising of animals, because cereal crops provide more food value if eaten directly than if given to an animal which could then be slaughtered for food. As a result, there is little grass for animals. The water buffalo, cow, bullock, and other work ani-

mals obtain their food from the stubble they can find in the wastelands and on the small dykes separating the fields, a diet which is
supplemented slightly with some cereal grains provided by the
farmer-owner. In some parts of Asia even the work animal is dis-
pensed with, and ploughing and furrowing is done by men and
women with hoes instead of ploughs. The food of a farmer takes
less space then the food of the buffalo or cow. Thus, most Asians
eat grains and vegetables at their daily meals. Even in those parts
of Asia where most families raise pigs, it frequently happens that
when a pig is killed most of the meat is sold for cash, and only a
few scraps are left for the family.

Rice or wheat is the basic food for the majority of the Asian
people. They eat very little meat or eggs, and in the interior, very
little fish. Many think of the Asians as being solely rice eaters.
Rice is the principal food for most of the Asian people, but wheat
is preferred by many others. Rice is the principal crop south of the
Yangtze River in Central China, but north of this river wheat,
millet, and soybeans are the principal crops, and wheat is the
favored food. Thus the saying: "He is a man who eats wheat flour
every day, why should he not have a smooth face!" In South
China, rice is the principal crop, and it is the preferred food. With
the exception of Burma, Thailand, and, prior to World War II,
Indochina, Asian countries are forced to import rice and other
food supplies to make up their food deficiency.

The Asians are always looking for ways and means to stretch
their available food supply as far as possible. One of the means of
making their rice last longer is by eating gruel, or *congee,* which is
a souplike rice dish containing much water but little rice, instead
of a more substantial portion of ordinary cooked rice. Rice gruel
gives a temporary feeling of repletion, but the feeling quickly dis-
sipates when work is required in the fields.

Barley, millet, corn, sorghum, and sweet potatoes are common
foods in Asia. Sweet potatoes have relieved more hunger pangs in
China than perhaps any one single food. They grow in all types of
soil and are prevalent everywhere. Where the American or European child is commonly seen and pictured chewing or sucking a
piece of candy, a Chinese child is frequently occupied in nibbling
at a cooked sweet potato. In North China, sweet potatoes are
planted immediately after the wheat has been harvested. Millet is
not the preferred grain for Asians, but it grows where wheat and
rice cannot be planted and therefore is common where the soil is
not good or where there is a lack of water.

For most Asians food is the center of their lives because they are never sure they will have enough of it to live. There are certain periods of the year when Asians have a chance to eat their fill of good food, as at funerals or weddings and during the sacred or secular festivals, such as New Year's and national holidays, but these periodic feasts are not daily occurrences. It is not surprising that food is often the dominant topic of conversation in Asia. Asians talk about all aspects of food: how to produce it—ploughing, hoeing, weeding, irrigating, harvesting, threshing, hulling, winnowing; the kinds of food to produce—rice, barley, sweet potatoes, wheat, millet, sorghum, soybean, and the hundreds of varieties of vegetables which are grown in Asia; the ways it should be prepared—broiled, steamed, fried, boiled; and the spices and sauces that should season it. Wherever Asians gather, there, sooner or later, either directly or indirectly, the conversation will shift to food.

Modern Asian leaders are striving desperately to solve the food problem besetting their people. Some are attempting to industrialize their nations and to introduce, in the fastest possible way, the new and unfamiliar machine into the lives of the people. But sometimes their goal may not be in the immediate interest of the people they govern. The money or capital to build modern plants and buy modern machines and machine tools comes inevitably from the peasant farmers who comprise the vast majority of the population. Since many of the farmers are living on the edge of famine and barely making enough to feed their families, any increased food tax inevitably pushes them nearer the starvation level. If priority is given to quick industrialization, food problems may afflict the country, as happened in the People's Republic of China. If, on the other hand, the farmers are permitted to keep more of their surplus food, their personal condition is improved but industrialization is delayed.

Some Asian leaders argue that if they can industrialize rapidly it will be possible to take care of surplus people by channeling them into plants and other productive work. This may be true. But industrialization does not come fast enough to take care of the millions now living who have no land and no prospect of ever possessing land. These landless millions are the ones who suffer first when famine grips the land. Industry must grow at a very rapid pace if it is to absorb even a small percentage of the increasing number of people.

The land must be made to yield even more food with the use

of modern agricultural methods and a more efficient use of artificial fertilizer. In the People's Republic of China the farms have been communized with the thought that larger farms using modern machinery and modern methods and worked by the cooperative efforts of all will result in greater productivity and more efficient use of the land. The Indian leaders have not turned to this method of solving the land problem, but they have given the development of irrigation and power systems top priority, and they have recommended progressive socialization of agriculture marketing and of processing industries in rural areas through the introduction of cooperatives. The government policy is to create and foster cooperatives in all possible aspects of agricultural operations. But at the present time the people are still increasing at a rate faster than the increased productivity of the land.

Throughout a vast part of Asia, national leaders are supporting the plantation system first introduced by foreigners. The only countries in which this system is of no special importance are Japan, Korea, and China. In all the other Asian countries plantations, which specialize in particular crops, usually tropical crops for export, are common. These plantations produce such crops as palm oil, tea, coffee, rubber, and sugar. Since the plantation system depends upon a large labor supply working with a relatively small number of tools, it reinforces the Asian emphasis on human labor.

The magnitude and immediacy of the food problem in Asia varies from country to country. Some countries in Southeast Asia, such as Thailand and Burma, are self-sufficient in food, and Japan is absorbing much of her manpower into a booming industry, but for most of the Asian leaders the question of how to feed a fast-growing population adequately is always paramount.

Health

Most Asians do not starve to death, but many are victims of malnutrition. They get enough food to keep them alive and working, but not enough to keep them healthy and efficiently working. As a result, many Asians are susceptible to disease and are not able to ward off the epidemics and sickness which are prevalent in Asia.

Most Asians receive their calories through grains and vegetables rather than by way of animal proteins. This is in contrast with some Western nations in which a great part of the diet comes from animal protein. Protein is essential for growth and life, and animal

protein is of greater nutritional value than vegetable protein. Westerners get much of their protein from meat, eggs, milk, cheese,
butter, and other foods. The amount of food consumed by the
various Asian populations as compared with the amount consumed
in the United States will give some indication of the inadequacy of
the Asian diet.

In the United States, the average man consumes about thirty-
one hundred calories per day, of which about 91.2 is the protein
level. The figures from Asian countries are much lower. The Japanese consumes around twenty-three hundred calories of which
about 69.3 is the protein level. The inhabitant of Sri Lanka (Ceylon) consumes about twenty-one hundred calories of which about
44.4 is the protein level, while the Indian eats about two thousand
calories of which about 51.5 is the protein level. These selected
figures are approximations and may be rapidly dated. Of course, in
Asia there are times of famine and disorder when the people eat
less calories and less protein. Occasionally, at weddings, funerals,
and other social events, they get a chance to eat an adequate
amount of food.

Most Asians at birth cannot expect to live much beyond forty-
five years of age. The baby born in Burma or Cambodia may expect to live around forty-four years, and in Thailand to between
forty-eight and fifty years of age. Japanese babies, however, can
expect to live to more than seventy-one years.

In the United States, a citizen can expect to live to 70.2 years
of age, and the average is rising every year. Americans of forty are
considered to have reached the prime of life and the most useful
period of their lives both for themselves and their communities.
Many Asians at this age have died or are about to die. This is a
tragic loss of talent and unreplaceable experience. Most Asians are
aware of this loss, for they give an honored place to those who survive and live to ripe old age. Age is respected in Asia, perhaps because it is relatively rare; those few who attain the age of sixty,
seventy, or beyond seem deserving of honor, praise, and attention.

The majority of those who die young in Asia are from the
poorer classes. The wealthy, a small minority, have a much better
chance of growing old. They eat better, they are able to afford
doctors and medicine. They receive much better care from their
children and relatives because the necessity to make a living does
not drive their family to work with the same remorseless regularity
as it does the poor.

The wife of a poor man cannot always take time to care for

her baby. It may lie untended for hours, often bitten by mosquitoes or insects of one kind or another. Sometimes the baby is cared for by the younger children who are willing, but untutored in child care. At times the mother has too little milk and cannot afford to hire a woman to nurse the baby for her. It is not easy for the mother to buy milk. On the other hand, the rich do not require the mothers to work in the fields, nor at domestic tasks for that matter. They can afford to hire servants to care for the house and men to till the fields. The mother has time for her baby. Should the mother lack milk, the family can buy it and feed the baby from a bottle or hire a woman who has abundant milk in her breasts to nurse the child. This woman is usually of a poor family and is willing to give her milk for extra money or food, for she too has babies to feed.

A great many infants die even before they reach one year of age. It has been estimated that one out of every four dies before the age of five. Of course, many infants in every part of the world die before reaching the age of one or five.

In the United States, about twenty-three infants per thousand live births die before reaching the age of one. In a number of Asian countries, it is estimated that between fifty to eighty-two per thousand live births die before the age of one. Japan has a low of eighteen per thousand.

Infants are peculiarly susceptible to disease during the first year of life. Many of the mothers of Asia have neither the time, the money, nor the facilities to practice the hygienic methods of some Western countries. Certainly they desire to follow the best practices, but they are prevented from doing so by their environment and circumstances.

Someday Asian mothers will be able to give their babies better care, and fewer babies will die. When this happens, the population of the Asian countries will take another leap upward. In this case, as in other instances of raising the standard of living in Asia, there arises the threat of overpopulation. Already the land of Asia is thronged. What will happen if, through increased food supply and better medical facilities, more infants survive and more people live to an advanced age?

There are few health services of the Western variety available for the majority of the people, but the services of doctors versed in native medical lore and trained in the traditional Asian manner are generally available everywhere in Asia. This is particularly true of China where a monumental *materia medica* evolved over the many centuries of China's growth. Most Asians rely upon their own Asian medical services or upon home remedies. The average Asian must be quite sick before he or she goes to the expense of calling in a doctor, either Asian or Western. Doctors and medicines cost money, and the ordinary Asian does not have money to spare for such expenses. Doctors and medicines mean that somebody goes hungry and that all will eat less this year.

From the viewpoint of sanitation and hygiene, Western medicine is more advanced than that of Asia. Also, preventive medicine is more advanced in the West. In many areas of internal medicine and in their *materia medica* the Asians have done some striking work for centuries. Many herbs used for medicine in Asia have been adopted by the West, although Western scientists have isolated the substance in the herb which is medically valuable, while the Asians continue to use the entire herb. Hence, Asian medicines are often bulky and given in soup and serving bowls, whereas Westerners generally take small pills.

Doctors versed in Chinese medicine are still in demand by Chinese everywhere in the world, even by those living in the United States and Europe. London, Paris, Chicago, New York, and San Francisco have Chinese herbs and drugs available for those who desire them. One of the most fascinating and sometimes efficacious medical practices both in China and Japan is *acupuncture,* the practice of sticking needles of gold, silver, or steel into various parts of the body to relieve pain and cure a variety of disorders. Western observers, including the author, have seen patients suddenly relieved of severe pain by means of acupuncture. While many Westerners scoff at acupuncture as a nostrum, millions of Asians continue to use it as a means of relieving pain. Recently, Western medical observers have been amazed at the widespread use of acupuncture as an anaesthetic in Chinese hospitals. In China and Japan the plant *moxa* is rolled into a small cone, set on fire, and applied to some part of the body as a cautery. The legs, arms, and backs of many Chinese and Japanese show scars from burning with *moxa.* It is believed to be a specific remedy for fainting fits, rheumatism, lumbago, arthritis, and many other ailments.

Large Asian cities like Bombay, Manila, Hong Kong, Peking, and Shanghai have hospitals and up-to-date medical services, but the great rural areas of Asia suffer from an acute lack of modern medical services.

Illiteracy

Widespread illiteracy in Asia is a tremendous obstacle in the path of modernization and industrialization. Modern technology and social progress require a population who can read and write. An illiterate society is not necessarily a primitive one, and certainly Asian society and people cannot be characterized as primitive. A society where many have an appreciation for opera and the classics, where exquisite courtesies are extended and expected, where many know the Vedas by heart and will sit all night watching the epics dramatized—this kind of society cannot be characterized by any term but *cultured.*

But the demands of an industrial society require that illiteracy be abolished. Asian nations are well-launched on a program of modernization which demands a reading and writing public. Thus, compulsory education is the law in most modern Asian nations.

Illiteracy is prevalent everywhere in Asia except in Japan where illiteracy is between 1 and 2 percent. When Japan started its rapid modernization program in 1868, a basic reform that was stressed rigorously was compulsory education. Japanese children of both sexes were required to take at least six years of schooling. The Japanese understood early that they could not create an efficient industrial society unless they had a literate people. The Philippines were made education-conscious by the Americans who governed these islands from the beginning of the twentieth century until 1946. Schools were established all over the islands and education was made compulsory. But even here the illiteracy rate is around 25 percent. The illiteracy rate for certain other Asian areas—Taiwan, Singapore, the Koreas, among others—is also rather low.

Elsewhere in Asia the literacy percentage is low. In India it is estimated that over half of the population is illiterate. Since the Indians are continuing their modernization program this figure should go down. A start, however, has been made, and there is no question that within several decades the great mass of young Asians will know how to read and write at least at an elementary level.

Everywhere, in India, China, Burma, Thailand, Indonesia, Vietnam, Malaysia, and Pakistan the top priority is being given to the building of schools and the training of teachers. The goal of all these nations is the eradication of illiteracy. Nevertheless, the number of people who require teaching and the lack of teachers and facilities will delay the total eradication of illiteracy for years.

The Cities

Although most Asians live in the country, there are great numbers of people who live in cities. Cities are growing in number and size. The following selected cities have a population which runs into the millions: Tokyo and Osaka in Japan; Shanghai, Tientsin, Canton, Peking, Wuhan and others in China; Karachi and Lahore in Pakistan; Manila in the Philippines; Jakarta in Indonesia; Bangkok in Thailand; Colombo in Sri Lanka (Ceylon); Bombay, Calcutta, Madras, and others in India; Singapore, Hong Kong, Macao, and still others not mentioned.

Most of these cities are ports and look to trade and to the sea for the preservation of their economy. These cities are the centers of political and economic control in Asian countries, and most of Asia's leadership lives in them. Many of these cities are Western in origin, attitude, and appearance. It is in the cities that the new ways of life are practiced extensively, and from them the currents of change and reform emanate. The cities of Asia are assuming more and more importance in this modern period of Asia's history.

The cities of Asia are also contributing more and more to environmental disruption in Asia. Wherever there is the burgeoning of cities and areas of industrialization, there one also sees growing pollution of all kinds. In replying to the question, "What does Tokyo lack most?" all candidates for a recent election replied, "Clean air and a clean sky." The Japanese use the term *kokai* to cover all environmental pollution and resulting unpleasant effects. *Kokai* is a much used term in modern Japan.

The cities of Asia also have some of the worst traffic problems in the world. One cannot visit cities such as Tokyo, Bangkok, and Manila, for instance, and not experience frustrations and tensions resulting from chaotic traffic situations. The Asians of the cities now also realize some of the disadvantages of modern cities.

But although there are great cities in Asia and they are growing in number and importance, the hundreds of thousands of villages housing hundreds of millions of people are one of the most significant features of the Asian landscape.

To see these economic and physical conditions of the Asians

in some perspective one should realize that similar conditions prevailed in the West a few centuries ago. Then, the European peasant, like the Asian peasant, lived at a level when a few bad harvests produced many deaths from starvation. And even in upper-class families a high proportion of children died. Up to the mid-eighteenth century many European visitors to Asia were impressed by a higher level of material civilization. The Asians are now trying to catch up with the changes which have revolutionized Western society in the last three centuries or so.

4

The Asian Village

Asia is a land of villages. It has been estimated that India has six hundred thousand villages: China alone has somewhat more than half a million villages and towns. The majority of Asians live in villages because of the predominance of agriculture as an occupation. The village encompasses a person's life. The Asian is born, grows up, marries, begets children, grows old, and dies within the boundaries of a village. Some individuals do get an opportunity to travel, and even go abroad, but they belong to a very small minority. The male adult frequently journeys to the market town a few miles away which serves the needs of his village, but the Asian female literally lives out her entire life within the confines of the village of her birth and her marriage.

Villages are the center of daily life for most Asians—Mahatma Ghandi spoke of the village as the heart of India—and the boundaries of the village are the boundaries of the individual Asian's life.

Villages in Asia are not planned; they just grow. For this reason a village is frequently a network of tiny winding lanes and alleys which lead to some courtyard and some door. These alleys and lanes are often filled with refuse and sewage and are seldom covered with anything but mud and filth. Sometimes cobblestones are laid, but they are usually uneven and irregularly spaced. The narrow avenues of a village permit only the passage of man and beast; there is no danger of a child being struck by a car as he or she plays and romps along the twisting lanes. Around the village lie the fields which the people of the village cultivate. During the working season, the villagers walk from their homes to the fields carrying their farming implements and often leading or driving before them a water buffalo, a cow, or a bullock. At dusk—sometimes later if they are very busy—they return to their village home with their implements and animals.

The social system is partly responsible for the haphazard growth and compact look of Asian villages. Most Asians have at one time or another practiced the joint or large family system and, even though the family may have divided the common property, the bonds of kinship still hold. When their common house became too small to accommodate the growing family, they merely built an extension to the house and moved in. Thus the village grew, with the closest kin generally living nearest to each other, and the houses were close together because they were extensions of other houses. This compact housing pattern served other purposes. In the first place, it provided better protection against theft and raids from bandits, deserters, and enemy villages. In some areas feuds start between villages over boundary problems, water rights, and fancied insults, and they can be very vicious and continue for years. The windows of the village houses were and are small and often barred, making entrance difficult for an intruder. Villages were thrown upon thier own resources in protecting themselves because, in the past, Asian governments afforded little protection to the villagers. Moreover, houses built close together conserved land. Good land is scarce in Asia, and land that is used for housing cannot be used to produce food. The result is a cluster of houses built close together, indentified by a name, and recognized as a social unit by the villagers themselves and others.

Some villages, particularly in Japan and South China, are stretched out like a string. They are ·laid out in rows on one or both sides of some natural or human phenomenon such as a river, dyke, or highway. Another type of village, found frequently in Japan, is made up of several clusters of houses. It is administratively one unit, although physically separated into several groups of houses.

The Asian village is primarily a group of farmhouses. Secondary activities, such as governmental work and manufacturing, are seldom carried on in the villages, though in some communities there are blacksmiths, weavers, workers in copper and metal, rope makers, pottery makers, and other artisans, and a number of villages have small markets where food, medicine, dyes, and other articles are sold. These village stores, generally very small, do not offer the variety and quantity or quality of products which are to be found in the larger market towns and cities. The villagers use their village stores in emergencies and for ordinary purchases. Some villages deliberately establish a small market section in order to keep money in the neighborhood. This market serves the neighboring village as well as the village of which it is a part.

In the past, many of the shops of the market town in China were run by people whom the villagers regarded as outsiders. Sometimes shopkeepers who had resided in the village for five or more generations were still regarded by the villagers as outsiders. When asked where their homes were, they often gave their ancestral provinces, which they might never have seen. Cantonese merchants were found in towns and cities all over China and when asked this question invariably replied, Canton city or Kwangtung Province. Canton is the capital of Kwangtung, and the people from Kwangtung are generally referred to as Cantonese. A provincial pride and spirit is still characteristic of many Chinese.

Houses

As a rule the villagers are poor and their houses are not pretentious. Many Asian houses are made of mud which is stamped and beaten into a tough consistency and then sun-dried and hardened. Sometimes mud bricks are used. The windows are generally small, barred, and frequently covered with thin paper rather than glass which is too expensive. In many villages the dwellings of the well-to-do and the ancestral halls, village centers, schools, and some shrines and temples are constructed of brick or stone. The roofs may be either thatch or tile, depending upon the physical resources of the area. The distinguished and sensitive author Gertrude Emerson wrote in *Voiceless India* a description of the thatching of her bungalow in India.

> Two Tharus [the name of an Indian tribal people living on the border between Nepal and India] sat on the ground and made rope of the fine grass. They held lengths of grass firmly with their toes and twirled the strands in their hands, feeding the grass lengths as needed. Bundles of this twine were tossed to the man on the roof. A number of bamboos, previously soaked in water to make them resistant to rain, had been split into narrow strips. These the Tharus tied down horizontally across strips. Then they took bunches of coarse grass and tied them firmly to the bamboos, with the loose ends streaming down like hair. They worked in one long line, beginning at the bottom and progressing upward. When they had finished, the thatch stretched over the Happy House [the name she gave her bungalow] like a field of cloth of gold, eight inches thick.[1]

Village houses differ in plan and room layout from country to country and from place to place within a country. In many parts of South China a house has three rooms. The front room is the largest and is used for a number of purposes. Rice is threshed in this room, guests are entertained and fed here, and traditionally the ancestral shrine occupied a prominent position in this multi-purpose room, though farm implements may also be stored in the corners. The kitchen, which is behind the main room, is generally smaller and contains stove, chimney, and miscellaneous kitchen goods. Behind the kitchen or beside the main room may be one or more bedrooms which are usually small and crowded with simple furniture such as chests, beds, and chairs. Outside the house there is a privy and sometimes small storage huts and manure pits.

Human waste is used extensively in many parts of Asia as fertilizer. Since most Asian farmers do not have access to artificial fertilizer nor the money to buy such fertilizer when it is available, they resort to human fertilizer as the cheapest and most abundant organic material available for fields and garden plots. Pits to store

[1] Gertrude Emerson, *Voiceless India* (New York: The John Day Company, 1944). Used with permission.

human excreta and the penetrating odors which accompany this custom are part of the village landscape and atmosphere. Though the practice is highly unsanitary, some method of storing and using a cheap fertilizer is necessary if the villagers are to continue to reap a harvest from an old and much worked land.

In many parts of Southeast Asia a typical house rests upon stilts at heights ranging from four to seven feet above the ground. It often stands in the middle of a fenced compound and is shaded by fruit and palm trees. Although located in a village, the houses are not as crowded together as in other areas of Asia. The house may have a roofed verandah which is open during the day but can be closed at night with a screen or lattice arrangement. There is also frequently a large front room which serves as a parlor, work room, and dining room and, when necessary, a sleeping room at night. Usually behind the front room there are private bedrooms which vary in number depending upon the size and wealth of the family. Should there be more than one family in the household, each family is assigned a private bedroom. Animals generally occupy the space beneath the house, but this space may also be used as an additional work area or for other purposes. The roof is usually thatched. Privies, bath facilities, and storage huts are located in the compound outside the house. This type of house has certain advantages. It provides protection against floods and pests of various kinds. It is adapted to the warm climate of Southeast Asia, for it permits a good circulation of air. Certainly it makes feeding the animals easier because they can be fed from above with little effort. Even if the compound in which the house sits is small, the privacy and sense of spaciousness experienced by the occupants is unknown to the families living in the more compressed villages.

Villagers in Asia have few material possessions in their houses. What they do have is practical and useful, rarely beautiful or unessential. The poor Indian home has been described as having a stove, a bench, a rope bed, a few brass pots, and nothing else. However, hovels in Indian cities are often worse than homes in Indian villages.

The villagers spend much of their time outside their homes, working, gossiping, and playing. It is a common sight in Asia to see villagers gathered together outside their houses at dusk during the slack season, conversing, smoking, or merely looking at the scenes of daily life around them.

Composition of the Village

Asian villages vary in size and composition. In the north of India, villages average about five hundred persons, but in the south, they average around one thousand. This variation in the size is true also of China, Japan, Korea, and the countries of Southeast Asia.

The composition of the village community ranges from a homogeneous group, all bearing the same surname and descended from a common ancestor, to unrelated individuals separated from one another by barriers of class and caste. The former holds true of some villages in China which may even be named after the family names—the Village of Wang, the Chang Village, the Li Village, and so on. More often the village is composed of individuals having several family names, with one or two or more families predominant.

In India the village may be made up of groups belonging to different castes. There are the cultivating castes, laboring castes, herdsmen, fishermen, basket and mat makers, blacksmiths, carpenters, washermen, barbers, and many others, all living together in a common village yet separated by the rigid barriers of caste. Outcastes live in the same villages, in a part separated by a strip of ground or a stream or some other demarcation. They are scorned by the other villagers and held in contempt. They live in hopeless poverty; to visit their homes is to visit a people condemned. Indeed, this is the way they are thought of—a people condemned to a life of hardship and pain by their sinful acts of a previous existence. They live as village scavengers and perform the filthy and degrading tasks that no other Indian villager or city dweller will do. They dress poorly, live in squalor, often stay at a distance from other castes, possess little land, generally have little to say about the government of the village, and regard the material future without much hope.

The government of India is trying to alleviate the wretched state of the scheduled castes, the official names for outcastes, but the Indian villagers generally continue to scorn them as inferior and insist that they live segregated from the rest of the village.

Although a variety of people lives in the Asian village, and although caste and class barriers separate the villagers from one another, there is a feeling among all of them that this is their village and that they have something in common. The villagers may not care to eat, talk, or associate with other villagers conceived as inferior, but all are regarded as members of a single community and as having a stake in that community.

In the past the village has been described as a self-sufficient community. The villagers grew the food they ate. Rice, wheat, barley, corn, and other cereal crops surrounded the village, and many of the villagers had private gardens where they grew such vegetables as turnips, squash, sweet potatoes, peas, and beans. Salt, sugar, and cooking oil were among the few food items which the community did not possess, and although some villages possessed facilities for processing these foods, most did not. Salt was a government monopoly in some countries and a principal source of revenue. Villagers usually made their own clothes. The women spent long days and nights spinning the yarn, cutting, sewing, and finishing the clothes for their men and their children. But here also the village depended upon outside sources, for often the dyeing of finished garments was done by a specialist.

The villagers are practical in their choice of clothes. They usually wear cotton, but they also have dress clothes of silk and wool which they wear during some special celebration or when visiting or entertaining others. In northern Asia, wool and padded, quiltlike clothes are worn for warmth, and children sometimes wear layer after layer of their ordinary cotton clothes in an effort to keep warm in winter. Some observers have jokingly remarked, and with some truth, that the children of North China wear their entire wardrobe from the beginning to the end of the winter season. But for most Asians clothes are not a major problem. Farmers work in the fields stripped down to shorts or an abbreviated piece of cloth. Children run around naked. Many go barefoot or use cheap straw sandals which are cool, light, and not very durable. Few villagers use socks or stockings and what clothes they do wear are full and open to the air. Loose and full trousers, shirts, and skirts are the villagers' answer to the warm climate in which they live.

Many agricultural tools are made in the village. Simple ploughs, hoes, spades, and shovels are beaten out by the blacksmith, who sometimes makes iron pots and cauldrons for cooking purposes. Workers in copper and pottery also make items for household and other uses. Weavers and dyers sometimes ply their skills within the village, especially if it is a large one and able to support them throughout the year. If the village is small, the villagers find it necessary to go elsewhere to buy tools, household equipment, and other necessary utensils. Sometimes the weavers, dyers, black-smiths, and workers in copper travel from village to village as need-ed, much like peddlers vending their wares from house to house.

In the larger villages services are sometimes provided by the various crafts. Often in an Indian village the barber, the washer-man, and the like receive a share of the village crop for their services. This is a cooperative endeavor and in a real sense symbol-izes the community feeling of the villagers and the social unity of the village. In other parts of Asia the villagers frequently cut their own hair or go to the market town where barbers practice their trade on a permanent basis. Since barbers often go from village to village cutting hair, it is commonplace in Asia to see a barber at work on a squatting customer on the side of a road or street. In most of Asia the village women wash their family clothes by hand. A group of women at a stream or river bank pounding the clothes on flat rocks with wide short paddles is a typical village scene. Pounding the clothes clean reduces the durability of the clothing, but for these women soap is too expensive.

Lenders of Money

The bankers of the village are the moneylenders or pawnbro-kers. These are among the most hated persons in Asia. They are considered parasites who have grown wealthy on the exhausting labor of the villagers. Without them, the villagers would not have facilities for borrowing money in times of emergencies; with them, the villagers frequently find themselves enslaved for years and sometimes for life. In some Asian countries today, moneylenders have either been eliminated or their activities more closely regu-lated.

It frequently happens in the villages that money is needed for celebrations such as weddings and funerals. When a son or daughter marries, the villagers expect the parents to follow local customs. As all know so well, the force of public opinion, especially in small communities, is strong. The villagers of Asia ostracize the person who does not follow local customs, and as the village is their life, the great majority of villagers dare not depart too far from accepted usage. Many Asians expect the family head in these instances to spend money rather lavishly on food, clothes, and other forms of conspicuous consumption. Since the villager has no reserve of capi-tal or food, he is forced to turn to the moneylender for the required cash. The moneylender is usually happy to lend it, especially if the man is a responsible villager and this is the first time he has borrowed money. The interest required on this loan might run as high as 10 to 15 percent per month. The villager may find himself in a desperate predicament when the time comes to pay off merely the interest on the loan, and it often happens that he must continue to borrow money even to pay off the interest which accumulates at a pace beyond measure. Finally, he becomes so deeply involved that he and his entire family can only look forward to a life dedicated to enriching the banker or moneylender. Funerals pose the same problem for the villager, particularly where the concept of filial piety has penetrated deeply into the mores of the society. The son is expected to carry out the mourning rites for the parents or other older relatives. He must invite the relatives to a banquet, hire mourners for weeping, buy a decent coffin, invite priests to chant prayers, hire pallbearers, and sometimes engage musicians to play during the procession to the grave. These expenses are heavy, but if the villager does not fulfill his obligations to the best of his ability, he will find it difficult to continue to live among neighbors who expect this obligation to be met. Accordingly, he borrows money and the trap closes around him. It is ironic that the villager who follows the "good path" as indicated by his village culture should end up almost inevitably in the awful trap of debt from which he may never escape.

Most people think that Asians are in debt only because of starvation and lack of food; few realize that such common occurrences as weddings and funerals are also inescapable reasons for borrowing money. The force of public opinion may be as frequent a cause for borrowing money as the force of hunger. This is a condition which could exist only where poverty is so prevalent and need so great. The moneylenders argue that high interest rates are necessary since the peasant is so vulnerable to calamities that may prevent him from repaying his debts. However, most moneylenders appear to make out rather well.

New Economic Forces

It cannot be said that the Asian village was ever completely self-sufficient, but it was relatively so in comparison with the cities and villages of today. This was evidenced in Japan, Asia's most industrialized nation, during and after World War II when thousands of city dwellers returned to the country to live with their families, relatives, or friends until the crisis was over. But with the coming of a money economy to Asia and the introduction of new Western-oriented ways of life, village self-sufficiency is lessening.

Cloth is available now at a price cheaper than the individual villagers can make it. It is often prettier and more colorful. The villagers now buy machine-made and machine-dyed cloth. Many no longer buy raw cotton but thread made in mills, thus saving the women much work. There are still millions of women who have the skill and do make their own clothes, but more and more of them are depending upon machine-made products. The villagers are relying more upon manufactured farm implements than upon hand-shaped ploughs, hoes, mattocks, and sickles. These farm tools are being made available to the farmer at cheaper and cheaper prices and are generally of better quality and more efficient than the tools made by hand. The blacksmith's place in the village economy is slowly decreasing in importance.

Asian villages are gradually being integrated into the economy of the entire country. They are no longer isolated from other villages nor from the cities and towns of the country. Fountain pens, locks, keys, pots and pans, combs, flashlights, batteries, nails, mirrors, and electric light bulbs are commonly found in many Asian villages, and the villagers are beginning to depend upon these imports. The price of their rice or wheat crop, the wages they receive from their farm labor, the fluctuations of the price of their main cash crop, are all now dependent upon the world and national market. A drop in the price of rice vitally affects each Burmese and Thai farmer. A drop in the price of peanuts alters the plans of an Asian farmer who is dependent upon this crop for the cash he needs to buy various essentials. No longer is it the price set in one or two market towns that influences the price of rice or wheat in the village. New roads, buses, railroads, radios, newspapers, telephones, magazines, technical education, and an increasingly bewildering variety of communications are invading the villages of Asia and breaking down their intellectual as well as social self-sufficiency.

Villagers still remain more self-sufficient than their city neighbors, and in a pinch can get along much better than city people. But the process of the integration of village and national economies is accelerating.

5

Ideology, Society, and Politics

Most Asians are preoccupied with the search for food and constantly beset by calamities which demand their unflagging attention to avoid and overcome. But the Asians, like all people, have certain beliefs and live in a community of their fellow humans, often very close to them in the land of compact villages. They also live within a

Religions play an important role in the lives of the Asians. Pakistan, Bangladesh, and Indonesia are the largest Muslim nations in the world in terms of population. India, although mostly Hindu, has about sixty million Muslims. Buddhism is the religion of hundreds of millions of Asians. There are Christians scattered throughout Asia, but most are concentrated in the Philippines. Also, many Asians continue to believe and practice various types of animism. See map on following pages.

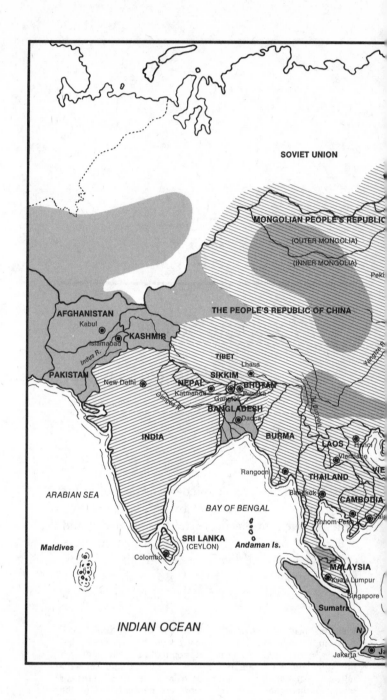

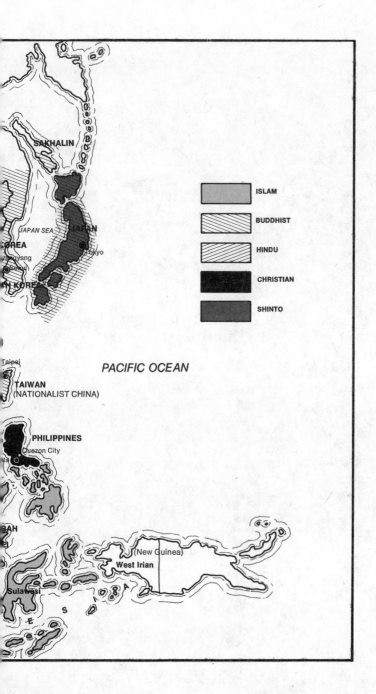

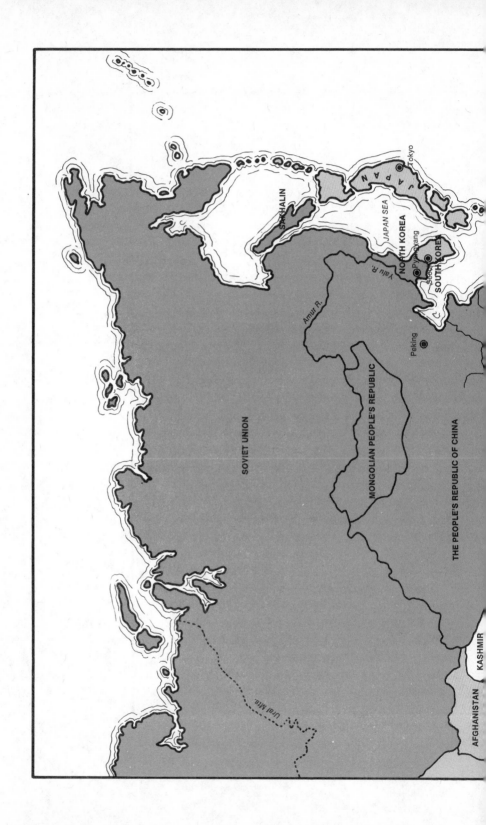

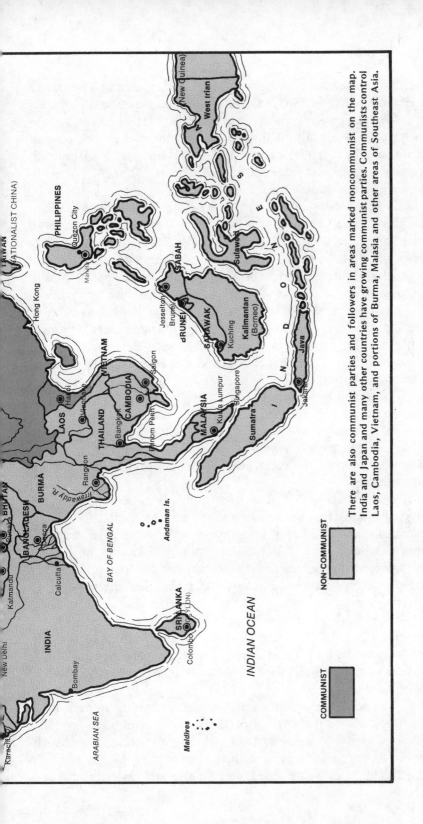

There are also communist parties and followers in areas marked noncommunist on the map. India and Japan and many other countries have growing communist parties. Communists control Laos, Cambodia, Vietnam, and portions of Burma, Malasia and other areas of Southeast Asia.

COMMUNIST

NON-COMMUNIST

TAIWAN
(NATIONALIST CHINA)

PHILIPPINES
Quezon City
Manila

Hong Kong

VIETNAM
Hanoi
Vientiane
Saigon

LAOS
THAILAND
Bangkok
CAMBODIA
Phnom Penh

BURMA
Rangoon
Irrawaddy R.

MALAYSIA
Kuala Lumpur
Singapore

Jesselton
Brunei
SABAH
SARAWAK
Kuching
Kalimantan
(Borneo)

BRUNEI

Sulawesi

I N D O N E S I A

Sumatra
Java
Jakarta

West Irian
(New Guinea)

BHUTAN
BANGLADESH
Dacca
Calcutta
Kathmandu
New Delhi
INDIA
Bombay
Karachi

BAY OF BENGAL

Andaman Is.

SRI LANKA
(CEYLON)
Colombo

INDIAN OCEAN

Maldives

ARABIAN SEA

political framework and atmosphere which is affecting increasingly their individual actions and future. To understand the Asians it is necessary to have a basic knowledge of their ideology and their social and political life which must be viewed not only in terms of their traditional beliefs, social customs, and political framework, but also in terms of newer ideas and practices usually imported from outside Asia.

Modern Western ideas have not permeated all levels of Asian life, for underneath these new thoughts still remain many layers of traditional belief. Asian thought cannot be understood merely from the philosophic base of the West; it must be studied in the light of its tradition and traditional ways of thinking if there is to be any understanding at all. The people of Asia live in a modern era, but they think in an old era. They know that the thinking of the West has challenged their traditional ideologies, and accepting the challenge, many Asians are incorporating the thought of the West into their traditional thought. The educated classes in particular are guiding their actions on many of the principles laid down by Western philosophers. But the great mass of the uneducated and many of the educated still cling to the traditional thought their fathers and mothers taught them. Although their national life is directed by men who are often steeped in Western ways and Western thought, the great mass of people think much as their ancestors did.

Two civilizations of Asia have influenced the thought of the majority of Asians—the Indian and the Chinese. India gave to Asia Hinduism and Buddhism; China reinterpreted and extended Buddhism and also gave to Asia Confucianism and Taoism. Both civilizations contributed other ideologies to their own national life, but these remained national or regional, rather than international, in character.

Islam has also had a tremendous impact upon millions of Asian people. Bangladesh, Pakistan, and Indonesia are three of the largest Muslim nations in the world, and there are millions of followers of Islam living in Malaysia, China, the Philippines, India, and other Asian countries.

The social life of the Asian people changed little over many centuries before the coming of the Western nations to the East. Their way of life was based on custom and tradition peculiarly suited to the agricultural base of the community. Classes were distinguished, roles well-defined, and for the vast majority of Asians the family was established as the center of social control and social activity. Today the social life of Asia is in the process of change. It has been substantially affected by the impact of foreign ideas, customs, and social attitudes. These new ways of life and thought have penetrated rather deeply into Asian society. The traditional has not been completely given up, and many Asians still cling tenaciously to the old social ways, but the change is obvious and continuous. The social life of Asia today cannot be described as exclusively traditional or modern. It is both, and something else—a compromise.

Traditionally, the joint or big family system was found throughout the entire region of Asia. Under this system the father, mother, unmarried children, and married sons, together with their wives and children, lived under one roof and had a common budget. This family system is still found throughout Asia, but industrialization, urbanization, and the impact of outside ideas are increasing the number of small Western-style families, especially in the cities. Traditionally, women in Asia were subordinate to the men, who dominated the political, economic, and social life of the country. In many Asian families the female was often less welcomed, less cared for, and less respected than the male. She found it difficult to get a divorce, rarely picked her own husband, and was often ill-treated by her frustrated and jealous mother-in-law. The subordination of women is still prevalent in many parts of Asia, but education, enlightened ideas embodied in the constitutions and legal codes of Asian countries, and, most of all, the fierce determination of Asian women to better their position are modifying this traditional attitude. It was also common custom in Asia for marriages to be arranged by families rather than by individuals. Marriage contracts were negotiated and concluded by the family heads, though the individuals concerned might be consulted at times. This practice is still common in many parts of Asia, but the young people of Asia are revolting against the custom. The struggle of modern young men and women to choose their own mates is another characteristic of Asian social life today.

Patterns of social life in Asia are changing. The old forms and relationships which were founded upon different values and ways of thinking are gradually being replaced and modified by newer forms and relationships founded upon more modern beliefs and philosophies. It is a time of social upheaval in Asia.

Traditionally, society in Asia was divided into the ruler and the ruled and their interests were rarely identical. The ruler did not regard himself as responsible for the welfare of the people, except perhaps in traditional China and areas governed by some Muslim rulers, and he never thought of himself as the people's representative. He was exclusively interested in preserving his position, maintaining control over the area he ruled, and increasing the wealth of his family and his favorites. The people existed for him, were not consulted about national and regional affairs, and were expected to obey his commands without question. The people did not think of themselves as members of a nation, that is to say, a group of people tied together by a common culture, common language, common tradition, and motivated by a desire to be politically independent. They were loyal to a village and a family, but not to any larger entity.

Today there is a difference. The people of Asia are thinking and speaking of *their* country and *their* policies and *their* political goals. In many areas of Asia the leaders and the people regard themselves as working together toward a common set of goals. Growing numbers of leaders think and speak of themselves as representatives of the people. The people, in turn, are coming more and more to look upon these leaders as their representatives. Moreover, Asian people are beginning to understand that it is *their* will that the government ought to express. Elections are being held in Asian countries, and although the choices are sometimes limited, the people do get a chance to vote in a formal manner. Frequently, they have responded enthusiastically and in India, Japan, Singapore, Malaysia, and other Asian countries have turned out in great numbers to express their opinion at the polls. Many of the new Asian leaders thus elected attempt to follow the will of the people in their legislative and executive acts. Of course, the people are still vague about the duties and functions of their representatives, and the leaders frequently act according to their own personal bent, but eventually the people will make their will felt in a more organized and decisive manner. The leaders today are interested primarily in raising the standard of living for their people and in making their nation a strong force in international affairs. At home and abroad, Asian governments have awakened the people to a sense of their importance and the importance of their nation-state in world affairs.

Because this is still a new political phenomenon, the traditional way of life remains an integral part of the present way of life. The past has left a legacy and that legacy is evident in the way millions of Asians continue to think and live politically. The new has not been completely grasped and assimilated, nor the past completely forgotten, and to understand the Asia of today, it is necessary to understand the Asia of yesterday. Because the traditional and the new are both struggling to maintain themselves in modern Asia, critical conflicts emerge. The political problems that face the Asian people today are many and complex.

In the chapters that follow an attempt will be made to outline the traditional aspects of Asian ideology and social and political life, as well as to describe the transitional complexities of the present.

In the following section the life and thought of the people of India, Pakistan, and Bangladesh in South Asia, and China and Japan in East Asia, are presented in some detail because these countries have had a great influence upon the life and thought of all Asia. A basic understanding of these civilizations is fundamental to an understanding of other Asian countries.

6

South Asia

South Asia includes the countries of India, Pakistan, Bangladesh, Nepal, Sri Lanka (Ceylon), Maldives, and some small Himalayan states. The republics of India, Pakistan, and Bangladesh are located on the mainland of Asia, while Sri Lanka is separated from the soutern tip of India by a few miles of water.

There is such a close physical unity between India, Pakistan, and Bangladesh that commentators writing about these three countries often treat them as one geographic unit. The republics of India, Pakistan, and Bangladesh were formerly one territorial area governed by Great Britain. For religious, economic, and political reasons this territory was divided in 1947 into three parts. Two parts, one in the extreme west, the other in the extreme east, became the Republic of Pakistan. In 1971, the former East Pakistan became an independent country under the name of Bangladesh. The third part, located between the other two, became the Republic of India. The political divisions thus created cut across railroads, highways, power lines, industrial facilities, and villages which were built formerly with one geographic area in mind. This neglect of geographic considerations has tangibly influenced the political relations and the economy of the three nations.

Sri Lanka (Ceylon)

In terms of physical geography Sri Lanka is the southernmost part of India. Technically an island, Sri Lanka is actually an extension of peninsular India, since the shallow waters separating it from India are dotted with many small bits of land. Because of its advantageous position in the Indian Ocean it has been used since ancient times as a port of call for ships passing east and west. About 270 miles long and 140 miles wide, it is only slightly larger than West Virginia.

Sri Lanka has a population of around fourteen million, the great majority of whom are Singhalese, the descendants of the original Ceylonese colonists who came from the valley of the Ganges River in north India around the sixth century B.C. The Tamils, who make up about 10 percent of the population, came to Ceylon at a later date from South India, many of them in the past century to work as laborers on the plantations. One of Sri Lanka's most vexing problems today is the tense relations between these two groups. The Singhalese are lighter skinned, are largely followers of Theravada or Hinayana Buddhism, and speak the Sinhala language which in 1956 was made the official language of Sri Lanka. The Tamils are darker, are predominantly Hindu, and speak the Tamil language of South India. In their drive to unify the country culturally, economically, and politically, the Singhalese aroused the alarm and antagonism of the Tamils, who fiercely resist assimilation lest their culture, language, and livelihood be endangered. There have been instances in recent years of riots, bloodshed, and violence between the two groups which have brought about adverse reactions on the social, economic, and political levels.

Sri Lanka achieved its independence in 1948 and is a member

of the British Commonwealth of Nations. Formerly under Portuguese and Dutch control, it came under British domination in the eighteenth century. Since independence the political situation in Sri Lanka has been in a state of flux. Until 1965 the prime minister of Sri Lanka was a woman, Mrs. Sirimavo Bandaranaike, widow of a former prime minister who was assassinated in 1959. Mrs. Bandaranaike was elected in 1960 on the Sri Lanka Freedom Party (Socialist) ticket. It is interesting to note that two women prime ministers in recent times were elected in Asia, where the position of the woman has traditionally been a subordinate one (Mrs. Indira Gandhi was first chosen prime minister of India in 1966. Mrs. Gandhi, who in 1971, led her party (Congress) to an overwhelming victory in India, continues to serve as prime minister.) Mrs. Bandaranaike's government embarked upon a policy of nationalization. Insurance, public utilities, newspapers, education, to mention a few, were brought or were slated to be brought under government control. Mrs. Bandaranaike sought the support of leftist groups in the country and formed a coalition government with a Trotskyite party. After a no-confidence vote in December 1964, Mrs. Bandaranaike dissolved parliament and called for new elections in 1965. She lost this election, but, in May 1970, once again became prime minister.

There is little industry in Sri Lanka because of a lack of essential raw materials such as coal. Tea, rubber, and coconut products are the country's main exports. The mountains of Sri Lanka intercept the monsoons from the southwest and the northeast, which sustain the growth of evergreen trees and the cultivation of tea, rubber, and rice. The former name Ceylon is synonymous with tea the world over, but the country is dependent upon imports for most of its manufactured needs and a large part of its food supplies. The Ceylonese are striving to diversify their industry and become agriculturally self-sufficient.

Friction between minority groups, rising costs of living, divided political parties, and strong labor unions have too frequently given Sri Lanka's domestic scene a chaotic appearance. Mrs. Bandaranaike has said that the "rising trend" of unemployment is her government's most pressing problem.

The Unity of South Asia

South Asia is not only a territorial unit in terms of surface features; it also manifests a definite unity in terms of climate, religion, and politics. The countries of South Asia depend upon the early summer monsoon which brings needed rain. All of Asia relies upon the monsoon, but this area is peculiarly dependent upon the regular coming of the rain-bearing monsoon winds. When the monsoon fails to appear on time, or brings too little water to the thirsty land, famines frequently result.

Culturally, the people of South Asia have much in common. They are a religious people. The great religions of Hinduism, Buddhism, and Islam have marked the land and the people. The Hindu temple, the Buddhist stupa, and the Muslim mosque everywhere give an otherworldly beauty to the landscape. The soaring simplicity of Muslim architecture is offset by the wonderful exuberance of Hindu art. The Brahmin, the Buddhist priest, and the Mullah are honored and respected.

Politically, the four principal countries of South Asia have the same heritage and the same aspirations. They are all former colonies of Great Britain, and won their independence at approximately the same time. They all manifest the same nationalistic aspirations and all profess to believe in a democratic form of government based upon modern Western examples such as England and the United States of America.

The location of the Indo-Pakistan subcontinent between Europe, Africa, and the Middle East, on the one hand, and the Far East and Pacific regions, on the other, early exposed it to many outside contacts. Northern India was convenient to the mainland routes between Asia and the West, while peninsular India lay actually astride the water routes between the Pacific and the Atlantic and Mediterranean areas. India was the eastern limit for Western trade and exploration, and the western limit for Far Eastern traders and travelers. Warehouses of Greco-Roman pottery have been found near Pondicherry on the southeast coast of India. This location gave the subcontinent the opportunity to receive cultural and ideological contributions from many civilizations. India has often adapted these new contributions to fit her civilization and, in many instances, has passed them along in an Indianized form to the other civilizations of both Asia and the Western hemisphere. Thus, Greco-Roman art forms were carried by the Buddhist missionaries to China, and the Indian names for rice,

South Asia is a region teeming with varieties of peoples, languages, customs, and attitudes. There is also a variety of landscape including mountains, deserts, jungles, rain forests, semiarid plains, rivers, lakes, and sea coasts. See map on following pages.

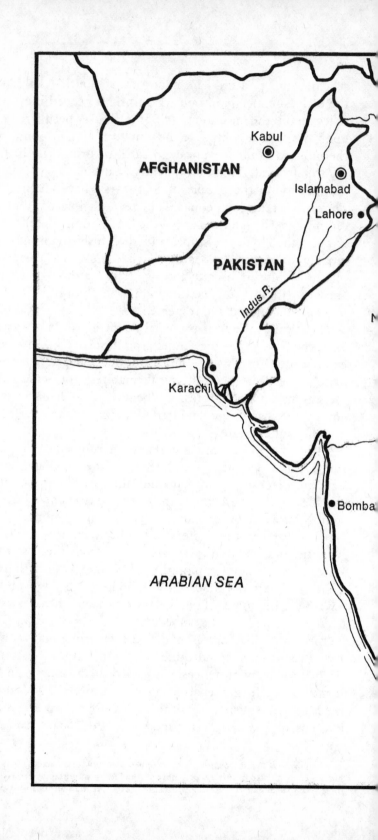

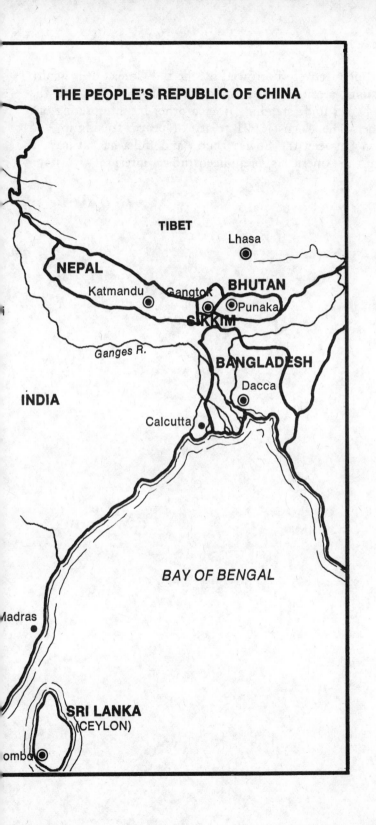

THE PEOPLE'S REPUBLIC OF CHINA

TIBET

Lhasa

NEPAL

Katmandu   Gangtok   BHUTAN

SIKKIM   Punaka

Ganges R.

BANGLADESH

INDIA   Dacca

Calcutta

BAY OF BENGAL

Madras

SRI LANKA
(CEYLON)

ombo

ginger, and pepper were borrowed by the old Greeks. It is significant that until recently India aspired to bring the East and the West to a better understanding of each other by interpreting one to the other. The August 1971 treaty of peace, friendship, and cooperation between the Soviet Union and India has, at least in the eyes of the Americans, prejudiced India's interpretative statements.

7

The Ideology of India

The ideology of the people of India is the result of a long and continuing search for the origin and meaning of life. Answers that Indian thinkers and sages have found to the questions of what, whence, why, how, and whither humanity and the universe make up most of the content of Indian ideology. Meditation on these fundamental questions has played a decisive role in shaping the Indian way of life.

Indians gave primacy to those who wrestled with these questions. Thought was more important than action; meditation was valued over the incessant search for material goods. Wealth and power were important goals, but spiritual realization and self-contemplation ranked higher in the scale of cosmic values. This attitude is demonstrated by the tremendous respect given to the ascetics and hermits who are found all over India; by the position of the Brahmins—the priestly group who has attained knowledge and renunciation—at the top of the hierarchy of castes; and finally by the overwhelming appeal of Mahatma Gandhi, who was famed for his self-discipline, ascetic life, and renunciation of worldly goods.

Indian sages were puzzled by the transiency of existence and the universality of suffering; they were intrigued by the unity that appeared to be manifest in the diversity that was the universe; they were challenged by the presence of an intangible soul or spirit coexisting with a tangible material world. Accordingly, they sought to explore the nature of humanity and the universe, of matter and nonmatter, of existence and nonexistence, and finally the ultimate reality of all things. Their findings form the substance of Indian ideology.

Philosophers in India dealt with the world of the spirit more often than with that of matter. Their thought assumed a spiritual and metaphysical character which has been a distinctive feature of Indian ideology. It is for this reason that the ideology of India provides for a religious way of life and furnishes such a creed and worship for the people that everything they do has a spiritual significance, and every act is for them, in a very real sense, a religious act.

One of the results of this search for the ultimate reality underlying the material world, this search for the ultimate truth and ultimate reason for existence, was the founding of two religions, two ways of life, which have influenced the beliefs and acts of countless millions living on the mainland and islands of Asia. These two religions are Hinduism and Buddhism.

Other religions arose in India, such as Jainism in the sixth century B.C. and Sikhism in the sixteenth century A.D., which continue to have a number of followers, but their influence is not comparable with that of Buddhism and Hinduism. Both Jainism and Sikhism were, like Buddhism, reform movements within the fold of Hinduism directed against the domination of the Brahmins, the priests of Hinduism, and the rigidity and artificiality of their ceremonials. Sikhism is also said to have been an attempt to bridge the gulf between Islam and Hinduism. Very eary in the history of India, Hinduism emerged as the dominant way of life for the majority of the Indian people.

Historical Buddhism was born later than Hinduism, in the sixth century B.C. It was both the child and the opponent of Hinduism. Hinduism and Buddhism were both concerned with the continuous process of change which appeared to be characteristic of the universe. Hinduism, however, held that beneath this change there was a permanent reality which gave unity and permanence to the world. Buddhism, on the other hand, taught that change was really the nature of things and that there was nothing permanent in the universe. All things were transitory and impermanent. Hinduism taught that each person had a soul. Buddhism denied the existence of an individual soul. Hinduism accepted many gods, while Buddhism denied the existence of all supernatural beings.

After its founding in the sixth century B.C., Buddhism spread rapidly. During the reign of Emperor Asoka, a devout Buddhist who ascended the throne in 273 B.C., and who was the grandson of the founder of the Maurya Dynasty (322 to 185 B.C.), Buddhism flourished in India and expanded abroad. Evidence of Asoka's vigorous proselytizing can still be seen in India in the form of stupas and tall sandstone pillars. The stupas are round-domed structures of brick and stone which house Buddhist relics and serve as memorials. The pillars, which stand as high as forty or fifty feet, are surmounted by capitals which are usually decorated with symbolic Buddhist representations. This symbolism continues to be represented in the design of the flag of India. Asoka, imbued with a missionary zeal, sent Buddhist missionaries to Burma, Sri Lanka, and as far as Egypt. Buddhism gradually penetrated most of Asia and became the religion of untold millions of people in Sri Lanka, China, Korea, Japan, Burma, Thailand, Cambodia, Laos, Vietnam, Tibet, and elsewhere in Asia and the world. It became one of the world's great religions and continues to hold the allegiance of millions in Asia today.

In India, however, Hinduism slowly made Buddhism a part of itself through absorption and assimilation. What was not incorporated into Hinduism was abolished by the proselytizing zeal of the Muslims who saw in the superstitions and magical practices of a corrupt Buddhism the devil of idolatry. Thus, Buddhism practically died in the country of its birth. Hinduism, the dominant thought of India for thousands of years, has, with the aid of Buddhism and other minor religions, remained an ideological framework within which the people of India live and work.

8

Hinduism

Reality is one; sages speak of it in different ways.
Rigveda I, 164

Hinduism attempts to be all things to all people. It tries to satisfy myriad needs and aspirations. It is a tolerant, accommodative religion, with a niche for every person and every god. Hinduism offers the scholar and mystic an opportunity for speculative thought on the most abstract level and for the most rarefied mystical experiences, at the same time providing the more literal-minded and worldly with a wealth of ritual, magnificent temples, and a god for every occasion. Detached and selfless seers are given identification with an Ultimate Absolute Reality as their final goal, while the less selfless have a personal God who loves and protects them on earth and finally rewards them with a place in heaven. Hinduism understands that individuals vary in their spiritual and intellectual capacities and that provision must be made for people on every level if all are to be satisfied.

Hinduism draws its inspiration and doctrines from a large body of ancient writings known as scriptures. These are divided into two parts—the Vedas, which are the primary and revealed source of Hinduism, and secondary scriptures which are authoritative elaborations upon the Vedas.

Much of the material in the Vedas was handed down for centuries by word of mouth. Finally put into written form during a long period of time extending approximately from 1500 to 500 B.C. or later, they are known to the Hindu as *Sruti,* or "that which is heard." The Indian sages heard the eternal truths from the Godhead and recorded them for future generations. There are four Vedas—the *Rigveda,* the *Samaveda,* the *Yajurveda,* and the *Atharvaveda.* Each is divided into three parts which generally follow a chronological order—the *Mantras,* which are the basic hymns and verses and the core of the Vedas; the *Brahamas,* which are ritualistic and interpretative explanations of the *Mantras;* and the *Upanishads,* which are profound mystical and philosophic extensions of the truths revealed in the basic *Mantras.* The *Mantras* are sometimes called the Vedas because they are the heart of the revealed truths and the basis for the later elaborations. The *Brahamas* are largely the work of priests and deal with ritual worship. The word *Upanishads* has the literal meaning of "sitting near," which conveys the idea of knowledge acquired while seated around a teacher. Teaching based upon the *Upanishads* is called Vedanta, which signifies not only the end of the Vedas, but also the peak of Vedic knowledge.

The secondary scriptures are known as *Smriti,* or "that which is remembered." These writings are not revealed but are authoritative and include digests of earlier writings, manuals of philosophy, commentaries, rituals, codes of law and conduct such as the law of Manu, sacred stories like the *Puranas,* and epics illustrated by the *Ramayana* and the *Mahabharata.* The *Mahabharata* is the longest poem in the world, and its most famous part, the *Bhagavad-Gita,* is one of the finest gems in world literature.

Unity in Diversity

The attempt to meet the needs of humanity at every level makes Hinduism a way of life that is bewilderingly diverse. The presence of thirty-three thousand gods—thirty-three thousand gods is an Indian way of saying "countless gods"—and innumerable religious practices which apparently have no relation to one another, confuses the untutored. The multiplicity of sects and sub-sects, cults and philosophies, commentaries, and commentaries on the commentaries, creates the first impression that the body of Hindu belief and practice is highly disorganized and incoherent. This incoherence, however, is merely on the surface. Beneath this diversity there is a certain common core of doctrine which gives Hinduism a basic unity of thought and belief. An example of this unity in diversity is found in the Hindu conception of their many gods as really many manifestations of One Absolute Reality.

One Ultimate Reality

Hinduism teaches that the thousands of gods revered and wor-shipped by the faithful merely symbolize and represent aspects of One Ultimate Reality that transcends the measure of form, name, and personality. The gods contained within the Hindu pantheon are limited portrayals of that which is unlimited. Hinduism senses that for most people the formless and nameless must be made con-crete. Only a select few have reached that level where the Absolute can be grasped as it is and not garbed in some particular body.

Three main gods represent the Hindu trinity; they possess their own heavens, wives, children, and servants. Representing three functions of the Ultimate Reality, they are Brahma, the Creator; Vishnu, the Preserver; and Siva, the Destroyer. Worship of these gods resulted in the birth of separate sects and cults dedicated to Vishnu and Siva and many forms of these two gods, but always there was the deep realization that belief in these gods as discrete personalities was a concession to the sense organs, a surrender to the demands of the human heart which required some material ex-pression of a reality that transcends human imagination.

Gods are not the only manifestations of an Ultimate Reality; all things in the universe, including humans, are but so many repre-sentatives of it. The Ultimate or Supreme Reality is the whole animate and inanimate universe. The cosmic character of Hinduism can be seen in this relationship between humans, the universe, and the Ultimate Reality, for neither human nor any material object, living or nonliving, can be viewed as standing apart from anything else.

In every person there is an essential self that is called *Atman.* It is divine and transcendent, beyond the mind, the body, and the senses, and one with the Ultimate Reality, or *Brahman.* Although no name can describe this Ultimate Reality, the Hindus generally refer to it as *Brahman,* Atman and Brahman are two names for the same thing—Atman is the Ultimate Reality viewed subjectively, while Brahman is the Ultimate Reality viewed objectively. Thus a person is one with all things in the universe because he or she is another manifestation of the Supreme Reality. The *Upanishads* exclaim: "The essential self or the vital essence in man is the same as that in an ant, the same as that in a gnat, the same as that in an elephant, the same as that in these three worlds, indeed the same as that in the whole universe."

Liberation from the Finite

Everything is really and essentially one; the multiplicity of material objects apprehended by the senses obscures and hides the true reality that pervades all things. In this illusory but tangible world, Hinduism teaches that the gods, the variety of rituals and creeds, and the other human accommodative institutions are not ends in themselves, but are means provided to aid people in reaching their ultimate goal of liberation from a particular body.

The essential self of a person is imprisoned in an individual body, mind, and understanding, which is finite, ignorant, and egotistical. The body is finite because it is limited to the world of the senses, ignorant because it views the world as so many separate objects distinct from each other, and egotistical because it thinks of itself as a particular individual reveling in its uniqueness. Hinduism teaches that the final goal of human life is *moksha,* or liberation from finite human consciousness to a high and divine consciousness of the Ultimate Reality or that of which everything is a part. A person's destiny is not happiness on earth or in heaven, nor is he or she destined for suffering on earth or in hell, but rather the ultimate goal is a realization that each is one with a Supreme Reality which encompasses both humans and the universe.

Each must rise above this body which obscures and conceals a self that is infinite and one with all things. All must liberate themselves from the concept of individuality and separateness from all other things and struggle to realize the true nature of themselves and the universe. When individuals realize that they are one with the Ultimate Reality, they are no longer subject to the limitations and restrictions of the body; each then becomes identified with Brahman, that is, pure existence, pure consciousness, and pure bliss. As one Indian has remarked, "We believe that the worst of all evils is the ego, the 'I am.' The more we can squash it, the better." The goal of every Hindu is to escape from the bondage of individual existence. This is not easy; for most people it is a long and complicated process necessitating a number of separate and varied existences before liberation is attained.

Rebirth

The Hindus believe in rebirth or the transmigration of self. The essential self of a person is really one with the Ultimate Reality; it has no beginning and can have no end. The self of a newborn infant is old beyond the conception of time; its body is merely a new form for an eternal spirit. Since the self is one with the entire universe, it is not restricted in the form it may assume. Like water, it may fit itself to any type of container. In succeeding generations, the self may reign as a god, destroy as a demon, bloom as a flower, crawl as a snake, wander as a tiger, or silently meditate as a Hindu seer.

The entire universe is a collection of temporary living quarters for selves struggling toward liberation and final release from their wanderings. Life is like a journey over a bridge, across which people must travel to reach their destination but upon which they do not build permanently. It is a lower stage of experience necessary before passing to the higher level of identification with a Supreme Reality. For Hindus, each individual existence becomes their primary burden, for it is a prison enslaving an essential self which should be free. There is always hope, however, for they know that each prison is merely temporary, and, if they use their time well, it may be their last temporary residence in the world of matter and multiplicity. Sir Edwin Arnold in *The Light of Asia* poetically catches this idea:

> Only, while turns the wheel invisible,
> No pause, no peace, nor staying place can be;
> Who mounts may fall, who fall will mount; the spokes
> Go round unceasingly.

Karma

The sequence of rebirths is determined by the law of *karma*. *Karma* literally means "action" and particularly action done in the past which determines the individual's present condition of existence. Karma operates like a moral law of causation whereby the present acts of an individual produce concrete results at some future time or existence. No deed is lost. No act is without result. Morally good acts produce good results; morally bad acts produce bad results. In a sense one's present life is determined because it is the result of the sum total of all one's previous acts. In another sense the present condition of the individual is self-created. "Each is his own destroyer or preserver, as he follows evil or good." In each current existence a person is fashioning his or her future life. Karma works with certainty and inevitability for the *Mahabharata* states: "As among a thousand cows a calf will find its mother, so the deed previously done will find and follow its doer." The *Mahabharata* describes karma as the unseen which shadows people everywhere.

> Yes, all the deeds that men have done,
> In light of day, before the sun,
> Or veiled beneath the gloom of night,
> The good, the bad, the wrong, the right—
> These, though forgotten, reappear,
> And travel, silent, in their rear.

A person's position in society and all the inequalities and sufferings of life are the results of the inexorable law of karma.

Spiritual Progression

Implicit in the concepts of rebirth and karma, or moral causation, is a certain spiritual progression, which reaches its culmination in the liberation of a person from the endless torment of the wheel of birth and rebirth. A human is closer to the Ultimate Reality than an animal, an animal is closer than a plant, and a plant is closer than a lifeless object. So a good person is closer to liberation than a bad person; and justice and mercy are valued more highly than injustice and cruelty. Spiritual values such as beauty, love, and righteousness are of more importance than intellectual values such as logic, keenness, clarity, and other skills. Below the spiritual and intellectual skills come biological values such as health and vitality and finally material values such as wealth and the like. Hinduism uses a spiritual and moral yardstick to judge and order the actions of people and society. This attitude is revealed in the caste structure, by which Indian society is organized, and in the institution of the stages of life called *asramas,* by which Hindus are supposed to order their lives. The belief that specific duties exist for each of the four castes and each of the four orders or stages of human life dominates Hindu social thought and practice.

Caste

A caste is a social group whose membership is determined by birth. The caste system developed early in Indian history. It is believed by some that the system had its origin in the division between the fair Aryans who invaded India many centuries ago and the dark-skinned non-Aryans whom they conquered. Scholars who accept the economic origin of the system maintain that the fourfold caste division of society is really based on a practical division of labor. The Brahmin caste was concerned with priestly and intellectual duties; the Kshatriya caste undertook the conduct of wars and government; the Vaisaya caste was occupied with commercial and agricultural pursuits; and the Sudra caste performed the more menial and servile work of the community. There were many subcastes, but theoretically, all Indians could be placed within these four groups. Finally, there were the outcastes, formally called the depressed or scheduled castes, who were the lowest of the low in India and who were deprived even of those few benefits that those in the lowest castes possessed. Even these groups divided themselves into separate divisions with special rules that regulated their lives.

Each caste is usually governed by an elaborate code of conduct which regulates most aspects of the lives of its members, such as drinking, eating, social intercourse with other castes, and like matters. Generally, the members follow the same occupation, marry within the caste, and confine their social activities to each other. All within the caste are brethren and are supposed to aid each other in time of need.

The caste system conforms to the law of spiritual progression because the most spiritual caste, the Brahmins, occupy the top position in the system, while the least spiritual, the outcastes, occupy the lowest position. Caste is regarded by most as determined by the law of karma. Thus, the good deeds performed by people in their present existence might merit for them a higher caste position in a future existence. Theoretically, this caste system, as ordered through the method of spiritual progression, is supposed to result in a harmonious Indian society arranged like a cooperative hierarchy. Each caste is supposed to carry out those special duties, whether intellectual and ruling functions or more servile tasks, which are commensurate with their spiritual capacities. Like most theoretical arrangements, this one represents a considerable departure from actual practice.

The caste system will be treated more fully when the social life of India is discussed.

Stages of Life

The concept of spiritual progression is manifested not only in caste divisions, but also in the division of the life of the individual into four successive stages called the *asramas*. Each stage of life is a progression from the baser to the more spiritual levels. These stages are: the student, the householder, the anchorite, and the *sannyasin*. The first stage is one of preparation and probation, in which students live an austere life and devote themselves to study and discipline. The second stage is one in which individuals carry out their responsibilities to society by raising and supporting families and by taking an active part in the affairs of the community and the state. After this active period, they withdraw from the bustle of life and enter the anchorite and third stage, where they engage in meditation and study for the second time. Finally, they enter the fourth stage of the *sannyasin,* wherein they completely renounce all possessions and attachments. At such a stage they are often found leading the life of a wandering ascetic. Since Hinduism holds renunciation and nonattachment to material objects as the highest of values, the *sannyasin* is believed to have reached the apex of spiritual life on earth, and for this reason is revered by the Indians above all others.

Dharma: A Guide for the Living

The practical and accommodative quality of Hinduism is strikingly illustrated in the provision of a rule or guide for people in their journey over the bridge of life. This rule is called *dharma.* The word *dharma* is translated in many ways and means different things at different times. It has been used to indicate duty, law, morality, conduct; it has sometimes embraced the conception of the entire rule of Hindu life and the whole duty of humans. It has been used to refer to the individual duty of a king or warrior, or the group duties of a particular caste; it has denoted both sacred and civil law. But no matter what the context or the particular meaning of the moment, dharma fundamentally acts as a guidebook directing people how to behave in this world of matter and the senses, while, at the same time, furthering their spiritual progress toward final liberation. Of course, the dharma for each in this existence is determined by a previous karma.

Hinduism realizes that beside a final goal of liberation from the bondage of the body, all have certain material ends which arise from the needs and desires of this same body they seek to escape. There are certain natural desires, instincts, and appetites of the flesh which a person must satisfy. Hindus accept this natural world in which they must work out their salvation. Although they seek to escape from it, they do not fight against it. They do not seek to control nature so much as they try to conform to it; they work with the natural processes rather than against them. Since nature is basically one with themselves, to struggle against nature is to struggle against oneself. The true Hindus are close to nature and they reveal their closeness in practices of bathing and eating and in honoring streams and mountains. There are also social demands, such as the maintenance of a family, aid to dependents and the needy, and other obligations that each must meet in this temporal world. Dharma regulates the expression of these natural desires and this search for material welfare in such a manner that both work toward the final goal—liberation. For instance, it advises a person to satisfy his or her appetites in a moderate and temperate fashion. It directs a man's method of gathering wealth for the support of his family so that this act is not a mere material action but is one infused with spirituality. In this way dharma attempts to bring spirit and matter together and to bridge the gap between the eternal and the temporal by making every act further both spiritual and material progress simultaneously.

Dharma, the Hindu guide to right conduct, is not only vitally interested in people's material and spiritual ends, their caste, and the four stages of life; it also directs their actions in other aspects of life. For instance, Hinduism emphasizes the virtues of truth, nonviolence, sacrifice, purity, and renunciation or detachment.

Truth is one of the most important virtues an individual may possess. It is a criterion by which the character of an individual may be judged. Nonviolence stems from the belief that essentially all things are images of one's own self and consequently should be respected. In modern times, Mahatma Gandhi advocated nonviolence not only for the individual, but also as an ideal for international life. Gandhi thought of Hinduism as the search for truth through nonviolence. Sacrifices are necessary if the world is to function properly. Purity is both ceremonial and moral, for all the purificatory practices prescribed by the Hindu scriptures were designed to bring about the *moral* purity of the individual. Perhaps, however, the greatest virtue a Hindu might practice is renunciation or detachment from all ties to this material world. This includes detachment from the good as well as the evil things of the world.

Hinduism synthesizes the spiritual and material ways of life by advising all to renounce the passion and attachment which accompany action, but not action itself. It believes that the renunciation of all earthly matters, along with an exclusive preoccupation with the contemplation of spiritual matters, can be reconciled with the individual's responsibility to participate in the affairs of the community and society. The Hindu ideal is to be in the world, yet not of the world; to act in the world, yet not be attached to these acts, or their results. When one works without attachment, no new karma is created. Thus, Hindus will further the progress of their society and the liberation of themselves at the same time.

9

Buddhism

No village law, no law of market town,
No law of a single house is this—
Of all the world and all the worlds of gods
This only is the law, that all things are impermanent.

Buddhism, unlike Hinduism, traces its origin to a
definite historical period and a single founder.
Historical Buddhism was founded in the sixth
century B.C. by Gautama Buddha, who is often
simply called the Buddha or the "Enlightened
One." The Pali spelling *Gotama* is frequently
substituted for the Sanskrit spelling *Gautama*.
Since the Buddha was a prince of the Sakya
tribe, he is sometimes referred to as *Buddha*

Eugene W. Burlingame, trans., *Buddhist Parables* (New York:
Yale University Press, 1922). Used with permission.

Sakyamuni, that is, "Buddha Sage of the Sakya Tribe." Much of his life is veiled by the myths that have gradually accumulated over the centuries, but certain aspects of his life are accepted as fact.

Gautama Buddha was the son of a chieftain of the Sakya tribe who ruled an area in the foothills of the Himalayan Mountains which was located within the boundaries of the modern kingdom of Nepal. Trained from childhood in those arts befitting his high station, especially war, he enjoyed all the advantages that power and wealth could procure at that time. He married, and when he reached the age of twenty-nine, his wife had a son called Rahula. The same year Gautama Buddha left his home and family, his wealth and power, and started on a quest that resulted in the founding of a new religion.

Tradition tells us that chance meetings in quick succession with an old man, a sick man, a dead man, and a religious beggar caused Gautama Buddha to realize for the first time the staggering truth that life is filled with misery and decay. The impact of these meetings was all the greater because, up to this time, Gautama's father had sheltered him from the harsh realities of the world. After this sudden awakening, he had no peace of mind but saw himself old while still young, poor while still rich, sick while healthy, and dead while living. This quick fading of happiness and pleasure into old age, suffering, and death troubled him deeply.

Haunted by the universality of suffering, the inevitability of decay, the passing of pleasure, and the brevity of life, he left his home and sought answers from scholars who tutored him in the Vedas and the *Upanishads,* the source of Hindu truths. Unsatisfied, he left them and tried to find answers in the practice of asceticism. Since this life of austerity merely ravaged his body and brought him nothing but a closer view of death and suffering, he rejected asceticism as sterile and unprofitable and began to follow a middle way between the two extremes of pampering and punishing the body. Then, one day, six years after he had begun his search, while sitting in meditation under a tree, he was suddenly enlightened as to the cause of man's suffering and the cure for these sorrows. With this inner illumination, he became the Buddha, or the "Enlightened One." From that time until his death about forty-five years later, he devoted himself to a life of service to his fellow man. He taught others the way he had discovered to escape from a sorrowful existence that had plagued the world for ages beyond count. This is Buddhism.

Buddhist Literature

The teachings of Buddhism are to be found in an extensive literature which was written after Gautama Buddha's death in both the Sanskrit and Pali languages. This literature was supplemented by later writings, largely in Chinese, Tibetan and Japanese. These are the languages of the people who, together with the people of South and Southeast Asia, responded most enthusiastically to the teachings and practices of Buddhism.

Buddhist literature is grouped around two major schools of Buddhism—*Hinayana* and *Mahayana.* Hinayana, literally "Lesser Vehicle," is sometimes referred to as Southern Buddhism because it is stressed in Ceylon, Burma, and Thailand. Southern Buddhists prefer to use the term *Theravada* instead of Hinayana when referring to the kind of Buddhism they follow. Hinayana or Theravada is more concerned with the literal teaching of Gautama Buddha and demands more of the individual. Mahayana, "Greater Vehicle," is sometimes called Northern Buddhism because it is emphasized in China, Tibet, Japan, and Korea in northern Asia. It appears to be more compassionate and demands less of the individual. Mahayana is concerned more with the example and heart of Gautama Buddha than with his teaching.

The Hinayana, or Theravada, canon, written in Pali around 80 B.C., is supposed to be a reliable presentation of Gautama Buddha's original teaching. This canon is known as the *Tripitaka,* or "Three Baskets." The *Basket of Discipline* contains the rules and precepts for members of the Buddhist order. The *Basket of Discourses* consists of discourses given by either Gautama Buddha or one of his disciples and includes the *Dhammapada,* a well-known anthology of Buddhist sayings. The *Basket of Higher Doctrine* contains seven works discussing principles and special doctrines. The Mahayana scriptures, a later development of Buddhist thought, were generally written in Sanskrit. The important works in this school include *Saddharmapundarika,* or "The Lotus of the True Doctrine," and *Sukhavativyuha* or "A Complete Description of the Blessed Land" of Buddha Amitabha. Amitabha Buddha is the compassionate lord of the Western Heaven to whom millions of Buddhists direct their prayers for mercy. *Prajnaparamitas,* "Perfection of Wisdom," is a collection of *sutras* teaching the doctrine of "Emptiness," *Sunyata.* These include *Vajracchedika,* or "Diamond Sutra."

Impermanence and Change

Buddhist writings teach that everything is impermanent and constantly changing. All things, animate and inanimate, human and divine, are transitory, momentary phenomena in the universe, mere passing scenes in the moving pictures of life. Gautama Buddha expressed this thought by saying "Whatsoever is an arising thing, all that is a ceasing thing." Not only are all things short-lived, but during their lifespan a constant process of change accentuates the fleeting character of their existence. Nothing remains as it is, for every moment witnesses the changing character of all things. The Buddhist refers to this change as the process of becoming. The youth of this generation become the aged of the next generation; the fresh plant of the morning becomes the withered plant of the afternoon; the soaring mountain of this age becomes the lowly hill of a future age. This is the nature of all things. All things are bound to the wheel of change and decay.

Humans are Soulless

Since they consider all things impermanent, the Buddhists logically hold that individuals have no permanent selves or souls. They are creatures made up of five *skandhas*, or components: 1) the physical body, 2) sensations or feelings, 3) perception, 4) volition or predisposition, 5) consciousness. A person is merely the embodied collection of five components and owes his or her existence to them. When these components fall apart, the individual dies. The death of the physical body signifies the final dissolution of that particular embodiment of skandhas, and no permanent self or soul lingers on.

Although Gautama Buddha did not believe that a permanent soul or self remained after death, he did teach that something continued, for he believed, like the Hindus, in rebirth or continued existence. It was, in fact, the purpose of the Buddha to free persons from the bondage of continued existence. Because he was vague on this point, this part of his doctrine has been explained in various ways. One theory is that a person's *karma* continues after death. Karma is that moral law of causation by which all the acts of a person have their good or bad effects in some future period, generally in another existence.

After the death of individuals, their karma, or the sum of all the good and bad results of their previous acts, enters into another five skandhas which together with the karma will live on as another individual. Karma is the result of actions and operates through skandhas just as electricity operates through metal and air. There are always skandhas being formed to receive karma. Individuals live on because their acts formed the karma which in turn united with five skandhas to create another individual. The present individual is identified with the individual of a former existence through the karma, but not through a soul or self. Viewed in this light, karma is the cause of the continued existence of individuals, and it will continue to be embodied until enlightenment is attained. The sum total of a person's actions in each existence keeps the wheel of life spinning through each successive existence.

The Four Noble Truths

Two major statements were made by the Buddha immediately after he was enlightened under the tree. These are expressed by the Buddhist as the Four Noble Truths and the Noble Eightfold Path. The Four Noble Truths are: 1) suffering is universal; 2) the cause of suffering is desire; 3) the elimination of desire is the cure for suffering; 4) the Noble Eightfold Path is a practical technique of action designed to help individuals eliminate desire.

The great overwhelming fact of suffering is every person's fate. Pain, sickness, and death are constant reminders of the endless sorrows of the world's people. Even the few pleasures that a person sometimes experiences are a cause of suffering, for the realization that all pleasures are transient brings sorrow. People are condemned to be frustrated until they overcome ignorance, for every pleasure, impermanent by nature, is merely the beginning of some sorrow. All things are doomed to death and decay, and to oppose this inevitable fate is to suffer inevitable sorrow. These sufferings are multiplied by continued existences, since suffering and existence go hand in hand. Only the termination of this continued existence by means of enlightenment can bring relief from continued suffering.

Desire is the cause of suffering. Desire also causes rebirths into other existences and hence continued suffering. The human heart craves all manner of things, riches and power, health and long life, things existing and things nonexistent. Craving for these things is the cause of suffering because such craving is founded on the hope of permanent satisfaction, either on earth or hereafter, and such permanent satisfaction can never be obtained on earth because change is a human's fate, nor in heaven because the gods are subject to the same law of impermanence and change as are humans. Besides, the individual has no self or soul which continues after death. The only way to avoid suffering and continued existence is to crush all desires and sever all earthly attachments. The person who has suppressed all his or her desires for permanent satisfaction, for existence, for individuality, will become an Enlightened One—a Buddha. When individuals are enlightened, when they realize that impermanence, change, and suffering are the rule of human existence, they understand that there is no self and that they must learn to dispel this illusion of self if they are to be free. When they comprehend fully the permanence of impermanence and change, they are ready to enter into that indescribable state of "Thusness" by which the Buddhists describe *Nirvana*.

To reach Nirvana is the goal of all. Nirvana has been described as a state of desirelessness and impersonal ultimate reality, but actually it is a state or condition that only those who have reached Buddhahood can completely comprehend. Literally, the term *Nirvana* means "extinction." One who has attained Nirvana has no desire of the senses, no craving for life, but an enlightened understanding of human nature and the universe.

Like the Hindus of his day, Gautama Buddha believed that salvation meant escaping to Nirvana. The flame blown out by the wind no longer exists; nor does the person exist who has been liberated from name and body. Such a one is beyond the Wheel of Life and is superior to any god who is still tied to continued existences. The destruction of desires breaks the karma-chain of continued existences, and to sever the karma-chain is to discontinue the existences of the individual and suffering. The mind approaching Nirvana has attained to extinction of all desires.

The Noble Eightfold Path

Gautama Buddha was a practical man. He gave to humans certain ethical guides and commandments to help them destroy all desires, escape the tragedy of life, and reach the final goal of Nirvana. Desire is suppressed by following the Noble Eightfold Path of ethical conduct and mental discipline. These precepts consist of 1) right knowledge, or a knowledge of suffering, its cause and elimination, and the absence of superstition or delusion; 2) right aspirations, or high and worthy intentions; 3) right speech, characterized by kindness, frankness, and truthfulness; 4) right conduct, which is peace-loving, pure, and honest behavior; 5) right livelihood, or practicing an occupation that does not injure any living thing; 6) right effort, or making an effort in self-training; 7) right mindfulness, or having an active, alert mind; and 8) right meditation.

Gautama Buddha did not teach a Godhead or even a real future life for the individual. Gods and heavens were subject to the same laws as all the universe, and therefore could provide little satisfaction for humans. They could not help people, for they too were impermanent and subject to change. Buddha was greater than any god. In fact, Buddha considered any speculation about the Godhead and the nature of God as a waste of time. His doctrine compelled people to walk alone in working out their salvation; it denied them all help from any supposed God or gods as well as a future heaven.

The Spread of Buddhism

Buddhism spread rapidly after the Buddha's death. Asoka (296 to 237 B.C.), a famous Indian emperor who was converted to Buddhism, devoted a great part of his life to the propagation of Buddhist doctrines. He sent missionaries to many parts of the world. Gradually, all India and the neighboring island of Ceylon were converted. Then Buddhism spread eastward and southeastward to the present lands of Sri Lanka, Burma, Malaysia, Thailand, Laos, Cambodia, Vietnam, and Indonesia. It entered China during the first century of the Christian era and became an integral part of Chinese life. During the seventh century A.D., Buddhism entrenched itself in Japan with the conversion of Prince Shotoku Taishi. During the eighth century, Buddhist missionaries introduced Buddhism into Tibet where it took a mixed form called *Tantrism.*

Buddhism still plays a prominent religious role in Asia, except in Pakistan, Bangladesh, Indonesia, Malaysia, India, and the Philippines. Pakistan, Bangladesh, Indonesia, and Malaysia are mostly Muslim today, Hinduism in India gradually absorbed Buddhism, and the majority of the Filipinos are Christians. In China, Buddhism was but one of several religions and philosophies that the Chinese harmonized. The Chinese were Buddhists, Taoists, and

Confucianists at the same time. Buddhism plays a much diminished role in the People's Republic of China. In Japan, Buddhism shares its religious role with Shinto, an indigenous religion.

In both China and Japan, Buddhism divided into various sects which gave different interpretations of·Buddhist doctrine. Many of these sects had their origin in China and were later carried over to Japan. There is no question, however, that Buddhism has greatly influenced the ethical and artistic development of all the areas it has penetrated.

10

Social Life in India

A surging river of new ideas and new practices is influencing the traditional social life of India. National and international events are impinging upon the daily lives of the people with increasing regularity and demanding change. But the people are resisting, for attitudes and customs buttressed by thousands of years of tradition are not easily overturned. Consciously or unconsciously, willingly or unwillingly, the Indian people today are in the process of meeting a challenge to their traditional social life, a challenge which they can neither completely accept nor completely reject. They are trying to adapt and absorb it in much the same manner in which they accommodated other alien challenges over the many centuries of India's past.

Change is evident in India—particularly in the cities—but the old social ways are still cherished and the new has not yet usurped the place of the old. Many of the traditional social institutions and customs endure with their vigor undiminished and their hold upon the people unbroken. To ignore their customary social life is to ignore and misunderstand the Indian people. To be unappreciative of the Indian's longing to preserve what has been held dear for many centuries is to be insensitive to the wellsprings of the Indian heart. The modern may be necessary and rational, but for many Indian people the old is necessary and sacred.

Change may not be wanted, but it is often necessary if a people are to move forward rapidly in their social, economic, and political development. Although the traditional caste system into which most of the Indian people are gathered is regarded as basic to Hindu society, and its perpetuation held a sacred duty, many Indian leaders believe it to be one of the greatest obstacles to the unification of the nation. Caste, with its rigid segregation of groups, tends to keep people apart rather than bring them together. One of the primary goals of the modern leaders of India is to unify the nation, because they realize that any substantial and rapid progress is contingent upon the united efforts of all, and they are patiently—sometimes impatiently—trying to moderate the divisive tendencies of communal groupings and harmonize their differences. Gandhi gave a spiritual and moral encouragement to this harmony when he bestowed upon the Untouchables—the outcastes of India—the name "Children of God" and pleaded that they be treated with more tolerance and respect by the more fortunate castes. Some leveling of the high barriers of caste will undoubtedly quicken India's progress toward the goal of a completely united people.

The family is also a basic social institution of India, and it is cherished and protected by laws, written and unwritten, customs, attitudes, and religion, which all combine to uphold its sanctity and integrity. Formerly in India its importance was heightened by the custom of estimating the population of an area in numbers of families rather than in numbers of individuals. Traditionally it was a large household, rooted deeply in the soil, and requiring many hands to wrest a living from the land. It was a *joint family,* for members joined together in eating, in worshipping, and in holding property. Today a great many Indians still live and die within the secure embrace of such families, but a growing number do not.

The exodus of people from the farming communities to the city, the absorption of many villagers into factories and plants, the advancement of education and the movement of the educated young into professions and skilled occupations, are taking large numbers from the traditional families and causing them to form new and smaller families that are more suitable to their physical environment and economic condition. The traditional family is still the pattern for large areas of India, but other family patterns are evolving in response to the changing times.

Greater opportunities and new national and international demands are broadening the scope of the traditional role of women in India. Obedience, sacrifice, and service still characterize the role of women in India, but many now render service to the community, the nation, and the world, not merely to their own home and family. Indian women are reaping the benefits of their country's new emphasis on education, and for some their horizons are no longer limited to home and village. It is true that the majority of Indian women are still devoting their whole efforts to the family and the home, but the number working in broader domains is increasing daily.

The traditional social life of the people has not been radically changed for most Indians, but all have been affected by the new forces to some degree. The absorptive talent of the Indians is at work, and when the process of adaptation is finished, if it ever is, the result will also be something new, and something Indian.

11

Caste in India

It is better to do one's duty badly than another's well.
—Manu X, 97

Caste is a word used to describe the system of social groupings into which most of the people of India are gathered. The Indian community is composed of a large number of distinct social groups, or castes. Basic to Hindu society, the caste system is the result of the association of many different types of people and numerous social and occupational groups within a common territory and cultural system.

It developed over a long period and in various ways. When the fair-skinned Aryans conquered

North India around 1500 B.C., it is thought that they introduced into Indian society a class division based on physical differences. The fair Aryans became the superior class; the darker-skinned aborigines were reduced to an inferior position in society. In the course of time other people entered India and took over a higher or lower place in the social system depending upon their power. Groups were also distinguished by their occupations and professions. Since people tend to associate largely with members of their occupation, early in Indian history classes were differentiated on the basis of function and work. From these occupational groupings there developed group customs, group attitudes, and a keen feeling of group solidarity which set the members of each occupation apart from other members of the Indian community.

Castes grew out of religious differences. Some were formed by breaking off from other castes, while others were formed by outcastes who had lost their own caste status for one reason or another. Primitive tribes responded to the more sophisticated economic and social system developing around them in India by holding themselves aloof and further emphasizing their own peculiar taboos and customs. At times some of these tribes became low-caste Hindus, entering the caste system as a body.

A complicated social system arose out of the associations of these physical, political, occupational, religious, and tribal separations. The Indian community divided into many distinct sections now referred to as castes. During the long course of India's history these castes grew and multiplied, as a continuous flow of new physical types, occupations, and other foreign elements had to be allocated a place within the community. Castes died out and new castes formed, but always the caste system remained the basis of the social order.

Social Hierarchy

Castes are arranged on a social scale rising from the Untouchables at the bottom to the Brahmins at the top. It is not aways easy to fix the the exact place of each caste on the scale, but Hindu society can be viewed broadly as a grouping of castes in different layers of the social strata. Three great caste groupings may be distinguished—the twice-born group, the once-born group, and the Untouchables.

The twice-born include the Brahmin, or priestly caste; the

Rajputs and those who claim descent from the *Kshatriya,* or military caste; and the *Vaisya,* or mercantile and agricultural caste. These are the elite castes of India. The Brahmin caste traditionally ranks first among this group and its members are generally regarded with honor. This group is called twice-born because its members have two births, a physical birth when they are born into the world and a spiritual birth when they are initiated into the mysteries of religion and given the sacred thread to wear. The sacred thread is a kind of string which is looped over and hangs from the left shoulder. The Brahmin's thread should be made of cotton, a Kshatriya's of hemp, and a Vaisya's of wool.

The once-born, or those who lack the second spiritual birth, are those castes who claim to be the modern representatives of the *Sudras.* Traditionally, the Sudras were supposed to serve the twice-born, but today this function is no longer descriptive. The members of this group are engaged in all kinds of skilled and unskilled work which has no connotation of service to the twice-born. This group includes people ranging from farmers, artisans, landlords, and moneylenders, to those engaged in all types of unskilled labor.

Untouchables constitute the lowest social layer of the Indian community. They were formerly known as the Depressed Classes, and are now officially called the Scheduled Castes. Ghandi called them *Harijans,* or the "Children of God." The Untouchable, as the name indicates, cannot touch anything without contaminating it. Belief in the contaminating power of an Untouchable is so great that, in South India, a scale of distances was worked out within which different groups of Untouchables may not approach a Brahmin. For example, one kind of Untouchable might not come within eight yards of a Brahmin, another twelve yards, and still another sixteen yards. The members of this group perform those jobs which the Hindus consider most degrading. Caring for and touching the dead, removing filth, sweeping, and working with leather.

Within each of these broad groups of twice-born, once-born, and Untouchables there is also an inner hierarchy. The Brahmin is the highest caste of the twice-born group and therefore at the apex of all the castes of India. The Rajputs and the present-day representatives of the Kshatriyas rank second, and the Vaisyas and their representatives rank third. The caste rank of the once-born is often determined by the relationship of a particular caste within this group to the twice-born. Generally speaking, the closer the relationship to the twice-born, the higher the rank of the caste within the once-born group. Thus, caste rank might be specifically indicated by the twice-born's acceptance or refusal of water and food from a particular caste member of the once-born group. Whether or not a member of a caste within the once-born group can touch one of the twice-born is also a criterion for judging the rank of that caste.

The Untouchables are divided into a bewildering number of divisions organized on a graduated social scale. The gap between the lower and higher levels of the Untouchable group is regarded by the members of this group as being as great as that between the Untouchables and the Brahmins.

The various castes are further divided into smaller divisions called subcastes. The members of these subcastes generally follow the same pattern of social life and use the same food and drink as the main caste. However, the subcastes are essentially exclusive social groups. Sometimes they are so exclusive that they consider themselves as separate castes. Subcastes are often further divided into smaller groups which have their own special rules and regulations. The factionalizing of Indian society has sometimes been carried to unbelievable extremes.

Membership in a subcaste or smaller subdivision may determine an individual's position in the main caste, but it is the main caste which determines the individual's position in the Indian society. The subcaste conditions a member's relations with those who belong to the main caste, but it has little influence upon the member's relations with other main castes in the Indian community.

Principal Characteristics of Caste

The principal characteristics of the caste system are: 1) members marry within the caste; 2) caste members eat and drink with each other and not with members of an inferior caste; 3) members practice a common occupation which is generally hereditary. Exceptions to all these characteristics can be found in India, especially with regard to the practice of a common occupation.

Marriage within the caste is the regulation most rigorously enforced today. Should a man or woman marry outside the caste, he or she may be expelled from the caste and become an outcaste, a most terrible fate for Indians. They are generally ostracized by their clan members and often by their own families. They have less security than the members of the lowest caste, and are often shunned and insulted by other Indians. The marriage of a woman to a member of a caste inferior to her own is considered an unnatural act, and even her parents are liable to be reduced to the inferior caste into which their daughter has married. A woman can marry a man of equal rank or a man of superior caste. The latter practice is known as "marrying up," or *hypergamy*. A high-caste man may sometimes marry down, but the female may marry only with her equals or superiors. Because of this restriction, it is often difficult to find suitable husbands for daughters, and parents are often forced to expend great sums of money on dowries in order to obtain suitable matches.

Hindu law permitted concubinage, especially when the wife was barren. Concubines were taken from outside the caste, provided the castes they came from were clean. High-caste males also took mistresses, provided these women were members of castes from which they might accept water and that these mistresses did not cook their food or eat with them. It should be noted that these practices are officially frowned upon by Indian leaders today.

Many of the young educated Indians today have no personal objection to marrying outside their castes, but the social pressure on their own and the womans' families are so great that they hesitate to do so. They resolve the conflict by marrying someone chosen by their parents who has also met their own approval. Intellectually, they reject the convention that forces such a marriage arrangement, but they conform because it is the practical thing to do under the circumstances.

Marriage outside the subcaste is much more common today than formerly. Although such a practice is generally frowned upon, it does not bear the same stigma as marriage outside the main caste. The furor over a marriage outside the subcaste often dies down after a short period of time, but the social ostracism that results from a marriage outside the main caste is generally permanent.

There is some change taking place in India. Some modern Indians are marrying outside their castes. It is not uncommon to see newspaper advertisements, inserted by Indians who are looking for mates, frankly stating that caste is no obstacle to marriage. A typical advertisement of this kind will read:

Matrimonial
Good match for handsome, highly qualified Brahmin, 27. Class I officer. Monthly income over rupees two thousand. *Caste no bar.* Girl main consideration.

In some studies made among college students it was found that one-half of the Brahmins and four-fifths of the non-Brahmins approved of marriage outside of caste. It must be remembered that these were college students and, as such, represent a very small minority of the Indian population.

Eating and Drinking

As a general rule, orthodox Hindus are required to dine with members of their caste only. The eating and drinking of the orthodox Hindu is carefully governed by regulations which apply to the food itself, the persons who cook the food, the hands which serve the food, and the company with whom the food may be eaten.

The kind of food that the Hindu is permitted to eat varies with locality and caste. The Brahmin should not eat animal food or drink alcoholic beverages. There are other castes that eat the meat of animals, especially mutton and goat's flesh. Most of the low castes in India are vegetarians, but this is a matter of necessity and not of choice. Most of them are too poor to buy meat.

The great majority of the Hindus will not eat the meat of the cow or peacock because they consider these animals sacred. The monkey is also honored and protected in many parts of India. The cow is revered by the Indians, and they commonly and lovingly refer to her as their "Mother." It is forbidden for Hindus to eat the flesh of a being they regard with such veneration and love. "May you eat beef!" is the worst curse one Hindu can fling at another.

Kachchi—Hedged with Regulations

Most of the restrictions with regard to the preparation of food and the company with whom the food may be eaten apply to the food known as *kachchi*. Kachchi is food, such as boiled rice, peas, beans, and wheat cakes, which is cooked in water. These items make up the daily food of the orthodox Hindu.

When preparing kachchi food, great care must be taken lest

even the shadow of an Untouchable fall upon the food and defile it. If this should happen, the food is immediately thrown away. Should it be touched by an unclean caste, a European for instance, it is also thrown away. Foreigners in India have had the embarassing experience of having even the lowest castes refuse to accept food from their impure hands. No orthodox Hindu will accept food from a European, or from a Muslim for that matter. Orthodox Hindus will eat with no one who is not a member of their caste or subcaste. If they cannot cook their own kachchi food, they must find a member of their own caste or subcaste or a Brahmin, who will prepare it for them. Brahmins are regarded as sanctified people and they do not defile the food. In fact, to have a Brahmin serve a caste is a sign of that caste's respectability. For this reason, Brahmins are much in demand as cooks. It is common to find Brahmin cooks in the various prisons of India because only a Brahmin cook is satisfactory to all the prisoners.

Before they eat, orthodox Hindus bathe their feet and hands carefully. Some eat with their waist bared; others eat completely stripped with the exception of a loincloth. Stories are told of orthodox Hindus who, even in the coldest weather, took off their clothes, bathed, and ate half-naked, exposed to the raw forces of nature.

Pakki—Less Regulated

There is another kind of food called *pakki* which is less susceptible to contamination. Pakki is food which is cooked in *ghee,* or clarified butter—butter that has been liquefied by boiling—and not boiled in water. It includes such foods as parched grains, curds, fruits, and sweets. This type of food can be eaten without much fear of contamination because it has been purified by being cooked with ghee, a product of Mother Cow. It can be eaten even after it has been touched by members of a caste regarded as clean but not, of course, after being touched by unclean castes. This is the kind of food which the orthodox Hindu traveler eats. It is jokingly said that Hinduism has one kind of food for the traveler and another kind for the Hindu who stays at home.

Other Ways of Pollution

Sea voyages pollute the orthodox Hindu because they make pure water unavailable. The orthodox will accept water only from those castes whose touch does not pollute it. The only type of water so holy that it cannot be polluted by any hands is water from the sacred river Ganges. Few can carry enough of the Ganges water to suffice for the entire ocean trip, and consequently many Hindus are polluted and lose caste by going abroad. When an orthodox Hindu returns from abroad, the caste may require that he or she perform purification ceremonies.

Hindus can be polluted by having something unclean come in contact with their mouths. For this reason orthodox Hindus will not lick gum or postage stamps, use toothbrushes made of pig's bristles, or smoke the water pipe of one who is not of their caste. The *hookah,* or water pipe, is a symbol of caste intimacy. Indians refer to the state of an outcaste as the condition of being cut off from smoking and drinking with caste members.

Eating and Drinking Today

Industrialization and education have done much to relax the attitudes of orthodox Hindus with regard to eating and drinking. Industrialization has created conditions which make the observance of food regulations extremely difficult. The building of factories which employ all kinds of castes and throw them helter-skelter together is one of these conditions. Industrialization is bringing increasing urbanization to India, and it is difficult to continue these elaborate ceremonial practices while away from home and living in a large urban area. The necessity of living in hotels and eating in public restaurants has accelerated the relaxation of Hindu eating habits. It is also difficult to avoid breaking caste rules when traveling on trains, ships, or planes. It is generally recognized that anyone who goes to a hospital for treatment must use hospital equipment. Spoons, glasses, instruments, which naturally have been used by other patients, do not defile the orthodox Hindu who has been hospitalized.

In a sample study of college students four out of five indicated that they would be willing to dine with anybody, regardless of caste or religion. Again, it must be remembered that the views of college students are more liberal and rational than those of the majority.

Occupations

Throughout the long history of India there has generally been some degree of craft-exclusiveness between castes. It is not uncommon even today to have an Indian give his occupation when asked to what caste he belongs.

In the self-contained and self-supporting villages of India, certain occupations are recognized as inherited caste callings. It is expected that at least one son of the family belonging to such a functional caste will follow in his father's footsteps and take up the caste trade. Such occupational groups include, among others, blacksmiths, barbers, potters, and washermen.

But caste is no longer a definite indication of a person's occupation. Rarely is a person's work equated with a certain caste. Any Hindu engaged in priestly duties is most likely a Brahmin, and any Indian found washing clothes, at least in North India, is most probably a *Dhobi.* However, modern Brahmins are to be found today working in a variety of occupations ranging from soldiering, police work, mail carrying, and work as messengers, to cooking and farming. Thus, although a man may be a Brahmin, he is not necessarily engaged in priestly work.

The increase in India's population and industrialization has led many Indians to desert the occupation of their forefathers. Over a long period of time too many people became occupied with making one product, with the result that the supply soon outstripped the demand, and the occupation would no longer support the number of people engaged in making the product. Also, the increasing number of cheap, machine-made products flooding India's markets has forced many of the native products off the market and abolished many trades and crafts. This process has forced many Indian artisans and craftsmen to seek other occupations.

Education and the ambition of lower castes to rise higher on the caste hierarchy have also affected occupational patterns in India. Many of the lower castes can elevate their status only by changing the character of their occupations. Any caste which deals with leather goods, sweeps the streets, or takes care of the dead must change its occupation to something else, say agriculture, if it wants to escape the low esteem in which it is held. Many castes have altered their standing in this manner, and this is another reason why castes and subcastes are continually forming and changing in India. Education is opening up more areas of work for the young Indian. India needs engineers, technicians, teachers, doctors, nurses, chemists, physicists, and a host of skilled workers to run the modern state. The leaders of India are encouraging young men and women to embark upon these new careers and thus lead the younger generations even further from the traditional paths of their parents.

Although there are still a number of functional castes in India which have hereditary tradition, many of the members of these castes no longer take up hereditary occupations. There is no obligation to do so at the present time. Modern Indians are entering those occupations which promise them rewards, not merely those formerly practiced by their parents.

Caste Government

The caste governs itself. It is an autonomous unit within Indian society which makes its own laws—many of them unwritten —and enforces them. The caste decides who will be members and who will not. It is the caste which expels members for one reason or another, and it is the caste which decides whether or not these members will be reaccepted into caste membership. The caste judges and condemns and the caste fixes the penalty for each offense.

The caste is commonly governed by a council composed of caste elders, prominent members, and a headman. Although the headman is sometimes elected, the office is more often hereditary. This governing body is called a *panchayat.* The number of members of this council is not fixed but varies from caste to caste. Generally there are as many councils as there are subcastes. The number of caste councils is determined by such factors as the amount of interdining and intermarriage, the size of the area, the availability of transporation, and the number of caste members. For instance, there may be several caste councils where the members are numerous and located over a large area.

Although the caste council performs executive and legislative functions, it is mainly concerned with judicial duties, and most of its time is spent in hearing cases. It sits as a tribunal with the headman presiding as judge and the directorate acting as a jury. Most of the cases brought before it are concerned with marriage, eating and drinking, improper performance of ceremonial requirements, smoking with men of another caste, and breaking one or more of the caste's innumerable social and religious regulations. Penalties fixed run from the very harsh to the very mild. The harshest penalty is expulsion from the caste. If the expulsion is permanent, the unfortunate one is condemned to a life of isolation and misery on earth. On death the person may be deprived of the spiritual ministrations of the Brahmin priest. If the expulsion is temporary, the person may be restored by performing certain purification ceremonies. Fines are sometimes imposed, as are painful ordeals like begging for food, being beaten with sticks, walking with heavy stones around the neck, and being exposed to ridicule.

The caste councils maintain strict discipline and watch their members carefully. Because of the close relationship that necessarily exists among the various members of the caste, it is comparatively easy to find out even minor infractions of caste regulations. The life of caste members is somewhat analogous to the glass-house existence of people living in small towns. Lower castes are much stricter in the enforcement of caste regulations than higher castes and much better organized in the government and regulation of caste affairs.

The Future of Caste in India

During lengthy periods of chaos and disorganization, the caste system gave India a stability and continuity essential to the survival of its civilization. No matter under what alien king or conqueror Indians were forced to live, they maintained a loyalty and devotion to the caste and in this way preserved Indian culture.

Caste has also given meaning and direction to the lives of the Indian people. Hindu writers often view caste as a cooperative rather then a competitive institution. For each person there is a special place in the community and a special function to perform. The acts performed by those in a previous existence have determined their special place and duties, and caste provides a framework within which these particular duties can be carried out conveniently and cooperatively.

Nationalism has influenced modern Indian attitudes toward caste structure. It is urging people to stop thinking of themselves as belonging exclusively to a caste or subcaste and to think of themselves instead as primarily citizens of the Indian nation. Rabindranath Tagore wrote as follows:

Nationalists say, for example, look at Switzerland, where, in spite of race differences, the peoples have solidified into a nation. Yet, remember that in Switzerland the races can mingle, they can intermarry, because they are of the same blood. In India there is

no common birth-right. And when we talk of Western Nationality
we forget that nations there do not have that physical repulsion,
one for the other, that we have between different castes. Have we
an instance in the whole world where a people who are not allowed to mingle their blood, shed their blood for one another except
by coercion or for mercenary purposes? And can we ever hope
that these moral barriers against our race amalgamation will not
stand in the way of our political unity?

Virtues such as loyalty, obedience, and devotion to the caste,
which in the past helped to preserve India's cultural values and
institutions, are now considered an obstacle in the path of India's
unification. It is difficult to create a united nation while Indian
society is divided. Therefore, Indian leaders argue, caste must go
because it is delaying the growth of India into a modern nation-
state. Modern India is dedicated to social progress. As long as millions of Indians are condemned to a lifetime of inferiority and
hopeless degradation, declare the Indian leaders, there can be no
real social progress in India. No society can make great social
advances while millions of its members are segregated. These are
the major reasons why many Indians think of caste as now being
detrimental to the nation and society of India. The new constitution of India forbids discrimination because of caste.

The caste system of India is a living institution. Caste is not a
rigid, unchanging system; it is a flexible system. It has survived because it has shown the ability to adapt to changing circumstances.
The caste system is undergoing a radical change today in response
to the shifting environment of the present time. Its religious or
metaphysical rationalization cannot endure unchanged in an industrial, scientific age. Modern times demand new forms of social
organization. Caste will remain at the basis of social life of India for
a long time to come, but it will be a changed and changing system.

12

The Family in India

With their teeth half-shown in causeless laughter,
And their efforts at talking so sweetly uncertain,
When children ask to sit on his lap
A man is blessed, even by the dirt of their bodies.
                                                —Kalidasa

The Indian family is part of the larger caste group. The family is basic to the caste, serving as the mechanism for enforcing the numerous caste regulations. In the family, caste members first learn their caste duties and are imbued with the caste spirit. It is the family which watches care-

Poem by Kalidasa reprinted from A. L. Basham, *The Wonder That Was India,* copyright 1954 by Sidgwick and Jackson, Ltd., London. Reprinted by permission of Sidgwick and Jackson and Hawthorn Books, New York.

fully over, the actions of the members and warns and exerts various pressures when the individuals of the family tend to stray beyond the caste limits.

The Joint Family

The family in India generally consists of parents, their married sons with their wives and children, all unmarried children, and sometimes other dependents such as aged parents, uncles, cousins, nephews, and brothers. This kind of family is commonly called a *joint family* because the family members join together in eating, in worshipping, and in holding property.

The average number of persons living in an Indian family is about six or seven, though in any given family there may be as many as fifty or more members and as few as two.

Common Property and Worship

Ancestral, and generally immovable, property is held in common. Family members are supposed to pool their resources and income, thus creating a common fund out of which each is given what is required for living purposes. The head of the family, generally the oldest male, is responsible for the supervision of the common property and finances. He does receive advice as to the disposition of the common property from other family members, especially the adult males. Though extremely powerful, he is restrained by sacred law and custom from making any use of the common property that might impoverish his descendants or the present individuals in the family.

From the earliest times provision has been made for the division of the common family property. In such close association of several families, quarrels, jealousies, suspicions, and envious comparisons are bound to arise, which may eventually culminate in demands to divide the family property among the members. When such divisions occur, the families split into individual units and become the creators of new joint families.

Individuals within the family may sometimes own property in their own right. Gifts, personal earnings, and jewelry may belong exclusively to the individual and not be included in the common fund. The jewelry that a bride has received from her parents and others customarily remains her personal property and cannot be taken from her.

Males of the joint family worship together. Sons, grandsons, great-grandsons, and others join together in commemorating their ancestors in a religious ceremony called *Sraddha*. This ceremony is extremely old and is similar to Chinese ancestor worship in that it links the living and the dead. Sraddha is another method of determining membership in a family group. Those entitled to participate in this ceremony by offering rice balls are regarded as genuine members of the family.

Headship and Responsibility

When the oldest male is too old or handicapped to remain as head, his eldest son assumes his position. If the grandmother is still alive, she often exerts tremendous influence, holding more authority than her eldest son and his wife, though technically and formally the headship descends in the male line.

Although the head of an Indian family carries great authority, he also bears great responsibility. From early childhood the individual has found his whole being and purpose revolving around family life. He has been indoctrinated with the necessity of preserving and continuing the family line. He finds it almost impossible to withstand the dictates of family duty even when this duty conflicts absolutely with his own ambitions. There are several instances of young Indians who gave up promising careers in order to take up family responsibilities. A brilliant young student had a magnificent future in psychology, but he was forced to give it up in order to ensure the future of his family. As the new head of a family he was compelled to undertake a career in business so that the family might have more income. Sacrificing his own future, he thus provided more opportunities for the other members of the family. Another promising young Indian retained his position as a clerk rather than jeopardize his family's financial state by taking time off for future studies.

Marriage and Family

Attitudes and customs with regard to marriage also indicate the importance of the family and the subordination of individual interests to its interests.

Marriage is thought of primarily in terms of protecting and preserving the basic family unit. It is not considered a private affair of romantic passion between two individuals but a family matter in which the individual has little, if any, choice. Traditionally, the bride and bridegroom do not see each other until the marriage ceremony itself. In India, unlike Europe and America, love is supposed to follow rather than precede marriage.

Because marriage is so essential to the preservation of the family, it is looked upon as a serious duty. Hindu parents have an obligation to find suitable mates for their children. Even though the head of the family is not a parent of the unmarried members, he still bears the responsibility of finding spouses for them.

The force of this obligation is so great that a Hindu family will often go into heavy debt in order to marry off a daughter. The expensive wedding of a high-caste Hindu is borne almost entirely by the bride's family. The social status of the bride's family generally determines the amount of her dowry, and a high-caste son-in-law is a high-priced item. He is expensive because there is no real necessity for him to marry early, whereas Indian girls are generally married off at an early age. In the past it was not uncommon for boys of ten to thirteen years of age to marry girls two or three years younger. In 1929, the Child Marriage Act was passed making it a criminal offense to arrange the marriage of a girl before she was fourteen or a boy before he was eighteen. In 1949, the Child Marriage Restraint Act raised the girls' marriage age from fourteen to fifteen. Many Indians circumvent these marriage laws by betrothing their daughters at any early age. Betrothal is tantamount to marriage. Since unmarried daughters are a continuous drain on the family resources that offers no hope of a return, Indian families are especially eager to marry them off early. The author has conversed with many Asian fathers and prospective fathers on the economic disadvantages of a daughter. A typical conversation with an expectant father might run something like this:

Prospective father: I hope it is a boy.
Author: Why not a girl?
Prospective father: It is better to have a boy. A girl is of little future value to the house. I must feed her, clothe her, take care of her, and then marry her off to another family. Her marriage costs me money too because I must give her a trousseau and make a feast. What do I get in return for all this money I have spent on her! Nothing. She may even come back and ask for more things if the husband's family is poor or stingy. No, I want a boy. He will stay home and work and, when I am old, care for me.

Many modern educated Indians have emphasized the necessity of decreasing the amount of money that is spent for wedding ceremonies, especially among high-caste Indians. The fact that certain wealthy men have agreed to keep the wedding expenses within one year's income of the bride's father gives some indication of the vast amounts that are expended in marriage ceremonies and practices. Among some of the lower castes this situation is reversed, and the bridegroom must pay a dowry to the bride's father.

Since the customs and ceremonies relating to marriage arrangements and weddings are regarded as important to the security of the basic family unit in India, the community demands their continuance, even though these customs place a tremendous financial burden on some families. This is another revealing instance of the importance of the family institution in India. No sacrifice is too great to maintain it.

Marriages in India are usually arranged between families with the help of a go-between. These go-betweens help families find suitable mates for their children and carry on all the many financial, religious, social, and other negotiations which are necessary to bring the marriage to a successful conclusion. The rise of cities has complicated the task of finding spouses, but the problem is partially met by the newspapers, which carry daily columns of matrimonial advertisements.

Generally speaking, whether the young man or woman is found by means of a go-between or a newspaper, certain conditions must be met. There is the all-important question of caste. Does the prospective mate belong to a caste into which the boy or girl can marry? What kind of family does the individual come from? Is it respectable? What is its economic condition? A family too rich or too poor can present complications for the future. Does the family live nearby? Indians, especially those in villages, prefer the in-laws to live in the neighborhood. Since the passage of the new laws regarding age, the age of the prospective mates is also an important consideration. All-important is the matter of comparing horoscopes. When a Hindu child is born, the position of the stars is plotted and a horoscope drawn up by an astrologer. Prior to the final decision the horoscopes of the boy and girl are compared by a Brahmin teacher or learned man. If the two horoscopes favor a union between the two young people, the marriage can take place without fear of dire consequences. Finally, financial arrangements must be fixed, including arrangements regarding time and form of payment.

It is only after all these questions have been settled that a marriage can be held. Throughout the negotiations the individuals to be married have usually not been consulted. This is not their affair; this is a family affair. The heads of the two families, with the advice of, their wives and other adult members, carry on the negotiations and make the final decision.

Many young modern Indians are following the Western custom of choosing their own wives. However, their number is still small, and the majority of Indian marriages are being arranged as in the past.

Marriage among Hindus is a tie not easily broken, especially if they belong to the middle or high castes. The high-caste Hindu will do everything possible to prevent the dissolution of a marriage. Such an attitude was especially characteristic of traditional India. Even in the case of a woman caught in adultery, the old Hindus thought it better to punish her severely than to divorce her. The stability and permanence of the family is still valued too highly by the majority of Indians to have it broken by divorce.

Nevertheless, the number of divorces is increasing. Separation by divorce was legalized under certain conditions by the Bombay Divorce Act of 1947. The new proposed Hindu Code Bill allows for divorce proceedings, but divorce remains rare.

Children and the Family

The child is living evidence of the successful continuation of the family—the important result of a duty well done. The families who arranged the marriage, the couple who participated in the marriage, have accomplished their aim—the extension of the family by the procreation of children. The child represents a link with the future as well as the past. In the faces of their children the family sees the creators of other families and a long, long line of other generations stretching endlessly into the future. The child is the happiness of the family.

A child is primarily a member of a family and only secondarily the specific offspring of a specific couple. He or she is responsible to a group, not merely to one or two individuals. For this reason relationships within the family are often quite blurred for the child. If the father has more than one wife, the child might refer to all the wives as mother. He or she uses the same word for both brothers and paternal cousins. The child might be as close to an aunt as to his or her real mother, and looks upon all females as having the same functions in the family. He or she finds happiness and security within the wide embrace of the large Indian family. Loved and cherished by the entire family, wrapped in great protective layers of affection, the child develops a sense of security which never leaves him or her throughout life. The male child is especially cherished and favored by the Indian family.

At this time the child imbibes a sense of responsibility and obligation toward the family which never really leaves him or her. It is not uncommon in India, or elsewhere in Asia, to see children of five or six taking care of even younger children. The teaching of the individual's duties with regard to the family starts early, and fundamental to all these duties is the preservation, stability, and continuation of the Indian family.

13

The Woman of India

As a general rule the horizon of the Indian woman is bound by the four walls of her courtyard. She is taught the truth that the highest ideal of life is service, but to her so often that means only service to her husband and her family.

—G. S. Dutt

The Indian woman leads a life of obedience, sacrifice, and service. She is taught from early childhood that she must sacrifice herself for the happiness of others. She thinks little of her own desires, but gives her attention, almost exclusively, to the needs and wants of her parents, her husband, her children, and her community.

G. S. Dutt, *A Woman of Bengal, Being the Life of Saroj Nalini* (London: The Hogarth Press, 1929).

The woman of India has both traditional and modern models of ideal womanhood which she is taught to emulate.

Traditional Models: Sita and Savitri

The foremost traditional model of Indian womanhood is Sita, the heroine of India's famous epic the *Ramayana*. "God bless you and may you be another Sita" is the lovely blessing that Indian girls often receive from older women. Sita gave up a comfortable life and followed her husband, Rama, into a jungle exile. She successfully resisted the seductive enticements of the demon-king of Ceylon who had kidnapped her, and after her rescue threw herself on a great fire to prove to Rama her innocence and constancy. Even after her innocence was proved when the fire rejected her, she suffered banishment and social ostracism. It would have been natural for her to have rebelled against her husband for his unjust treatment, but Sita remained a submissive, obedient wife and in all things bowed to the will of her husband. "She did as Rama told" is the crowning compliment paid her by the Indian community.

Another well-known model of the ideal Indian woman is Savitri. She also gave up high station and wealth and shared a life of exile in the jungle with her husband, Prince Satyavan. When she married him, she was told that one year from that date he would die. Savitri, a courageous, persistent woman, prayed and fasted during that first year of marriage that the gods might spare her husband's life. She still refused to accept the decree of destiny even after the Lord of Death, Yama, came and separated Satyavan's soul from his body, bound it with a cord, and led it away. Savitri followed Lord Yama, pleaded and argued with him, and refused to stop her stubborn pursuit. Struck by the magnitude of her love and devotion, Lord Yama released the soul of Prince Satyavan and permitted him to return to the world of the living. To this day an Indian bride may be called upon to be another Savitri.

Modern Models: Ramabai Ranade and Saroj Nalini

Ramabai Ranade, the wife of a prominent Indian official, is a modern model of Indian womanhood whose autobiography reveals a gifted and devoted life. Besides performing her many household tasks, she spent long hours educating herself, primarily to increase and improve her service to her husband. Ramabai sums up her philosophy of life in these words: "A wife's truest obligation is to protect her beloved husband from suffering of any kind at any time. This is her desire throughout her life, and to this she bends every effort in things great or small. This is her blessed privilege and her religious duty."[1]

Saroj Nalini, another modern ideal for the woman of India, made herself into a well-educated woman in order to be of greater service to her husband and to society. She was a devoted wife and mother and loved her husband with self-sacrificing passion. She wrote of him, "I only want your love while I live on earth, and your feet to lay my head on when I pass away."

Saroj Nalini not only provides a model for Indian women to follow in serving their immediate relatives, but also exemplifies for them the new woman who serves the greater community of the nation and the world. Rabindranath Tagore, the great philosopher-poet of India, stated that the modern ideal is no longer that of the woman who is merely a housewife and nothing else, "but the woman who works for the wealth of the home and community alike." He believed that this ideal was realized in Saroj Nalini's life.

Service in the Home

Although increasing numbers of Indian women are giving more time and effort in the service of their nation, the majority of them still spend most of their energies within the home. It is only a few highly educated professional women that serve the community exclusively. Most Indians, especially villagers, still consider marriage the only respectable career for an Indian woman, and most Indian girls are taught to look forward to a life of married service. The majority of females are married or widows.

Even the formal education of Indian girls is designed to prepare them for marriage. In this transitional period, the husband sometimes wants a bride who can be a companion as well as a manager of the household and a mother of his children. Consequently, education is often stressed because it helps procure husbands for the girls. The schools generally reinforce the ideas of obedience, sacrifice, and service with which the girls are first indoctrinated in the home.

[1] Ramabai Ranade, *Himself, An Autobiography of a Hindu Lady,* translated by Katherine Gates (New York: David McKay Company, 1938). Used with permission.

The girl of India is generally well prepared to assume the duties required of a good wife. She has been well trained in the art of cooking and in the care of the home. Even in homes where there are servants, wives take great delight in preparing dishes for their husbands and children. Village girls are taught a variety of duties associated with the farming home. One of the first tasks the village girls are introduced to is the preparation of cow dung for cooking. Straw is mixed with dung, stuck against a wall to dry, and then heaped in piles. Dung makes a good fire and burns with an intense, smokeless flame. The girls are also taught to husk rice, grind grains, and help with the harvesting and planting of the fields. Most girls learn these tasks early, and what they do not learn the mothers-in-law soon teach them.

The Indian bride must be a virgin. From puberty on she is taught to maintain a certain reserve and distance from all men with the exception of her closest relatives. In traditional India care was taken that the boy and girl did not meet before their marriage, and the girl rarely, if ever, saw her husband prior to the wedding night.

Traditionally, the Indian girl has little choice in picking her husband. It is the duty of the parents to choose a husband; it is the duty of the girl to serve well the husband selected.

Certain changes are evident in modern India. Occasionally, love matches take place but these are the exceptions rather than the rule. Wherever such cases occur, there is often conflict between the young couple and their two families because of the radical break with customary ways. In present-day India, the engaged individuals are shown photos of each other, and sometimes they see each other in person before the marriage night. In the cities, and particularly among the young educated set, betrothed couples go out together, but this practice is still frowned upon. Even after the marriage has taken place, the woman is supposed to maintain a modest demeanor in the presence of men.

The Woman in the Family

The position of the woman in the family varies from stage to stage of her existence in the household. Each passing stage of life in the family brings new duties, new responsibilities, and new authority.

When she arrives in the family as a new bride, she is quiet, unobtrusive, and self-effacing. She is expected to show deep respect to the parents of her husband and to observe strict propriety toward her brothers-in-law. She must observe numerous restrictions and regulations. She should not cook or serve rice to the older members of the family. She should not prepare the offerings for ritual worship. Neither she nor her husband should manifest any affection for each other in public. No matter how great the provocation, she must always obey her husband and mother-in-law.

When she becomes a mother, her status changes. She is given a greater amount of freedom and is treated with much more respect. Children are a mark of success. Now she is prized more by the entire family because she has fulfilled her duty as a woman and a wife. Motherhood is revered in India. Gandhi expressed this reverence when he said: "Today the Gita is not only my Bible or my Koran; it is more than that—it is my mother. When a woman becomes a mother, she becomes a goddess. For woman is the eternal field in which the self is born." A woman is proud to be a wife and a mother. She lavishes tender care and devotion on her child, her husband, and her family. The child never forgets the love and care he or she received from his or her mother, and the most cherished memories of Indian men revolve around their mothers. There are innumerable examples of self-effacing love of the wife for her husband, and a gentle solicitude for his health and welfare is a quality that suffuses the women of India.

As she grows older in the household, she wins more and more freedom until she may eventually rule the domestic matters of the house. She may assume the position of mother-in-law and have daughters-in-law of her own to rule and teach. She finally attains the fullness of dignity and respect when she becomes the ruling matriarch of the family, and her influence continues to increase with age and experience.

When a woman becomes a widow, she enters a period of sorrow that often endures until her death. Social custom forbids Indian widows to remarry. This custom, formerly applicable to high-caste women, has gradually grown to include all widows, no matter what their caste. Usually this custom does not cause undue hardship to a widow whose children are grown, because she can continue to live, relatively happy, in her own household, surrounded by her children and grandchildren. If, however, she has no children of her own and is still young, she is often unhappy. India has many millions of widows. An Indian commentator, S.

Chandrasekhar, has written: "The paucity of females keeps up the custom of early marriage for girls. Early marriages customarily involve considerable disparity in age between husbands and wives. This difference in age increases widowhood. Since widows cannot remarry, widowhood increases the shortage of eligible brides, which accentuates the paucity of females. Thus the vicious wheel whirls on."[2] The young widow is expected to live a life of severe simplicity. Depending on caste, time, place, and circumstances, a variety of restrictions govern her way of life. She should wear a white sari without a border and never adorn her body with jewelry. She must eat only one meal a day, which is cooked by her alone. This meal should contain no meat, fish, honey, wine, or salt. Perfumes are forbidden, and many widows cut their hair very short. A widow is expected to spend her time in prayer and meditation and religious exercises. She should not attend the Indian festivals which the Indians enjoy very much, nor should she manifest gaiety or joy. A widow is believed to bring bad luck, and consequently is seldom welcomed by others at their gatherings. She is condemned to a life of austerity, unhappiness, and frustration.

Remarriage of widows has been legalized in India, but the pressure of public opinion operates to prevent such a practice, especially in the rural areas. Virgin widows do occasionally remarry. Marital advertisements appear from time to time in the newspapers stating that virgin widows are acceptable. Some effort is being made in modern India to train young widows to take up constructive work that will benefit the nation and the community.

Subordination of Women

It is customary to speak of the subordination of the women to the men of India. An old Indian saying states, "As a girl she was under the tutelage of her parents, as an adult, of her husband, and as a widow, of her sons." Even the Buddhist nun, advanced in age and sanctity, is regarded as subordinate to the youngest male novice of the order. The Law of Manu, the canon law of India, stresses this subordination in harsh, unyielding language, stating that "She should do nothing independently even in her own house."

The Indian woman usually accepts the authority over her,

[2] S. Chandrasekhar, "The Family in India," *Marriage and Family Living*, Vol. 16, November, 1954, pp. 336–342. Used with permission.

whether from her parents, her husband, or her elders. She must find satisfaction and pleasure in her dependent role of service and in being needed, loved, and approved by those close to her. Most Indian women do not regard themselves as inferior to any man, but as having a different function to perform in life. Most do not desire to take over male functions, but do desire recognition that their role in life is also important. They consider that it is not a question of equality of rights, but a question of different functions which carry their own unique duties and rights. When each individual performs his or her assigned duties, a harmony of social life results. The duty of the woman of India is to transmit the cultural heritage and create new families.

Moreover, it is not entirely true to say that all decisions are made by the husband. Here as in many instances, there is a gap between theory and practice. The wife has a great deal to say about the upbringing of the children, their work and play, and their future employment and marriage, and she exerts a strong influence in the management of the house. It is the women of India who transmit to the children the old traditions and legends of India and give the children their religious instruction.

It is the Indian women of the villages who often block modern progress because of their conservatism and reluctance to change traditional ways of life. Reformers have found time and time again that reform was only possible after they had convinced the women of the benefits of change. Women have died rather than leave the seclusion of the *purdah,* and women still remain the bulwark of Indian traditional values.

Ultimate decisions are formally announced by men. The women, however, exercise great influence in the making of these decisions and often exercise a veto power after they have been made.

Conflict and Change

Many traditional attitudes in India with regard to women are now being modified. The forces of conservatism and progress are in conflict. Generally speaking, it is the city people and the educated classes—these two groups are usually synonymous—that favor the progressive changes. Great Indian leaders like Gandhi, Nehru, and Ram Mohan Roy were exponents of this progressive, educated Indian class. They even permitted their children to marry outside the caste. Opposed to this educated class are the great mass of Indians living in the villages, especially the womenfolk of these villages. However, even the educated classes do not favor a quick, radical change, but a slow, orderly modification of social customs.

The problems created by the current campaign to educate Indian girls highlight the conflict between these two forces. The goal of compulsory education for all conflicts with the work requirements of the poorer villagers who need the girls to help in the farm and household work; every hand is needed to keep the spectre of hunger from the family. Moreover, the villagers feel that they do a better job of training the girl for marriage than could a formal school. Many of the schools are becoming coeducational, a practice contrary to the customs of the Indian people who strive to keep the girls separated from the boys, especially from the time of puberty onward. Education takes girls from the home and makes them independent. Many modern girls are starting to work toward a career which requires long years of preparation unhindered and undistracted by the duties of marriage. Marriage is delayed, and many boys will not marry girls who are extremely well educated. Villagers view a single woman over twenty with suspicion and her family with disfavor.

These problems engender conflict within the girl's family and within herself. She has been indoctrinated from early childhood with the conviction that marriage is her primary duty in life, and she knows that by refusing to accept this duty she is rejecting her purpose in life as conceived by the Indian community. But the desire for education is irresistible. Even women in *purdah* learn to read and write. A male teacher in India solved the problem of teaching one group of women secluded by *purdah* by putting up a cloth curtain between them and himself and teaching them blindfolded. In the cities it is now normal for girls to go to school. In the villages the rate of literacy among the girls is rising.

The combination of education and increasing industrialization has created a situation in which conflict is inevitable. Girls are taught not to compete with boys, but to cooperate with them by concentrating on specific duties assigned to them as females. Emphasis is placed upon distinction of function, cooperation, and harmony. On the other hand, increasing education brings them into competition with men. New careers are opening up for them in fields formerly dominated exclusively by men. Thus, changing circumstances are bringing a new emphasis upon independence, competition, and individual initiative, as opposed to submissiveness, cooperation, and group harmony.

Expansion of the communication system in India has introduced other new elements into the life of the Indian woman. It is practically impossible for her to keep at a distance from men while traveling in crowded buses, trains, and airplanes. More and more girls are traveling by themselves on bicycles, in cars, and in public vehicles. This was rarely done in traditional India.

Changes are occurring within the family circle. Formerly, men and women did not eat together. Today it is not uncommon. Although most Indian men and women do not address each other by their first names, this practice is beginning to creep into the conversation of educated Indians.

The father is assuming more responsibility for the care of the child. Although some of the more conservative women grumble at this usurpation of their traditional functions, the father's participation in caring for the child was not unknown in ancient India. The Maina Canon speaks of fathers holding children in their arms and staggering around like weak camels under their squalling sons. The Canon went on to say that fathers got up in the middle of the night to put their child to sleep and scrubbed their baby's dirty garments. There is no doubt that many Indian fathers today are staggering around in the middle of the night trying to put their howling children to sleep.

Some Indian women responded to the call for independence from Britain with the same single-minded devotion that they formerly reserved to the service of the family. Some went to jail, marched in the streets, participated in civil disobedience programs, and rallied all classes behind the independence movement. The numbers of such women are destined to increase. India's rapid industrialization, broadening education, and political crises—all the social and economic requirements of a great emerging nation—are slowly modifying traditional attitudes. The social life of the Indian people is changing, and the Indian woman is changing, too.

One characteristic of the Indian woman has not changed. She is still dedicated to a life of service. But this aim is now expanding beyond the home to embrace the nation and the world. The choice of Madame Indira Gandhi as prime minister of India in 1966 and again in 1971 symbolizes the growing status and expanding horizons of the women of India.

14

Politics in India

A king should not attempt
to gain the earth unrighteously,
for who reveres the king
who wins unrighteous victory?
Unrighteous conquest is impermanent,
and does not lead to heaven.
—Mahabharata

Political thought in India today uniquely combines ideas and institutions imported from the West and attitudes and concepts inherited from classical times. This marriage of classical India and the modern liberal West has resulted in a political product which is both old and new.

Excerpt from the *Mahabharata* reprinted from A. L. Bashan, *The Wonder That Was India*, copyright 1954 by Sidgwick and Jackson, Ltd., London. Reprinted by permission of Sidgwick and Jackson and Hawthorn Books, New York.

117

Because of the strong and lengthy influence exerted by the British upon India, the political philosophy and institutions of the Republic of India bear a close resemblance to those of Great Britain. Many provisions of the Indian Constitution of 1950 reflect the principles upon which British, American, and other liberal democracies base their political institutions. The preamble to this Constitution declares that the purpose of the Republic of India is ". . . to secure to all its citizens: Justice, social, economic, political; Liberty of thought, expression, belief, faith and worship; Equality of status and opportunity; and to promote among them all Fraternity assuring the dignity of the individual and the unity of the Nation."

Despite these expressions familiar to Westerners, the leaders of modern India are steeped in the wisdom and spirit of classical India. Mahatma Gandhi, the father of India, exemplified intense spirituality, an ascetic attitude toward life, and adherence to a code of conduct peculiarly Indian in form and content. Since the past has played an important role in shaping their attitudes and opinions, and since India's present stems from ancient roots, there can be no real grasp and appreciation of her contemporary political life until something is also known about her past political life.

India's Past

Archeological discoveries show that civilized people lived in India and Pakistan as early as 3000 B.C. In the 1920s, two of their long buried cities were uncovered—Mohenjo-Daro on the Indus River some two hundred miles north of Karachi, and Harappa about one hundred miles southeast of Lahore, Pakistan. Because of their locations, this civilization has been called various names: Indus Valley Civilization, Harappan Culture, and Indus Culture. The people who created this civilization are often named Dravidians. These cities were centers of a civilization covering an area of around one-half million square miles, and from them this civilization extended southeastward to the Gulf of Cambay close to Bombay on the west coast of India. It reached westward following the coastline of the Arabian Sea to the boundaries separating Iran and Pakistan, and northeastward, perhaps as far as the river Ganges.

It is believed that these ancient civilized people were of many physical types, and that the color of their skins varied from very dark to a light brown. Perhaps they were a mixture of people who had migrated to India by land and by sea over the centuries. We cannot speak with certainty about their origins, but we do know that the advances of these civilized people were startling for that time.

Their main cities were well planned with streets running north and south and east and west in regular fashion. The one- and two-story houses which lined these streets had open interior courtyards and advanced sanitary facilities. They obviously prized cleanliness, for their private and public baths and toilets were connected to a network of sewers which were lined with baked brick. They possessed a script which has not yet been deciphered. They worked with gold, copper, silver, and bronze. The imaginative toys they made are enduring witnesses of their love and devotion to their children. Their religion was centered on the fertility and life-giving features of their earth. They traded over the wide expanse of their civilized region, and they traded with those who lived beyond their cultural borders. On the island of Bahrain, in the Persian Gulf about a hundred miles south of the mouth of the Tigris and Euphrates Rivers, a civilization has been uncovered which has characteristics of both Indus Valley and Sumerian civilizations. The Dravidians also built an impressive dock at Lothal, on the Gulf of Cambay, which extended more than seven hundred feet and enabled them to load and unload cargoes during both high and low tides.

Then, around 1500 B.C., this Indus Valley Civilization began a rapid decline. Most probably there were a variety of causes for the deterioration, but some of the remains of their buildings and skeletons suggest the ravages of war. It was around this time that a people from Central Asia, called Aryans, began to assume a political and cultural dominance over much of this ancient civilized region. And from the meeting and mingling of these two groups, there emerged the early cultural foundations of the later Indian people.

The period from around 1500 B.C. to about 500 B.C. or later is known as the Vedic Period of Indian history. It was during this long interval that the *Brahmanas* and early *Upanishads* were written and the foundations of Indo-Aryan culture were laid.

The Aryans were originally a pastoral people, divided into many tribes, who came into India from the west and northwest— the historical invasion routes into India. They gradually penetrated much of North India, settling on the plains watered by the Jumna and Ganges Rivers. They drove many of the former inhabitants to the east and south of the country. Today those whose native languages are Tamil, Kanarese, Malayalam, and Telugu trace their language roots back to the old language of the Dravidians.

Development of Kingship

The Aryans slowly pushed over northern India and organized themselves into broader political groupings as families, villages, and tribes joined to form well-defined territorial units. Some of these units evolved into kingdoms; others became oligarchies and republics. Thus, early in India's history, North India served as a breeding ground for the development of the country's political thought and culture. Throughout India's long history, it has been the center of India's political life, and it is not strange that the capital of the Republic of India, New Delhi, is located there now.

Kingship became the characteristic political institution of the Aryans. North India divided into a number of territorial units which were almost continually at war among themselves and with others. Disunity and disorganization, fear and unrest were the rule rather than the exception, and the people needed the unity and power that result from working together under one leader to protect themselves from the conditions of anarchy that then prevailed. Kingship was necessary to counteract the "law of fishes," which is the metaphorical way the Sanskrit language describes a state of anarchy, in which the larger fish swallow the smaller without hindrance. Only the legally established coercive power of the king could prevent the chaos that existed under the "law of the fishes." This concept is still fundamental in the political thought of the Indian people.

The idea that kingly power is a trust is one of the basic principles of Hindu political thought. Since kingship arose in India to satisfy certain needs of the people, the king was judged in terms of his performance in meeting these needs. He retained his office if he efficiently carried out the duties assigned him; he was deposed if he failed. If a king did not carry out his duties, he was regarded as unrighteous and would eventually perish from the earth. Some Indian political theorists even held that an unrighteous king could be assassinated. The conviction that political leaders may be removed from office if they do not fulfill the functions assigned to them is still a cardinal principle of the Indian political system.

Assemblies of the People—Samiti and Sabha

Early Vedic kings were checked by two powerful institutions known as the *samiti* and the *sabha*. The *samiti* was an assemblage of all the people; it had the power of electing or appointing a king, and deposing him. The *sabha* was a council of influential men to whose advice the king was bound to listen. Generally Brahmins, or priests, and the elders of the community, they advised the king on political and other matters.

From around 1000 B.C., to about 600 B.C. the influence of the *samiti* and the *sabha* slowly decreased. Continual wars plaguing North India during this period led to a consolidation of the king's authority. Kingship became hereditary, and the two assemblies were superseded by a council of ministers appointed by the king. The *samiti* disappeared as a political institution, and the *sabha* was transformed into a royal agency entirely dependent upon the king's will and exclusively devoted to carrying out his commands. The king became the central authority in the state and the people looked to him rather than the assemblies for their protection.

The Village in Politics

The village has given a certain degree of continuity and stability to the political life of India. It was the basis of the *samiti,* or general assembly, and it enjoyed a great deal of autonomy during the Vedic Period. Whenever a strong central government administered India, as during the Maurya Dynasty (321 to 185 B.C.), and while Great Britain ruled India in recent times, the independence of the village was somewhat curtailed, but village self-government has been fundamental in Indian political life from the Vedic Period to the modern era.

Usually, the village had a council, known as the *panchayat,* which governed it. It functioned inside the village no matter what government was in power. Traditionally, the *panchayat* consisted of five of the most respected people of the village, and a headman who frequently represented the central government. In some localities, the village was governed by committees chosen by lot or operated under a form of constitutional government; in others, all householders actively participated in the decision-making process.

In all periods of India's history, the village community worked together on public projects such as irrigation, roads, temples, collecting taxes, or caring for community land. The Republic of India is now trying to encourage the villagers, who make up the vast majority of the population, to work on the national level with the same enthusiasm and spirit that sparked other work on the local level. As one method, it is trying to revitalize the *panchayat* councils.

Republican Institutions

Republican institutions started to develop around the eighth century B.C. and survived in some areas, especially the western part of India, into the fifth century A.D. These republican institutions developed at the same time as political power was being consolidated in the person of the king. The Sakyas, the tribe to which Gautama Buddha belonged, had a republican form of government. Gautama Buddha himself preferred the republican type of political organization and based the organization of the Buddhist clergy on a constitution borrowed from some Indian republic, perhaps his own.

The character of these republics varied from place to place. Some republics held large assemblies where all the important political decisions were made. It is reported that, in one instance, there were five thousand councillors in a parliament. In another republic, political power was limited to less than eight hundred families, while the total population was over a million and a half. In some republics, political participation was hereditary; in others it was not. Some republics had a house of elders, and in another the leadership of the army was vested in an elected chief.

No systematic theory of republicanism developed in ancient India, and the Guptas, who rose to power in North India in the fourth century A.D., finally succeeded in destroying both republics and republicanism in India. Rule by king and royal authority continued to dominate the political history of India down to modern times, when the idea of republicanism was revived by the entrance of Western nations, particularly Britain.

Division and Unity

Divided and disorganized throughout most of her history, India has been the battleground of many warring kingdoms. From the time the Aryans arrived in India to the time of the Muslim invasions, which began in the eleventh century, a period of over two thousand years, there were only three relatively short periods of unified government in North India.

In the fourth century B.C. Chandragupta Maurya unified India under one ruler for the first time in its history. Asoka, the grandson of Chandragupta, brought the Maurya Dynasty to the apex of power and prestige. He combined in his person the powers of a monarch with the duties of a Buddhist monk. His great goals of life were the propagation of the teaching of the Buddha, the consolidation of royal power, and the renunciation of warfare as a means of conquest and Indian expansion.

The substitution of royal ministers for the people's assemblies, and the invasions from Central Asia and elsewhere, pointed up the need for a unified front under one leader. The new religions of Buddhism and Jainism also supported and increased Asoka's authority because they needed his help against the Brahmins, advocates of the established religion. Finally, Asoka himself undertook to increase his own authority by fostering the spirit of unity among the people of India. One of the means he used was to set up pillars all over India on which he wrote ethical precepts in one language, Pali.

Asoka's renunciation of war at the height of his fame has had an enduring influence upon the political thought of the Indians, an influence which was dramatically evident during the latter part of Gandhi's life when he and his followers stressed the concept of nonviolence as a means of obtaining political ends. The dramatic picture of thousands upon thousands of Indians sitting passively under the blows of British policemen, as they followed Gandhi in a campaign of civil disobedience, was striking evidence of the power of the idea of nonviolence. It worked. This ideal is still basic to Indian political thought, although India supports an army, navy, and air force and has sometimes used them to achieve a political goal.

Asoka also established a policy of toleration. He published an Edict of Toleration which stated in part:

King Priyadarse (Asoka) honors men of all faiths, members of religious orders and laymen alike, with gifts and various marks of esteem. Yet he does not value either gifts or honors as much as growth in the qualities essential to religion in men of all faiths.

This growth may take many forms, but its root is in guarding one's own speech to avoid extolling one's own faith and disparaging the faith of others improperly or when the occasion is appropriate, immoderately.

The faiths of others all deserve to be honored for one reason or another. By honoring them, one exalts one's own faith and at the same time performs a service to the faith of others. By acting otherwise, one injures one's own faith and also does disservice to that of others.[1]

The Indian people have preserved this heritage of toleration. One of the most attractive features of Hinduism is its tolerant acceptance of other religions and other beliefs. It is fundamental to the teaching of Hinduism that there are numerous roads to the liberation of the spirit. Within its wide embrace there is room for all, no matter what their spiritual needs or beliefs. As in Asoka's time, there are still those today who are fanatical in their beliefs and intolerant toward others. But, toleration was bequeathed by Asoka to the Indian people, and this heritage still retains great vitality and commands respect in India.

Asoka is so highly regarded that the new Republic of India has adopted the capital of an Asokan column for the device of its state seal. The emblem on the national flag is the Buddhist wheel which stands for the law and which was copied from an Asokan pillar.

Cultural Unity and War

The Maurya Dynasty left behind it the ideal of a universal emperor, but it also left behind a number of kings who thought they were destined to become that universal emperor. Consequently, it became customary for kings to assume such titles as "Great King of Kings" and "Supreme Lord." Even unimportant princes called themselves by sonorous titles. It was a world of many states competing with each other, but acknowledging a common culture and way of life. This condition is not very different from that of the Western world which generally admits to a common culture but is politically divided.

Conflict and intrigue characterized the relations between the various kingdoms in this political climate. Although Asoka renounced war as an instrument of policy, the martial tradition grew, and war became the chief occupation of statesmen and kings. It was regarded as part of the warrior's duty, or *dharma,* and good in itself. Such ideas helped to keep India a jungle and prevented the unification of the nation under one emperor.

The Doctrine of Circles

The basic concept which underlay the relations of one kingdom with another during this period might be termed the "doctrine of

---

[1] Quoted from *The Edicts of Asoka,* ed. and trans. by N. A. Nikam & Richard McKeon, University of Chicago Press. Copyright 1958, University of Chicago.

circles." Briefly, this doctrine taught that neighboring contiguous kingdoms were natural enemies, while kingdoms beyond these neighbors were natural allies. Thus, it was common practice for the Indian king to ally himself with the kingdom beyond his neighbor for the purpose of encircling and destroying the kingdom between them. Of course, its destruction made the allies neighbors of each other, and the process started all over again with the former allies now enemies and targets for each other. Under these circumstances, all alliances were temporary, and all friendships impermanent.

The accepted Indian political structure was that of a dominant political unit in the midst of a circle of kingdoms. When the highly centralized Maurya Dynasty fell, this was the type of system that prevailed in India. A large kingdom directly administered a central core of territory, while around it were grouped a circle of vassals who acknowledged this overlordship of the central kingdom. Kingdoms became vassals by conquest and to acquire more vassals became the king's principal ambition. Of course, these surrounding vassals were a constant source of trouble and a real threat to the overlord, for any ruler who wanted to keep his dominant position had to be careful lest he in turn become the vassal of a former vassal or a neighboring kingdom.

The Gupta Dynasty—the Second Unity

Beginning with Chandragupta in 320 A.D., most of India was once again united under one rule, the Gupta Dynasty. This dynasty reached its peak under Chandragupta II (375 to 415 A.D.) and coincided with the most glorious period of classical Indian civilization. During this period Indian art and literature reached full maturity. Indian sculpture of this time rivals the finest in the world. Colleges and universities were filled with students, and Nalanda University enrolled students from all over Asia. A Chinese visitor, Fa-Hsien, commented on the atmosphere of peace prevalent everywhere, the lack of crime, and the fact that there was little, if any, oppression of the people.

By 550 A.D., continued invasions from the northwest finally overcame the Gupta rulers, and the dynasty disintegrated into the familiar pattern of many kingdoms that made war on each other for supremacy. With the exception of the period when King Harsha became emperor in 606 A.D. and ruled for forty-one years, not until much later was India to realize again the ideal of a unified country under one beneficent ruler. To the turmoil and dissensions that already plagued India were now added the additional troubles of sustained Muslim invasions.

Followers of Islam

From the beginning of the Muslim invasions of India from the northwest in the tenth and eleventh centuries until the establishment of the Mughal Empire in the sixteenth century, India was torn apart by the quarrels of kingdoms and warring princes, seeking to grasp a throne. Muslim Turks, Muslim Persians, Muslim Afghans, and Muslim Mongols in successive waves stormed into India looting, killing, and seizing territory. It is true that some Arab Muslims came to India by way of the sea and peacefully for trade, but these Muslims were never politically powerful.

For over five hundred years the Muslims could not establish a stable regime under one leader. Rule over the city of Delhi and the surrounding lands was the prize sought by all, but the authority of the Delhi throne was slight and its occupants in continual danger. Both the rulers and the frontiers of the Delhi kingdom were perpetually changing. More often than not, the governors of the various provinces, nominally subordinate to the Delhi throne, actually ruled as independent sovereigns in their own right.

This scene of disunity began to change when Babur, a descendant of the famous Turkish conqueror Tamerlaine, brought great parts of North India under his control. His grandson, Akbar, conquered more of India and established the Mughal Empire upon a firm base. Akbar became emperor in the middle of the sixteenth century and his reign coincided roughly with the rule of Queen Elizabeth of England and Philip II of Spain.

Akbar, an energetic and capable ruler, brought to much of India the first peace and unity that the people had known for a thousand years. The Mughal Empire maintained itself firmly in power until the middle of the eighteenth century when anarchy, chaos, and disorder once again became widespread in India.

Although the Muslim rulers were in many ways tolerant and understanding, they usually regarded the native Hindu civilization with a measure of contempt. Hitherto, the Indians, though continually weakened by factional quarrels which left them an easy prey for invaders, were usually able to absorb their conquerors eventually and thus win final victory. They failed with the Muslims. Probably because of the character of their religion, the Muslims firmly resisted assimilation. But not entirely, for they did acquire some Indian characteristics which had their source in Hinduism.

This resistance to assimilation, together with the heritage of struggle, kept high the barrier between the Hindus and the Muslims. The division between the two cultures was preserved when, in 1947, the territory of old India was split between the new Muslim-dominated state of Pakistan and the Hindu-dominated Republic of India. These two new nations reflect also the impact of Western nationalism.

Western Nations in India

The first Western nation in the modern period to reach India was Portugal, whose sailors landed on Indian soil in the latter part of the fifteenth century. Portuguese, Dutch, French, and British entered India in greater and greater numbers, and by the middle of the nineteenth century all India, including the nominally independent princes, was subject to Great Britain. British rule in India lasted until 1947 when India and Pakistan were established as free and independent nations with dominion status within the British Commonwealth of Nations. India became a Republic in 1950; Pakistan, in 1956. Prior to independence, the British were the primary source of Western thought and attitudes in India.

Hindu Reaction

Indian Hindus reacted to the coming of the West to India in three ways:

1. A small group of well-educated Indians almost completely abandoned their former way of life and thinking for that of the West. In the beginning this group was very influential, but gradually, as nationalism grew in India, their influence over policy making waned. There are still many Indians, living mostly in large urban areas, who are little affected by the classical tradition of their ancestors, but their influence is negligible.
2. The Brahmo Samaj group attempted to create a synthesis of the best in Hinduism and Christianity. Ram Mohan Roy, sometimes called the father of the Indian renaissance of the nineteenth century, was the leader of this group. He started his career after witnessing his sister burn to death on the pyre of

her dead husband. This practice, called *suttee,* has now been abolished in the new India. Roy's followers were influential in the nineteenth century, but in the twentieth century they also declined in prestige and influence.

3. Another group reacted in an actively hostile manner to this infiltration of Western ways of thinking and acting. Fearing that this alien culture would eventually destroy India's classical tradition and civilization, members of this group became the leaders in reviving Hindu culture and in calling attention to the glories of the past. Their vehement rejection of foreign concepts and renewed loyalty to the classical Indian tradition became one of the bases of modern militant Indian nationalism, which swept over India and finally culminated in the sovereign Republic of India.

Nationalism

One of the most significant results of the impact of the West on India was the growth of nationalism. Indians for centuries have recognized their cultural unity, but it was only after the British established their rule over India that they learned to consider themselves as members of a common nation as well. There were many reasons for this growth of nationalism. British common law and administration brought to different Indian factions and groups a sense of unity because all were forced to follow similar behavior. The British established an educational system in India which stressed Western culture, history, attitudes, and beliefs. Eventually Western-trained Indians aspired to live by Western ideals of freedom and liberty. British rule in India was an obvious contradiction to British teaching. Then, too, the British were giving the Indians a knowledge of the West at a time when Western nationalism was flourishing.

They also gave India a common language at least for the educated and the officials. Formerly, India's multiplicity of languages and dialects prevented even educated Indians from communicating with one another and constituted one of the most serious obstacles to national unity. The problem persists, but the imposition of English as the common language proved to be a partial solution. It facilitated the creation of the Indian press which provided the Indians with a medium for molding public opinion, an outlet for their grievances, and an excellent means of propaganda. Thus, by establishing political unity and educating the Indians in their way of life, the British also fostered national feeling and helped to develop the intense patriotism which motivates many Indians today.

Modern Government

The British example of parliamentary government resulted in the establishment of a representative government in India. Since the British ruled India for such a long period of time, it was natural for Indians to think of democracy in terms of British political institutions. As does Great Britain, India has a cabinet which performs the executive tasks of government and is responsible to a legislative body made up of two houses which are collectively known as parliament. This parliament is elected by the people. The members of the cabinet must also be members of parliament.

Instead of a queen or king, as in England, India has a president who presides as titular head of the state. The president of India, however, has little actual political power. In India, as in Great Britain, the Prime Minister is the functioning head of the government. As in England, he or she is head of the largest political party in the country or the party which holds a majority in the lower house of parliament. The late Jawaharlal Nehru was the first Prime Minister and also headed the Congress Party which yet holds a majority of the *lok sabha*, the lower house of the Indian parliament.

The British brought to India the idea of rule by law to replace the concept that the king was the sole giver and interpreter of the law, with no appeal from his ruling except by rebellion and force.

The new Constitution of India contained many provisions guaranteeing the freedoms and rights of the individual. Among those freedoms and rights were freedom of speech, freedom of assembly, freedom to form associations, freedom to move throughout India, and a number of others. The Constitution, however, also contained emergency provisions which permitted the government to suspend these freedoms and rights if the government thought it necessary. In 1975 and 1976, the government of India, under the leadership of Prime Minister Indira Gandhi, suspended a number of these rights and freedoms.

Indira Gandhi, the daughter of Jawaharlal Nehru who was the first Prime Minister of India, became Prime Minister in January 1966. In the years that followed she became the dominant leader of the reorganized Congress Party. She stated that the "chaotic conditions" prevailing in the country required the government to issue these emergency decrees. She declared that the country now needed a national discipline. She has also said that the British-style democracy inherited by India should be modified to fit the special conditions of the Indian people. What modifications will take place in the following years is a matter of speculation. Perhaps there will be a return to more traditional ways of government in India.

The interaction of old and new forces in India is resulting in a synthesis of the traditional and the modern. This synthesis has expressed itself in many ways. For instance, the scientific spirit has been rekindled in modern India. Indian scientists, like all modern scholars, now emphasize the necessity for an attitude of rationality and for scientific analysis based upon empirical evidence. Yet Indian philosophers and thinkers have preserved their aptitudes for exploring the soaring reaches of human thought, explorations which demand intuition and imagination of the highest order. The negative aspects of India's classical tradition which bound some of her finest minds in the chains of rigid customs have been slowly eroded. But the social and cultural traditions developed over thousands of years cannot be erased in a short period of time. They continue to influence the lives of the Indian people. There is change. But it is change that is uniquely Indian and rooted in the old traditions of the Indian people.

15

Pakistan and Bangladesh

The founder of Pakistan, Quid-i-Azam Mohammad Ali Jinnah, expressing the will of the people, declared that Pakistan would be a democratic State based on Islamic principles of Social Justice.

—Preamble to the Constitution of Pakistan (1962)

Pakistan and Bangladesh (formerly East Pakistan) are the geographic expressions of a Muslim fear of Hindu dominance. When Great Britain prepared to give independence to the people on the South Asian subcontinent, the Muslims became greatly fearful of Hindu dominance and absorption because the Hindus represented the overwhelming majority of the population. To escape

131

this prospect, the Muslims urged a division of the former united territory based upon religious affiliation. This was done. The borders of Pakistan and Bangladesh follow rather closely the Muslim concentrations on the subcontinent. Not all Muslims, however, were included within the borders of Pakistan and Bangladesh nor all Hindus excluded. It is estimated that around ten million Hindus, or approximately 13 percent of the population, stayed in the area now known as Bangladesh at the time of partition. Both Pakistan and Bangladesh have small minorities of Christians, Parsis, and Buddhists. Nor did all Muslims migrate from India at separation time in 1947, and approximately sixty million or more Muslims live in India today.

Although Muslims are to be found scattered throughout the area of South Asia, they are concentrated in two widely separated parts, namely in the western and eastern extremities of the subcontinent. Accordingly, when the new state of Pakistan was created by the partition of former British India on August 14, 1947, both of these separated Muslim communities were placed within the one state of Pakistan. As a result, Pakistan, until 1971 when the new state of Bangladesh came into existence, was composed of two distinct land units—one in the east, East Pakistan, and the other in the west, West Pakistan—which were separated from each other by over a thousand miles of Republic of India territory. Pakistan was born physically divided.

The roots of the force that created Pakistan go back to the rise of Muslim power in India in the tenth and eleventh centuries A.D. Gradually, under the leadership of a succession of dynamic and able generals and statesmen, most of India was brought under the control of the followers of Islam. Their successes culminated in the establishment of the Mughal Empire which brought to India an administrative unity it had not possessed for centuries.

The invaders of India who preceded the Muslims had no culture or belief comparable with the Indian's in distinctiveness and appeal and therefore were usually absorbed into the cultural and religious life of India. The Muslims were different. They possessed a religion which had spread over much of the civilized world and a culture of Middle East and Persian origin which was the equal of the Indian's and in some ways superior. Under the sponsorship of the Muslims, this Persian culture eventually pervaded the middle and higher levels of Indian society so that Persian language and literature, Persian art and architecture became an integral part of the cultural life of India. The Muslims were imbued with a deep pride in their religion and regarded the Hindu and Buddhist religions as inferior to their own. Moreover, millions of Indians embraced Islam. They believed that it offered them more hope, freedom, and tolerance than the Hinduism with which they were familiar, and they were drawn by its social teachings. It appealed to the women because Islam demanded that wives be given fair treatment and maintained in a reasonable state; daughters could inherit property, and women could divorce their husbands if necessary. All were drawn by the Muslim's conceptions of racial equality and the brotherhood of man, for many Indians found the caste system of India a heavy burden to bear, and Islam had no castes. Within Islam, the race, social status, or economic condition of a person is immaterial; all individuals are equal before God.

Some Indians, of course, became Muslims to enhance their chances of advancement under Muslim rule, but their numbers were relatively few. It was not essential to become a Muslim to attain power; many Hindus have held positions of high authority under Muslim rulers. The famous Muslim emperor Akbar bestowed power upon numerous non-Muslims during his reign in India. Nor is it correct to say that Islam converted by the sword in India. Although incidents of this nature might be cited, they remain the exception rather than the rule. The majority of Indians who were converted to Islam saw in Muslim beliefs and practices something that appealed to them.

Thus the Muslims brought to India a new faith and system of practices which were embraced by a quarter of the entire Indian population at the time of partition in 1947. During the centuries they lived together in India, Hindus and Muslims influenced each other's thought and practices, but Islam and Hinduism retained their distinctive religious features, and their followers remained separated by distinctive ways of life.

With the disintegration of the Mughal Empire in the eighteenth and nineteenth centuries, Muslims declined in power and wealth. Their empire had sustained them for many centuries, and when it was lost to them, they were forced to renew the basic sources of their faith and to turn to other means for the preservation of their heritage and communal feeling. They reemphasized the values that undergirded Islam and the unique characteristics which differentiated it from Hinduism. They proceeded to cooperate more with the British, who had succeeded to the Mughal Empire, in an effort to counteract the greater numerical strength of the Hindus. Many of them came to feel that the Congress Party, which was founded in 1885, was a threat to their independence of thought and action because it was dominated by a Hindu majority. In 1906, they established the Muslim League, which eventually became their primary political instrument in advancing their cause. Rahmat Ali, a graduate student in England, proposed the formation of a new Muslim nation in 1933. He called it Pakistan. Muhammad Iqbal, a great Muslim poet who died in 1938, also proclaimed the idea of a homeland for the Muslims in India where they could practice and renew their faith without hindrance. He, too, called it *Pakistan,* "Land of the Pure." Then Mohammad Ali Jinnah, the father of Pakistan, led the modern movement which culminated in the creation of the state of Pakistan.

The Hindu leaders of the Congress Party underestimated the deep emotional appeal a separate Islamic homeland would have for all Muslims and the tenacity and organizational ability of Jinnah. They appeared to forget the history of Muslim and Hindu separateness and the lengths to which the Muslims were willing to go to establish their own nation where there would be no danger of absorption and no possibility of domination by others. The Hindu-dominated Congress refused to part with any of its power, and so an impasse was reached which even British diplomacy could not solve short of the partition of India. The Muslim League, under the leadership of Jinnah, held the same power over much of Muslim India as the Congress Party did over Hindu India, and it was adamant in its demand for a separate state. Finally, on August 14, 1947, the British Parliament gave dominion status to both India and Pakistan, and the Muslims of India had their homeland.

A few months after the birth of Pakistan, Mohammad Ali Jinnah summed up the motivating force that sustained him and his Muslim followers during the arduous and often tense months and years prior to independence. "The creation of a State of our own was a means to an end and not an end in itself. The idea was that we should have a state in which we could live and breathe as free men and which we could develop according to our own way of life and culture, and wherein the principles of Islamic social justice could find free play."

The principles of Islam are basic to the Republic of Pakistan.

The preamble to Pakistan's Constitution, as published in 1962, begins:

In the name of Allah, the Beneficent, the Merciful; Whereas sovereignty over the entire Universe belongs to Almighty Allah alone, and the authority exercisable by the people is a sacred trust. . . .
And whereas it is the will of the people of Pakistan that . . . the principles of democracy, freedom, equality, tolerance and social justice, as enunciated by Islam, should be fully observed in Pakistan. . . .
The Muslims of Pakistan should be enabled, individually and collectively, to order their lives in accordance with the teachings and requirements of Islam. . . .

This is not to say that Pakistan discriminates against other religious groups or minorities, because the Constitution of Pakistan provides for religious and personal freedom, and the first president of Pakistan, General Iskander Mirza, stated that "As long as I am Head of State, I will regard the honor of my Hindu Pakistani brethren as my own and I shall be personally responsible for their well-being and safety." However, there is no doubt that every official act of Pakistan is infused with the spirit of Islam.

The religion of Islam was a unifying factor among the people of West and East Pakistan for some years, but there were other secular conditions which tended to divide them. The most obvious divisive element was the division of the country into two distinct geographic units separated by over a thousand miles of land and sea. The divisiveness of this physical separation was reinforced by cultural and linguistic differences, and by mounting convictions on the part of the then East Pakistanis that the politically dominant West Pakistanis were governing the country for their own selfish purposes and neglecting the East which contributed much, they thought, to the economy of the country.

The physical and cultural differences between the land and the people of the eastern and western portions of the country were striking. The land area of Bangladesh (I shall refer from now on to the former East Pakistan as Bangladesh, and the former West Pakistan as Pakistan) is only one-fifth the size of that of Pakistan, yet its population is larger than that of Pakistan. Bangladesh is well watered, and two major rivers, the Ganges and the Brahmaputra, flow through and merge to form a delta as they empty into the Bay of Bengal. Between June and December when the rivers flood, much of the area around Dacca, Bangladesh's capital, is like a sea. As the floods recede they leave a rich loam. Moreover, from around the middle of June until October, the monsoon brings torrents of rain to the land, and it is estimated that this region receives more than 80 inches of rain annually. On this fertile, generously watered earth, the people harvest two and three crops of rice. About 85 percent of their cultivated land is used for growing rice. Jute, their cash crop, is also extensively cultivated here. There are also extensive tea plantations in the country.

The majority of the people speak Bengali and, in almost all cultural and physical characteristics except religion, are closest to the people of West Bengal who live near them but across the border in India. Calcutta is the main city of West Bengal. The citizens of Bangladesh are a cultured people with a fine literary tradition, and they take passionate pleasure in the creation of poetry, music, and the arts. Their climate, physical environment, housing, clothing, diet, cultural orientation, and language mark them as culturally distinct from the people of Pakistan in the west. It was the strong bond of religion that held the two peoples together for so long a time.

Much of Pakistan is mountains or high plateau in contrast to the flat plains of Bangladesh. A great part of Pakistan is arid or semi-arid, and the farmers depend upon the waters of the Indus and other rivers for their irrigation. In Pakistan the major crops are wheat, barley, millet, and corn, and some rice. The land presents an appearance of drab browns, and in certain periods of the year many Pakistanis are harassed by stinging storms of sand. Although Urdu is the official language, most people converse in one of the many dialects prevalent in the country. There are many differing ethnic groups in Pakistan, and they speak many differing dialects and languages. The varieties of people are known by a variety of names—Punjabis, Sindhis, Baluchis, Pathans, Hunzas, and others. Although many of the people have been deeply influenced by the culture of the Persians, Moghuls, and Indians, and appreciate poetry, music, dance, and the arts, there are many others who are oriented more toward the military arts and virtues. For centuries these warrior people have found their pleasure and their gain in battle, and the British recruited many of them into their armies when they controlled India. It is not surprising, therefore, that the military have played a large role in the government of Pakistan since the very early days of independence. Nor is it surprising that the military leaders of the country took drastic military action when their citizens in the eastern portion of the country demanded greater autonomy in running their part of the country, including levying and collecting taxes, issuing money, organizing a militia, and other privileges. The result was a disaster for these military leaders and a tragedy for millions of people in Pakistan and Bangladesh.

When in 1970 and 1971 the Bengalis of then East Pakistan insisted on fiscal, economic, and political autonomy, the West Pakistani military rulers were reluctant to respond favorably to their major requests, and the resulting anger of the Bengalis snowballed into a clamor for secession and complete independence. Troops were dispatched from West Pakistan to check this movement. Eventually, their activities in the eastern portion resulted in turmoil within the country, the exodus of large numbers of refugees to the safer haven of India, and confrontation between the armies of India and the occupying Pakistan troops. Finally, in early December 1971, the armies of India invaded East Pakistan and, in a short time, their superior military forces defeated the Pakistan troops. The Pakistani forces surrendered and with their surrender, the former East Pakistan became the reality of Bangladesh.

After the war, Pakistan's President Yahya Khan, a military man, resigned and was replaced by Zulfikar Ali Bhutto, leader of the Pakistan People's Party. President Bhutto released Sheikh Mujibur Rahman, leader of the majority Awami League of Bangladesh, from prison in Pakistan and permitted him to return to the new country of Bangladesh to head the government of the new country.

The leaders of both countries have had to cope with grave economic, social, and political problems since their division into two independent countries. Conditions in Bangladesh were particularly deplorable. Many were starving; millions more were living at a minimal level of existence. During the following years there was continual unrest and little improvement. In 1975 there were two military coups. In the first, Mujibur Rahman was killed. Later another military coup brought new leaders to power. The leaders of both countries do not have an easy task in bringing progress and hope to their demanding millions of citizens.

16

Islam

God is most great!
God is most great!
I testify that there is no god but Allah.
I testify that Muhammed is the prophet of Allah.
Arise and pray; arise and pray.
God is great;
There is no god but Allah!
                    —The Call of the Muezzin to Prayer

Islam is an important ideology to millions of
Asian people besides those who live in Bangladesh and Pakistan. The followers of Islam are
found in Indonesia, Malaysia, China, the Philippines, and other Asian areas. The Republic of
India has a population of Muslims estimated at

around sixty million. It is important that an ideology that has created nations and is still influencing the thought and activities of so many Asians be understood and appreciated.

Islam is a complete way of life. It embraces the social, political, economic, and cultural life of its followers as well as their belief in God and the divine commandments. Islam is concerned with the total person, and all acts receive their justification and direction from the teaching that is ultimately embodied in the Koran, the holy book of the Muslims, which contains the final and complete revelation of God's truth to humans. The Koran is filled with laws which should govern the daily practical affairs of people, for Islam is vitally interested in how people should live together and in their individual material welfare. Islam deals explicitly and in detail with the treatment of women, the conduct of war, race relations, the quality of the individual, marriage, interest rates, health, and a host of other matters. Islam seeks to bring the total life of an individual into harmony with God.

Misconceptions About Islam

Islam is a much misunderstood and misrepresented religion. Over the centuries it has been portrayed by many Western writers and speakers as an anti-Jewish and anti-Christian religion, while in fact Islam teaches religious tolerance. In his charter to the city of Medina, Muhammed, the prophet through whom God revealed the truths of Islam, said: "The Jews who attach themselves to our commonwealth shall be protected from all insults and vexations; they shall have an equal right with our own people to our assistance and good offices." He also stated that both Jews and Christians shall be permitted to practice their religion as freely as the Muslims. The Islamic Republic of Pakistan has given concrete expression to this creed of toleration by guaranteeing religious freedom in its Constitution.

Islam recognizes the truth that is contained in the doctrines of Judaism and Christianity and confirms Abraham, Moses, Isaiah, Jesus, and others as true prophets of God who preceded Muhammed. Muhammed was the last and final prophet and therefore is called "the Seal of the Prophets." Islam holds that the Old Testament of the Jews and the New Testament of the Christians were revelations from God, and those who believe in them are called "People of the Book." But these revelations are incomplete, and thus the necessity for the Koran, which embodies the complete and uncorrupted revelation from God. Although Abraham correctly revealed the oneness of God, the Jews who came after him forgot this revelation and took to themselves golden idols. Jesus was chosen by God to reveal this and other truths, but his followers made him a god, thus dehumanizing him and humanizing God. Jesus, like Muhammed, was a true prophet and a man, not a god.

Western novels and serious historical and religious works have often indicated that the sword was the primary instrument of conversion for Muslims. They allege that it was the practice of the Muslims to give the nonbeliever two choices—conversion or death. There have been incidents when Muslims, caught up in the fury of war or lacking knowledge of the basic tenets of Islam, have used force to convert others to their faith, but the history of many religions is strewn with zealots who have utilized torture and force for this purpose. The followers of Islam have probably sinned less in this regard than the disciples of other religions. Muslims, as a rule, adhere closely to the injunction of the Koran: "If it had been thy Lord's will, they would all have believed,—all who are on earth! Wilt thou then compel mankind, against their will, to believe!" (Surah X, 99) And in the Koran it is also stated: "Let there be no compulsion in religion." (Surah II, 256) And "Unto you be your religion, and unto me mine." (Surah CIX, 6)

A conception of Muslims as addicts of war has also grown up in Western minds. Islam does permit its followers to resist evil, and those who injure others wrongly may be punished to the full extent of the injury. The Muslims also believe in the concept of a *jihad*, or "holy war," in which those who die become martyrs and go immediately to heaven. But this holy war must be a defensive one or waged to right some wrong. The Koran states: "Defend yourself against your enemies; but attack them not first: for God does not love transgressors." (Surah II, 190) Even when they are engaged in a righteous war, Muhammed required his followers to spare the women and children, sacred objects, and fields of grain and orchards, and to refrain from mutilating the wounded and the dead. Maddened by the passion of war, many forgot the precepts of Muhammed, but these are the basic teachings of Islam on the conduct of war.

Islam has been repeatedly slandered as a degrader of women and a refuge for lascivious men whose libidinous desires may be fully and legitimately satisfied under the protective cloak of religion. Numerous historical romances, past and present, employ this stereotype of Islam to inject sex and spicy incidents into the story. Thus an image of Islam as basically carnal is passed on from generation to generation of Westerners. The only feature of Islam known by many Westerners is that it permits polygamy. Such an image does not present a complete and true picture of Islam's teaching and practice with regard to women. At the time Islam was born in Arabia in the seventh century, women were in a most degraded state. They were at the complete mercy of their husbands and fathers to do with as they liked; they had no inheritance rights; infant daughters were unwanted and frequently killed; and marriage was often conditional and temporary with no recourse for the woman should her husband divorce her, as husbands frequently did. Women were looked upon as mere playthings or work animals to be discarded when their usefulness was over. Muhammed did much to mitigate this evil. He prohibited the killing of daughters and demanded that they have the right of inheritance of the family property. His enlightened laws gave to the women of his day and later a status much higher than formerly and prepared the way for the astounding progress that the modern Muslim women are making today toward full equality with men.

Islam views marriage very seriously. A woman must give her full consent before she can be married to any man even if he is a king. Although divorce is permitted in Islam, it is not regarded as a routine solution but as an exceptional one. Before most Muslim marriages, the prospective husband is required to set aside for his future wife a certain sum of money which might be termed a dowry. She may take this dowry at the time of marriage, but it is hers to claim whenever she desires it. Should they be divorced, she may take possession of this dowry, if she has not already received it at the time of the marriage or thereafter, and the former husband must support her until she remarries. The Koran states "For divorced women maintenance should be provided on a reasonable scale. This is a duty for the righteous." (Surah II, 241) Wives are also permitted to initiate divorce proceedings themselves. Islam has elevated the status of women from its previous deplorable depths and given them a certain degree of social, legal, and economic security. But what about polygamy?

The Koran does state: "You may marry two, three, or four wives, but not more." (Surah IV, 3) But Islam lays down a hard condition for those who desire more than one wife, for the Koran also states that if a man cannot deal equitably and justly with more than óne wife, he shall marry only one. (Surah IV, 3) This means that a man cannot have more than one wife if he cannot give them all the same material benefits, the same love, the same respect, and the same treatment. Since this is an almost impossible condition for the ordinary man, the true follower of Islam cannot generally practice polygamy. This hard qualification has oriented most Muslims toward monogamy, and today there are relatively few Muslims who have more than one wife.

Muhammed: The Prophet of Allah

Muhammed was the man through whom Allah (God) transmitted the teachings of Islam to His people. Though a prophet only, he was not an ordinary prophet, for to him God gave the special task of revealing His truth and His divine law in its *most complete form*. There were other prophets before him—Abraham and Jesus were two—but he was the last and final member of this chosen few. He was "the Seal of the Prophets."

Muhammed was born in Mecca, a city located within the present boundaries of Saudi Arabia, about 571 A.D. His father, mother, and grandfather all died before he reached the age of nine. He was then brought up by a kindly uncle for whom he worked as a shepherd. Although he grew up in an atmosphere of lawlessness, sensuality, treachery, and war, he managed to remain aloof and unscarred by the atrocious practices of his time. He is described as a youth of mild and kindly disposition whose charity and helpfulness made him beloved by all who knew him.

When he was twenty-five, Muhammed was employed by a rich widow named Khadija. They grew to esteem each other's qualities and finally married, even though Khadija was fifteen years older than Muhammed. Muhammed was married to her for twenty-six years and took no other wife until after her death. He always spoke of her with endearment, and to all Muslims she is the epitome of the faithful and devoted wife. A man who, in a social environment which favored polygamy and temporary marriages, remained married to one wife for so many years cannot be said to have been overly inclined toward polygamy. Although Muhammed did take other wives after the death of Khadija and in the last years of his life, there is no evidence that he was motivated by sensuality. His later wives were, for the most part, widows of his followers who had died in the cause of Islam, and he married them primarily to provide them with economic security and to prevent them from falling into evil hands. He married an African woman in order to teach his followers that Islam believes in racial equality. Islam is not color-conscious, and the spectacular successes it has had in Asia and Africa attest to the efficacy of its teaching on racial equality. It is reported that Muhammed treated all his wives with the same consideration and respect.

History of Islam

From one point of view the history of Islam starts with God. God was the real founder of Islam, and the truth that was revealed through Muhammed is a truth that always was and always will be. Much of this divine truth had already been revealed to humans through such prophets as Abraham, Moses, Isaiah, and Jesus, but Islam was its confirmation and culmination. The Koran states: "This Koran is not such as can be produced by other than God; on the contrary, it is a confirmation of revelations that went before it and a fuller explanation . . . wherein there is no doubt—from the Lord of the Worlds." (Surah X, 37)

Muhammed traced the ancestry of the Arab people back to Adam through Abraham. Abraham had two sons, Isaac by his wife Sarah, and Ishmael by his other wife Hagar. Sarah forced Abraham to banish Ishmael and his mother from the tribe, and they went to Mecca. Thus Ishmael became the progenitor of the Arabs, while the descendants of Isaac are the Jews.

From an external or historical point of view, the history of Islam began in the seventh century of the Western calendar, when God revealed his truths to Muhammed. Muhammed was upset and puzzled by the barbarism and savagery which characterized the world into which he was born. Why must these conditions exist? What could be done to mitigate and modify the evil and folly of man? He sought answers everywhere to these troubling and perplexing questions, but mostly he sought within himself. He found a lonely desert cave outside of Mecca, and there he meditated for long periods of time on the vexing problems of life. There must be a reason and a solution for these evils which afflict humans, for they were created largely by people.

Muhammed found the answer to his questions but not in himself; he found the answer in God. As he thought and fasted in his quiet cave, sometimes for nights and days without pause, the reality of God became more and more the content of his contemplation. God soon became the silent and unseen companion of his vigils, and then one night God spoke to Muhammed through one of His angels. "Proclaim!" the voice said. Muhammed was startled, and replied. "I know not how to proclaim." "Proclaim!" the voice repeated the second time. Muhammed was now thoroughly frightened, and again answered, "I know not how to proclaim." "Proclaim!" the voice demanded a third time. Muhammed could resist no longer, and timidly he asked, "What shall I proclaim?" The answer came quickly:

> Proclaim—in the name of your God
>   The Creator,
> Who created man from a clot
>   Of congealed blood.
> Proclaim! Your God
>   Is most generous,
> He who has taught man
>   By the pen
> Things they knew not.
>   —Surah, XCVI, 1–5

From that moment on Muhammed knew no rest or peace on earth, for he was destined to cry out to all people, both present and future, the hope and glory and truth of Allah. He was committed to the divine purpose of bringing Allah to humans, and humans to Allah, and he could not pause while even one person did not know the revelation of Allah. The voice that was heard by Muhammed in the stillness of his desert cave so many years ago is still heard around the world today when the *muezzin* cries out, "I testify that there is no god but Allah. I testify that Muhammed is the prophet of Allah."

The citizens of Mecca did not find the new mission of Muhammed to their liking. His revelations of Allah demanded too much of the individual, threatened the established customs of their society, and, more important, might impede the flow of pilgrims into Mecca and wealth into their coffers. Pilgrims came to Mecca because of many gods, and if one God superseded them in Mecca, the number of pilgrims would certainly dwindle, for many gods have a greater pulling power than merely one. The pilgrims journeyed to Mecca to pay homage to their gods at the sacred shrine of Kaaba. Originally, the Kaaba was built by Abraham and Ishmael and dedicated as a place of worship to the one God, but over the years the original meaning of the Kaaba was obscured, and it became a shrine of many gods. After the citizens of Mecca accepted Islam, Muhammed rededicated the Kaaba to Allah, and it became Islam's most sacred shrine. Today's pilgrims pour into Mecca from every part of the earth in numbers far exceeding those who came prior to the teachings of Islam. The power of the one God was a greater attraction to pilgrims than the power of many gods.

But Muhammed's fellow-citizens did not know this at the time, and they savagely persecuted him and his followers, who were beaten, starved, imprisoned, and finally driven from the city. The cruelties and tortures inflicted upon the early Muslims rival some of the sufferings of the early Christians. Thus in 622 A.D. Muhammed and his followers were forced to flee from Mecca to Medina where he was welcomed and honored. This migration is known as the *Hijra,* and the Muslims date their calendar from this year, using the symbols, A.H., "After Hijra." This migration was the beginning of the amazing spread of Islam, and when Muhammed died in 632 A.D., or 10 A.H., all Arabia belonged to Islam. A century after his death the people of Armenia, Persia, Syria, Palestine, Iraq, Egypt, and Spain were ruled by the followers of Islam. They even crossed into France where their advance was checked by Charles Martel at the Battle of Tours in 732 A.D. But although frustrated in Europe, Islam continued to expand in Asia and Africa. Today there are about five hundred million Muslims throughout the world, but the greatest concentrations of them are found in Asia, Africa, and the Middle East. Islam is a dynamic, living religion which continues to attract millions of men and women.

The Koran

According to the teachings of Islam, Muhammed was the last of the prophets through whom God's message was transmitted to humans. He was not God but the instrument God used to convey His truth to all people, and although Muhammed is revered and honored by all Muslims as Allah's prophet, he is not worshipped. God's revelation as spoken through the voice of Muhammed was recorded in a holy book called the Koran (*Qu'ran*), which is the final authority in Islam, and for all Muslims the written word of

God. The Koran has 114 chapters, or *surahs,* which range in length from four to 286 verses. Most Westerners find the Koran difficult reading, but to the Muslim it is an incomparable work. Many Muslims think that in the translation of the Koran from Arabic, the original language, to other languages much is lost of the symbolism, poetry, richness of imagery, and nuances of thought. Perhaps it is for this reason that so much time and effort is spent in teaching the followers of Islam to read the Koran in the original Arabic. God gave a complete revelation through Muhammed, and it is the sacred duty of Muslims to ensure that it is known completely. Even after a quick reading of the Koran one is struck by the fact that Muhammed, who could neither read nor write, dictated a book which reveals an amazing knowledge of Jewish and Christian traditions and history, and a penetrating insight into the psychology and nature of humans. The laws and ordinances that are promulgated throughout the Koran have withstood the vicissitudes of time and are still applicable. The social and ethical teachings of the Koran possess the stamp of permanency because they continue to meet the needs of the community and the yearning of the human heart. Of course, the good Muslim would not be amazed by the wisdom displayed in the Koran because it contains the words and knowledge of God, not Muhammed. The voice was the voice of Muhammed, but the thought and the words were of God. Nonetheless, the voice had a magnificent tone and it reverberates through the pages of the Koran. For such a message, God chose a man whose voice could be heard through the ages.

Very early in the history of Islam, problems in the interpretation of the Koran and in the adjustment of the Muslims to the requirements of Islam arose. As a result, another authority developed, based upon tradition and anecdotes, which describes what Muhammed said, did, or tolerated among his followers. This authority is called the *Hadith* or *Sunna.* The *Hadith* supplements the Koran and is equally authoritative in matters which are not treated in the Koran.

Basic Beliefs of Islam

Islam teaches that there is but one God, Allah. Belief in the oneness of God is fundamental to the Muslim religion, and the primary purpose of Islam is to remind all that God exists and should be worshipped and obeyed. The opening surah of the Koran reads:

> In the name of Allah, the Beneficent, the Merciful.
> Praise be to Allah, the Cherisher and Sustainer,
> The Beneficent, the Merciful.
> Master of the Day of Judgment,
> Thee alone we worship; and Thine aid we seek.
> Show us the straight path.
> The path of those on whom Thou hast bestowed Thy grace,
> Those whose portion is not wrath,
> And Who go not astray.
>
> —Surah I, 1–7

God is eternal, God created heaven and earth, and is all-powerful, all-merciful, and all-just. God is unique. Having no equal, God should have no rivals. From the time of the Prophet himself, the Muslims have reserved their harshest criticism for those who worship so-called gods, for they veil the ultimate truth *of the one God.* In .the early days of Islam, Muhammed and his followers were continually harassed by the worshippers of many gods who feared and detested the revelation that there was but one God. When the Muslims invaded India, the more extreme among them took every opportunity to destroy what they conceived to be the idols of Hinduism and Buddhism, which they found in temples and public places. They scolded the Jews for forgetting the revelation of Abraham that there was but one God, and they reproved the Christians for deifying Christ, for they should know that he was but a prophet, although a great one. That there is but one God, is the eternal foundation of Islam.

Islam teaches that God created humans and endowed them with immortal souls. Each soul is an individual soul. Islam values the individual: it does not, as Hinduism, regard the individual as impermanent or transitory, but as having a permanence that is eternal. Every person is differentiated from every other person by the quality of uniqueness bestowed on each by God. Islam stresses the duty of each individual to work out his or her own destiny. Each is responsible for his or her actions. This is not to say that people should not help each other—Islam very emphatically commands its followers to provide others with all possible material and spiritual assistance in their efforts to reach God—but it is to say that, ultimately, it is the decision of each individual whether he or she follows the will of Allah or not. The Koran points out that "If anyone sins, he alone is responsible for his sin." (Surah IV, 111)

Islam teaches that there is a life after death for every person born on earth. Eventually, all must go to one of two places: heaven or hell. The Muslims believe that heaven is an abode of eternal delight where people may live forever together with God in rapturous peace and happiness. God does not dwell in hell, which is a place of eternal sorrow, torment, and despair. There are two paths which a person may walk in life—one is straight and leads to heaven and God, the other is crooked and leads to hell. It is for the individual to select, for the Koran says: "Whoever strays, he bears the full responsibility for his straying." (Surah X, 103) At the end, God will judge which of the two paths a person has chosen to walk.

Islam seeks to guide people through life by encouraging them to undertake good deeds. Essentially, the good life for a Muslim is founded upon the five pillars of Islam.

The Five Pillars of Islam

The first pillar is the creed, "There is no god but Allah, and Muhammed is His Prophet," which should be recited daily by the faithful. Generally, Muslims say this creed many times in the course of a day, but essentially it is only required to say it with faith and understanding once in a lifetime. The teachings of Islam are based on the fact of one God, and it is necessary for all Muslims to affirm this God with their tongue, at least once, but preferably every day and many times a day. The oneness of God must be indelibly engraved on the minds and hearts of every Muslim.

". . . and Muhammed is His Prophet." Muhammed was the man chosen by Allah to reveal His Word to man and has, therefore, a most honored place in Islam. By the frequent recitation of his name and title, Muslims recall that it was under his leadership and direction that Islam was born in the hearts of humans and that he merits their esteem and remembrance. But this recitation also recalls to them that he was a prophet only and must not be deified.

The second pillar of Islam is prayer. The Muslim should pray five times daily—before sunrise, at noontime, during the midafternoon, at sunset, and after sunset. Islam permits deviations from this schedule if, for example, adhering to it is likely to bring serious harm to the petitioner. One of the striking human qualities of Islam is the fact that it permits exceptions to many of its requirements under extenuating or abnormal circumstances.

Muslims can pray anywhere. Although there are thousands of magnificent mosques scattered around the globe, it is not required of Muslims to pray in a mosque. The whole world is a mosque for them, and they are urged to spread prayer rugs and to pray whereever they find themselves at the scheduled hour of prayer.

Muslims should pray facing toward Mecca. This practice symbolizes the unity of Islam and is a respectful remembrance of Abraham. Before starting prayer they should wash themselves—hands, mouth, face, behind their ears, neck, arms up to the elbows, and feet up to the ankles. One should be as pure and as clean as possible before approaching God in prayer. Here, as in other matters, Islam permits an exception, for if there is no water, and the Muslims of the desert might often find it impossible to obtain water, the Koran urges them to go to clean, high ground and rub their face and hands with its earth. The practice of compulsory washing instills in the Muslim the habit of cleanliness, and it is characteristic of Islam that, in this and other instances, it links together what is good for the body and what is good for the soul.

Muslims stand with their thumbs touching the lobes of their ears, saying three times, *"Allahu akbar"* ("God is most great"). Still standing, but with their hands clasped on their chests, they then recite the opening surah of the Koran, followed by a shorter surah of their own selection. An example of a short surah is the CII:

> In the name of Allah, the Beneficent, the Merciful.
> Proclaim the Allah, the One!
> Allah, the Eternal, Absolute.
> He begetteth not, nor is He begotten;
> There is none that can compare to Him.

They then bow placing their hands on their knees, saying, "Praise be to God, the Most Great." They stand again, praying, "Allahu akbar." They then kneel down, place their hands and faces on the ground, saying, "Praise be to God, the Most Great." They also recite other prayers. They return to a kneeling position, sit on their heels, and pray again. They repeat this ritual several times, always accompanied by prayer. They conclude by turning their heads first to the right and then to the left, saying in each position, "May God watch over you and bless you."

The frequent prayers are designed to keep the Muslims ever mindful of God and the duties required of them. The ritual is symbolic, but it also serves to keep them alert and conscious of the prayers they are reciting. When they turn their faces to the right and to the left at the conclusion of prayer, they are bestowing the peace of Allah upon their neighbors, whether there be anyone present or not, and thus they are reminded of the brotherhood that must exist within Islam.

Charity is the third pillar of Islam. Muhammed established a graduated tax of 2.5 percent on the entire holdings of each person, a tax which adds up to one-fortieth of the entire wealth a Muslim possesses. Those who have must give; those who have not are excused. This is a high tax, and far exceeds the taxes which many modern states impose upon their citizens. In a real sense, Muhammed instituted a share-the-wealth plan which incorporates old-age pensions, social security, and other features of the welfare state. The money collected from this tax is used to succor the poor and the needy and to provide for the aged. The tax is also a kind of insurance because it is used to liberate debtors from their debts. In a sense Islam acts like a benevolent aid society, for the tax money is also used to assist wayfarers and to free captives from their bondage. Islam's teaching on charity helps to knit the family and the community more closely together, for it is the responsibility of Muslims to provide for their parents, impoverished kinsfolk, and neighbors. The funds collected are also utilized for religious purposes, such as the building and maintenance of mosques and the spread of Islam. In this use it resembles the tithing system of the Christians. Good Muslims, who faithfully and religiously observe the teachings of Islam on charity, do not find it easy to amass wealth.

Observing the month of Ramadan is the fourth pillar of Islam. The ninth month of the Arabic lunar calendar, Ramadan is important because, during this month, Muhammed received his revelation from God, as embodied in the Koran, and made his momentous *Hijra,* or migration from Mecca to Medina. In memory of these two most significant events, every Muslim, except those who are sick, involved in war, taking a journey, or excused by other exemptions, must fast from sunrise to sunset. No food, drink, smoke, or anything else should pass their lips during this period.

After sunset it is permitted to take food and drink. Islam imposes this arduous fast upon people to teach them self-discipline and to remind them that they are in reality weak creatures who constantly require the sustaining nourishment of God. It also compels them to experience the searing and sickening pangs of hunger so that they will feel compassion for the hungry ones they meet, or who seek them out, and provide for them.

Pilgrimage to the holy shrine of the Kaaba in Mecca is the fifth pillar of Islam. All Muslims who can, should visit Mecca and the Kaaba at least once in their lifetime, to renew their faith on the sacred ground which was blessed by Abraham when he erected the original Kaaba to the one God and where Muhammed was born and God first spoke to him. Here, the two sheetlike garments which all pilgrims must wear when approaching the Kaaba hide distinctions of status and wealth and publicly proclaim the equality of all before God. This same theme of equality and fraternity is evident when the Muslims pray within their mosques, as they usually do on a Friday. There is no reserved place in the mosque for the rich or the powerful. The possession of material goods or earthly power means nothing in the sight of God, and rich and poor, peasant and king, pray side by side, paying homage and adoration to their common God. The gathering of Muslims in Mecca from the far corners of the earth is a dramatic expression of the international brotherhood that links Muslim to Muslim within the shelter of Islam.

Because it affords an opportunity for Muslims from many different lands to meet and talk with one another, the pilgrimage to Mecca promotes international understanding within Islam. The unifying factor of one religion permits them to exchange ideas and information with less suspicion and antagonism than if there were no common ideology. Thus, the fifth pillar of Islam not only provides for spiritual growth, but also furthers the concept of international brotherhood and understanding.

Conclusion

Islam is an accommodative ideology. It does not try to mold all into one strict pattern of life, and it allows for individual and cultural differences, provided the basic teachings of Islam are preserved. It realizes that people live in different environments, and it adjusts itself to this diversity without sacrificing basic doctrines. Islam is a complete way of life for all who believe.

17

East Asia

East Asia is a term used to designate that part of Asia controlled by the political units of the People's Republic of China (Communist), North and South Korea, Japan, and Nationalist China based on Taiwan. The People's Republic of China and the Koreas are mainland nations, while Japan and Taiwan are island territories lying near the eastern and southern coasts of the mainland. The nations included in this area are close to one another geographically, and, generally speaking, the lives of the people reflect certain common physical and cultural characteristics.

Congestion on "The Good Earth"

Since only a small portion of the total land is suitable for farming, most of East Asia's millions are confined within a small land space. China has a population of more than eight hundred million, most of whom live in less than one-third of its land area. Japan, about the size of California, has over one hundred million people, most of whom are concentrated in about 15 percent of its land. The heavy pressure of tremendous numbers of people on a small portion of the land has led to an intensive cultivation of the soil, a great waste of human labor, and some of the highest food yields per acre in the world.

Farming is the main occupation of the people, except in Japan. The search for food is continuous, unending. Much is demanded of people and the land. Asian farmers exhaust themselves in a prodigal effort to gain a living from the soil; sometimes they even become beasts of burden, pulling the ploughs themselves. Every little bit of land is coaxed into producing as much food as possible, not only once, but in some places two and three times a year, and often more effort and tender care is lavished on the good earth than is given to the children or wife of the farmer.

This concentration of great numbers of farmers in the same areas has resulted in the establishment of numerous villages. The villages in many rural areas are located so near each other that the resulting scene resembles a rambling and loosely structured urban settlement, rather than a rural farming community. This congestion of villages is usually found in the rice-producing regions of East Asia, which are located south of the Ts'inling Mountains in China, generally south of the island of Hokkaido in Japan, and wherever there is good soil and adequate water in Korea and Taiwan.

Most of Korea's farmland is located in South Korea; North Korea, which has a Communist government, also has farming lands, but it is more noted for its industry and natural resources. The food-producing area of Taiwan is located on its western shores facing the southern coast of mainland China. North of the Ts'inling Mountains in China, and in the Hokkaido part of Japan, where wheat is a more important crop, the farms are larger and the villages located farther apart.

In the Mongolian People's Republic, around a million and a half people occupy a land area of six hundred and four square miles. The nation embraces the old homeland of the conquering Mongols,

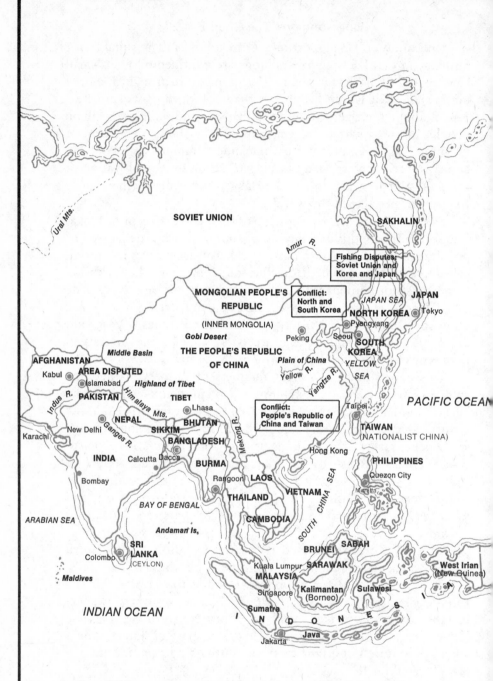

Soviet and Chinese armies confront each other along their long border. Chinese on the mainland and Chinese on Taiwan confront each other with propaganda and guns. The two Koreas face each other in armed array, and all Koreans continue to regard the Japanese with varying degrees of suspicion.

who by the thirteenth century ruled a vast territory reaching from China to Western Russia. As their power gradually declined, they became subjects of the Chinese; but after the establishment of the Chinese Republic in 1911, they drove out the Chinese officials. In a treaty with Russia in 1945, the Chinese relinquished their claim to Mongolia, and the Mongolians now rely on Russia to protect them from China. The Russians are reported to have stationed troops in Mongolia, and to have constructed airfields and other military installations there. The people continue to cherish a nomadic way of life, herding their flocks and driving their horses over vast stretches of their land. But more and more of them are gathering together in collective settlements and living in their few but growing towns and cities.

China

China is the outstanding geographic, cultural, and political fact of East Asia. All but a small fraction of East Asia's land area belongs to China. The great rivers, the great mountains, the great plains, the great deserts, and the great plateaus of East Asia are all found within her borders. These borders contain 3,691,500 square miles and a population of more than eight hundred million that is increasing by twelve or fifteen million a year. The civilization of East Asia is to a degree the civilization of traditional China. For centuries China possessed the most important civilization in East Asia. Highly original, it grew and matured largely independent of other cultures because barriers of mountain, ocean, desert, and jungle separated East Asia from the rest of the world. The geographic proximity of the countries of East Asia facilitated the spread of Chinese civilization to Japan and Korea.

Korea was visited early by Chinese immigrants who carried their language, culture, and customs with them. Gradually all of Korea came to be dominated by the culture of these settlers and their descendants. Korea is separated from Japan only by a relatively narrow body of water, and the Japanese were soon attracted by this culture. Korea thus served as a bridge over which the early civilization of China traveled to Japan. The languages, the arts, the philosophy of Korea and Japan all reflect the cultural penetration of China into these areas of East Asia. The literature of Korea and Japan is written in ideographs which were borrowed from China. Confucianism, the dominant Chinese philosophy, was incorporated into the official ideology of Korea and Japan, and to this day it influences millions of Koreans and Japanese. There is a striking similarity between the art and architecture of China, Korea, and Japan. Even the clothes which the Japanese wear today, with the exception of Western dress, are thought to be copies of old Chinese costumes.

This dominant cultural position of China was strikingly shown in its contemptuous attitude toward its neighbors, whom it generally referred to as "barbarians." It was right and proper that these barbarians should come to China to learn about civilization, and thousands of students from Japan, Korea, and other neighboring lands went to China where they studied, among other things, philosophy, art, calligraphy, literature, and government. They took this learning back to their own countries where they became focal points of Chinese learning which they spread among their fellows.

For many centuries China's neighbors also acknowledged its political dominance. Every year many countries, both far and near, indicated their subordination to the Empire of China by sending tribute to the court at Peking. China graciously acknowledged this tribute by sending back better gifts than were given it. The exchange of gifts served to stimulate trade and commerce between China and the other lands surrounding it, and in time there developed an economic interdependence in this area.

China has also contributed much to the world in technology and in science. Among these contributions are the efficient equine harness, the technology of making iron and high-grade steel, the inventions of gunpowder and paper, the mechanical clock, and basic engineering devices such as the driving-belt and the chain drive. The Chinese created segmental arch bridges, nautical techniques such as the stern-post rudder, and the magnetic compass. They were among the first to use successful immunization techniques, kept remarkably detailed astronomical records of novae and supernovae, and utilized the seismograph from around the second to the seventh centuries A.D. They were the first to print books utilizing inked wood blocks, and the oldest printed book found to date is a Buddhist work which dates back to around 868 A.D. Later, in the eleventh century, the Chinese invented a movable type made of clay characters and, still later, movable types made of metal. The crossbow, the stirrup, the wheelbarrow, canal locks, weaving and milling machinery, the technique of deep drilling, side wheels on boats, and a host of other inventions were used in China many centuries before the Westerner discovered them.

It would be incorrect to say that the Chinese were not influenced by the thought and actions of other Asians and non-Asian people. Probably the greatest impact made by India upon any people was the gift of Buddhism to China. Buddhism permeated the life of the Chinese and exercised an influence upon them that is immeasurable in its depth and breadth. Buddhism penetrated China during the first century of the Christian era and slowly became an integral part of Chinese religious life, finally blossoming into full flower during the Tang Dynasty, one of the greatest periods in Chinese history. The Chinese interpreted and modified the Buddhism they had received and transmitted it to the Koreans and the Japanese who, in turn, molded it to fit their own special needs.

More recently, from the West has come the political thought of nationalism, democracy, and communism. Supreme authority during the two thousand years of imperial China was lodged in the emperor; who was ultimately the supreme law of the land. Under the leadership of Dr. Sun Yat-sen, the father of the Republic of China, the imperial system was abolished and a more modern government established based on his political ideas. From 1911 until approximately 1949 his "Three Principles of the People" were the official political philosophy which guided the leaders of the Chinese people. Since the establishment of a Communist government in China, the followers of Chiang Kai-shek have carried on a government in Taiwan formally based upon Dr. Sun's political philosophy.

The present government on the Chinese mainland is based upon the principles of communism as enunciated by Marx and Lenin and interpreted by Mao Tse-tung, the leader of the Chinese Communists. In view of the long and strong influence that the Chinese have had upon the thinking and actions of many East Asians in the past, it is not surprising that they continue today to influence the political, economic, and social life of their neighbors.

18

Chinese Ideology

Confucianism, Taoism, and Legalism, the major schools of Chinese philosophy, can all be characterized as human centered and thus world centered. They are almost exclusively preoccupied in seeking to establish right principles of conduct which, if followed closely, must necessarily eventuate in a better human life on earth. In their optimism about the chances of achieving this better life, they differ significantly from Buddhism, an Indian import, which is deeply pessimistic about human prospects for earthly happiness and looks to a nonearthly existence for an escape from suffering.

The Background of Chinese Thought

A partial explanation for the singularly "practical" nature of the great Chinese philosophies may perhaps be found in the circumstance that all of them originated between the fifth and third centuries B.C. This was a troubled period for China, characterized by civil war and profound disturbances in economic, social, and political life. It was a transitional period when old institutions had seemingly lost their value but nothing new had yet taken their place. The people of China had two basic needs: to end the bloody wars between the states, and to establish a new social order. It was with these very real human problems that Chinese ideology was concerned.

To understand these ideologies it is essential to have some awareness of the historical circumstances which determined the character of Chinese society. After they had defeated the Shangs in the twelfth century B.C., the Chou kings established a feudal system in China in order to hold the conquered people in subjection. They placed vassal lords in charge of areas which varied in size and population and gave these lords rank generally commensurate with the size of the territory they governed. On condition of a strict obedience to the Chou king in matters affecting the kingdom, they were given full authority over their domains. The right to rule was, or soon became, hereditary. Political authority was retained by the descendants of the Chou kings and the ruling families within the feudal states assigned to them. The right of the old and noble families to rule derived from the belief that only they could invoke the supernatural aid required for the prosperity of the state in peace and war. They alone, according to popular belief, could make the sacrifices at the ancestral temples and at the altars of the land and the grain. If the rulers' sacrifices should cease, it was thought that the state would fall on evil times. The feudal order of society was thus secured by the partnership of the hereditary aristocrats and the spirits to whom they made sacrifices.

Gradually the foundations of the feudal order were whittled away. By the eighth century B.C. the royal authority was seriously diminished. During the period 772 to 481 B.C., the vassal lords acted more and more like state sovereigns. The basis of political authority became no longer spiritual sanction, but superior military force. By the time of Confucius in the fifth century B.C., the feudal kingdoms of the Chou Dynasty had been replaced by a group of independent states engaged in a struggle for political

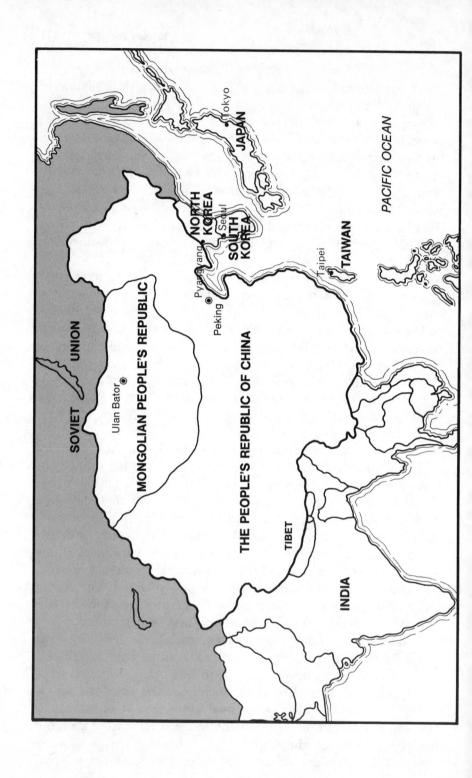

mastery of all China. The period from 481 to 221 B.C. in which this struggle took place is known as the Warring States Period. It ended with the triumph of the state of Ch'in over all other states and the unification of China under one emperor.

It can be seen that the fifth century B.C. was an age when the customary ways of living and thinking associated with feudalism had broken down and a new concept of society was desperately needed. Perceptive individuals of intellectual talent and humanitarian concern rose to the challenge of disorder. The great schools of Chinese philosophy were born.

Looking at the chaos around him, Confucius proposed a new political system and a new society which would retain many of the old rituals and diplomatic formalities but would be grounded in the moral responsibility of the ruler for the welfare of the governed. Viewing the same ruins, the Taoist concluded that the evils of the time were the inevitable consequences of any ordering of human life for social or political ends. They taught that people could be happy only in the absence of a convention-oriented society. Under similar unhappy circumstances the Legalists decided that the solution lay in increasing the power of the ruler. They developed skill in the organization and supply of armies and the use of diplomacy in the interests of the state.

From the time of Confucius in the fifth century to the second century B.C. these three philosophies and a number of other schools of thought competed for supremacy, although none of them were accepted as orthodox. This era is known as the Period of the Philosophers. Around 100 B.C. Confucianism was adopted as the orthodox Chinese philosophy. The years between this date and the twentieth century are known as the Period of Classical Study because during this time the development of Chinese philosophy focused on the interpretation of Confucian, Taoist, and Buddhist writings rather than on the discovery of new institutions and ideas. China was now a unified nation with a single orthodox ideology based on a modified Confucianism.

Buddhism Met a Need

Buddhism entered China around the beginning of the Christian era. At first it was frowned upon because it was thought that the

East Asia includes the People's Republic of China, Mongolian People's Republic, North Korea and South Korea, Japan, and Taiwan. China has been recognized politically as a world power. Japan is recognized as the third greatest economic power in the world.

concept of reincarnation was a fantasy and that the celibacy of monks was a disgraceful practice since it prevented a man from having descendants. Moreover, the authorities feared that the spread of this foreign religion would seriously threaten their power. It expanded rapidly, however, especially among the common people, and by 381 A.D. most of the people of northwest China were Buddhist. Winning converts also among the rulers and scholars, by the time of the T'ang Dynasty Buddhism was found everywhere in China.

There are a number of reasons why this religion found a home in China and attained such a prominent position in Chinese life. From the second to the sixth century A.D. the people were beset with famine, wars, banditry, and political oppression, and Buddhism brought them hope. It taught that life was evil and death was only a pathway to a glorious heaven. It offered to rich and poor alike such compassionate deities as Amitabha Buddha and Kuan-Yin. Promising that justice would ultimately triumph, it taught that there was a rule of law throughout the universe and that everyone would be rewarded and punished according to strict justice.

Buddhist teaching dealt with fields of speculation which Confucianism and Taoism had generally left untouched, namely, the hereafter. Confucianists and Taoists did not regard this life as preliminary or probationary to another life in some hereafter. They were primarily interested in bettering human society and handling human problems. Interested in the dead only from the viewpoint of making them happy and obtaining blessings from them for themselves, they did not emphasize the question of death or give an answer to the problem of suffering.

Mayahayana Buddhism, on the other hand, painted a graphic picture of the heaven and hell that awaited the good and bad people of the world. In this sense it possessed a more comprehensive doctrine than Taoism and a more spiritual character than the ethical code of Confucianism. Buddhism provided the Chinese of this period, from the second to the sixth century A.D., with a hope of material and spiritual benefits which attracted great numbers of them to the Buddhist faith.

19

Confucianism

Do not do to others what you do not wish yourself.
—Confucius

Confucianism takes its name from Confucius, the Latinized name of its founder, Kung Fu-tzu. Confucius was born in 551 B.C. and died in 479 B.C. During his lifetime he attracted a number of disciples who, with later followers of his doctrines, are called Confucians.

From the time of Confucius until the second century B.C., the Confucians were engaged in a struggle to put their ideas into practice throughout China. The Legalists, the chief philosophical rivals of the Confucians, won a temporary victory when the state of Ch'in, 221 to 207 B.C., established a unified empire based on Legalist principles. Soon after the fall of the Ch'in Dynasty the Confucian philosophy was established as the official doctrine of the imperial government (early in the Han Dynasty, 202 B.C. to 220 A.D.). Only with the destruction of the old educational system early in the twentieth century did the cult of Confucius become weakened. Confucianism lost its favored position with the institution of the Republic of China in 1911, when a mixture of Confucianism and Western liberal thought, as propounded by Sun Yat-sen, became the official political theory of the state.

The content of Confucianism comes from many sources. Many ideas came from a period prior to the time of Confucius. For example, ancestor worship, sacrifices to the dead, spirits, and ceremonials were handed down from early Chinese times. Confucianism later drew on other schools of thought, including Legalism, Taoism, and Buddhism. Generally speaking, however, the Chinese have traditionally held that nine ancient works were intimately associated with the Confucian tradition and contained the essential principles of Confucian teachings. They have sometimes been referred to as the Confucian Canon. These nine works are generally divided into two groups known as the *Five Classics* and the *Four Books.*

The *Five Classics* are among the earliest works of the Confucian Canon. The *Shih Ching*, variously known in English as *The Book of Poetry, The Book of Odes,* or *Classic of Songs,* is a collection of 305 poems or songs which were composed most probably some time between the tenth and seventh centuries B.C. Although ostensibly folk poetry, the sophistication of form and content indicates that they were written by urbane and literate persons.

The *Shu Ching* or *Book of Documents*, the second of the *Five Classics,* is also known as the *Shang Shu* or *Book of History.* It purports to provide an historical foundation for ancient sages and events in China's remote past through documents and statements. Modern scholars, however, have discovered that much of the classic was forged by later writers. However, a portion of the work may date from about 1000 B.C.

The *I Ching* or *Book of Changes* was intended primarily as a manual for diviners or soothsayers. The treatise is based upon eight trigrams and sixty-four hexagrams. This classic has become rather popular in contemporary times. Much of the work may date back to 1100 B.C., but it is thought that the appended philosophical explanations may have been added some centuries after the death of Confucius.

The *Ch'un Ch'iu* or *Spring and Autumn Annals,* the fourth of the *Classics,* covers certain major happenings at the court of Confucius' native state of Lu between the eighth and fifth centuries B.C.

The *Li Chi* or *Book of Rites*—sometimes called *Record of Rituals*—deals with ceremony and ritual. It is the fifth of the *Classics.* Although the rituals and ceremonies contained in this *Classic* are thought to be of much earlier origin, the work itself was most probably compiled around the second century B.C.

Modern scholars dispute the claim that Confucius either authored or edited any of these *Five Classics.* Many think, however, that he drew inspiration and learning from some of them, particularly the *Book of Poetry,* the *Book of Documents,* and the *Spring and Autumn Annals.*

The *Four Books* of the Confucian Canon were gathered from Chinese classical writings many centuries after the end of the Chou Dynasty as containing the essential principles of the Confucian teachings. The first *Book* is the Lun Yu, or *Analects,* sometimes known as *Sayings* or *Conversations of Confucius.* The work is mostly a record of Confucius' responses to a variety of questions put to him by his disciples on a variety of subjects. It is the principal and primary source for what knowledge we have about the man himself, his life, and his teachings. It was in part written by his immediate disciples, in part by their disciples, and perhaps expanded later from oral tradition.

The second of the *Four Books* is known as *Mencius* or the *Book of Mencius.* Mencius (372 to 289 B.C.) was one of the greatest exponents of Confucianism. His additional contributions to the thought and practice of Confucianism laid a deep imprint on the future life and thought of the Chinese. Humans are born morally good, he said, it was a corrupt society and environment which later corrupted them. People had the right to revolt and change their rulers, he proclaimed, when their government was oppressive and hurtful of the people.

The third and fourth *Books* are *Ta Hsûeh* or the *Great Learning,* a short treatise on Confucian ethics; and *Chung Yung* or *Doc-*

trine of the Mean, which deals with universal harmony and ethics.

Sympathy and the Five Relationships

Confucianism teaches that humans are compelled by their nature to live in the company of other humans, that is to say, in society. Only unnatural and abnormal people live outside the communities. This social way of life is the best way to live, because it is only in society that people reach their fullest development and realize their potentialities. The universal human quality which leads people to live in society is called by Confucians *jen.*

The Chinese character *jen* combines the symbol for *man* and the symbol for *two,* a combination which conveys the idea of a relationship between persons. The meaning of this word has been rendered in English as "benevolence," "human-heartedness," "person to personness," and "perfect virtue." All catch part of the meaning, but no single word conveys the whole meaning of *jen.* "Sympathy" is perhaps the one word that best expresses the idea. Sympathy expresses such a close relationship between persons that whatever affects one, similarly affects the other. Sympathy is the entering into and sharing of the feelings and interests of another; it is a mutual affection and understanding that arises from a common nature and temperament. The quality of *jen* has all these meanings and more. *Jen* to Confucians was and is the very root of society. *Jen* implies a shared humanity that can find expression only in human relationships.

Jen also includes the desire to help others. Since it is a universal quality possessed by all, all have the ability to help one another. You merely look into yourself for the answers to the problems of others. In a sense you contain all people in yourself; self-understanding leads to an understanding of the fears and hopes of others. *Jen* involves a desire to aid others to achieve their ends. The Confucians taught that "The man of *jen* is one who, desiring to develop himself, develops others, and in desiring to sustain himself, sustains others. To be able from one's own self to draw a parallel for the treatment of others; that may be called the way to practice *jen.*"

In its negative formulation the quality of *jen* is restated as a practical Confucian maxim. "Do not do to others what you do not wish yourself."

In both its positive and negative aspects *jen* points the way to action. When one's feelings are in harmony with those of others, to assist others one has only to examine himself or herself. There is a beautiful example of this sympathetic feeling for others in a poem of Tu Fu, one of China's·greatest poets, who lived in the T'ang Dynasty, 618 to 907 A.D. In a poem written to a relative he says:

> Please allow your western neighbor to pluck the
>   dates from the trees before the hall;
> She is a woman, without children and with no
>   means of support.
> Were it not for dire poverty, she would hardly
>   have come for these fruits;
>
> And to save her from embarrassment, we have to
>   be especially kind.
> She is of course needlessly afraid of a stranger
>   from a distance;
>
> I recall her complaints of the taxation that has
>   made her poor to the bone;
> The burdens of war on such persons! It makes me
>   shed bitter tears.[1]

It is apparent that the Confucians wanted *jen* to be expressed in action.

"Right action" is defined by Confucians in terms of the duties and obligations implicit in five basic social relationships. These five relationships are: ruler and subject, father and son, elder brother and younger brother, husband and wife, friend and friend. All of them except the last involve the authority of one person over another. The inferior owes loving obedience and loyalty to the superior, and the superior owes loving responsibility to the inferior. However, it is the duty of the inferior to advise the superior as to the right course of action. Confucius described right action in a positive manner when he said:

In the way of the Superior Man there are four things, to none of which I have as yet attained—to serve my father as I would require my son to serve me; to serve my prince as I would require my minister to serve me; to serve my elder brother as I would require my younger brother to serve me; and to offer first to friends what one requires of them.[2]

[1] *Tu Fu, China's Greatest Poet*, translation and commentary by William Hung (Cambridge: Harvard University Press, 1952). Used with permission.

[2] B. S. Bonsall, *Confucianism and Taoism* (London: The Epworth Press, 1934). Used with permission.

Addressing himself to the idea expressed in the maxim "What you do not want done to yourself, do not to others," Confucius wrote:

> What a man dislikes in his superiors, let him not display in the treatment of his inferiors; what he dislikes in inferiors, let him not display in the service of his superiors; what he hates in those who are before him, let him not therewith precede those who are behind him; what he hates in those who are behind him, let him not therewith follow those who are before him; what he hates to receive on the right, let him not bestow on the left; what he hates to receive on the left, let him not bestow on the right: This is what is called "The principle with which, as with a measuring square, to regulate one's conduct."[3]

Confucianism insists that the names father, son, ruler, subject, elder brother, younger brother, husband, wife, and friend indicate a certain type of conduct. When a son is lovingly obedient to the father and the father dutifully responsible for the son, the Confucians say that the names father and son have been rectified. If a man does not act like a father, a husband, an elder brother, a friend, then he is not really one, because the reality does not conform to the meaning of the terms. This is true for all other human relationships. The continual process of individual adjustment to a well-defined traditional role is a distinctive feature of Chinese society. A perceptive author, Mr. Francis L. K. Hsu, in his book *Americans and Chinese* has observed that "The Chinese tends to mobilize his thought and action for the purpose of conforming to the reality, while the American tends to do so for the purpose of making the reality conform to him."

The "just action" in a particular situation is called *yi*. When it has been decided upon, it should be carried out because it is just, but the correct decision can be made only if the weighing of the facts has been inspired by *jen*, that is, combined with a feeling of humane concern. Confucian justice is not a cold intellectual principle, nor merely a written code like that of the Legalists, but a kind of compassionate wisdom. The Chinese have many codes of law, but above and beyond the written law is the quality of sympathy which must enter into each decision.

Confucianism is, in many ways, a rule by humans rather than by law. The concept of an impersonal abstract law which is binding upon all persons at all times and in all situations is alien to Confucian thought. The maintenance of peace and harmonious

---

[3] *Ibid.* Used with permission.

relations within a community is more important than a notion of absolute human rights. Consequently, peacemakers and go-betweens are continually mediating disputes and settling all sorts of conflicts everywhere in China in accordance with the prescriptions of established custom and tradition and the circumstances of the particular case. Justice was what local public opinion thought fair and reasonable to all concerned under the circumstances, and decisions were made only after arbitration and compromise. No one party was considered completely right or completely wrong.

Ceremonial and Religious Aspects

Li is the specific manner in which the just action should be performed. *Li* has several meanings and is translated into English as "etiquette," "ritual," "ceremony," and "sacrifice." Both Westerners and Taoists have sharply criticized this ceremonial aspect of Confucianism. The West has represented it as a tiresome routine of ritual and pedantry and described it as superstitious, meaningless, and mumbo-jumbo. They detested the Confucians for their rituals and ceremonies, charging that they distort people's feelings in the interests of social conformity.

It should be made clear, however, that, dear as ritual in social relations is to the Confucian, it is not considered important in itself. Ritual and forms are important as language is important. They furnish a standard vocabulary for the expression of feeling; and it is a rich vocabulary.

Their use implies the existence of a norm of human behavior. Confucians believe that it is normal and right that one should experience certain feelings of respect or solicitude or sorrow in certain situations. Whereas the Taoists deplored mourning for the dead as a useless ordeal performed out of ignorance, the Confucians believe that one ought to experience a sense of loss on the death of, say, a father or mother, and that rites and forms of mourning supply a medium for the sincere and dignified expression of sorrow. If for some reason people do not experience sorrow, rituals are worthless, and those persons should look into themselves for the reason for their indifference.

To the Confucians the regular reverential observance of *li* cultivates the reverential feeling that graces social relationships and the exercise of political authority. Thus, *li* has an educational importance. In the *Li Chi,* a Confucian classic which provides a rich source of ceremonial forms, Confucius is reported as saying, "The instructing and transforming power of ceremonies is subtle; they stop depravity before it has taken form, causing men daily to move towards what is good, and keep themselves farther apart from guilt, without being themselves conscious of it." In addition to expressing these feelings, the rituals and ceremonies provide a specific guide for normal behavior.

Confucius himself was not much concerned with religion as such. He mentioned it only incidentally, and although he appeared to believe in heaven and ancestors, he spoke little about these beliefs. However, when Confucianism became the orthodox doctrine of the empire, religious functions were incorporated into it. Confucius, along with his ancestors and his famous followers, became objects of worship and veneration. Confucian temples were erected all over the empire, tablets to Confucius and his followers were placed within these temples, and sacrifices and rituals were performed before these tablets and elsewhere.

In the Confucian cult one of the most important duties of the emperor was to maintain the proper relationship between himself and heaven. Heaven is generally interpreted to be an impersonal force. With this interpretation of heaven a Confucian could be an agnostic, and even an atheist. Heaven was, however, regarded as the governing authority of the universe and the final judge of right and wrong. The universe was resolved into a trinity of heaven, earth, and humans. Heaven directs, earth produces, and humans cooperate. When they cooperate, they prosper. When they fail to cooperate, they destroy the harmonious arrangements of the universe and suffer the consequences in the form of national disasters and calamities such as floods, droughts, and famines.

The emperor was charged with a particular responsibility in this regard. If he fell away from the state of moral perfection, heaven would cause the world to suffer its displeasure. To prevent this, the emperor was obliged to undergo a tiresome round of ritual observance, performing ceremonies and sacrifices by the calendar throughout the year. When the emperor fulfilled his role, the officials and common people theirs, and served the emperor well, the empire was a harmonious society in which all people were tied together by bonds of right feeling.

The Confucian cult differed much from other cults in Asia and in the West. It was very rational. Little was said about an after life; there were few visible objects of worship, and there was no god to save or condemn, or to whom responsibility could be relinquished. The cult was mostly limited rather sharply to the scholar class, which was tied together by the bonds of a common education and culture. The cult did not demand an unflinching faith in some fixed creed, but permitted the individual great freedom of personal belief. So long as Confucius remained the model of the scholarly class, and the ceremonies were performed reverently and regularly, little more was demanded of the Confucian scholar.

The Family and the State

Confucians give an important place to the family as a moral community. It is in childhood that personality has its main development, and a family life is a kind of social school in which children encounter the problems of responsibility and privilege that they will meet in other forms in the world at large. Since Confucians believe that the state is an extension of the family, the same attitudes toward authority and obedience that are valued in the family are also valued in the state.

In the days of the empire, the emperor and all the officials under him were referred to as the parents of the people. Subjects owed the same loyalty to the political authorities that they owed to the seniors in the family. The emperor sacrificed for the whole people much as the head of the family sacrificed for his particular family. In the Confucian view, if one learned to accept and perform the standard roles in relation to members of their families, they could understand and honor the obligations and privileges of public office.

The Master (Confucius) said: "In their nature at birth men are nearly alike, in their habits they are vastly different." (*Analects,* 17:2) The Confucians, knowing that these habits were the results of experience, emphasized the importance of education in forming character and in cultivating a moral standard. Education was largely ethical, for family heads and the political officials were responsible for the moral state of the people under their authority.

Confucians aimed to turn people into good family members and good subjects of the emperor. The officials were to provide a good example for the people, and the emperor was to show the way for all to follow. If he failed in this, the state must fall into decay.

Confucius said nothing explicitly about social classes, but he did discuss the relationship between the ruler and the ruled. He believed that the wisest and most humane persons should rule because only they could be relied upon to rule in the interest of all. The educated man was honored above all others in China. Teaching and government service, professions which required a great deal of education, were the most honored professions. True, there were always corrupt officials who met the formal Confucian tests of office in order to enrich themselves, without thought for the people they governed. But what Confucianism aimed at in government was a tradition of selfless service. Adherence to the tradition would administer the empire and guide the emperor himself. In the course of time, and perhaps inevitably, the scholar-officials, or *literati*, came to form a distinct social class. Inclusion in this class was not limited by heredity, but by learning as tested in examinations of the imperial civil service. Most Chinese, by reason of poverty, were unable to learn Confucian literature and were thereby denied admission to the ruling group. Thus Confucianism became the special concern of a social class as well as the official philosophy of an empire. The dogmatic development of Confucian ideas was given impetus when Confucians came into their own as administrators of the Han Dynasty, 202 B.C. to 220 A.D. Complicated ritual and etiquette are a handy and not uncommon device to exclude outsiders from a social class or group. Many people today use such means to maintain the so-called purity of their group.

Confucianism is sometimes dismissed as a mere rationalization of political authority by an exploitative ruling class. However, taking all things into account this estimate of Confucianism fails to gauge the truth of its basic propositions or objectives in the light of common human experience.

In the days of the empire the practical object of Confucianism was to promote and conserve a happier and a better ordered society through government. The basis of good government was the virtue of the ruler. The good example expressed by the ruler was a positive force capable of transforming people and making them better. This rule by example and popular response was stated by Confucius in a short sentence: "As the wind blows, so bows the grass." The need for virtue and rule by example was not confined to the emperor but also applied to the ministers who aided him. In politics, Confucius was not concerned so much with techniques as with morality. The business of government was as much to reduce corruption by moral education and example and, when needed, by punishment as it was to keep up irrigation works and defend the empire.

A Confucian state exhibits some features that distinguish it sharply from the nation-state of the West. "State" in the Western sense of that term implies definite territorial limits and sovereignty. The Confucian state was a universal state. All people ought to give their allegiance to the emperor. Foreigners and Chinese alike owe all they have to the service of the emperor. Racial or ethnic origins are theoretically irrelevant. Yellow, white, black, or red—all started off alike. A person was not born a Chinese. But each might learn to be one. Being Chinese was a matter of culture, of obedience to the emperor, not of nationality. Naturally, this involved full acceptance of the customary role of the Chinese subject. Such an official philosophy led to two results: a remarkable degree of homogeneity and a marked absence of racial prejudice. A common culture, not a common skin, made all brothers and sisters within the political family of China.

Successful revolution was justified by the Confucians. It was called the "Mandate of Heaven." This drastically limited the sovereignty or ultimate authority of the state. There was in fact no absolute sovereign in the Chinese system unless it was heaven itself, before which the emperor must himself bow as its adopted son. In effect, the emperor must always subordinate his authority to the principles embodied in the Confucian canon and the precedents in the historical records compiled by Confucian scholars. No Emperor could say, without violating the Confucian estimate of his position, "I am the state."

Neo-Confucianism

Starting with Han Yu (768 to 824 A.D.), and ending with Chu Hsi (1130 to 1200), there developed a school of thought within the Confucian doctrine and system known as Neo-Confucianism. From the thirteenth century onward this interpretation of Confucianism gradually became the orthodox doctrine throughout China, and it lasted until the twentieth century.

This was a period when the Chinese scholars and philosophers turned their full attention upon the old and traditional Confucian teachings. They were moved to reexamine their old doctrines by the challenge to find answers within their traditional philosophy to certain Buddhist questions about good and evil, heaven and hell, the nature of humans, and other fundamental matters. This was also a period of intellectual ferment, a questioning time when, for one reason or another, persons of perception turned inward and looked thoughtfully at their value systems and institutions.

They found what they wanted in the old classics of China. They never claimed that they were introducing something new into Confucianism, but rather that they were rediscovering meanings that had been lost over centuries of time. However, they were influenced to a certain extent by both Taoist and Buddhist thought. Many of them had been students of Buddhism and Taoism, and they frequently utilized the terms and conceptions of these two ideologies to explain and elaborate on their new Confucianism.

They discovered in the *I Ching* the term *t'ai chi* which became for them the Supreme Reality, the First Cause, from which all else derived. It had no personality; it was a moral force. Chu Hsi, the final arbiter of neo-Confucianism, thought of this moral force as *li* undergirding the myriad forms of all things. He called the matter or the materials which made the forms concrete, *ch'i.*

There was a debate over human nature. Chu Hsi decided that Mencius was right in his conviction that human nature was good. Some had claimed that human nature was bad, or neither good nor bad, but like water which takes any route it can find for outlet regardless of the goodness or badness of the circumstances. Chu Hsi argued that the *li* underlying human nature must be good and the source of all the basic virtues. The physical manifestation of a human, or *ch'i,* must of course be carefully educated and cultivated so that the benevolent virtues of *li* may shine forth. Thus, the need for a good social order, a well-taught officialdom, a moral leader, a family-centered society and state, and all of the other Confucian values and institutions so necessary for a harmonious and happy society.

By the beginning of the fourteenth century, the thought and teachings of Chu Hsi had become the orthodox interpretation of Confucianism. The scholars and educated classes became quite skeptical about the existence of supernatural beings. There was a decline of Buddhism in China. This new interpretation of a basically old Confucianism became central to the education system in China, and it was rigidly upheld until the time of radical changes in China during the twentieth century.

The Conservative Nature of Confucianism

The unity and permanence of Chinese civilization is in large measure due to the contribution of Confucianism. For the past two thousand years Confucianism has been the ideology of countless generations of scholar-officials. A good knowledge of Confucianism was the only path to fame and the most influential positions in Chinese society. Anyone could obtain this knowledge if he had the desire, the opportunity, and the will. Regardless of racial origin or ethnic group, no matter what class of society he was born into, if a person successfully proved knowledge through tests, he took his place among the leaders of Chinese society. With few exceptions, China had a male-led society.

The family, which gave permanence and stability to Chinese civilization, was emphasized in Confucian thought. Confucians considered it the most important moral unit, and the state merely an extension of it. They protected family unity by law and custom; they encouraged its growth through the grant of privileges; and they prevented its breakup by reserving the harshest sanctions and punishments for those who violated family regulations and traditions.

The privileged position of the Confucians led at times to conservatism and arrogance. Since it was Confucianism that kept the scholar-officials and the leaders of the community in power, these men were strongly impelled to oppose ideological changes. Furthermore, the Confucians sincerely believed that they were the only civilized community in the world, that all beyond the boundaries of their culture were barbarians who had nothing to give the Confucians, but to whom the Confucians had much to give. To hold such a belief is to become arrogant and contemptuous of other beliefs and other cultures. One of the reasons for China's reluctance to change her way of life when first exposed to Western culture and technology was the degree to which Confucianism had permeated Chinese life and thought.

20

Taoism

The duck's legs are short, but if we try to lengthen them, the duck will feel pain. The crane's legs are long, but if we try to shorten them, the crane will feel grief. Therefore we are not to cut off what is by nature long, nor to lengthen what is by nature short.

—Chuang Tzu

The philosophy of Taoism takes its name from the Chinese word *Tao* meaning "The Way." It is the first word of the Taoist book *Tao Te Ching,* "The Classic of the Way and Its Power." The three principal teachers of this Chinese philosophy were Lao Tzu, Tang Chu, and Chuang Tzu. Traditionally, Lao Tzu, "Old Master," was the founder of Taoism and the author of *Tao Te*

Ching. Tang Chu lived about the fourth century B.C. Chuang Tzu lived approximately 369 to 286 B.C.; he is considered Lao Tzu's most distinguished disciple and is believed to be the author of the book of *Chuang Tzu.*

According to tradition, Lao Tzu was an older contemporary of Confucius, but modern scholars have questioned his very existence. They believe that the books attributed to Lao Tzu and Chuang Tzu were written after the period when Confucius lived by later members of the Taoist school.

The Natural Way

Taoism taught that the best way to live is the natural way. They are happiest who live in accordance with their nature. People's fears, sufferings, and problems are the result of an unnatural life. Humans can be truly free only when they liberate themselves from all artificial restraints. Taoism, which is also described as "The Way of the Uninhibited," stresses such words as "naturalness," "spontaneity," and "simplicity."

It is barely possible to suggest what the Tao is. The early Taoists never directly defined it because they believed language incapable of adequately determining its precise meaning. "Those who know the Tao do not speak of it; those who speak of it do not know it." Chuang Tzu stated that he should not seek precision in trying to understand the Tao, for although he had journeyed across it, he still only knew where it began, and although he had wandered in its vastness, he did not know where it ended. The Tao lies beyond shape and feature like an uncarved block and is eternally nameless. Taoists spoke of it as "a shape without shape, a form without form." The Tao is the unseen power beneath the life and movement in nature. It is like the quiet unconscious processes of nature which flow without motive, without effort, and without end. Chuang Tzu states this idea poetically: "The sun and moon simply shine, and the four seasons pursue their courses. So it is with the regular phenomena of day and night, and with the movement of the clouds by which the rain is distributed." The Tao is like the stream of time, drifting along without goals and without purpose, and just as unexplainable. Certain of the Tao's properties are suggested by analogy with moving water. As water overcomes obstacles in its path by flowing around them, so the Tao overcomes by yielding; as rivers and oceans are great because they occupy the low places of the earth, so the Tao is great because it is lowly. The Tao, because it is the ultimate reality, is present everywhere in all things, in the fly, in the earth, in the wastes of body and kitchen. It is also infinite, for if you go back and back, you cannot discover its beginning, and if you go forward and forward, you will not find its end.

Flowing unceasingly and effortlessly in nature, the Tao is also the force that gives life and their particular nature to all beings. The nature of any particular being is found in the Tao's manner of producing and sustaining it. It is the nature of a fish that it cannot exist out of water. It is the nature of humans that they must breathe air. Things differ in their natures and natural abilities. A duck is different from a crane, a horse is different from a human, and a dog is different from a cat. Although the Tao is continually changing the physical forms inhabiting the universe, the change is always in accordance with the individual nature of each form. To overrun this nature and act contrary to its commands is harmful because such actions interrupt the unconscious, natural, sustaining flow of the Tao. For instance, to subject horses to hunger and thirst, to force them to race and walk together in regular order, to place a bit in their mouths and lash them with a whip must harm them because all these things are contrary to the nature of a horse. Something is contrary to the nature of a being when it is artificial and human-made, external rather than internal. "What is of nature is internal. What is of man is external. . . . That oxen and horses should have four feet is what is of nature. That a halter should be put on a horse's head, or a string through an ox's nose, is what is of man." To try to shorten a crane's legs, or to try to lengthen a duck's legs, is contrary to the nature of these animals and therefore can only cause them pain.

Taoism affirms the right to spontaneous expression of one's individual nature and abhors social restraints. The fact that people live in society with conventional rules of behavior is contrary to the dictates of their natures and therefore harmful. Social conventions are external to humans and artificial and therefore must be considered unnatural. The early Taoists could not describe precisely the nature of human, or any animal for that matter, but they could teach what it was not. The wood of the living tree, unspoiled by alien hand, was the Taoist symbol of the natural state of humans whose natures have not been inhibited by conventional values.

In its negative theoretical aspects, Taoism was a revolt against society by withdrawal from it. It did not preach a withdrawal from the physical presence of others; rather it denied the validity of the social relationships established by them.

The Taoists, like other dissident groups in China, attributed their principles to a past golden age in order to make their philosophical innovation seem conservative and therefore more palatable to the people of their time. People once lived naturally, wearing clothes they had woven and eating food they had grown, and all creatures of earth and sky lived together in harmony. People wandered over the land like wild deer. Virtue was practiced unconsciously and knowledge was not valued. All things acted naturally without knowledge, without purpose, without unnatural desires, and without artificial restraints. All things were in harmony because all were unrestrained in the spontaneous expression of their natures. After the coming of the culture heroes—the inventors of conventions and morality and the seekers after knowledge —the perfect community became disrupted and was gradually forgotten. Then all submitted their natures to the harness of convention. The world became confused because the Tao, the True Way, was obscured and hidden by artificialities. The Taoists were in revolt against society as an agent of the corruption of humans which separated them from their true natures.

The Taoists denied the validity of conventional notions of good and evil. They saw conventional good and conventional evil as opposite sides of the same coin. The standards of value that society invented created an evil for every good they defined.

The true good of all was the free expression of their proper natures, and if they should fail in this, nothing good could be said concerning their condition. The conventional paragon and the conventional thief were both of them pitiable distortions of their natural selves.

The Taoist Sage

Taoism asserts that another way by which people are led astray from the paths of their true natures is by the improper use of the senses. Improperly used, sense perception leads to the illusion that things, which are merely manifestations of the Tao, have an existence independent of the viewer and other things. Thereupon two forms of perversion become possible: 1) to desire things or fear them, and 2) to have knowledge of them as things. Taoist sages, possessing all things because of their union with the Tao, were not troubled by the illusion that they had a separate existence and were therefore devoid of all fear, desire, and false knowledge. This is not to say that the Taoists had no human feelings or lacked natural appetites. The sages rejoiced in the spontaneous expression of their nature and the satisfaction of their natural appetites. But the only true knowledge for the Taoists was the realization of oneness with the Tao that eliminated the distinction between knower and known.

Taoist philosophers contrasted the tranquil happiness of the sage with the gnawing anxiety and fear endured by those whose nature had been corrupted. One of the joys of sagehood, perhaps the greatest of them, was the attainment of a sense of immortality. The corrupted ones, ignorant of the Tao, held fast to illusory and impermanent selves. The everpresent threat of death intensified the pain of their striving with the knowledge that they must someday lose everything. It was quite otherwise with the sages. Since they felt themselves to be one with the eternal Tao, they knew that death was merely a change of form and had small significance. They awaited it without fear.

The practical consequence of the corruption of people by society and by errors arising from their senses is that they deliberately exert themselves for unnatural ends. They embroil themselves in politics and loud arguments, they fight with one another, and feel frustration in their search for fame. They arouse envy and constantly live in fear of death. The Taoist sage, on the other hand, never had the intention of seeking or doing anything, but did all things naturally and not for a purpose. Similarly individuals should act without the intention of acting, they should give without the intention of being generous, and smile without the intention of pleasing. In other words, every act should flow spontaneously from the individual's nature as the processes of nature flow in their inevitable course. The true Taoist's mind did not stop to pass judgment on itself. The thought should be as unthought of by the thinker as the well-fit shoe is unthought of by the foot that wears it.

One might reasonably suppose that the Taoist philosopher's impassioned rejection of society implied a corresponding rejection of politics. On the contrary, the Taoists developed a historically important theory of politics. Soon after Taoist philosophy was founded, Taoists yielded to the very human desire for political power. This power they based not in social virtues, or in ancestral spirits, but in the Tao. The Taoist sages, they believed, would of necessity be masters of the world. Quiet, humble, and nonwilling, they would be one with the Tao and therefore in complete control of the myriad things of the universe. The sage-ruler would govern without appearing to govern, and would restore to the people the felicity of the golden age by filling their bellies and emptying their minds. This doctrine was eagerly taken up by the Legalists who found in it a theoretical basis for their totalitarian techniques.

Popular Taoism

Taoism is an imaginative philosophy that has its best expression in the poetic system of the *Tao Te Ching* and the *Chuang Tzu*. Taoist philosophers tried to liberate the minds of their listeners from conventional habits of thought that obscured the truth. In carrying out their mission of liberation, Taoist philosophers used startling paradoxes and vivid analogies, often in dialogue form, to excite the minds of listeners. A typical paradox states: "The Tao in its regular course does nothing, and so there is nothing which it does not do." The Taoist delighted in speaking of the usefulness of the useless, the importance of the unimportant, the intelligence of the stupid, and the sight of the sightless. The analogies found throughout the early writings of Taoism show a feeling for life and movement in nature. Thus, the speaker in the book of *Chuang Tzu* illustrates a point by saying: "The tailorbird makes its nest in the deep forest, but only uses a single branch; the mole drinks from the Ho River but only takes what fills its belly."

Later Taoists gave a religious turn to the mystical aspects of the original doctrine. Many important Chinese gods, such as the gods of rain, fire, medicine, and agriculture, and the kitchen gods, arose from the Taoist school. The impersonal and infinite force beneath nature became transformed into individual, finite human souls that, after death, became powerful spirits. The popular Taoism of later times increasingly filled the need for the magic that people often turn to when other resources fail them. Chinese peasants sought the help of unseen powers because they lived on a narrow economic margin, and hard work and skill were not always enough for survival. As a consequence, the average person began to associate the Taoists with the world of spirits who must be placated and appeased. The Taoists were called upon more and more to select lucky days for weddings and funerals, to choose sites for housing, and in general to regulate those human activities peculiarly related to the world of spirits.

The debasement of Taoism in its popular form was clear in the Taoist practitioners' search for the elixir of immortality. They and their clients showed a fear of death that would have shamed such philosophical Taoists as Lao Tzu and Chuang Tzu. Further, Taoist alchemists profaned their philosophic heritage by attempting to transmute base metals into gold and silver.

Popular superstitions were not the only additions to Taoism. Ideas and practices of other schools also attached themselves to the Taoist tradition. Ritualistic practices, possibly of Indian origin, can be found in later Taoistic writings. Buddhism greatly influenced Taoism because of the mystical quality common to both schools of thought, and the Taoists in later days borrowed much of the external trappings of Buddhism, such as monasteries, statues, and the organization of priesthood.

Philosophic Taoism has remained through the ages of Chinese history a subject of study and meditation for the scholarly class of China. The Chinese scholar, like the Western scholar of Chinese thought, is intrigued and stimulated by the imaginative and acute criticisms that Taoism levels against many aspects of society and by its view of the nature of the universe. Taoism has also been reflected in Chinese poetry and painting. In their contemplative moods and in their love of nature the Chinese owe more to Taoism than to Confucianism.

21

Legalism

> When the guiding principles of the people become un-
> suited to the circumstances, their standards of value
> must change. As conditions in the world change, different
> principles are practiced.
>
> —The Book of Lord Shang

The Chinese called Legalism "the school of law" because it was a philosophy that stressed laws, imposed and interpreted by the ruling sovereign, as standards for the people's actions. Three works contain the main collection of Legalist writings: *The Book of Lord Shang*, traditionally attributed to Shang Yang (d. 338 B.C.); *Han Fei-Tzu*, compiled by Han Fei-Tzu (d. 233 B.C.), the most famous of the Legalist writers; and *Kuan Tzu*, which was probably written by a number of Legalist writers.

Legalism was the first Chinese philosophy that became the official ideology of the country. It provided the direction and philosophical foundation for China's first unified empire, the Ch'in Dynasty (221 to 207 B.C.).

Totalitarian Philosophy in China

Legalism was a philosophy of expediency that had no place for permanent or absolute moral standards. The ruler should stand alone and be all-powerful. He was not subject to any higher authority. The ruler should lay down the standards by which the people of the state were to govern their lives. The Legalists believed that if the ruler based his actions upon absolute moral standards his authority would soon be lost and the state weakened.

The determining factor in all matters, the Legalist held, was the ruler's needs for the moment. These needs varied with time and circumstance; in each situation only those actions should be justified which helped to maintain or increase the ruler's power. The question of right and wrong in this context was determined by the individual ruler. The same act might be right for one ruler but wrong for the other. Schools of thought that sought in a real or imagined past for ways to solve the disorders of the Warring Period (481 to 221 B.C.) were rebuked by the Legalists who said that "There is more than one way to govern the world and there is no necessity to imitate antiquity, in order to take appropriate measures for the state."

The Legalists believed that society formed the individual. As social conditions changed, so the people changed. Any solution for the problems of life must take into consideration this fact of a changing society. Because they believed that their teachings were based upon this fact, the Legalists thought of themselves as completely realistic.

They held that two problems not present in former ages complicated the social and political life of their time: the scarcity of material goods, and the increased value of state offices, especially that of the emperor. With regard to the first problem, the Legalists taught that material goods were abundant in former years, and because of the small population all had more than they needed. Therefore there was no disorder, for there was no need to compete with others. With the passage of time, as the population grew, the amount of material goods which could be shared by the people decreased. Competition, which then became the normal relationship between the people, grew so intense that it obscured the long-range goals of the general welfare and blinded the people to all things except their individual and immediate interests. Han Fei-Tzu referred to the people as babies who were incapable of understanding why their heads were shaved or their boils lanced, who did not realize that these operations, though painful, were for their own good. The second great problem, according to the Legalists, was the struggle, then tearing the country apart, to obtain the office of emperor of China. They believed that in former times the office of emperor was not so lucrative as in their times, that formerly the emperor lived in a rough hut, ate the poorest foods, wore the clothes of a gatekeeper, and worked like a slave. In time, however, even the office of district magistrate provided enough to keep a family comfortable for generations. Of how much more value was the office of emperor. Consequently, the various independent states of China were engaged in continual warfare, each seeking the ultimate goal of hegemony over all the other states and each ruler seeking the position of emperor.

Virtue by Legislation

The Legalists thought that the solution to both problems lay in the establishment of a strong centralized government under the control of one ruler. Such a government would simultaneously increase the power of the state in relation to other states and in relation to its own citizens. The three important factors in the organization and maintenance of a strong centralized nation were: *fa*, or law; *shih*, or authority, position, power; and *shu*, or statecraft, methods or art of government.

The Legalists held that law was superior to virtue, morality, or ritual as an instrument for controlling the citizens of the state. *Jen*, or benevolence, did not enable a father to keep his children in order, much less could it enable a ruler to keep his subjects in order. Law, however, gave strength to a state: "No country is permanently strong. Nor is any country permanently weak. If conformers to law are strong, the country is strong; if conformers to law are weak, the country is weak." The laws promulgated by the legalists were intended to safeguard the power of the state; they were not instituted for the protection of individual rights or privileges. They were, in the last analysis, penal laws, instituted for the purpose of concentrating power more firmly in the hands of the ruler and enabling him to conquer other states.

Shih (power, position, authority) was another essential factor in the establishment and preservation of a strong centralized government. *Shih* represented dominance over others; the ability to influence and control people's actions. The office of ruler was the concrete manifestation of this power. No one could command the people's obedience until he had occupied the office of ruler. Thereupon he possessed the authority to rule the people through punishment or reward.

The Legalists thought that people were moved to action only through motives of self-interest, that is, through the hope of some reward or the fear of some punishment. Subjects obey their ruler, not because they love him, but because they fear him, and it was on this basis that the ruler must govern. In employing punishments no affection or extenuating circumstances must be taken into consideration. Even the smallest of infractions must be punished severely, and there were many instances of severe punishments for relatively small violations of the law, such as having a hand cut off for throwing ashes in the street or being cut in two for neglecting to denounce a culprit. The thought behind this attitude was that if small infractions were punished with severity, no one would dare commit grave infractions. Punishments and rewards, like the law, should be made known to the people clearly, simply, and in great detail. They should be definite, adequate, and inevitable so that there might be no ambiguity and confusion.

Shu (statecraft, method or art of government) was the third essential factor in the creation and preservation of a strong centralized state under the dominance of one ruler. Since the ruler was the key individual in the state, the one who set the standards, gave directions, and kept the people in line by his application of rewards and punishments, the wisdom of his actions was the most important factor in the Legalists' philosophy of expediency. In their books many pages are devoted to describing the manner in which he should rule and the relationship that should exist between him and his ministers. Well aware that the ruler needed men to govern the country, the Legalists advised him to delegate all his duties to them. He should do nothing but maintain the system of rewards and punishments and see to it that the ministers carried out the duties required by the offices they held. In fact, the ruler who truly understood the art of government could pass the time hunting and carousing, for his country would not suffer from his lack of attention to administrative details. This is the Legalist interpretation of the Taoist idea that the ruler rules by doing nothing; yet there is nothing that is not done. The ruler did not need to do anything after the methods for selecting and promoting personnel, and the duties of each office, had been spelled out in the law and backed up by a code of rewards and punishments that covered every situation. Certain other recommendations were stressed. The ruler should tell no one his wishes, not even his son, lest his ministers use this information for their own purposes. He must beware of corruption and bribery on the part of his ministers, especially with regard to his favorite concubines and mistresses, lest he be influenced while drunk or during some particularly tender interlude. He was cautioned against the attempt of ministers to advance their cause through his relatives and friends by gifts and palaces, trappings for his horses, or clothes for his wives.

People Exist for the State

The Legalists contended that, in a world of competing states all striving for mastery, only two occupations should be encouraged by the central government—war and agriculture. The Legalist sage should mobilize the people to concentrate exclusively on agriculture at home and war abroad. Agriculture contributed directly to the strength of the state since food was essential for life, and war was the pathway to the control of all China. When the people were single-minded in these pursuits, the road to becoming emperor of all China was clear of all major obstructions.

The Legalists solved the difficult problem of recruiting people into these strenuous and sometimes dangerous occupations by resorting to their theory that people were actuated solely by self-interest. The ruler should make certain that profit came only from the soil, and fame solely through war. People, they believed, spend most of their lives scheming for profit and, when near death, are very desirous of a high reputation and fame. The ruler should bring about such harsh conditions at home that the people find life bitter when not tilling the land and dangerous when not fighting the country's battles. When this ideal condition was realized, the state would be strong and orderly at home, respected and victorious abroad. There should be no classes or occupations standing outside the law; only the ruler stood above it. Advancement should come only through proficiency in war and agriculture. Consequently, the Legalists attacked the aristocrats, artisans, hermits, innkeepers, merchants, soothsayers, scholars, and philanthropists. Artisans, who pander to the tastes of people through luxuries, were useless to the state, as were the hermits, who spend their days in foolish meditation. Innkeepers served only restless people who were probably plotting against the state; and merchants, scheming in their own interest, harmed the state through the creation of artificial scarcities.

The Legalists reserved some of their harshest criticisms for the Confucians, whom they termed the "good people." By "good" the Legalists meant those who would loyally protect friends and relatives who broke the law rather than denounce them to the state. This practice made the people stronger than the law and thus weakened the state; it was only when the law was stronger than the people that a state was strong.

Philanthropists were denounced as weakening the state by encouraging laziness and extravagance. It was wrong, said the Legalists, to tax the rich, who through thrift and hard work had won success, in order to feed and clothe those who through idleness and extravagance had become poor. The Legalists also opposed appeals to supernatural agents and insisted that private quarrels cease because the law alone determined guilt or innocence, reward or punishment. Everything must be subordinated to the good of the state, even the luxury of revenge.

The Legacy of Legalism

In the Ch'in Dynasty, established in 221 B.C., Legalism saw its doctrines triumph. The state of Ch'in, by utilizing the methods advocated by the Legalists, conquered the other independent states of China and set up one nation headed by a ruler who significantly took the name of "The First Emperor." The country was divided into a number of administrative districts, laws and regulations were promulgated throughout the country, weights and measures were standardized, and all measures taken to unify the country under the control of one ruler.

After eleven years the emperor died, and by 207 B.C., the Ch'in Dynasty had lost control of the people. The Chinese did not take kindly to the rigorous punishments inflicted by the Ch'in rulers, and soon many of them revolted against this severe regime. Under the Han emperor Wu, who came to the throne in 140 B.C., Legalism, disguised by Confucian trappings, became again the dominant ideology of the state. But after Wu's death it passed away as an independent philosophy and exclusive ideological foundation for the government.

Legalist philosophy, however, left a legacy in codified laws, the unification of language, standardization of weights and measures, the destruction of the feudal domains, and the division of China into administrative districts headed by men of ability. It lived on in such concepts as individual land ownership, the taxing of the individual farmer by the state, and the development of irrigation projects which benefited the important occupation of agriculture. It also lived on in Chinese rulers who used their absolute power to oppress the people in order to advance themselves and the nation.

22

Buddhism in China

Thou perfect master,
Who shinest upon all things and all men,
As gleaming moonlight plays upon a thousand
    waters at the same time!
Thy great compassion does not pass by a
    single creature.
Steadily and quietly sails the great ship
    of compassion across the sea of sorrow.
Thou are the Great Physician for a sick
    and impure world,
In pity giving the invitation to the Paradise
    of the West.
                    —Prayer from Mass for the Dead

When Buddhism passed from India to China,
Korea, Tibet, and Japan, it changed from a reli-

From *Buddhism, A Religion of Infinite Compassion*, edited by
Clarence H. Hamilton, copyright © 1952 by The Liberal Arts
Press, Inc., reprinted by permission of the Liberal Arts Press
Division of the Bobbs-Merrill Company, Inc.

gion demanding much of people to a religion of compassion promising much to all who were faithful and devoted. This form of Buddhism is known as Mahayana Buddhism.

Mahayana Buddhism follows the example and heart of the Buddha more than his rigid teaching. It is concerned with the Buddha who, after his enlightenment, spent the remaining forty-five years of his life telling others about the path of freedom. His followers interpret this action as a social goal and ideal.

The story spread that, ages before, he had taken a vow to become enlightened in order to rescue suffering humanity. Before he was enlightened, he was a *Bodhisattva*, that is, one striving for enlightenment to fit himself to aid fellow humans. By heroic deeds in previous existences, he accumulated the merit which resulted in his enlightenment in his final rebirth. A Buddha is not accessible to human beings once he has entered Nirvana, but there are those, Bodhisattvas, who defer entrance into Nirvana and remain behind on earth to help those who suffer. Buddhas and Bodhisattvas are both enlightened beings. The difference between them is that Buddhas are those who have entered into Nirvana, while Bodhisattvas continue their cycle of birth and rebirth in order to gain merit for others and guide them to enlightenment.

According to Mahayana Buddhism, the true follower of Buddha is one who follows the example of Buddha and becomes a Bodhisattva. Anyone who is moved by the suffering of others and seeks enlightenment for their benefit may become a Bodhisattva or Buddha. Buddhahood and Bodhisattva are stages open to all—merchant, banker, farmer, lawyer, or laborer. This spirit is caught in a poem:

> O that I might become for all beings
> the soother of pain!
> O that I might be for all of them that
> ail the remedy, the physician, the nurse,
> until the disappearance of illness!
>
> O that by raining down food and drink I
> might soothe the pangs of hunger and
> thirst, and that in times of famine I
> might myself become drink and food!
>
> O that I might be for the poor an inexhaustible treasure!

> All my incarnations to come, all my goods, all my merits,
> past and present and future, I renounce with indifference,
> so that the end of all beings may be attained.[1]

There are few great Bodhisattvas; and with the exception of Gautama Buddha who stayed on earth for many rebirths, Buddhas are beings in the heavens rather than on earth. The common people began to rely upon the merits of those whose compassion and pity were conceived to be infinite. Buddhas and Bodhisattvas became deities who were worshiped, adored, and prayed to. They were clothed in all the formal garments of an organized religion. Examples of these are: Kuan-yin (Japanese, Kannon), the Goddess of Mercy; Wen-shu, the Lord of Wisdom; and Ti-ts'ang, who goes to hell (which the Chinese added to Buddhism) to save the suffering ones. These Bodhisattvas are found under other names in Japan, Korea, and Tibet.

Amitabha: The Compassionate Buddha

The greatest and most popular god is the Buddha Amitabha (O-mi-t'o in China, Amida in Japan). Ages before, he had taken a vow to save others, and through his good deeds done in countless ages, he created the "Pure Land" or "Western Paradise," a heaven where all will go who call upon his name. There, in the western part of the universe, he reigns with his faithful in perfect happiness.

> It is called the Land of Supreme Happiness because all beings there do not suffer from any mental or physical pain and only enjoy pleasure and happiness of all kinds.
>
> In this land of Supreme Happiness there are seven lakes, all adorned with gems. The lakes are filled with water which possesses the eight good qualities. . . . The bottoms of the lakes are strewn with golden sand. On the four sides of the lakes there are paths and steps of gold, silver, beryl, and crystal, white corals, red pearls, and diamonds. In the lakes the lotus flowers grow as big as wheels of chariots. . . .
>
> In this land of Supreme Happiness the musical instruments of heaven are often played on grounds of gold. Three times a day and three times a night Mandarava flowers drop down like rain. . . .

Thus is described the Western Heaven which is ruled over by a

---

[1] René Grousset, *In the Footsteps of the Buddha* (London: Routledge & Kegan Paul, Ltd. 1932). Used with permission.

Buddha of infinite compassion, Amitabha Buddha. All good Chinese Buddhists, those who call with faith and constancy upon the name of Amitabha Buddha, go to this magnificent place.

Another well-known compassionate being is Kuan-yin, the Goddess of Mercy, who also is ready and willing to succor the afflicted who seek her aid. Kuan-yin was originally a male deity known in India as Avalokitesvara, or "the Merciful One Who Surveys the World with Pity," but somewhere along the passage from India to China this divine being changed sex. Kuan-yin has sometimes been compared to the Madonna of the Christian faith. These two merciful beings are representatives of Mahayana Buddhism who captured the imagination and loyalty of the Chinese people in the past and who, along with the Western Heaven described above, continue to hold a favorite place in the hearts of millions today.

All of the Buddhas and Bodhisattvas are the physical embodiments of Mahayana mercy and compassion. Mahayana Buddhism is a religion of compassion because it does not require people to rely solely upon themselves for salvation. Prayer and worship are an integral part of Mahayana Buddhism. Prayers are said continually to the various Bodhisattvas requesting them to aid petitioners in their efforts to obtain salvation. The verse addressed to Amitabha which heads this chapter is from the *Mass for the Dead* and vividly illustrates the deep faith of the people in his infinite mercy. The emotion, the hope, the humanity of Mahayana Buddhism were preferred by the Tibetans, Chinese, Koreans, and Japanese to the middle way and self-discipline of Hinayana or Theravada Buddhism.

Buddhism Becomes Chinese

Buddhism in China played down its foreign elements and made itself as Chinese as possible. The abstract concept of Nirvana—the state or condition of desirelessness—was minimized, and a concrete place of happiness, like the Western Heaven of Amitabha Buddha, was given prominence.

It built on the foundations of the other ideologies popular during the early part of the Christian era. Since Taoism was popular among the commoners and intellectuals alike, Buddhists used Taoism as an instrument of conversion by taking over Taoist terms, writing commentaries on Taoist books, and identifying Buddhism with Taoist teaching and practice. The common elements in Taoist and Buddhist doctrine were deliberately stressed over and over again. At times, indeed, the truth was stretched in order to make Taoism and Buddhism agree. They honored Confucianism by speaking of a Bodhisattva as being an incarnation of Confucius, by naming a temple after Confucius, and by stressing the virtue of filial piety as an aspect of Buddhist teaching. Buddhist monks pointed out the similarities between Confucian and Buddhist morality, even going so far as to set up ancestral tablets in a special hall to honor the memory of their dead monks.

Buddhism attracted the scholarly class because of its speculative nature and enticed the common people because of its ritual and ceremonial observances. Its appeal was reinforced by the literary labors of numerous Indian and Chinese Buddhist missionaries who made a determined effort to translate Buddhist literature into Chinese and to relate Buddhism to the observances and attitudes of the Chinese. Two Chinese Buddhist pilgrims famous for their travels between China and India are Fa-Hsien, who left China in 399 A.D. and spent fifteen years in India, and Hsuan-tsang, who left China in 629 A.D. and lived for sixteen years in India. Both of these famous travelers carried Buddhist books and manuscripts back to China with them. It is said that Hsuan-tsang and his pupils translated more than a thousand volumes into Chinese.

Buddhism showed its desire to coexist peacefully with the rulers by not developing an administrative machinery in the monastic order and by not attempting to wrest the administrative machinery of the country from the Confucian scholars.

By showing itself not as an exclusive religion, but as a complement to other Chinese beliefs, Buddhism penetrated and permeated Chinese life and became as Chinese as the native philosophies of Confucianism and Taoism. The Chinese were never thereafter at any particular period either Confucianist, Taoist, or Buddhist—they were all three simultaneously.

Buddhism was a tremendous intellectual force in China. It gave the Chinese a new look at the universe, at the individual, and at life. It provided the Chinese with a new literature and stimulated the production of new forms of music and religious art. It influenced Chinese painting and architecture, brought to China a message of justice and hope, and imbued the Chinese with a love and respect for all living things. It also served as a vehicle for carrying the culture of India and China to Korea and Japan.

23

Chinese Social Life

Patterns of social life are changing in China. The old forms and social relationships are gradually being replaced or harmonized with newer forms and relationships which are founded upon different values and ways of thinking. It is a time of social upheaval when generalizations previously used to describe many aspects of social life in China are no longer completely valid. Descriptions of such social institutions as the gentry, the family, the clan, marriage, and the status of women must be modified in light of the swift changes that have taken place in China in recent years. However, the amount and pace of change vary with locality. Cities and urban areas have

195

experienced greater and faster changes than the rural areas, for the farmers do not change quickly, and the ways and attitudes hallowed by the centuries press them to follow the traditional paths.

Traditional customs and mentality linger on in a changing, modern government. The modern stress upon companionship and equality between men and women in China has resulted in more mingling of sexes prior to marriage than was previously the case, and many couples now become engaged without their parents' approval. However, these same couples are extremely shy about showing their affection for each other in public, an attitude reminiscent of old Chinese social life. In negotiating marriage preliminaries, the tractor boss, or foreman, or member of their discussion group, may serve as the go-between for the two individuals. The go-between is traditional in China, but he or she usually negotiated between families rather than individuals. Instead of bowing before the elders of the family and the ancestral tablets during the marriage ceremony, many couples now bow before a picture of Mao Tse-tung and proclaim their intentions to serve the state instead of the family.

A new emphasis was given to social change when, in the summer of 1966, Mao closed the schools of China and called upon the youth of the nation to become the vanguard of a new revolution formally named "The Great Proletarian Cultural Revolution." He told them to search out the enemies of Mao's thought, whether inside or outside the party. Armed with his words and authority millions of young people, mostly between the ages of fifteen and twenty-five, swarmed over the land, harassing those whom Mao and his followers considered revisionists, capitalists, and opponents of his thought. Except for Mao and his few chosen leaders, no one was safe from the probes and the attacks of these enthusiastic and energetic Red Guards. As a result of their activities, many officials, including the Chief of State, Liu Shao-chi, fell from power, and many were compelled to undertake "thought rehabilitation." Finally, in late summer of 1967, the Maoist leaders in Peking informed the Red Guards that their goals had been reached and that they should return to their schools and homes. Committees consisting of soldiers, workers, and peasants were established to bring order to the countryside and the cities and to carry on the Cultural Revolution. Gradually, under the leadership of the People's Liberation Army (PLA), a certain amount of stability and order was restored to the country. By the middle of 1969 millions of young people had returned to their schools or had been sent to the rural areas and the wastelands to release their energies in producing food and in developmental projects. In the meantime, the old social order had been shaken and shocked to its roots by the roaming millions of Chinese youth.

In Nationalist China, and among the Chinese living elsewhere in the world, there is also change. But it is more gradual, evolutionary rather than revolutionary, and more of the traditional practices are honored and retained.

The social life of the Chinese cannot be described as either traditional or modern. The old and new are reacting upon each other to form a composite of the alien and the indigenous, the traditional and the familiar.

24

Gentry and
Peasantry in China

Those who earn their living by labor are destined to be ruled.

—Mencius

The gentry and the peasantry were the two main classes of traditional Chinese society.

The gentry class, at the top of Chinese society, represented a way of life which all Chinese sought to attain. The hope of the various classes in China, especially the peasant class, was to become a member of the gentry class and follow gentry customs. Membership in the gentry class was open to the peasants, and a constant stream of peasants ascended into the gentry class during all periods of Chinese history. This may be one of the factors which helped to preserve the gentry as a vital class for so many centuries. One of the means by which members of the peasantry entered the gentry class was through education and government service. It was not uncommon for a bright peasant boy, educated through group effort, to pass the examinations and embark upon a government career. This achievement immediately placed him and his family in the gentry class. Other stepping stones were the acquisition of political power, military promotions, or wealth. The sons of these politically or economically powerful families would be educated, established in government careers, and thus introduced into the gentry class. Gentry families might also descend to peasant status. In almost every peasant family in China there are tales of some ancestors who were members of the government or prominent scholars in a particular field. Thus, a certain degree of mobility between gentry and peasantry was a striking feature of the social life of the Chinese people.

The gentry and peasant ways of life differed in many respects. The gentry led an easier existence, had more time to engage in social activities, and carried out the traditional ceremonies with greater pomp and on a more lavish scale. They were more concerned with political affairs and devoted much more time to cultural activities such as poetry, painting, essays, and the art of calligraphy or brush writing. Other economic, social, and political characteristics distinguished the gentry from the peasantry.

Economic Characteristics of the Gentry

The gentry derived their income from land which they did not cultivate themselves or from means that did not require physical labor. In imperial China one of their principal sources of income was a government position of one kind or another. This was also true of China under the Republic, but during this period industrial, commercial, and banking organizations also served as sources of income. Members of modern professional groups such as lawyers, doctors, engineers, and professors were considered members of the gentry class. Rents collected from their tenants varied with locality but were generally quite high, permitting the gentry to purchase such luxury items as paintings, musical instruments, porcelains, jewelry, and art objects of all kinds.

Great numbers of the gentry lived in towns. They moved there to increase their income, to be close to the political and cultural center of the community, and to lead a leisurely life with congenial companions.

Gentry families who stayed in the country and lived solely off the land soon became rather poor. These families, like all gentry families, grew fast, and eventually the family property was divided among the male heirs, creating a number of small landowners where there had been only one large one. By moving into the towns and supplementing their rentals with another source of steady income, the family could divide its property without radically impairing the economic status of its members.

Members of the gentry often supplemented their incomes by opening shops, frequently pawnshops and rice shops. Pawnshops were a common sight in Chinese towns. Because the Chinese were subject to periodic economic crises of one kind or another and frequently needed ready cash, the pawnshops were convenient sources of money and served as banks or lending agencies for the community. Their interest rates were high. Rice shops were also very profitable. Their owners bought rice cheaply immediately after the harvest and stored it until it was in short supply. Then they sold it at a high price or loaned it out at a high interest. Often twice the amount of rice was demanded in return, and if the loan was not repaid within a fixed period, the percentage of rice interest was increased accordingly. This rice plus interest was generally payable at the next harvest, usually three or four months later. It was not uncommon for the original sellers to have to buy or borrow the same rice they had grown.

Since the gentry were the source of scholar-officials who administered the government of imperial China and were the leaders and patrons of the intellectual and cultural life of the country, it was only natural that they should gravitate to the towns, which were centers of the administrative, political, and cultural life of the area. Towns also provided the opportunity and setting for living a gracious life of leisure. The gentry were a leisure class, abhorring physical labor. This aversion was one of the factors which for many years retarded the industrial development of China because the educated gentry youth refused to perform the physical labor so often demanded by the engineering and technical professions.

Economic Characteristics of the Peasantry

The peasantry obtained their income mainly from the cultivation of the land and other physical work. It included owners of small pieces of land, tenants who cultivated the land for others, and farm laborers who received a salary.

The average Chinese peasants were a hard working group. They spent most of their time working in order to produce enough food to feed their families. Often they were compelled to find ways to increase their income. Before the Chinese town and countryside were flooded with cheap machine-made products, the peasants supplemented their income by various types of handicraft work. They worked at night and in the slack season when the fields did not demand their attention; often the entire family participated in weaving, embroidering, working with silk, basket making, or other skilled and semi-skilled tasks. They generally sold their home-made products in the nearby towns. Without this supplementary income many peasants would have sunk to an unbearable economic level. This was especially true of those peasants who had gone into debt and were attempting to pay off both the capital and the high interest on the loan. The supplementary income helped to keep them out of debt or, if they were compelled to borrow, permitted them to repay their loan without sacrificing their land. More often they used this additional revenue to buy the necessities of life. They seldom had enough to buy the nonessential items which the gentry purchased.

The constant and intensive work required to wrest a living from the land, and the necessity of augmenting their income by a handicraft of one kind or another, kept the peasants close to home. They went to town merely to buy the few supplies they could not produce at home and to sell the few surplus things they produced. Otherwise, the town had little to offer them. The teahouses, the theaters, the restaurants, the house of pleasure, and the sing-song girls of the towns were not for them. They had little money and little time to spare. Such places of entertainment were primarily set up to provide amusement for the wealthy and the gentry. Occasionally, during festive occasions such as New Year's, theatrical companies would visit the villages or smaller market towns where the peasants came and watched the performance. Storytellers also roamed from village to village. Sometimes during the slack season the peasants would spend a little time in teahouses and in visiting neighbors. Funerals and festivals also provided an opportunity for feasting, gambling, and gossiping. However, in all these cases the entertainment was mostly confined to the rural areas.

Peasants looked at the towns with pleasure and displeasure.

They liked the towns as concrete symbols of the way of life toward which they were striving. They dreamed of the day when they too could sit at leisure in a teahouse and enjoy the town pleasures. But they disliked the rents, the taxes, and the interest that flowed from them to the town gentry. From their point of view, towns were the living quarters of parasites, and they did not like to dwell on the idea that the pleasures of the town demanded a horrible price in flesh and bone and sinew from their bodies.

Political Characteristics of the Gentry

Since the gentry were the educated group, government officials in China were recruited mainly from this class. The officials drawn from the peasant or other classes were automatically incorporated into the gentry class when they became scholars and officials.

Scholars and educated men stood on the summit of Chinese society. The Chinese placed the scholar first on their social scale, the peasant and farmer next, then the artisan and merchant, and the soldier and others, like actors, at the bottom. The position of the soldier at the bottom of the Chinese social scale has caused both Nationalists and Communists much difficulty in recruiting good people for their armies. Both governments have been forced to wage widespread propaganda campaigns to make the soldier a person of distinction in China.

The gentry, through the scholar-officials, controlled the intellectual life and ideology of the country. The scholar-officials administered the civil service examinations which had to be passed before an applicant could become a recognized scholar and be accepted for government service. The questions which the scholar-officials asked determined what the budding scholar and official must study before taking these all-important examinations. Of course, these questions concerned the traditional philosophy, attitudes, values, ideals, and beliefs. Young minds were thus indoctrinated early with the traditional and controlling ideology of China. So effective was this system of perpetuating an ideology that, even now, the traditional ideologies continue to have a strong hold on millions of Chinese.

Teachers all over China were also drawn from the gentry class. They were held in such high respect as to be considered one of the five objects worthy of worship; the others were, heaven, earth, emperor, and parents. Even today, many Chinese use the term "teacher" as a courteous form of address equivalent to our term "Mr." (In the People's Republic of China the preferred form of address is "Comrade".) Because Chinese teachers indoctrinated their students with the same concepts and values that were featured in the civil service examinations, even those students who did not take the examinations but merely learned to read and write were taught to revere and respect traditional values and ideals.

Politically, the gentry functioned in two ways: they checked the absolute power of the emperor, and they acted as an extension of the central government on the local level.

Theoretically the political power of the emperor of China was great. All power in the country was lodged in his person; there was no command he could not give, no veto of his laws, no appeal from his judgment. When he was a strong figure, he often made use of his tremendous power in awesome and terrible ways. However, most of the time the emperor was not a very strong figure, and it was then that the power of the gentry-scholar-officials to check imperial ambition was most evident. Even during the regimes of the stronger emperors this power was quite effective, for the gentry controlled the machinery of government. When the emperor gave orders that were detrimental to gentry interests, they evaded, delayed, and choked those commands in the red tape of their administrative machine.

Moreover, gentry families tightened the bonds among themselves through expedient marriages. Connections among the gentry were extremely important, and marriage was a convenient method to arrange alliances between strategically placed families. Since all the gentry families engaged in such practices, the web of interconnected families eventually covered most of the officials in administrative posts.

When the people of any given locality in China were threatened with exorbitant demands from the central government upon their goods and services, the gentry of that locality immediately swung into action to soften these demands. The local county representative of the central government, the county chief, was informed that the gentry of the area thought the requests extravagant. Often this information was sufficient to cause the official to find ways of moderating the demands without impairing his own position in the administration. If the county official stubbornly insisted upon the full measure requested of the people, whether it be taxes or conscription, the gentry used their web of alliances to reach his superior. Since the county official himself was a part of this web and since he was dependent upon his superior for advancement and other favors, this action was usually sufficient to moderate the original demands.

The gentry class had most to lose from the unchecked power of an emperor or his followers, for they possessed the money, land, and other objects of value that ambitious emperors might covet. To protect their property, wealth, and high economic status, the gentry sent an unceasing stream of candidates to fill the high and low positions of government. Thus, between the emperor and his subjects there was interposed a deep layer of self-perpetuating bureaucrats who were dedicated to the purpose of checking and modifying the demands of an "all-powerful" emperor.

Until very recently the chain of formally appointed administrative officials reached down only as far as the head of the county, who was usually called the magistrate or mandarin. The mass of people lived in numerous villages scattered throughout the country. With the small staff at his disposal, and the lack of any formally appointed village officials to serve as his assistants, it was only natural that the magistrate should turn to the gentry to aid him in carrying out his duties. The gentry were in a unique position to act as an extension of the central government and as assistants to the magistrate. They were well connected with the government administration through their web of alliances; they were regarded by the peasants as the leaders of the community since they were the larger landowners, the politically connected families, and the arbiters of fashion and morals; and they were concerned with the problems of the peasantry and knew well the intimate affairs of the people of their countryside. Moreover, the gentry were pleased to act in this capacity since it strengthened their position in relation to both the administration and the peasantry. They were needed by both. The administration needed them to aid in such duties as collecting taxes, erecting public works, and preserving the peace. The peasants needed them to mediate for them when taxes were oppressive, conscription was heavy, and other demands were troublesome. The gentry also acted as informal arbitrators in land quarrels, feuds threatening lawsuits, and the thousands of matters with which the local governments dealt. Thus, the gentry were the administrators of an informal countryside government which considerably reduced the formal functions and services of government and kept government interference in local affairs at a minimum.

Political Characteristics of the Peasantry

The peasant has traditionally thought of the people of China as being divided into two classes—the ruler and the ruled. During the imperial period the ruling class consisted of the emperor, the royal family, and the gentry class from which the government officials were recruited. Today, the ruling group comprises the members of the two parties, Communist on the mainland and Kuomintang on Taiwan, and their sympathizers and supporters. Those ruled are the peasants, who make up 75 or more percent of the population, and smaller groups such as laborers, artisans, civil servants, soldiers, and other groups.

In imperial China the peasants shied away from government and governmental activities and scrutiny. They regarded government with deep suspicion, associating it in their minds with evils such as taking their scarce food for taxes, taking their needed strength for public works, taking their sons for the army, and often taking their land by means of lawsuits. As a result, they worked on the assumption that the less they had to do with the government, the better off they were. In present-day China many of the peasants still cling to this view of government. However, modern Chinese leaders are striving to change this attitude of suspicion and aversion. They are attempting to give the peasants a feeling of participation in government and to convince them that this is *their* government, *their* policies, and *their* administration.

Peasants are a conservative force in the community. The rural environment in which they live provides little stimulation, reason, or means to change their ways of thinking or acting. This conservatism is one of the greatest barriers to those who seek to remold China. The peasants are generally content to live in their accustomed pattern of life, even when they have given their support and help in overturning a dynasty or regime. In the past, the peasants rose many times when their lot became unbearable and there was no other way to alleviate their condition. During these uprisings they were as fierce, as cruel, as unyielding, and as devoted to their cause as any modern revolutionaries. But they were interested primarily in throwing out their incompetent and unjust rulers, not in changing the political system itself. Once the rulers had been changed, the injustices remedied, and the country was calm and peaceful again, the peasants resumed their customary traditional way of life.

Chinese peasants were independent individuals. Their political, social, and economic environment compelled them to be self-sufficient and self-reliant. Few people were available to help them financially, physically, or politically. They depended upon their own initiative, their own labors, their own spiritual and physical resources. They did not have the united strength of the large joint family which was characteristic of the gentry. They tried to solve their many problems without recourse to government. They found other ways to settle disputes with others over land and money. Their social security came from their sons, and daily living from their own foresight and labors. They cared for and built their own irrigation ditches, planned and carried out their own flood-control measures, and made their own fertilizer. When problems arose which they could not handle alone, they sought the help of the gentry or the village elders and not the government.

Social Characteristics of the Gentry

The gentry lived in large families that sometimes included four or five generations. A patriarch ruled over the family much as an emperor ruled over the state. A definite social hierarchy within the family ranged from the lowest female member to the male patriarch himself, and an elaborate and rigid code spelled out the relationship between the various members. A great amount of time and attention was given to teaching and disciplining the younger members so that they might know and practice the ceremonies and etiquette required of them. Stress was laid on ritual and proper behavior toward both the dead and the living.

Large families gave the gentry the unity and solidarity necessary to maintain their position at the top of Chinese society. Family property and family wealth were preserved as a unit and not scattered over a dozen small families. Within the large family all worked in supporting and maintaining the economic and social status of the household. Each depended upon the other. There was no necessity for individual self-reliance and no urge to be independent, such as existed among the members of smaller families.

But forces of division also worked within these large families. The presence of so many different interacting personalities under one roof, living on a common budget and holding common property, gave birth to continual bickering, envious comparisons, jealous maneuverings, and malicious intentions. Very often the wives of the male heirs, insecure and ambitious, worked through their husbands in an effort to have the property divided and the families independent. Generally, the patriarch of the family was able to hold the diverse families together, but after his death those seeking division of the property often won out over the forces of unity.

Social Characteristics of the Peasantry

Although they aspired to live in the gentry manner, few peasants could afford to do so. They lived in small families. The tiny bits of land they cultivated could not support a large number of people, and many found it difficult even to support aged parents. To preserve intact this small piece of land they often permitted only one son to inherit the property, in contrast to the gentry practice of permitting all male sons to inherit equally.

The peasantry did not have time, education, or means to follow the elaborate code of etiquette practiced by the gentry. They respected these rules of social intercourse, and they practiced them when they could, but they could not adopt them as fully and completely as the gentry. They offered sacrifices to their ancestors when they could, at least once or twice a year. They stretched their resources to the utmost to follow the wedding and funeral rituals and regulations, and they tried to make their festivals, especially New Year's, as gay and correct as their economic condition would permit.

Economic necessity forced the male peasant to place more importance on obtaining a strong helpmate than upon obtaining important and influential relatives. His almost complete preoccupation with the matter of making a living determined his major concern—the efficiency of the family as a working group. The physical makeup of a wife was very important to the peasant and his family. She needed a strong back, sturdy legs, and firm hands. Her relatives were important, of course, but her health and strength were more important. The peasant had no reason to make strategic political marriages because he had no high position in Chinese society to protect.

He respected the ideals of kinship, and he paid at least lip service to the formal requirements of etiquette in relation to sex, age, and generation. He, too, was a formal member of the clan, and he had a wide number of relatives to whom he was connected by marriage and blood, but he did not require these relatives as much as the gentry did, who needed the web of kinship and marriage ties to shore up their power in the community and in the nation. With little, if any, power to lose, the peasant regarded such ties as relatively unimportant and sometimes even troublesome.

Both peasantry and gentry were bound by the same code of ethics and the same philosophy of life. Both were more interested in stability and the status quo than in changing a political system. Both were more interested in their own particular families and kinship groups than in a national unit called a state. Both required supplementary incomes to maintain themselves. Both were more loyal to their locality and neighborhood than to the ruler. Both held to the same ideals and tried to follow the standards imposed by these ideals to the best of their ability.

In more modern times a spirit of nationalism, foreign ideas, aggressive actions by foreign nations, lack of a strong central government, and recurring crises such as famines, floods, and wars have forced both the gentry and the peasantry to rebel and to take other drastic measures to protect their interests. The majority were primarily interested in solving their immediate problems and not in changing the traditional social order of China. Many were surprised when it became evident that a solution to their problems involved radical and, sometimes, strange changes in their traditional way of life.

25

The Clan in China

Practically all the families in my village bear my surname.
We are all descended from the same ancestor and the lines
of descent can be clearly traced in the genealogy....
—Hsien Chin Hu

The clan includes all classes of Chinese. Membership is determined by ties of blood and marriage
rather than by the economic and educational
considerations which distinguish the gentry and
the peasantry. Thus class conflicts are often harmonized and class divisions often spanned by
the blood links of the clan.

The clan is an organized and united group of
people who trace their ancestry back to a com-

mon ancestor. The group is often very large, some clans having thousands of members. Descent is patrilineal, that is, traced back to the father's ancestor rather than the mother's. Some clans trace their first ancestor back to a legendary figure in the mythical period of Chinese history, others to some prominent emperor or official; but few genealogies go beyond the Sung Dynasty. Generally, the clan is limited to the descendants of that ancestor who came to the region first. It does not embrace all those people in China who bear the same surname, but only those of the same surname who are descended from a common ancestor who settled first in a given locality.

Chinese names are generally made up of three characters. The family or surname is written first, the second character is common to all cousins and brothers of the same generation, and, the third character is unique to the individual. The importance of the family name is stressed by putting it first. The ties of blood indicated by the same surname are emphasized by the traditional custom of discouraging marriage between those of the same surname even if the individuals concerned were of different clans and came from widely separated parts of the country.

The relationship between the members of the clan was demonstrated by means of a genealogy, the chart and written history tracing the clan's descent from a common ancestor. In drawing up a genealogy the Chinese did not confine themselves merely to tracing the descent lines of all present descendants from the original paternal ancestor. Genealogies also included the age of the individuals at death, the number of their sons and daughters, the family names of wives, and the family names of sons-in-law. Biographies of prominent men and women, and outstanding achievements of individual clan members were also given. Maps and diagrams showed the location of the clan graves. The history of the ancestral hall, moral and ethical statements, pertinent data regarding the common property, and any other items which the clan leaders thought important were also included. Keeping clan genealogies up-to-date required long hours of research, meticulous labor, and often much travel. In 1937 there were over 180,000 descendants of Confucius scattered in more than 246 communities, and divided into sixty branches. One clan in Kwangtung is now composed of 118 divisions. The genealogy of this clan traces the movements of these 118 different divisions from the time of the Sung Dynasty to the present. When it is remembered that much more than a genealogical chart is incorporated in these genealogies, the true magnitude of compiling and maintaining a genealogy can be appreciated. In modern times, 109 members of the Tseng clan in Hunan worked on the last edition of its genealogy.

The Ancestral Hall

The ties of blood and kinship were strengthened by ancestral ceremonies, common property, and a common interest in preserving and increasing the prestige of the clan and the welfare of its members. There usually was a clan center where the ancestral hall was built and where most of the ancestral graves were located.

The ancestral hall, like the clan itself, served many functions. It was a convenient place for the clan leaders to discuss clan matters. Records of births and deaths and other personal data concerning the clan members were stored in the hall which thus served as a bureau of vital statistics for the clan. The hall was sometimes given a personality; gifts were sent to, and cases judged by, the "ancestral hall." Most important, however, was a ceremonial hall where the tablets of the dead ancestors were kept and where the so-called ancestor worship was carried out. Each ancestor possessed a tablet, a rectangular piece of wood, upon which was written his name, title, and birth and death dates. While ancestor rites were performed, the spirit of the dead ancestor was supposed to be in the tablet. For this reason these tablets were known as "spirit tablets." More recently, portraits are sometimes used instead of tablets.

Once or twice a year, in the spring or autumn or both, the clan met to honor their common ancestors. Termed "ancestor worship" by most Western commentators, it was actually more a memorial service which indicated, by means of ceremonials, the respect and reverence of the descendants for their ancestors. There was no intent to worship the ancestors in the sense that Christians, Jews, and Muslims worship God.

The Chinese believed that the ancestors continued to live in another world as spirits and that they depended upon their descendants for certain necessities of life. These ancestor spirits had the power to help their descendants if the proper rites were rendered them. Otherwise the ancestors would cease to live or might roam about as hungry ghosts. The descendants would then suffer misfortune. It was most important, therefore, that the Chinese have male descendants who would carry on the proper rites for them after their death. Mencius, the most famous disciple of Confucius, stated that the most unfilial act was to leave no posterity. This feeling was engraved so deeply on the Chinese mentality that an individual, if he had no children of his own, would adopt a son to carry on his line and conduct the ancestral rites.

Memorial service was one of the reasons why the Chinese paid such great respect to the aged. Since they were only a step away from becoming ancestors themselves, the aged were felt to be entitled to great honor and homage. The clan supplemented the family in carrying out the ancestral ceremonies. The family usually honored the preceding four or five generations only, but the clan rendered memorial service to all the ancestors, even the remotest ones. Consequently, no ancestor was deprived of the rites, and all clan members were blessed by the help of the comforted ancestors.

The location of ancestral graves was important. A favorable location helped ensure the prosperity of the descendants, while an unfavorable location might very well result in their ruin. A location was selected by someone who had a gift for picking a lucky site. This person was versed in the art of *feng shui,* which is literally translated "wind and water." *Feng shui* is founded on the assumption that everywhere there are forces and spirits which affect people for good or bad. The *feng shui* expert was skilled in the art of finding the places where these forces were most favorable. In picking a spot, the patterns of mountains and waterways and many other factors were carefully calculated. The best site for a house, a place of business, or a farm was determined by the same influences. The Chinese have long felt that nature has a vital bearing upon their pattern of life and were willing to go to extreme lengths at times to ensure a favorable location. The author knows of a case in China where the mother of a governor of a province tore down and rebuilt her house four times in order to correct the *feng shui.* The rational Confucianist was opposed to such superstitious practices and attributed them to the pernicious teaching of Taoism. The Confucian philosopher Chu Hsi commented perceptively when he said that "divining the auspiciousness" of a place is merely "to divine the beauty or ugliness of the location. If the place is beautiful, then the spirit will be happy and the sons and grandsons prosperous." He advised the Chinese that the only consideration in choosing a grave site was the likelihood that at some future date a road or a wall might be built on the site, a ditch dug there, or some farmer's plough might turn up the bones.

Graves had to be kept in good condition. Once a year, on the Ch'ing-Meng festival in the spring, the descendants sweep and tidy up the graves. Here they offer up sacrifices of food and wine to their ancestors. The clan kept maps of these graves and set aside suitable burial land for its members. This was especially intended to help those members who had insufficient funds to bury their dead in a suitable place.

Ritual Land

In addition to the ancestral hall, which was built and maintained by contributions of clan members in the form of money, labor, or kind, the clan often held in common productive land, bequeathed by wealthy members, which provided a regular income for the support of the clan activities and the continuance of the required sacrifices and memorial services. Such land was called ritual land and was sometimes referred to as the "property" of the ancestral hall. The rents from this land were used in part for clan charities which embraced a wide range of welfare activities. The clan provided for orphans, indigent widows, childless members, and those unable to work. In times of crisis, during wars, floods, famines, droughts, and other human or natural calamities, the clans did what they could to help out their members. It was a common practice in traditional China to provide for the proper burial and marriage of clan members. Sometimes clan funds were used to further the education of the youth.

Nothing enhanced the prestige of the clan so much as the number of its members who received a formal education. Many clans, both in the imperial period and under the Republic, established schools and engaged tutors to educate their promising youngsters. Some of them set aside a certain amount of land called "school land" to support these schools and tutors. They often paid the traveling expenses of their scholars when they went to Peking to take the final examination. Both clans and government favored these welfare activities, the clan because they helped unify its members, and the government because it believed these welfare services were necessary to maintain order and stability in the community.

Sometimes abuses crept into the administration of clan property, and it was used to further the economic interests of the clan leaders and administered as if the property were their own. The poorer clan members resented the exclusive character of the supervision and use of the common property. Moreover, when the lands were tilled by members, friction sometimes developed over the amount of rent. Clan members insisted that the rent should be low because they were, after all, part owners and entitled to preferential treatment. The clan leaders, on the other hand, argued that if the tillers did not pay the going rate the entire clan would be the loser. Consequently, to avoid constant bickering and obtain the fullest amount possible, clan leaders commonly rented the common lands to people outside the clan. This practice, of course, incensed the poorer members and increased their hostility toward the wealthier clan leaders.

Government of the Clan

The gentry were the leaders of the clan because they were men of education and wealth and knew the proper ancestral rites. They were the spokesmen for the clan in dealing with the outside world of government officials and the leaders of other clans. They wielded the same moral influence and enjoyed the same prestige within the clan as in the society at large outside the clan.

Clan members were usually physically concentrated in the neighborhood of the ancestral hall and the ancestral graves. Even when living in distant places, they were spiritually attached to the ancestral neighborhood. Old scholar-officials who had given years of their life to public service and government work looked forward to the time when they could retire to their ancestral homes and spend their remaining years honored and untroubled in the protecting shadow of their ancestral hall. Chinese living in America, Europe, Southeast Asia, and elsewhere, still often think of themselves as attached to an ancestral home somewhere in China. From time to time they visit these ancestral homes and often request that they be buried there. These attitudes are especially true of the Chinese who come from Kwangtung, Fukien, and other parts of southeast and central China. It is in these areas that the clan organization developed most extensively and put down the deepest roots.

The ancestral hall sometimes served as a courtroom where civil and criminal cases affecting clan members were judged. Traditionally, the Chinese government left the teaching of moral and ethical doctrines, and punishment for crimes against them, to the family and the clan. The government reserved to itself the power to step in and take over whenever it seemed necessary, but this was rarely done. The government was seldom called in even when the dispute was between clans rather than within them. Clan leaders considered it better to compromise and to settle the matter by informal discussions and in committees than to call in even the local government.

Each clan had regulations which the members were expected to follow. They concerned unfilial conduct, property disputes, thefts, and other offenses. Sometimes these regulations prohibited the members from gambling, smoking opium, consorting with prostitutes, drinking excessively, wasting money on luxuries, and other practices considered harmful to the solidarity of the family and the clan. When members offended against these regulations they were subject to judgment by the clan leaders in the ancestral hall. Punishment varied with the offense, ranging from verbal reproofs to expulsion from the clan, either temporary or permanent. The latter was a serious punishment because the expelled individuals could not participate in the ancestral rites, enjoy the common funds, and have their tablets in the ancestral hall or their names in the genealogy. A person without a clan in China was in many ways like a person without a country.

The Clan Today

The Nationalist government, under the leadership of Sun Yatsen and, later, Chiang Kai-shek, did not attempt to remove the clan institution from China. They wanted the Chinese to give their loyalty to a state as well as a clan, but it was not their purpose to abolish this cherished Chinese tradition. The Nationalists are in this, as in other matters, more traditionally Chinese than the Communists.

With the coming of the Communist government to mainland China the power and influence of the clan have decreased. There can be no sharing of political power with social units and social institutions like the clan. Such sharing of power, the new leaders believe, can only further the process of decentralization that has been characteristic of China's political history. Consequently, the clan has been shorn of many of its functions, its power and influence decreased, and its leaders—the gentry, the wealthy, and the aged—have been removed or deprived of their prestige.

Nevertheless the clan group, though less organized, continues to exist wherever there are Chinese. The ties of blood cannot be sundered overnight. The clan still lives, and ancestral rites are still practiced in thousands of ancestral halls inside and outside China. The welfare, educational, and judicial functions of the clan have been curtailed, but clan sentiment based on genealogies and ancestor reverence still exists. As long as it exists, there will be clans.

26

The Family in China

The root of the empire is in the state. The root of the
state is in the family.

—Mencius

The family, the basic social unit in China for
thousands of years, was so important that not
only the clan, but even the state was regarded as
an extension of it. Chinese thought of the interests of their families as the basis for all their
judgments and decisions. What was advantageous
and good for the family was permitted; what
was disadvantageous and bad for the family was
prohibited. Individuals thought of themselves as
members of a family, and they were viewed by

217

others in the same light. The success or failure of an individual reflected upon the famly and increased or decreased its prestige. The family was responsible for the acts of its individual members and was held accountable for them by the community and the government. In this sense traditional China was composed of a large number of families rather than of individuals.

Confucian philosophy emphasized the fundamental importance of the family. Of the five basic social relationships necessary to the right functioning of Chinese society, three were family relationships—the relationship between father and son, elder brother and younger brother, and husband and wife. It was in the family that individuals learned their roles in Chinese society, or not at all. "Inside the smaller doors leading to the inner apartments are to be found all the rules [of government]. There is awe for the father, and also for the elder brother. Wife and children, servants and concubines, are like the common people, serfs, and underlings."

Economically, the traditional Chinese family was a joint productive effort. All members were supposed to do what they could for the common family, and they were supported from the common funds. There were three important variations of this economic family in China: the small or conjugal family, the middle-way or stem family, and the large or joint family. The small family usually consisted of the parents and their unmarried children. It was similar to the family common in America and the West. The middle-way family was composed of the parents, all their unmarried children, and one married son with his wife and children. The large or joint family included the parents, both married sons and unmarried children, and all the wives and children of the married sons. Sometimes other close relatives, such as grandparents, uncles, aunts, cousins, and nephews, might live in this family. The head of the family, usually the father but sometimes the elder brother, supervised the common property and watched over the moral life of the members.

Ideal and Practice

The large or joint family was the traditional ideal family. From the time of the T'ang Dynasty until very recently, the large family system was praised and encouraged by the leaders of society as the ideal family arrangement. The presence in one family of six or more generations who functioned together as one economic unit was the highest expression of this system. Few families achieved this aim. Most large families never included more than three or four generations, and only certain wealthy families were able to achieve this goal.

There are a number of reasons why the Chinese were seldom able to realize the ideal of living together in a large family. Members of the families of the poorer classes were subject to a higher mortality rate than the richer classes and few of them lived very long. Malnutrition, diseases of one kind or another, natural calamities which destroyed their crops and brought famine and starvation, were the common fate of the poverty-stricken peasants and artisan families of China. Only the very strong and the very lucky lived to a ripe old age. Many children died young; it is thought that, prior to the coming of modern health practices, over half of all the children in China died before the age of five. Owing to unsanitary conditions, many mothers died at childbirth. Furthermore, the small amount of land which the poor possessed was insufficient to support large numbers. Even in gentry families, the frequent division of wealth kept the number of members down. As a consequence the vast majority of the Chinese people lived in small and middle-way families which numbered on the average from five to seven members.

Probably a typical Chinese family on the mainland today would include the two parents and up to three or four children. It is also not uncommon for aged parents to live together with one of their children, usually a son. After the advent of the Communist government in China the members of the former gentry class, who most frequently lived in large or joint families, disappeared from Chinese society. Their land, which was the source of their wealth, was redistributed, and they could no longer support the practice of large families. As a result, the small family, so common in America and the Western world in general, is also becoming typical in present-day China.

Family Relationships

Until recent times the parents had almost complete authority over their children. Society sanctioned whatever steps parents took to enforce their commands, and public opinion permitted harsh and prolonged physical punishment when the children rebelled against parental edicts.

However, when the grandfather retained headship of the family, he often protected his grandchildren from the arbitrary dictates of the father and mother. It was common for the grandchildren to scurry to the loving shelter of a grandparent when the father threatened or attempted to punish his children. Others in the older generation, such as uncles and aunts, were also in a position to protect the child from harsh discipline. This was true even when the old one had relinquished formal supervision of the family. The aged were revered and their wishes and desires granted whenever possible. Thus, love for the child was diffused over a wide range of relatives. The children found early that they often received more warm affection from grandparents, uncles, and aunts than from their own father.

Traditionally, Chinese fathers were regarded by the sons with a great deal of fear. Since untrained and undisciplined sons gave the community a bad impression of the father, Chinese fathers were often severe and inflexible in training their sons to assume their future role in society and the family. Since the father did not have the same responsibility to discipline and indoctrinate the daughter in her future family duties, the relationship between father and daughter was usually warmer and closer. In some of the more wealthy families it was not uncommon for the father to teach his daughter to read, write poems, and compose music.

The relationship between the mother and her children, both girls and boys, was generally one of warm love and affection. She acted as an intermediary between the children, especially the son, and her husband, and often protected them from his wrath. In poorer peasant families, the love of the daughter for her mother was so great that, many times, the daughter would take something from the family of her husband in order to give her mother a few more material comforts. This act of "borrowing" was one of the seven valid causes for divorce in traditional China.

Parents were obliged to train their children to assume their proper stations in Chinese society. For each generation, for each age, for each sex, there was an accepted pattern of behavior which each Chinese individual had to be taught. Thus, from about four to fifteen or sixteen years of age, the children were taught their future duties. The boys of gentry families were sent to schools or put under the guidance of tutors, to start the long and difficult task of scholarship. The boys of the peasant families were taught field work at an early age and instructed in all the arduous tasks demanded of the farmer-peasant in China. The boys of both gentry and peasant families were taught the ancestral ritual. Both peasant and gentry girls were taught the household duties of sewing, cooking, washing, and cleaning. The peasant girl, in addition, learned to help in the fields during the planting and harvesting seasons. It is a common sight in China to see a long row of bending women planting the delicate rice shoots in the water-covered rice fields.

Arranging marriages for their children was one of the primary obligations of the parents. The boys must be married in order that the family line might be continued and descendants created to perpetuate the ancestral rites. Girls must be married so that they might fulfill themselves as women and strengthen the family fortunes. Gentry families were interested in making a strategic family alliance. Peasant families desired money for their daughters and were reluctant to marry them to families who owned or rented little or no land. Marriages were arranged by the families concerned. The prospective bride and groom had little say about either the choice of their mate or the marriage arrangements. In fact, they rarely saw each other before the marriage. A meeting of the two before marriage was sufficient reason for calling off the ceremony, because it violated the custom of separating the sexes and compromised the girl. Marriages were contracted between families on the basis of convenience. The social and financial position of the families concerned was carefully scrutinized before the marriage contract was signed.

A go-between always negotiated the marriage. He or she—the go-between could be either male or female—did the talking and bargaining, carried messages, and conducted all the many delicate but necessary negotiations required to bring the marriage preliminaries to a successful conclusion.

When the bride's parents agreed to the proposed match, they sent, via the go-between, a card bearing the girl's eight characters to the boy's family. These eight characters, which represented her name, and the hour, day, month, and year of her birth, were then compared with the boy's personal data by one skilled in such matters. If the comparison indicated future harmony and happiness for the two individuals, negotiations to connect the two families through marriage began in earnest. One of the most important questions to be settled, especially for the poor peasant families, was the size of the dowry to be paid by the family of the bridegroom to the family of the bride. The girl's family used part of the dowry money to purchase the bridal outfit and, if there were unmarried sons in the family, often used the rest as dowry money again, to obtain wives for them. The wealthier gentry families used all the dowry and much more besides to outfit the bride. The more furniture, chests, household equipment, clothes, and other articles that were carried in the bridal procession when she was escorted to the home of the bridegroom, the greater the prestige that devolved upon her family.

Marriage preliminaries were concluded with the fixing of the date of marriage and the signing of the betrothal contract by the family heads. The marriage day was selected by an individual skilled in the choosing of lucky days for important events. On that day the bride was carried in a long procession, together with her personal property and bedroom equipment, to the home of the bridegroom.

When she entered her new home, she was obliged to adjust to a new environment and a new set of relationships. Usually, she had not seen any of the family members before, including her husband. She was surrounded by unfamiliar objects, unfamiliar faces, and unfamiliar mannerisms and expressions. The sudden and sharp change from a secluded, familiar life to this rather public, unfamiliar life frightened and confused her. Her most difficult adjustment was to her mother-in-law. Chinese mothers-in-law were often awe-inspiring individuals within the family. They were the rulers in the home, especially with regard to the daughter-in-law's training, discipline, and duties. Since the men of the family were not supposed to give their wives any undue attention beyond the bedroom door, a public show of affection between husband and wife was frowned upon by Chinese society. Consequently, the young bride was forced to spend most of her time in the company of her mother-in-law, trying to meet all of her demands and to bear her scoldings with tact and patience. Stories are told of some mothers-in-law whose nagging and cruelty drove their daughters-in-law to flee from the home or even commit suicide. Filial obligations required the son not to interfere in his mother's treatment of his wife. Both husband and wife stood in a subordinate position with relation to the mother-in-law. Should the husband support his wife against his mother, he aroused jealousy that only intensified the harsh treatment of his wife. Moreover, Chinese society did not favor such action by the son against the mother, to whom he owed loving obedience no matter what the provocation.

In Chinese thought children must do everything possible to ensure the comfort and happiness of the parents. The lives of the son's children, and even his own life, should not be valued over the lives of the parents. Chinese children are told stories of filial sons who cut off portions of their living flesh in order to provide their parents with food and medicine. One of the strictest and most important filial obligations was the support of parents in their old age. Another important duty was faithfully to carry out ceremonial rites to them after their death. Confucius said, "When the parents are alive, serve them with propriety; when they die, bury them according to propriety; and sacrifice to them according to propriety." Greatly prized and respected, the aged in traditional China were valued even over children. Children could be had again, but the aged could not be duplicated, and they soon would become powerful ancestors who could be of great aid to the family. The most important birthdays in an individual's life were at sixty, seventy, eighty, and up. To reach the age of one hundred was the crowning achievement for both the person and the family.

The Chinese lived in anticipation of old age, for growing old was pleasant. Age was respected. It was a time of leisure and of little responsibility. There was no superior over the aged except the dead ancestors, who rarely spoke. The aged were supported and not requested to support anyone else. There were only two periods in the life of a Chinese male when he possessed maximum security and minimal responsibility—infancy and old age. Of the two, old age was the better because one was conscious of the pleasure to be derived from such a tranquil and, from a Chinese viewpoint, satisfying period.

The woman also achieved respect and superiority with increasing age. The young bride, cowed and afraid, grew into a mother-in-law or female head of the household. She was no longer a stranger and she had sons and daughters-in-law of her own. She was an authority in the family and her position was buttressed by the whole weight of Chinese society. All members of the family owed her respect, obedience, and support.

New Attitudes Toward the Family

Traditional attitudes toward the family are being modified in China in response to the changing pattern of modern life. Individuals are now encouraged to think in terms of loyalty to the nation rather than to the family alone. This is especially true of the People's Republic of China. The welfare of the state is the final basis for all decisions and acts, and when there is a conflict of interest between it and the family, the Chinese are taught to place the interests of the state first. Theoretically the relationship between the individual and the state is of more significance than the one between the family and the state. The failure of individuals should no longer reflect upon the family, but solely upon themselves. Most Chinese, however, continue to feel that the family is also responsible.

Though families are still held responsible for teaching their members their new roles in society, other institutions are beginning to perform this function. More and more nurseries, schools, clubs, discussion groups, committees, indoctrination courses, party work, unions, cooperatives, and other groups and institutions outside the home and family are molding the character and values of the modern Chinese. He or she is in the process of becoming a different person, oriented outside the family rather than inside.

Modern Chinese no longer give the same regard to the aged as formerly. Yesterday's China admonished the young to be quiet listeners at the feet of her ancient sages. Today's China admonishes the old to be more quiet since the ancient learning is no longer always applicable. The young in China are hailed as the forerunners of a new society; they are lauded, showered with attention, and sometimes placed in positions of authority. It is also true that elderly men have held the top leadership posts in modern China; Mao Tse-tung was born in 1893, Chou En-lai (now deceased) in 1898.

Marriage laws promulgated by the new regime express another conception of marriage. The sexes are equal. Each spouse may retain his or her family name and personal property. Each may freely work in any occupation and engage in political and social action. The two people concerned may choose their own mate without interference from a third party. There shall be no compulsion on the part of either party. The interests of the children shall also be safeguarded. "Children born out of wedlock shall enjoy the same rights as children born in lawful wedlock." Husband and wife shall live together as companions and one will not be dominant over the other. Husbands shall have only one wife.

In old China most Chinese were monogamous by economic necessity. But many of the wealthy possessed concubines. Secondary wives were often introduced into the house when the first wife proved barren or had not borne any male offspring. The introduction of a number of wives under the same roof was generally the signal for the beginning of disturbances for the household. Furthermore, many secondary wives under one roof was another instance of the traditional subordination of women. Most women shunned the prospect of becoming concubines. For these and other reasons, the modern Chinese have forbidden more than one wife per husband.

Marriages need no longer be arranged by the families concerned. When a boy reaches the age of twenty, and the girl the age of eighteen, they can legally marry voluntarily. There are still, in many instances, certain ceremonies attached.

Whereas marriage was formerly a family affair, it is now often an ideological affair, especially if one or both persons are party members. One of the members of their party cell, or their discussion or work group, may act as a go-between in the marriage preliminaries. Instead of judging the marriage from the point of view of the family, the suitability of the match may be discussed in terms of the advantages that their union will bring to the party and the state.

Where formerly the marriage ceremonies took place in the family household of the male, today they are often conducted in a public hall decorated with flags and the pictures of Mao Tse-tung and other important political dignitaries. The couple, if they are laborers or workers, frequently wear their regular work clothes and publicly announce at the ceremony what they intend to do after their marriage to benefit the community. This practice is generally not followed by the Chinese living outside the mainland. For many Chinese, marriage is still a festive and colorful occasion.

Divorce has always been permitted in China. Generally speaking, however, it was a family and clan matter; the wishes of the individual were secondary. Furthermore, divorce was a privilege enjoyed almost exclusively by the male. The wife was practically helpless when her husband decided to put her away, and it was almost impossible for her to divorce her husband.

However, she was not entirely defenseless. The husband was not supposed to divorce his wife except for the following reasons: disobedience to his parents, failure to bear children, adultery, overt jealousy, a repulsive disease, loquacity, and theft from the family (in order, usually, to help her mother). Moreover, divorce was rather rare. Public opinion did not approve of it, and it was usually more convenient for the man to take other women into his home than to brave public opinion and the anger of his wife's relatives and family.

Divorce is also permitted in modern China. It is now a matter to be decided by the husband and the wife, not by the family. The new attitude is that divorce shall be granted only when both the husband and wife want it. Should it be the desire of only one of the parties, then the state becomes a party to the divorce affair. The new law states explicitly: "In the event of either the husband or the wife insisting upon divorce, it may be granted only when mediation by the subdistrict people's government and the subdistrict judicial organ has failed to bring about a reconciliation."

Encouraged by the government and new social attitudes, young women are now working in places sometimes far removed from their ancestral villages and homes. In the words of Mao Tsetung, "In order to build a great socialist society, it is of the utmost importance to arouse the broad masses of women to join in productive activity. Men and women must receive equal pay for equal work in production. Genuine equality between the sexes can only be realized in the process of the socialist transformation of society as a whole." This is a radical break with the tradition which required young girls to stay close to the village and the home until the time of their marriage. Separated from the eyes and ears of the hometown relatives and neighbors, they became more independent, more receptive to new ideas and attitudes, and, sometimes, a bit daring. They frequently meet males whom they like in the factories where they work or at union and party meetings, and marry them. They settle down in a small government-owned apartment where the rent is cheap, and both husband and wife continue to work and save for such desirable articles as a transistor radio, a sewing machine, and a bicycle. They practice birth control, for they want only two or three children. If needed, the wife may have an abortion in a government hospital or clinic at a cheap price or without any charge. Stylish clothes and cosmetics have been discouraged because they connote Western and bourgeois tendencies, and such tendencies must be eradicated if the "New Chinese Communist Person" is to ever emerge in China. The new wife is freed from the once dominant mother-in-law because often the husband's family is elsewhere. Should the husband's mother live with them, she generally does not possess the unquestioned authority she commanded in the past. The workers are the heroes of today, and the dominant aged of yesterday must follow their example and teaching. Change is evident in the modern Chinese families.

Although the Chinese society is undergoing change, it has not completely changed everywhere. The most radical changes have taken place in mainland China. Elsewhere, in Taiwan, Hong Kong, and Southeast Asia, many Chinese still retain the old customs. The importance of traditional attitudes in shaping Chinese families today varies with the individual, the circumstance, and the locality.

27

Politics in China

For forty years I have devoted myself to the cause of the people's revolution with but one end in view, the elevation of China to a position of freedom and equality among the nations. My experience during these forty years has firmly convinced me that to attain this goal we must bring about a thorough awakening of our own people and ally ourselves in a common struggle with those people of the world who treat us on the basis of equality.

—Sun Yat-sen

Marxism should not be applied subjectively and dogmatically.... The point is to grasp the general truths of Marxism and apply them to the concrete practice of the Chinese revolution.... Chinese culture must have its own form, that is, a national form.... During the long

Excerpt from Sun Yat-sen reprinted from *Three Principles of the People,* translated by Frank Price (London: Routledge & Kegan Paul Ltd., 1928). Used with permission.

period of its feudal stage of development China built up
for herself a glorious ancient culture. . . . We should respect our past and never deny our history. But to respect
our history is to give it a certain scientific esteem; to respect our cultural past is not to negative our present
with a view to praise everything in the old including the
poison of feudalism. Therefore, it is important for us to
teach the people and the young student, in the main, not
to look backward, but to look forward.

—Mao Tse-tung

Today two governments claim to be the only lawful government
of China. One, officially known as the Republic of China, is the
Nationalist government, formerly headed by Chiang Kai-shek and
his local supporters, and is located on the island of Taiwan. The
other, officially called the People's Republic of China, is the Communist government, which was long headed by Mao Tse-tung and
his supporters, and controls the mainland of China.

Both of these governments represent a compound of native
and foreign elements. The native elements were inherited from the
traditional political system of China; the foreign elements were received from the West. The resulting political system has often the
appearance of Western politics and institutions but is permeated
with spiritual and political conceptions from old China. These conceptions date back to very ancient dynasties which ruled China
many hundreds of years before the birth of Christ.

Historical Background

The Shang Dynasty, ca. 1766 to 1122 B.C., had a monarchical
form of government, and the king combined both religious and
political duties in his person. The succeeding Chou Dynasty, ca.
1122 to 249 B.C., is famous for three important events in Chinese
history: 1) the beginning of feudalism in China; 2) the promulga-
tion of the doctrine of the Mandate of Heaven, or the right of the
people to overthrow a wicked ruler; and 3) the initiation of the
traditional major Chinese political philosophies—Confucianism,
Legalism, and Taoism, among others.

After the defeat of the Shang Dynasty, the country was divided into many territorial units ruled by loyal retainers of the
Chou emperors. This arrangement gradually grew into a feudal
system in which the loyal retainers had more power than the

emperors themselves. The House of Chou justified the overthrow of the Shang Dynasty by teaching that it was right to depose an emperor who had lost his virtue. The Chou ruler was merely carrying out the will of heaven when he threw out the wicked Shang ruler. This idea was later incorporated into Confucian teaching. According to this (Mandate of Heaven) doctrine, the emperor ruled by reason of heaven's favor. If he lost this favor because of a lack of virtue, the people had the right to revolt. The mandate to rule was then given to a more righteous person.

The three philosophies of Legalism, Taoism, and Confucianism first made their appearance in systematized form at this time. These philosophies, especially Confucianism, formed the ideological foundation upon which the Chinese built their political institutions.

Legalism, a totalitarian philosophy that justified any act a ruler thought necessary for the retention of his power, was the first of these philosophies to be used as the official ideology of a Chinese government. It was the orthodox political doctrine of the Ch'in Dynasty, 221 to 207 B.C. Styling himself "First Emperor," Ch'in conquered the warring states of China and united the country. By destroying the feudal organization that had grown up during the Chou period and concentrating all power in his person, he laid the foundations of a united, centralized, bureaucratic Chinese empire, which, with some modifications, continued to the present. He also showed future Chinese leaders the advantages of using ideology as an instrument of control. Finally, to ensure conformity and centralization he standardized everything he could, including language, currency, weights and measures, and even the size of the wheels of the carts that traveled over Chinese roads.

But when Ch'in, First Emperor, died, his empire fell apart. During the Han Dynasty, 202 B.C. to 220 A.D., that followed, a modified form of Confucianism became the state philosophy. From this time to the twentieth century, Confucianism was the controlling social and political ideology. It became a political cult used to support the continuation of such political institutions as the monarchy. The government was administered by scholar-bureaucrats steeped in Confucian knowledge and practice.

After the Han Dynasty fell, there followed a rather long period of general unrest and disunity which was marked by invasions and civil wars. This period, known as the Dark Ages, lasted for about four centuries. The country split into rival kingdoms, some in the north ruled by barbarian tribes, though even these barbarians gradually adopted Chinese culture and forms of organization. This ebbing of power from the emperor continued until China was reunited under the Sui Dynasty, 589 to 618 A.D. With the beginning of the T'ang Dynasty, 618 to 906 A.D., power began to flow back again to the emperor.

During the T'ang Dynasty—the golden age of traditional China —much attention was given to improving the administrative machinery of government. The principal improvement consisted in placing the civil service system on a merit basis. The passing of civil service examinations became the main avenue for obtaining government posts. To provide the civil service with an adequate supply of trained personnel, the educational system of the country was reorganized and expanded. The Imperial University at Ch'ang-an was given the emperor's patronage and encouragement, and prefectural preparatory schools and provincial colleges were expanded. The purpose was to place the administration of government into the hands of educated individuals who had gained their official posts through merit rather than by way of political patronage or corruption. (This is not to say that there was no political patronage or corruption in China. They had many opportunistic and greedy officials over the many years of their history.) The T'ang rulers separated the civil and military administration and introduced a new supervisory administrative unit at the local level called the "circuit." It was designed to assure a closer connection between the local and central government.

The remaining dynasties, the Sung, 960 to 1279 A.D., the Yuan, 1260 to 1368 A.D., the Ming, 1368 to 1644 A.D., and the Ch'ing, 1644 to 1911 A.D., which was the last of the imperial dynasties, continued the process of concentrating power in the person of the emperor.

The civil service system was further developed, expanded, and refined. The scholar-officials who staffed the civil service rarely attempted to usurp the emperor's power, though they protected the interests of the gentry class which they represented. Only scholars indoctrinated with Confucianism could become a part of this system. Since the content of the civil service examinations was almost exclusively Confucian, government administrators were completely indoctrinated with this philosophy, and they saw to it that these teachings were transmitted to the people. Confucianism buttressed the imperial government of China. Attempts were also made to bring about a closer tie between the local and central government. During the Yuan Dynasty, headed by the Mongols, closer supervision of local government was obtained by the establishment of provinces. With some modifications, this provincial system continues today. During the Sung Dynasty, a rather effective means of local control called the *pao chia* system was established. Originally devised as a defense measure against foreign invaders, this system became an effective method for internal control because it made neighbors responsible for the acts of one another.

Efforts to enforce greater control over the local units of government were counteracted by strong forces working for decentralization. This tug of war between central and local governments runs throughout Chinese political history. There are several reasons for this struggle. China is a large country. Prior to the modern age there were no quick means of communication between the central government and faraway provinces. Thus a certain amount of autonomy had to be given to the local government officials. The degree of local autonomy varied from time to time, depending on the strength, or lack of it, of the current dynasty. Moreover, the central power was inherently weak because government itself was minimized in the daily life of the people. Most of the daily affairs of the Chinese were carried on by nongovernmental institutions such as families, clans, villages, and guilds. Land disputes, suits, quarrels between villages, the collection of taxes, and most of the everyday activities of life were taken care of by the leaders of of these units. The magistrate, the central government's representative at the lowest level of local government, the county, had only to make sure that the taxes were collected and forwarded, the peace kept, and public works maintained.

Impact of the West

China's native political evolution was drastically modified by the intrusion of Western influences. These began in the sixteenth century and have continued to the present. The Chinese, proud of their old culture and civilization, struggled long to resist this cultural penetration by the West, but internal weakness coupled with strong pressure from the West broke down their defenses and permitted Western science and philosophy to spread throughout the land. Their rapid sweep left the Chinese confused, upset, bitter, and desperately groping for a synthesis that would tie the old and the new together in some effective but understandable form.

The establishment in 1912 of the Republic of China marked the beginning of almost fifty years of political confusion and discord as the Chinese struggled to formulate a political philosophy and establish political institutions which would combine both Western and Chinese elements.

Dr. Sun Yat-sen, the father of modern China, was chosen president of the new republic. Because he lacked organizational backing, he resigned his office to a strong military leader of the old regime, Yuan Shih-k'ai. Yuan mocked the new republican institutions by ruling as a dictator until his death in 1916. After his death, warlords rose all over China. They kept the country in a state of turmoil for about ten years as they struggled with one another for control of the nation. Patriotic Chinese were frustrated and embittered by the weak and chaotic condition of the country, and throughout this period more and more Chinese intellectuals and students turned to the study of Western ideas and practices for a solution to their national problems.

Under the leadership of Dr. Sun Yat-sen and his followers, this knowledge and bitterness of the people were channeled into a nationalist movement which eventually succeeded in uniting most of China under one government. Dr. Sun's Kuomintang Party, founded in 1912, and the Chinese Communist Party, founded in 1921, banded together from 1924 to 1927 in a loose association for the purpose of defeating the warlords and uniting the country under one head.

During this period the organization of the Kuomintang was revised along Communist lines. Student, labor, and peasant organizations were formed, and soldiers were trained. At the time of the split between the Kuomintang and the Communist parties in 1927, a large part of China had already been brought under the control of the associated groups. Under the leadership of Chiang K'ai-shek, who assumed control of the Kuomintang Party after the death of Dr. Sun, most of China was gradually united, at least formally, under one government.

Neither the Nationalist nor the Communist government has ever controlled all of China. From the time of their breakup in 1927 until the present, with the possible exception of the brief United-Front Period beginning in 1937, there has been constant conflict between these two groups. The Communists were never completely destroyed, although they were forced to retreat from the south of China to the sparse northwest, where for some time they struggled to survive as an independent state within a state.

Today, the Communists control the mainland, and the Nationalists have been compelled to retreat to the island of Taiwan off the southern coast of China.

Political Legacy of Traditional China

From traditional China contemporary Chinese leaders have inherited the conviction that the best method of governing is through an enlightened leadership, that collective responsibility should be enforced, that government should be centralized, that government is personal in character, that the individual should be judged in a social context, and that a common ideology is essential to the proper functioning of the government.

These new leaders operate on the theory that it is necessary for an enlightened elite to rule on behalf of the people until such time that they, too, comprehend the political, economic, and social values and philosophy which support the new practices and attitudes. Confucianism justified the rule of the scholar-official as being in the best interest of the people. Although the Chinese use the term "democratic" and describe themselves with it, they ascribe to it a different meaning than is commonly given this term in the West.

The belief in the right to revolt is still implicit in the political system of China. Both Nationalists and Communists proclaim that their revolutions were justified by the wicked behavior of the former rulers. The Nationalists condemned the Manchus as rulers without virtue, and the Communists condemned the Nationalists as unworthy to continue governing the people. According to this modern application of the Mandate of Heaven doctrine, the present governments are entitled to the power they hold because they carried out the will of the people (will of heaven) when they expelled their predecessors.

The device of collective responsibility, known formerly as the *pao chia* system, has been taken over by modern Chinese governments to ensure greater control of the people by the central government. Groups of households or block and other committees watch one another because they are held responsible for one another by the government.

But the historical tendency toward political decentralization in China still hampers the efforts of the present Chinese leaders to centralize their control of the mainland—it also hampered the Nationalists when they were in control—and they are using all sorts of administrative devices to counter this tendency. In addition to using the collective responsibility method of "people's associations," which is similar in purpose and principle to the *pao chia* system mentioned above, they have experimented with administrative units intermediate between the provinces and the central government. It was also thought that the establishment of a commune system would provide, among other advantages, a greater degree of control in the rural and urban areas. And, recently, revolutionary committees composed of soldiers, workers, and peasants were instituted to assist the government leaders in administering the various levels of government in the country. Mao Tse-tung believed that a greater involvement of the people in their government would benefit all Chinese and would lead to a lasting and beneficial relationship between the people and their officials.

Government in China remains personal in character. Relations between people and officials, and between members of the bureaucracy and their leaders, are extremely important to the proper working of government. Bureaucracy is not yet a cold, impersonal machine; it is a group of human beings performing their duties on the basis of personal relations as well as on the basis of the administrative regulations. Emphasis is placed upon personal leadership, personal virtue, personal contacts. In this kind of atmosphere, judgments are often made on the basis of feelings, sympathies, and obligations rather than on the basis of detailed regulations. The personalities of Chiang Kai-shek and Mao Tse-tung were vitally important in shaping the character and spirit of their respective parties and governments. To understand Chinese politics, it is essential to understand the personalities who make Chinese policy and the relations among them.

Government in China is also concerned with social conduct. Under the Confucian system, only right conduct gave the emperor the power to govern. Since the Confucian scholar knew the rules of right conduct, he was important to the traditional system of government. The worth of the individual continues to be measured in social terms. Has the individual benefited society? Has he or she conformed to the rules of right conduct? Do individuals play their roles well in relation with others? These are important questions when the character and worth of an individual are being discussed. Government in China is dedicated to the improvement of society.

The use of ideology as an instrument of social control has been carried over from the traditional system to the present. Political indoctrination is considered essential by modern Chinese leaders. They have bolstered their rule by championing an ideology and indoctrinating the Chinese with its principles. The Nationalists have, for the most part, formally founded their political system upon the "Three Principles of the People" formulated by Dr. Sun Yat-sen. The Communists, of course, base their government upon the ideology of Marxian Communism as interpreted by Mao and Lenin. The Communists have also, at various times, interpreted the "Three Principles of the People" to harmonize with their beliefs.

The Three Principles

The doctrine of the "Three Principles" is an attempt to synthesize the best of traditional China with the best that the West has to offer. The core of this philosophy is made up of three principles commonly translated as nationalism, democracy, and people's livelihood.

Sun Yat-sen received his inspiration for these principles from Lincoln's Gettysburg Address which speaks of government of the people, by the people, and for the people. Dr. Sun interpreted this statement to fit the Chinese scene. Government of the people meant national independence or nationalism; government by the people meant a democracy; and government for the people required that the nation use its power to ensure the people's livelihood, to ensure that the needs of all are supplied by the efforts of all.

Nationalism

Nationalism, the first principle, was primarily an appeal to the Chinese to think of themselves, not only as members of a family, clan, and race, but primarily as members of one large political state to which they owed their loyalty and devotion. This was a Western thought.

Dr. Sun insisted that the Chinese people become patriotic; otherwise the nation-state of China would never become independent and strong. The signing of unequal treaties with foreign nations, the establishment by outside powers of spheres of influence, and many other limitations on China's sovereignty were due, in large measure, to the lack of a unifying feeling of patriotism. Chinese independence and continued self-rule depended upon the rapid growth of Chinese patriotism. He believed that China was in imminent danger of being overrun by the Great Powers and feared that the Chinese race would be swallowed up and absorbed by the rapidly increasing "white hordes." He looked forward to the time when the Chinese would relieve China's neighbors of the white imperialist burden that now lay so heavy upon their lands and replace this burden with the civilizing influence of China.

Chinese nationalism was to be preserved by a revival of the old Chinese ethical philosophy, which was to be broadened by the addition of Western techniques and science.

As a Confucianist and a Christian, Dr. Sun stressed virtue and high ideals. He believed in the natural goodness of people and their reasonableness. He emphasized loyalty, filial devotion, kindness, love, faithfulness, justice, harmony, and peace as the motivating forces of the revolution. He hoped that this ideological nationalism would make China a leader among the nations of the world, capable of fostering the kind of peaceful cosmopolitanism that prevailed in earlier days in East Asia.

Democracy

Democracy or popular sovereignty, the second of the three principles, defined liberty in a special manner. To be sure, it provided for a representative form of government, with the administration of government by elected officials and with the power of election, initiative, referendum, and recall in the hands of the people. But it stressed the duty of all Chinese to subordinate their interests to the interests of the state. The individual did not need liberty in China; it was the state that needed liberty.

Dr. Sun held that the Chinese historically enjoyed a large measure of local autonomy and personal freedom. Generally speaking, the only interference with individual freedom in traditional China came from either the family, the clan, or the guild, not from the government. Theoretically, the central government was all-powerful, but it rarely used this power at the level of the people's daily life.

On the other hand, Dr. Sun thought that the Europeans and Americans prized personal freedom because, until comparatively recently, they had been oppressed by feudal lords and despotic kings. As a result Western tradition emphasized the concept of natural freedom and the right of every person to do as he and she pleased provided there was no infringement upon the rights of someone else. In the past the Chinese had enjoyed too much of this kind of freedom; what they needed in the future was freedom to work on behalf of the Chinese nation-state.

Dr. Sun felt that people are not equal, that they can be divided into three classes: 1) those who "know and perceive beforehand," the creators and inventors, the people of wisdom and insight who think independently; 2) those who "know and perceive afterward" and cannot initiate or create; and 3) those who "do not know and perceive" and, like the blind, must be led by the more knowing and perceiving people. They act but do not think. The great majority of people are in the last group. With this conception of the inequality of humans, Dr. Sun, quite naturally, followed the practice of the Confucianists in separating the people into two classes—the ruler and the ruled. The acting but unthinking mass should be governed by the wise and creative thinkers.

Yet the masses should be given an opportunity to participate in politics so that they could learn to practice democracy and become a progressive force in China. Dr. Sun believed that the people were capable of learning and felt that there must be some check on the elite ruling class lest it become despotic and unresponsive to the requirements of the common good.

Dr. Sun distinguished political power from administrative power. Political power or sovereignty, expressed specifically in terms of election, initiative, referendum, and recall, was lodged in the people. An elite ruling group checked by the sovereign power of the masses formed the essence of what he called popular sovereignty. He compared the government to a factory or corporation which is managed by competent individuals but in which the final power is retained by the owners—the shareholders. "This general manager is an expert who has the ability; the shareholders simply keep a supervision over him. The people of a republic are shareholders, the president is general manager, and the people should look upon the government as an expert." Government by experts, and the division of the society into the rulers and the ruled followed Confucian tradition rather closely.

Although this political system was ultimately subject to the will of the people, the people were not yet trained in the art of government. Therefore, Dr. Sun proposed a tutoring period during which the Kuomintang Party would teach the masses about the "Three Principles of the People" and constitutional government. When the people became capable of governing themselves, the Kuomintang would abdicate its position as sole acting head of the government, and the people would then elect their own officials. The authoritarian but competent government of the Kuomintang would be replaced by democratically elected but competent representatives of the people. The period of tutelage was divided into three stages: the military period, which would last only as long as military operations continued; the political period, during which the people would be taught the art and the theory of government and their new powers; and the final period of democratic and constitutional government.

Sun Yat-sen crowned his proposals with regard to democracy with the recommendation that there be five separate and distinct departments of government—the legislative, the executive, the judiciary, the examination, and the censorate or control department. The first three departments are customary in Western political systems; the latter two—the examination and control departments—were customary in the traditional Chinese political system. Dr. Sun was convinced that this combination of Western and Chinese institutions would make the finest and most complete government in the world.

Livelihood

Livelihood, the third principle, embodied the idea of providing the Chinese people with a decent standard of living in terms of food, clothing, shelter, and transportation. It was also designed to enrich and strengthen the entire nation-state. Dr. Sun recommended two programs that he believed would meet both needs—equalization of land ownership, and government regulation of capital.

The first was important because China was predominantly an agricultural country and there was a grave inequality of land holdings which was a primary cause of many of China's economic evils. Sun Yat-sen recommended that the government purchase land at a fair price and equalize its ownership. After the land had been divided, its value should be fixed, and any future increase in its value which did not stem from the owner's own efforts should revert to the community. He also urged a number of reforms to increase farm production.

Sun Yat-sen thought that the government should regulate capital. He favored state action to develop industries and enterprises that the country needed. He desired the nationalization of heavy industries and the communication and transportation system, the development of consumer cooperatives, and improvements in the condition of the laboring classes. He also mentioned progressive income and inheritance taxes. He believed the people should be protected against exploitation by the regulation of private industrial capital. He wanted Western nations to invest in China, although he opposed any Western exploitation of the Chinese people.

The principle of "livelihood" in its broadest sense is summarized in the Nationalist Constitution of China, which states that the "national economy shall be based on the principle of the people's livelihood for equitable distribution of land ownership and control of capital in order to obtain a well-balanced development of public economy in private livelihood."

Communism

Chinese Communism represents a more radical departure from the political philosophy of imperial China than the "Three Principles of the People." Less effort is made to synthesize traditional Chinese thought with Western Communism as interpreted by Lenin and Stalin. Chinese Communists theoretically accept the major Marxist assumption that economic factors determine the political and cultural organizations of any society, but they have had to adapt Communist theory and practice to the special political and social conditions prevailing in China. "We are not idealists," Mao Tse-tung declared. "We cannot place ourselves above the conditions of present-day life."

Mao accepts the orthodox Communist theory that for China and other undeveloped nations there must be a dual revolution, one from feudalism to capitalism and one from capitalism to socialism, but does not believe that the revolutionary transition from feudalism to the new democratic stage must be led solely by a dictatorship of the proletariat, or factory workers.

He taught, prior to the Communist victory in China, that the first stage of a new democracy in China should be led by a "combined dictatorship of all revolutionary classes." Of these the peasants were the most important. Mao early recognized their key value by shifting the Communist base in China from the urban proletariat to the peasantry. He held that other progressive groups were the proletariat, the *petite bourgeoisie,* and the national capitalists. The *petite bourgeoisie* embraced government employees, professionals, intellectuals, artisans. National capitalists were Chinese industrialists who operated production facilities and who desired the development of China's industry free from foreign domination. Enemies of the state were the imperialists, feudalists, and bureaucratic capitalists. They were called reactionary groups who could not be assimilated into the socialist society.

The government based on a coalition of anti-imperialist and anti-feudal elements was termed a "democratic dictatorship." It was democratic, according to the Communists, because these groups understood the "real interests" of the people. It was a dictatorship because they controlled absolutely the imperialist and feudal groups of the nation. In practice this stage ended by 1956 when all trade and industry was nationalized.

This new "democratic republic" practices *democratic centralism.* Generally speaking, democratic centralism means that the people are permitted to discuss policy and elect representatives of each level of political life, but that once a decision has been made, and the election certified from above, complete obedience is demanded. The people may criticize and discuss the manner of implementing a policy, but the policy itself is immune from any adverse comments. Discussions and elections form the democratic content of democratic centralism; the requirement of obedience represents the centralist content.

Mao tried at one time to harmonize Communist theory and practice with Sun Yat-sen's "Three Principles of the People." He declared that "the principles of the minimum program of the Communist Party are fundamentally and consistently the same as those of the Three Principles of the People." He advocated control of capital and equalization of land, two basic ideas of Sun Yat-sen's third principle of "people's livelihood." Land was to be divided and given to the peasants as their own property; state ownership was to be limited to banks, industries, and commercial organizations too large for private owners to handle. This was another example of Mao's policy of not placing himself "above the conditions of present-day life."

Since Dr. Sun's teachings had become widely accepted and understood throughout China, Mao's "acceptance" of them undoubtedly helped him in spreading Communist doctrine.

Quotations From Writings of Mao Tse-tung

Mao Tse-tung has been Chairman of the Communist Party of China since the early 1930s. He is of peasant stock, a realist, and a dedicated Communist. Under his leadership, the Chinese Communists eventually defeated the armies of the Nationalists, and in 1949 assumed control of mainland China. Despite the internal factional disputes and external pressures that beset the country, Mao continued to grow in stature and in influence until he became the single most important person in all of China. His pictures, statues, and words are to be found everywhere in China, and he is regarded as the final arbiter of the thought and deeds of his people. Here are certain selections from the best-known book in China, *Quotations From Chairman Mao Tse-tung.*

We must have faith in the masses, and we must have faith in the Party (Communist). These are two cardinal principles. If we doubt these principles, we shall accomplish nothing.

No political party can possibly lead a great revolutionary movement to victory unless it possesses revolutionary theory and a knowledge of history and has a profound grasp of the practical movement.

The ruthless economic exploitation and political oppression of the peasants by the landlord class forced them into numerous uprisings against its rule . . . It was the class struggles of the peasants, the peasant uprisings, and peasant wars that constituted the real motive force of historical development in Chinese feudal society.

A revolution is not a dinner party, or writing an essay, or painting a picture, or doing embroidery; it cannot be so refined, so leisurely and gentle, so temperate, kind, courteous, restrained, and magnanimous. A revolution is an insurrection, an act of violence by which one class overthrows another.

The serious problem is the education of the peasantry. The peasant economy is scattered, and the socialization of agriculture . . . will require a long time and painstaking work. Without socialization of agriculture, there can be no complete, consolidated socialism.

Apart from their other characteristics, the outstanding thing about China's . . . millions of people is that they are "poor and blank." This may seem a bad thing, but in reality it is a good thing. Poverty gives rise to the desire for change, the desire for action and the desire for revolution. On a blank sheet of paper free from any mark, the freshest and most beautiful characters can be written, the freshest and most beautiful pictures can be painted.

Our state is a people's democratic dictatorship led by the working class and based on the worker-peasant alliance.

The only way to settle questions of an ideological nature or controversial issues among the people is by the democratic method, the method of discussion, of criticism, of persuasion and education, and not by the method of coercion or repression.

War is the highest form of struggle for resolving contradictions, when they have developed to a certain stage, between classes, nations, states, or political groups, and it has existed ever since the emergence of private property and of classes.

"War is the continuation of politics." In this sense war is politics and war itself is a political action; since ancient times there has never been a war that did not have a political character. . . . It can therefore be said that politics is a war without bloodshed while war is politics with bloodshed.

History shows that wars are divided into two kinds, just and unjust. All wars that are progressive are just, and all wars that impede progress are unjust. We Communists oppose all unjust wars that impede progress, but we do not oppose progressive, just wars.

Every Communist must grasp the truth, "Political power grows out of the barrel of a gun."

To achieve a lasting world peace, we must further develop our friendship and cooperation with the fraternal countries of the socialist camp and strengthen our solidarity with all peace-loving countries. We must endeavor to establish normal diplomatic relations, on the basis of mutual respect for territorial integrity and sovereignty and of equality and mutual benefit, with all countries willing to live together with us in peace . . . As for the imperialist countries, we should unite with their peoples and strive to coexist peacefully with those countries, do business with them and prevent any possible war, but under no circumstances should we harbor any unrealistic notions about them.

Our principle is that the Party commands the gun, and the gun must never be allowed to command the Party.

The people, and the people alone, are the motive force in the making of world history.

The masses are the real heroes, while we ourselves are often childish and ignorant, and without this understanding it is impossible to acquire even the most rudimentary knowledge.

To link oneself with the masses, one must act in accordance with the needs and wishes of the masses. All work done for the masses must start from their needs and not from the desire of any individual, however well-intentioned.

Our congress should call upon the whole Party to be vigilant and to see that no comrade at any post is divorced from the masses. It should teach every comrade to love the people and listen attentively to the voice of the masses; to identify himself with the masses wherever he goes and, instead of standing above them, to immerse himself among them; and, according to their present level, to awaken them or raise their political consciousness and help them gradually to organize themselves voluntarily and to set going all essential struggles permitted by the internal and external circumstances of the given time and place.

Weapons are an important factor in war, but not the decisive factor; it is people, not things, that are decisive. The contest of strength is not only a contest of military and economic power, but also a contest of human power and morale. Military and economic power is necessarily wielded by people.

We must never adopt an arrogant attitude of great-power chauvinism and become conceited because of the victory of our revolution and certain achievements in our construction. Every nation, big or small, has its strong and weak points.

On what basis should our policy rest? It should rest on our own strength, and that means regeneration through one's own efforts.

We stand for self-reliance. We hope for foreign aid but cannot be dependent on it; we depend on our own efforts, on the creative power of the whole army and the entire people.

To win country-wide victory is only the first step in a long march of ten thousand li. . . . The Chinese revolution is great, but the road after the revolution will be longer, the work greater and more arduous. This must be made clear now in the Party. The comrades must be helped to remain modest, prudent, and free from arrogance and rashness in their style of work. The comrades must be helped to preserve the style of plain living and hard struggle.

Where do correct ideas come from? Do they drop from the skies? No. Are they innate in the mind? No. They come from social practice, and from it alone; they come from three kinds of social practice, the struggle for production, the class struggle, and scientific experiment.

It is man's social being that determines his thinking. Once the correct ideas characteristic of the advanced class are grasped by the masses, these ideas turn into a material force which changes society and changes the world.

Knowledge begins with practice, and theoretical knowledge which is acquired through practice must then return to practice.

In this world, things are complicated and are decided by many factors. We should look at problems from different aspects, not from just one.

Only those who are subjective, one-sided and superficial in their approach to problems will smugly issue orders or directives the moment they arrive on the scene, without considering the circumstances, without viewing things in their totality (their history and their present state as a whole) and without getting to the essence of things (their nature and the internal relations between one thing and another). Such people are bound to trip and fall.

Don't wait until problems pile up and cause a lot of trouble before trying to solve them. Leaders must march ahead of the movement, not lag behind it.

The world is yours, as well as ours, but in the last analysis, it is yours. You young people, full of vigour and vitality, are in the bloom of life, like the sun at eight or nine in the morning. Our hope is placed on you . . . The world belongs to you. China's future belongs to you.

The young people are the most active and vital force in society. They are the most eager to learn and the least conservative in their thinking. This is especially so in the era of socialism . . . Of course, the young people should learn from the old and other adults, and should strive as much as possible to engage in all sorts of useful activities with their agreement.

An army without culture is a dull-witted army, and a dull-witted army cannot defeat the enemy.

Knowledge is a matter of science, and no dishonesty or conceit whatsoever is permissible. What is required is definitely the reverse—honesty and modesty.

Complacency is the enemy of study. We cannot really learn anything until we rid ourselves of complacency. Our attitude towards ourselves should be "to be insatiable in learning" and towards others "to be tireless in teaching."

The Drive Toward a Powerful State

Theoretically, supreme authority in China rests with the National People's Congress, which is elected every four years. In fact, the members of the Congress, numbering over a thousand, merely serve to provide a united front for the decisions of the Communist party. Administration is carried on by the State Council, which is headed by the Premier of China; but actual power is concentrated in the Communist party.

The party includes over twenty million Chinese, although millions more support its principles and programs. It is controlled by a Central Committee that is elected by national party congresses. The Central Committee, in turn, elects a Standing Committee that is composed of the most powerful leaders of the party and that is the real focus of power in China. All state organs are subject to the commands that issue from a few top leaders of the party. Usually, the top officials of the government and the leaders of the Communist party are the same persons. The authority of the party is evidenced by the person of Mao Tse-tung, who held no official post in the government but controlled the state through his position as head of the party. Wherever there is a government official who is not a member of the party, there is near him a deputy or a secretary who is a member, and this arrangement carries downward through the various levels of government to the basic administrative units of the communes at the local level.

In 1949, the Communists gained control of a country made desolate by years of war. Gradually, they curbed inflation and restored and improved the transportation system. By confiscating the properties of businessmen, industrialists, and foreign investors, they brought under their control much of the industrial production of the country and increased the revenues of government. By 1952, they had rehabilitated the economy of China, but they lacked the capital and skilled manpower needed for rapid industrialization. To implement their First Five-Year Plan, they therefore turned to the Soviet Union for financial and technical aid. The Soviets advanced a credit of 130 million dollars that, together with 300 million advanced earlier, made a total loan of 430 million, part of which the Chinese had to start paying back in 1954. Another aspect of the First Five-Year Plan that was to plague the Chinese at a later date was its emphasis on heavy industry at the expense of light industry and agriculture.

During the period of the First Five-Year Plan, the Chinese began to collectivize agriculture. Beginning in the spring of 1953, they began to organize the villagers into temporary mutual-aid groups, then into permanent mutual-aid teams, and then into agricultural producers' cooperatives. The farmers worked on the basis of joint ownership of their pooled property, were paid in proportion to what they contributed, and had the right to withdraw their property from the cooperatives if they wished. Soon after, joint ownership became common ownership; they could no longer withdraw their original property; and they were paid on the basis of their work rather than on their capital investment in the common holdings. By the end of 1957, the leaders reported that over 95 percent of the peasant households were members of collective farms.

Although food production barely kept ahead of the rapidly increasing population between 1952 and 1957, industrial production during this period increased at a yearly rate of around 4 percent. Emboldened by this success and convinced that collectivization was right, the government announced a Second Five-Year Plan for the period 1958 to 1962. In February 1958, they proclaimed "a great leap forward."

To accomplish this "leap," thousands of party cadres were sent into the fields to mobilize the masses. Workers labored fourteen or even sixteen hours at a time to meet production goals. Peasants worked in the fields from dawn to dusk and then tended backyard furnaces far into the night, producing inferior iron and steel. To mobilize labor more efficiently, the leaders changed the cooperatives into communes, each commune including about five thousand households. Since the communes permitted labor allocation on a massive scale, millions were mobilized to repair roads and build railroads, to the accompaniment of clashing cymbals and stirring music.

As a result of the great leap forward, new cities sprang up overnight near industrial centers. At the same time, the people were driven to exhaustion, and food shortages began to plague the cities and the countryside. The people became resentful, and the leaders were finally forced to relax their pressure. The commune was decentralized into three levels of ownership. It continues to own factories, public buildings, and power plants to which all in the commune have contributed. The production brigade, a subdivision of the commune, owns its own land and tools and whatever factories and public buildings have been constructed with brigade funds. The production team, which is a subdivision of the production brigade, about the size of a peasant village, owns its own animals, houses, and local property. The leaders of the commune and its subdivisions are elected. They need not be Communist party members, but they must be sympathetic with the party's agricultural objectives.

Agricultural productivity and economic development were somewhat curtailed when, in August 1966, Mao summoned millions of Red Guards to spearhead the Great Proletarian Cultural Revolution and ferret out his enemies in the party, bureaucracy, communes, unions, factories, and elsewhere. The zeal and excesses of the crowds of Red Guards often led to work stoppages in the factories, violence in the cities and rural areas, and to fear and the abrogation of decision making in the administrative ranks. The military, aided by the peasants and the workers, brought a measure of stability to the land by early 1969.

The Chinese leaders regard the Soviet Union as their principal threat on the international scene. The antagonistic relationship between China and the Soviet Union is evidenced by the sporadic violence between their soldiers and citizens along portions of their long common border. The intrusion of Soviet Power into the Indian Ocean, Soviet support of India during the 1962 boundary conflict between China and India, the 1971 friendship treaty between the Soviet Union and India, the continuing attempts by the Soviet Union to obtain port facilities and areas of influence in Southeast Asia, and their wooing of Japan politically and economically, have all led the Chinese to conclude that the Soviet Union has embarked upon a policy of limiting or containing Chinese power in Asia. This conviction has been further reinforced by other actions and statements of the Soviet leaders such as the renaming of Siberian towns which formerly bore Chinese names.

Soviet leaders suddenly withdrew all of their technical experts working in China and left many projects uncompleted. At times they called for a change in the leadership of China, and some of the Soviet military leaders have thought out loud about a preventive strike against China's nuclear establishment. The Soviet leaders accused the Chinese of being "sectarians" and "splitters" and condemned their brand of Communism as being incorrect. The Chinese responded to these words and acts with bitter statements of their own, vied with the Soviets for leadership of the Communist movement, positioned their troops along their common borders with the Soviet Union, and made tremendous efforts to prepare themselves for a possible war with the Soviet Union.

Until recently, the Chinese also regarded the United States as one of their principal enemies. The long history of U.S. support of Chiang Kai-shek, head of the Nationalist government based on Taiwan, and recognition of his regime as the only legal government of China, was a major concern to the Chinese mainland leaders. The confrontation between U.S.-led forces in Korea, and the presence of U.S. military power in South Korea, Japan, Taiwan, Vietnam, Thailand, the Philippines, and Okinawa led them to the conviction that the United States was a real threat to their security. They also suspected that the Soviet Union and the United States had reached an understanding about working cooperatively in the containment of China. The words and acts of President Richard Nixon, however, eased the suspicions and softened the convictions of the Chinese leaders about the future policies of the United States toward China.

Not long after President Nixon assumed office, he made an address to the nation outlining his objectives and proposing solutions to the war in Vietnam. He negotiated a peace settlement with the North Vietnamese and Viet Cong and withdrew all American combat troops from Vietnam. He made other statements that indicated a lessening military presence of U.S. troops in all parts of Asia, and implied that future conflicts among Asians should be settled by Asians without the involvement of outside military forces. He concluded an agreement with Japan which returned the great military base of Okinawa to the Japanese government. He supported the seating of the People's Republic of China (Communist) on the Security Council of the United Nations and, although he also supported the continuation of the Republic of China (Taiwan) in the United Nations, this act represented to the Chinese a substantial change in U.S. policy toward them. The Chinese began to develop a new and more positive viewpoint with regard to future Chinese-U.S. relations.

In February 1972, the leaders of the People's Republic of China welcomed President Nixon in China. While there he spent long hours in consultation with these leaders, especially the Prime Minister, Chou En-lai. He also met with Mao Tse-tung, Father of the People's Republic, and the ultimate authority in the country. The leaders of the People's Republic of China and the United States agreed to the establishment of liaison missions in Peking and Washington which in every way but in name, are de facto embassies. In April 1973, the first members of the U.S. Liaison Office in China reached Peking. In December 1975, President Ford also visited China and reaffirmed a U.S. intention to maintain a positive relationship with China. After many years of hostility and antagonism, the statesmen of these two countries have continued a real movement toward a more harmonious relationship between them. The future is always rather uncertain, but certainly a peaceful and cooperative arrangement between the United States and China should lead to a more peaceful era in Asia and the world.

28

Korea

Korea, "Land of High Mountains and Sparkling Streams," has the more ancient name of Cho-son, which was given to it in the twelfth century B.C. by the first Chinese to govern the country. Cho-son means "Land of the Morning Calm" or "Morning Radiance." Because the country isolated itself from the rest of the world for many years, outsiders often referred to it as the "Hermit Kingdom."

Korea is a mountainous peninsula jutting out from the eastern coasts of the Eurasian Continent. It lies between the Yellow Sea, which separates the peninsula from China on the west, and the Sea of Japan, which separates it from Japan on the east. Chinese Manchuria covers most of the northern boundary of Korea with the exception of a narrow strip in the northeast which is bordered by Soviet Russia.

The Korean peninsula is approximately eighty-five thousand square miles in area and about six hundred miles long and one hundred and thirty-five miles wide.

There are two political Koreas today—North and South Korea. North Korea is officially known as the Democratic People's Republic of Korea and is ruled by a Communist government. South Korea is officially named the Republic of Korea and is ruled by an elected government.

The population of Korea is between forty-five to forty-six million. Of this number over thirty-one million live in South Korea below the thirty-eighth parallel, and about fourteen million in North Korea above the thirty-eighth parallel. Most of the people derive their living from agriculture, and the great bulk of the population is rural in character. Pyongyang, located at the mouth of the Tadong River, is the capital of North Korea. Seoul, located on the mouth of the Han River, is the capital of South Korea.

Because of its location Korea has served as a bridge connecting Japan with the religious, political, and social ideas of China. Korea was originally settled by various peoples, but it was the Chinese who most influenced the Koreans' language, culture, and customs. But, over the centuries, the Korean people have evolved their own unique language, culture, and customs from this original heritage. The Japanese owe a great debt to the Korean people for having transmitted to them so much of the wealth of Chinese philosophy, religion, art, and architecture.

The location of Korea has influenced both its own historical development and the political relations between Korea, China, Japan, and Russia. China, Russia, and Japan at one time or another have sought to control Korea because of the country's unique geographic position. Japan has thought of Korea as a possible staging area for outside invaders. China thinks of Korea as a nation uncomfortably close to its industrial area of Manchuria. Russia believes that control of Korea would help to secure its position in East Asia. Because all three have long felt that Korea is necessary to their security, its land has been saturated by the blood of many armies.

Most Koreans had looked to a period of peaceful independence and greater prosperity after the defeat of the Japanese who had ruled their country as a colony since 1910. This was not to be.

The Allies were victorious in 1945, but Korea was divided. The Russians occupied northern Korea south to the thirty-eighth parallel, and the Americans occupied the land from there southward. After prolonged and strenuous efforts by the Americans and others to bring into being a United Korean government had failed, the Russians established a Communist government in their area, and the Americans encouraged the formation of a democratic form of government in South Korea. In June 1950, a few years after the establishment of the two governments, the North Koreans invaded South Korea, thereby initiating a war which eventually drew into its vortex many of the nations of the world. Communist nations poured military supplies, advisors, and many thousands of soldiers—mostly Chinese soldiers—into supporting North Korea. Defending South Korea were a number of nations, headed by the United States, who fought under the banner of the United Nations. After the fighting and bombing stopped three years later in July 1953, both Koreas lay ravished and still divided; two economic, political, and social wrecks.

The fate of South Korea was most deplorable. Much of the war was fought on its soil; its fields were mined, its crops destroyed, its cities leveled, and multitudes of people killed by pestilence, starvation, bullets, and bombs. Life went on somehow after the war, but frustrations mounted as hope receded and morale dropped.

These frustrations showed up on the domestic political scene when Syngman Rhee, the aged, paternalistic first president of the republic, was forced to resign his position after the April Revolution of 1960 and leave the country. In May 1961, the government which succeeded the Rhee regime was taken over by the military who were disgusted by the inefficiency and corruption they observed at every level of government. In October 1963, General Chung Hee Park was elected President of the Republic. He was reelected for a second term of office in 1967, and a third four-year term in 1971.

Under the dynamic leadership of new leaders and with American aid, the economic position of the country dramatically improved. Economic growth averaged over 7 percent in the first four years of President Park's rule, and some report that the real gross national product (GNP) increased at an annual average of 9 percent during these years. Industry expanded at a rapid rate during this same period, and the Koreans began manufacturing a wide variety of products, ranging from textiles and footwear to steel rails. This diversified industry was reflected in the export trade which more than quadrupled during these years. The Koreans substantially improved their food production. New irrigation projects, the introduction of modern farming techniques, and abundant use of chemical fertilizers resulted in continuous increases in food yields each year.

There are, however, many grave problems to be solved. Population continues to increase at a rate slightly over 2 percent annually, and it is no easy task for most of the over thirty-one million people to make a decent living. Per capita annual income is estimated around 227 dollars and continuing inflationary trends threaten the people's present standard of living. Housing is drab and scarce. There is a developing crisis in unemployment, and imports are far exceeding exports. The South Koreans have not yet achieved self-sufficiency in food production, and there has been a massive migration of rural people to the cities resulting in congestion and conflict in the urban areas. There has also been the constant fear of war with the North Koreans which has led to the creation of a large military establishment and an additional heavy burden on their scarce financial resources. Recent indications however, indicate that both the North and South Koreans are moving toward a more harmonious and peaceful relationship.

Kim Il Sung, a Manchurian-Korean who fought with Chinese Communist guerrillas against the Japanese and was later trained in the Soviet Union, is the premier and Communist party leader of North Korea. Kim seems determined to maintain a certain flexibility of policy and action amidst the conflicting interests of the Soviet Union and China. Under his rule, the North Koreans are striving to achieve the maximum amount of independent action. He has been called both pro-Chinese and pro-Soviet, but as he has said, he sits in his own "Korean chair." Of course, the physical location of North Korea does place restrictions on Kim's national and international policies.

Traditionally, North Korea has been the industrial part of the peninsula and, in the past, depended much upon the half now known as South Korea for agricultural products, textiles, and light-industry goods. At present, the North Koreans must rely upon their own efforts and those of other countries to supply these products. North Korea is stressing increased agricultural production, and the farms have been collectivized. North Korea exports steel, other metals, machinery, chemicals, fuel, and textiles. Most of its trade is with the Soviet Union, China, other Communist countries, and Japan. There is no evidence of starvation in the country, but rationed rice and clothing, and the demands of the leaders for continued austerity and increased production do not indicate an easy life for the people of North Korea.

Recent speeches by Premier Kim focused on many problems which are obstructing the progress of the country. There is an insufficiency of energy, fuel, and raw materials. There is a critical shortage of technical experts and other manpower. Management is inefficient in many areas; and the people continue to cry out for more consumer goods, more food, more comforts, and to manifest other "capitalistic" and "bourgeois" tendencies. A six-year plan was inaugurated in 1971 to solve some or all of these problems. These problems, together with an economically burdensome military establishment and the Nixon plan to gradually withdraw a number of American troops from South Korea may have led Premier Kim to temporarily soften his hostility toward the South Koreans and the Japanese.

In August 1971, representatives of the South and North Korean Red Cross met in Panmunjon to work toward an easing of the problems of relatives (ten million of them) who were separated by the partition of Korea into two separate states. They eventually agreed to have their future conferences in Pyongyang, capital of North Korea, and Seoul, capital of South Korea, at alternate times. In 1972, high government representatives of the two countries met in Pyongyang, and agreed to establish permanent committee-relationships with the ultimate goal of unification of the two nations. Furthermore, the North Korean government, in 1971, granted Japanese reporters the right to live in Pyongyang, and delicately suggested that Japan and North Korea establish formal and normal relations in the near future.

During the following years, however, continuing incidents and statements on the part of North Koreans indicated a persisting hostility toward the South Koreans and Americans. The Chinese cautioned Premier Kim of North Korea to seek reunification of the country by peaceful rather than violent means. The Chinese do not want to be drawn into another conflict with the United States at this period of their development and tense relationship with the Soviet Union.

29

Japan

The Japanese call their country Nippon, which means "Land of the Rising Sun." Geographically the country is an island group of approximately one thousand islands. The major part of the area is included in the four main islands of Honshu, Hokkaido, Kyushu, and Shikoku.

Japan is one of Asia's most important countries. During the past hundred years it has practically lifted itself from among the least known countries in the world, to one whose influence is felt throughout Asia and the world. Despite its meager land area—slightly smaller than California —and the relative paucity of its natural resources, Japan has become one of the world's great industrial countries. Japanese products are to be

255

found in every country in Asia and are familiar to most Westerners. The quality of these products has improved over the years, and today their cameras, lenses and motorcycles are regarded as among the best in the world. Japanese technicians are to be found in many Asian countries helping in the establishment of small industries and sharing their technical knowledge with their Asian neighbors.

The Japanese are assisting today in the rehabilitation of many Asian countries which about three decades ago they had conquered by force of arms. Thirty years ago the Japanese were regarded as one of the great military powers of the world; they occupied and controlled, for a period of time, a great part of Asia. The combined power of the Allies eventually wrested these areas from the Japanese, but not before Japanese actions and ideas had changed the political face of Asia by destroying the underpinnings of Western colonialism in this region.

The Japanese have been accused of excessively imitating others and described as lacking in originality. It is true that the Japanese have taken ideas from others and copied products produced by others, but they have also originated concepts and products which have been widely accepted and imitated by others. Nor have they imitated slavishly, for in many instances they have practically and esthetically improved the original foreign product through additions created by their own inventive and artistic minds. Ideas which have flowed in upon them over the centuries from Asia, particularly from China, have been modified to fit the Japanese scene. Their present great industrial complex, which was rebuilt so rapidly from the rubble of war, is a tribute to the skill, persistence, intelligence, and imagination of the Japanese people.

It is essential to understand something of the thought and way of life of a people who have created a key country in Asia, who have since the late nineteenth century shaped the destiny of so many millions of Asians and non-Asians through their military and political activities, and who will continue to play a major role in the evolving life of the world.

30

Japanese Ideology

Japanese traditional thought is a composite of indigenous beliefs grouped under the name of Shinto, or "Way of the Gods," and a number of foreign ideologies of which Confucianism and Buddhism are the most important. From the fusion and interaction of these concepts has come what the Japanese like to refer to as the spirit of Japan, a spirit which they believe has made the land and people of Japan unique. Because it has a mystical character and includes the whole corpus of sentiment and belief that moves the Japanese people to action, it is impossible to define this spirit, but certain of its aspects can be described.

Reverence for Nature

Shinto, the native religion, and Taoism, an ideological import from China, have given the Japanese a deep and reverent feeling for nature which is revealed in the tender, patient care they lavish on their islands. These resemble gardens that have been trimmed and trained to be natural scenes of beauty. Trees have been shaped to serve as frames for islands, lakes, and mountain tops. The forest paths ramble gracefully, the brooks speak in soft, pensive tones, and even the small stone is perfectly placed to give an artless but harmonious appearance of grace. The beauty that is Japan is the result of an abiding love and respect for nature and for the divinity which lives within it.

The mingling of Shinto and Buddhism has stimulated the holding of many festivals which bring added gaiety and charm to an already lovely group of islands. Nature, festivals, and joy are intimately related. The great festivals are occasions for celebrating the changes of season or the generous harvests that divine nature has bestowed upon the Japanese people. The emperor of Japan participates personally, as an intermediary between his people and the gods of nature, in both the spring and autumn festivals. He seeks the blessings of the gods for the new planting, and he gives thanks for the benefits the people have already received in the form of food.

There are many festivals. There are the flower festivals which are celebrated once a month, there is the doll festival, the children's festival, which honors Gautama Buddha as a child, the moon festival, and the New Year's festival, which lasts for a month, and many others. These festivals are not merely Shinto or Buddhist—they are Japanese festivals.

Bushido

Bushido, or "the Way of the Warrior," is the name for a code of behavior and morals which had its origin in the military history of Japan. It developed from the intimate relationships that existed between the early landholder and his armed retainers. Gradually it evolved into an expected pattern of behavior that governed soldiers under the stress of war. From vague beginnings in the early feudal and prefeudal period to the seventeenth century, this creed of Bushido served as a well-known social guide, rule of life, and set of ideals for the *samurai,* or military class.

With the establishment of the Tokugawa shogunate in 1603, Bushido was codified and given a definite philosophical base. It became a system of practical ethics which was to serve not only as a guide for the samurai, but as a set of high ideals for all good Japanese citizens. It was an ambitious attempt to apply the code of the warrior to civilians. Taken from the context of war and battle, it became somewhat elaborate, ceremonial, and complex, but the ideal and spirit of Bushido still remains a part of every Japanese.

Bushido incorporated elements from Confucianism, Buddhism, and Shinto. Confucianism stressed the quality of loyalty which should exist between the inferior and the superior in social and family relations. The "five relationships" predominated. The son owes obedience and loyalty to his father, the younger brother must be loyal to the elder brother, the subject must be loyal to his emperor and to his lord, the wife to her husband, and a friend to a friend. The Japanese taught that the loyalty of the vassal to the lord transcended all other loyalties and that this loyalty passes on from father to son and from generation to generation. For a mother or father to substitute their son for their lord's son who was threatened by an assassin, and to watch him being killed with no show of emotion, was not only ethical but an act highly praised. The Japanese people possess a strong sense of obligation and generally subordinate their individual desires to the claims of society. The struggle between obligation and natural affection is a common theme of Japanese tragedy.

"The Way of the Horse and the Bow," another name for Bushido, also incorporated qualities from Zen Buddhism and Shinto. Zen teaches that enlightenment is achieved only through one's inward efforts, and consequently it stresses self-discipline, self-control, and self-conquest. These were the qualities that military men made an essential part of their code. Shinto bequeathed to Bushido its great reverence for nature, its simplicity and lack of ostentation. From Shinto, Bushido also obtained its strong attachment for the land of Japan and all that it stood for, and this sentiment still grips the people and leaders of Japan.

From earliest times to the present, Japanese rulers have typically made use of religion to serve their own political ends. The Yamato rulers, the dominant clan of early Japan, fostered a belief in the superiority of their divine ancestress, Amaterasu, the sun goddess, in order to justify their assumption of the rulership of all Japan. In the sixth century, the Saigo family used the new religion of Buddhism to further their political fortunes, while the Nakatomi and other clans upheld the native gods as a counterbalance. The Tokugawa rulers stressed Buddhism because it upheld their policies of maintaining unchanged the Japanese social and political structure. Later, the group of samurai who overthrew the Tokugawa rulers used the ancient religion of Shinto to justify the revolution and to strengthen their right to rule. All political leaders stressed those elements of loyalty and obedience found in Confucianism and emphasized the superior-inferior relationships which were an integral part of Confucian doctrine. In modern times, those types of Western constitutions and ideas found favor with the Japanese authorities which gave a great degree of power to the ruling executive body.

31

Shinto

The roots of Shinto, "the Way of the Gods," are deeply embedded in the legendary past of Japan. For centuries Shinto teachings were handed down by word of mouth; it was only in the eighth century A.D. that Shinto beliefs and observances were put into writing. Basic works are *Kojiki,* "Record of Ancient Things," and *Nihonshoki,* "Chronicles of Japan." The *Manyoshu,* or "Collection of a Myriad Leaves," an anthology of eighth-century verse, contains some parts of Shinto ritual and faith. A handbook of Shinto prayers and sacred rites entitled *Engishiki,* or "Origin of Rites," was written in the tenth century.

The *Kojiki* (712 A.D.) and the *Nihon-shoki* (720 A.D.) are our principal written sources of information about early Japanese beliefs and customs. Both works are written in Chinese characters because the Japanese had not yet evolved their own script at this early period. They were written primarily to strengthen the dynasty of the reigning Yamato sovereigns and the social position of the seventh-century aristocracy. Early myths, legends, and events were chosen which tended to buttress the legitimacy and prestige of the ruling king and his clan; genealogies were included to provide the emperor and the important clans and families with gods for ancestors. The compilers planned well, because these two books have been used throughout Japan's long history as documentary proof of the divine origin of the Japanese people and their leaders. In the nineteenth century these same two works provided a firm foundation for the growth of Japanese nationalism.

The Shinto Story of Creation

The *Kojiki* and the *Nihon-shoki* relate the story of the creation of the land and people of Japan. Out of chaos came heaven and earth, and then a succession of divine beings ending with the god Izanagi and the goddess Izanami. These two deities stood on the bridge of heaven and dipped a spear into the waters beneath them. The drops that dripped from this spear piled up and formed the islands of Japan. Then these two divine beings descended to this land, married, and produced such offspring as the mountains, rivers, and forests of Japan. Izanami gave birth to Amaterasu-o-mi-Kami who shone so brightly that her parents sent her to heaven where she rules as the sun goddess. Thus the sun was created. A younger brother was also sent to heaven where he shared power as the moon god with his sister Amaterasu. Thus the moon was created. Izanami then gave birth to Susa-na-wo who was so fierce and cruel that he was sent to rule the world of darkness. Izanami then gave birth to the fire god who burned her so seriously that she died. This did not stop the creation of gods and nature, however, for from her excreta and the tears of her husband more gods were born.

Japan's legendary history continues with the uncouth behavior of Susa-na-wo in his sister Amaterasu's palace. He so shocked and angered his sister that she fled and hid herself leaving the whole world in darkness. The gods tricked her into revealing herself again by having one of their female members perform an indecent dance in front of her hiding place. Hearing the laughter and shouts of the gods watching the dance, she looked out to see what was taking place. They seized her, pulled her out into the open, and light shone again upon the world. Susa-na-wo was banished from heaven to his land of darkness, but before he returned, he went to Japan where he begot many offsprings who ruled over these island lands.

A decision was made in heaven to send Ninigi-no-Mikoto, the grandson of the sun goddess, to rule Japan. He came first to the island of Kyushu bearing three treasures given him by his grandmother Amaterasu—a jewel, a sword, and a mirror. Ninigi married, and had children and grandchildren. One of his great-grandchildren, Jimmu Tenno—Tenno literally means "Sovereign of Heaven" and is the common name for emperor in Japan—moved eastward from Kyushu to central Japan where he is said to have set up the state of Yamato on February 11, 660 B.C. This is considered the foundation date of the empire of Japan, and Jimmu is regarded as the first emperor.

As the Yamato clan gained supremacy over other Japanese clans, the legendary stories became accepted as true and the three treasures—the jewel, sword, and mirror—given by Amaterasu to her grandson Ninigi became symbols of imperial authority. These legends also formed the basis for popular belief in the divinity and natural superiority of the Japanese people. The origins of most modern Shinto deities and much Shinto ritual are traced by the Japanese to the *Kojiki* and the *Nihon-shoki.*

Nature is Divine

Shinto teaches that nature bears divinity within itself. Shinto deifies all natural forces and regards all things animate and inanimate as divine and the product of deities. Mountains, trees, stones, winds, lightning, birds, and plants are reverenced and worshipped as carriers of a divine spirit. This kind of religion—usually called animism—may at various times have been universal among early mankind, but in Shinto the Japanese have brought animism to its most civilized and sophisticated form.

The Japanese gave the name *kami* to the gods of heaven and earth and to the spirits that dwell within natural objects. *Kami* literally means "superior" or "above," and the Japanese applied this word to all things they thought superior regardless of whether they were living or dead. The early Japanese, impressed by such natural forces as raging seas and frightening storms, and awed by the majesty of mountains and the vast sweep of forests, thought of these expressions of nature as something superior and above them. Kami implies respect and reverence, and it came to be applied to anything that was mysterious, awesome, and strange. The Japanese gradually endowed all nature's manifestations with the divine presence referred to as kami.

In order that the awesome expressions of nature might be more approachable, the Japanese gave them an anthropomorphic character. The sun became the sun goddess, the moon the moon god, and Japan's beloved Mount Fuji became Fujisama—"the Mountain Goddess." Besides these well-known deities there were the earth god, the food god, the fertility god, and other gods and goddesses who were members of the Shinto pantheon.

Ancient Shinto has no images. The mountain, valley, stone, or tree was worshipped in its natural state. Later, objects thought to be bearers or symbols of divinity were enclosed in a crude manner with sticks or branches of trees. Still later, under the influence of Buddhism, Shinto housed the symbols of divinity in more elaborate and colorful structures. However, for the most part, the religion retains much of its original simplicity. The great Shinto shrines at Ise are torn down and erected every twenty years in their original form with unpainted wood. These are the national shrines of the sun goddess and the food goddess. They are merely large huts, with no place for congregants to sit, and the people simply stand outside the shrine to worship. After washing their hands and rinsing their mouths, the worshippers generally stand outside the shrine, make an offering, clap their hands, bow, clap their hands again, and leave. Sometimes the ringing of a bell substitutes for the hand clapping.

None of the gods and goddesses of the Shinto pantheon is sharply defined, for Shinto has little speculative and philosophical content. The obscurity and vagueness which surrounds Shinto deities continues even today as new functions and new identities accumulate. This vagueness does not worry the Japanese worshippers. It is enough for them to know that the shrine encloses a divinity which brings the good things of life to themselves and their country. Except in the case of the more prominent deities, Shinto shrines are essentially a means by which the worshipper gets in touch with the unseen.

Shinto is much concerned with natural processes. Birth, growth, and life are blessings which should be sought from the gods and for which thanks should be given when obtained. Death, decay, sterility are to be shunned and guarded against in every possible way. The chief evils are those that interfere with the productive forces of nature; the chief blessings those that encourage them. The prevalence of phallic symbols in trees and stones is due to this emphasis upon the constructive processes of nature. The greatest and most joyous festivals in Japan are those that deal with the planting and harvesting of crops.

Shinto is a religion of love and thanksgiving, but it is more—it is a religion which shows a striking appreciation of nature's beauty. Nature provides a feast for the eyes as well as food for the stomach. The Japanese felt that anything so beautiful must be godlike, and they honored the valleys, mountains, rocks, and streams of their land by making them divine. The earth and sky, the land and sea, the sun, moon, and stars are bearers of a beauty beyond the power of humans to express, and the Japanese considered them to be among their greatest deities. The gods of nature were givers of life and beauty, and the Japanese could only love, praise, and be grateful. There was little need for fear; there was a great need for thanksgiving.

An example of the appreciation of beauty which permeates the Shinto religion is the lovely setting of its shrines. They are often set in a serene landscape and surrounded by ancient trees. Some Japanese have stated that the real spirit of Shinto can be felt best among the old whispering pines that girdle and shelter their shrines. Often these shrines are framed by a torii which separates the secular from the divine and is a sign that one approaches a sacred place.

This love of beauty which fills the Shinto religion is found everywhere in Japanese life. An attractive simplicity is revealed in the arrangement and service of food and in the tea ceremony which is carried out in a very clean little room surrounded by a miniature garden. Many homes in Japan have carefully planned gardens, which may sometimes be small but are always tasteful and show the work of patient, artistic hands. A home is so designed that it becomes a part of the surrounding scenery; there is no jarring note, only a harmony of man and landscape.

Ritual Purity

Ritual purity is the heart of Shinto ceremonial. Before people can worship, they must be purified. Pollution is offensive to the gods, and the avoidance of anything that will defile a person is an integral part of Shinto observances. Some of the many things that can soil a person are uncleanliness, menstruation, sickness, and wounds or injuries of all kinds. This is an actual physical impurity. The uncleanliness that needs to be washed away is something that can be seen, something that is physically repulsive. There is no sense of sin or feeling of guilt such as Westerners might possess. In the moral sense the problem of evil does not exist for the Japanese. The early religion of the Japanese was almost completely free from abstract ideas of morality. Shinto worshippers had to be purified of their physical uncleanliness; there is no abstract guilt to be forgiven. It is a ceremonial matter rather than an ethical or moral compulsion.

Purification is obtained in three ways—through exorcism, cleansing, and abstention. An unclean worshipper can be cleansed by a priest who waves a wand and pronounces a formula of purification. An offender is cleansed of defilement by washing or by sprinkling of salt and dirt. Abstention is practiced most often by the priests and consists of the avoidance of anything that might defile a person, such as sickness or certain kinds of food.

Chinese Influences

Shinto has been influenced by foreign imports. From Confucianism it obtained ancestor worship, emphasis upon loyalty to the emperor, and a guide for social behavior. From popular Taoism it received magical practices and sorcery. Other Chinese imports were the theory of the dualism of the *yin* and *yang—yin* represents a female or negative element, while *yang* symbolizes the male or positive element—and the theory of the five elements of wood, earth, fire, metal, and water which influenced divination, fortune telling, and augury. The greatest influence was Buddhism, which overshadowed Shinto from the ninth to the nineteenth century. These foreign ideas brought ethics and philosophy to Shinto, added foreign gods to the Shinto pantheon, and sometimes veiled the original simplicity of Shinto shrines and objects by introducing a tendency toward ornateness and complexity.

From the moment these foreign ideas entered Japan there began a process of harmonization which has continued to the present day. This process was so successful that today the Japanese can, and often do, consider themselves at the same time Shintoists, Buddhists, and Confucianists. A good example of this process can be seen in the early harmonization of Buddhism and Shinto.

When Buddhism first entered Japan around 552 A.D., it clashed with Shinto, not because of doctrinal differences, but because they were both used as a justification for strife in a struggle for power between several Japanese clans. When the clans upholding Shinto were finally defeated, support for Buddhism in Japan was guaranteed. Buddhism spread very rapidly, especially in the court circles. The native cult of Shinto continued strong among the common folk. Then the eclecticism of the Japanese and the assimilative quality of Mahayana Buddhism became manifest.

The Buddhists declared that the native gods of Shinto were really incarnations of Buddhist deities, and they frequently and specifically identified these deities. The Japanese monk Gyogi reconciled the two religions by stating that they were merely two different forms of the same faith. Acting upon this theory Buddhist priests took part in Shinto rites, and an empress of Japan publicly proclaimed that the cardinal duties are "first to serve the Three Treasures—Buddha, the doctrine, and the order (Buddhism) —then to worship the gods (Shinto), and next to cherish the people." She saw no objection to the participation of Buddhist nuns and priests in the important Shinto feast of the Great Festival of the First Fruits which is celebrated at the beginning of each reign. On one occasion a prominent Shinto deity was conveyed from western Japan to the capital, Nara, where he was installed in a special shrine and attended by a priestess who was also a Buddhist nun. For seven days, forty Buddhist priests prayed at the shrine of this Shinto deity.

Today shrines and temples exist peacefully together, representing to the Japanese mind not contradictions but only differences of function. Today in Japan a new baby may be taken to a Shinto priest for a religious service, but should he or she die, the funeral will be conducted by Buddhist priests. Many homes have both Buddhist altars and Shinto sacred shelves.

Political Aspects

The ascendancy of the Yamato clan raised its clan deity, the sun goddess, to the preeminent position of ancestress of all other clans. Gradually she became regarded as the ancestress of the entire race. More and more Shinto became a vehicle for official ritual and stressed the functions of the emperor as the intermediary between the people and the ancestral gods. It became an institutional religion supported by the ruling classes and tied closely to the political system of Japan, and a national cult developed centered in the sun goddess who was the ancestress of the ruling family.

In 1882, Shinto was divided into Shrine Shinto, often referred to as State Shinto, and Sect Shinto, the traditional native religion. State Shinto was the official cult sponsored by the government for the purpose of inspiring in the Japanese single-minded obedience and loyalty to the emperor and, through him, to the state. Although it was placed above all other beliefs in Japan, officially it was declared not to be a religion. This distinction was somewhat artificial, because the same deities were worshipped and the same shrines honored in both sects; the division between the two Shintos was more political than religious.

The administration of about one hundred thousand shrines was placed under the Home Ministry. Certain family shrines were taken over by the government, and officials placed in charge. Often there was no change of personnel, merely of title. Priests were graded and given court rank according to the shrine they served. The government also gave detailed instructions with regard to the performance of rituals and ceremonies. This nationalist trend affected some shrines more than others, but in most cases emperor worship was added. The shrine of Ise, which is dedicated to the sun goddess, became the greatest shrine in Japan. The emperor and government officials traveled to the shrine of the sun goddess on important occasions.

The aim of this movement was to revive loyalty to the emperor as over against the shogun and feudal lords. *Shogun* literally means "Barbarian-Conquering General" and was the title given the military dictator of Japan during the feudal period. State Shinto was a means of obtaining national unity and stability. The ruler was viewed not only as a political head, but also as the chief priest of the nation—the main intermediary between the sun goddess, his ancestor, and the people. Article III of the 1889 Constitution declared: "The Emperor is sacred and inviolable." The emperor possessed divine virtue and had the quality of infallibility. The emphasis placed upon divine rule led many Japanese to think that the emperor was destined by heaven to rule the world.

Prior to the war there were numerous Shinto sects and sub-sects with a total of about seventeen million members. Although all the sects teach certain common doctrines, such as ritual purity and divinity in nature, they differ in their emphasis upon such things as the tradition of ancient Shinto, Confucian elements, worship of sacred mountains, purification, and faith healing.

State or Shrine Shinto, abolished in December 1945, is attempting to become Sect Shinto, a religion with an ethical content and an organized priesthood. Most of its individual shrines are now incorporated as religious bodies, and thousands of them have formed an association with headquarters in Tokyo. Shrine Shinto is also giving a good deal of attention to social work of all kinds.

Shinto is not dead in Japan. It continues to grow and change and influence the lives of the Japanese people.

32

Buddhism in Japan

No matter how many beings there are,
  I vow to rescue them;
No matter how endless the passions,
  I vow to destroy them;
No matter how great the depths of the Dharmas.
  I vow to know them;
No matter how much beyond my reach the truth of
  Buddha,
  I vow to know them;

                  —The "Four Great Vows,"
       —recited by the Zen monk after every service

Buddhism was carried to Japan from Korea
around the middle of the sixth century A.D. At
first it was not graciously received, but it soon
took root and flourished under the protection of
the Soga family and the patronage of Shotoku

Taishi (593 to 622 A.D.). As a result, Shotoku, the prince regent during that period, is often called the founder of Buddhism in Japan.

By and large Buddhism was supported and encouraged by the ruling group in Japan. In 685 A.D. the court instructed the people to set up a Buddhist shrine in their houses which would serve as an object of worship and to which food might be offered. Even now most Japanese houses contain such a shrine. During the Tokugawa Period (1603 to 1863) the shogun patronized Buddhism as a stabilizing force in the country, and every household was required to belong to some Buddhist sect. As a result of this requirement, the temples became storage houses for the vital statistics of the nation, because each temple recorded the births, marriages, and deaths of its members.

Buddhism entered Japan as both a bearer and an aspect of Chinese culture and is fundamentally the same as in China. It is divided into various sects, of which the largest is the Shin-shu. Shin-shu follows the Chinese type of Mahayana Buddhism and teaches salvation by faith in Amitabha Buddha. It is a ceremonial and pageant-loving sect. A second important Buddhist sect in Japan is Zen, which differs radically from Shin-shu because it teaches that salvation is the result of one's own efforts rather than the outcome of a faith in some supernatural deity. Zen traces its origin to Ch'an Buddhism which started in China around 400 A.D.

Zen Buddhism

Zen teaches that the Buddha-nature is everywhere, not only in some Western Heaven or Pure Land. All living things possess the Buddha-nature, and all may attain Buddhahood. Zen belief in the universality of the Buddha-nature is vividly exemplified in the story of a Buddhist monk who entered a temple and spat on the statue of Buddha. When he was reproved for this insulting behavior, he answered: "Show me a place to spit where there is no Buddha."

Humans have the power within themselves, says Zen, to discover this Buddha-nature. When they come to understand the true character of their own nature, they will be enlightened. But they must achieve their own salvation; no one can achieve it for them. Thus Zen differs from the general teaching of Pure Land and Shin-shu Buddhism, which stresses dependence upon others, and more closely resembles the original teaching of Gautama Buddha who stated that individuals must reach enlightenment by their own efforts.

The followers of Zen believe that enlightenment comes suddenly, but only after a lengthy and rigorous period of meditation sometimes lasting for many years. The story is told that Bodhidharma, an Indian sage who first brought Zen doctrines to China, sat for nine years in meditation facing a blank wall. Because of the prominent place of meditation in Zen Buddhism, it has been poetically described as "the Philosophy of Silence."

Because it believes that absolute truth cannot be expressed in words or analyzed by means of sacred scriptures, Zen Buddhism has little use for books, scriptures, discussions, and writings of any kind. Neither good works, nor faith, nor prayer can substitute for meditation in reaching a knowledge of the Buddha-nature that is the foundation of life. Meditation is helped by simple and self-disciplined living. In Japan, Zen monks feel that such pursuits as tea drinking, gardening, and contemplation of nature lead in some manner to the final goal of enlightenment. The simplicity, austerity, and self-conquest that is required of followers of Zen appeals to the tastes of many Japanese, especially those of the military class.

Meditation is preliminary to the final goal of sudden enlightenment. Zen masters often hit or shout at their students when it seems that they are on the verge of the intuitive flash which signifies a sudden comprehension of the Buddha-nature. This enlightenment has been described as a sudden revelation in which the bottom seems to fall out of everything and in which the mystery underlying all things is revealed in a blinding flash. Although outwardly the enlightened continue to act like ordinary persons, they are no longer attached to this world. They are sometimes described as those who continually eat but swallow not a single grain, who always clothe themselves but touch not a single thread.

Buddhism showed the same adaptability in Japan that it showed elsewhere in Asia. It penetrated all levels of Japanese life, influencing and being influenced in a reenactment of the same process that took place in China. Shinto deities, for example, were referred to as Bodhisattvas and Buddhas, and ancestral worship became a part of Japanese Buddhism. Prince Shotoku stated that Shinto was the roots of the tree, Confucianism the stem and branches, and Buddhism the fruits and flowers. Japanese Buddhism differs from that of China not so much in doctrine as in the strong position it continues to hold in Japan in contrast to its decline in China.

The religion founded by Gautama Buddha continues to be an inspiration to the Japanese people. Although it was relegated to a secondary position by the government from 1868 onward, and although its resources and prestige were crippled by World War II and by postwar occupation reforms such as religious freedom (hundreds of temples seceded and became independent), land reforms, and the separation of church and state (many temples were deprived of their principal income), Buddhism is still a major force in Japan. The monasteries do educational work ranging in level from the kindergarten to the university; the people still flock to the Buddhist temples and priests for funerals and memorial services; and the Buddhist monk remains a common sight. One Buddhist sect, the Sokagakkai, became very influential on the religious as well as on the political scene in Japan. Claiming many millions of members in Japan and elsewhere in the world this modern Buddhist sect is dramatic witness to the dynamic and durable spirit of Buddhism.

33

The Japanese Family

The Japanese belongs to his personal family, which, in turn, belongs to the national family of which the Divine Emperor is the kind father.

—Helen Mears

The Japanese were long taught to regard themselves as one large family headed by a divine emperor. Since the same duties and loyalties that bound together the members of a Japanese family were regarded as also serving to bind together the members of the state, the nation literally became an extension of the family, and Japan was viewed as populated by a number of

From *Year of the Wild Boar* by Helen Mears, published by J. B. Lippincott Company, copyright 1942.

families ruled by fathers who in turn were subordinate to the great father of all—the emperor. This conception was reinforced by religion, for primary in the life of the community was the religion of the family rather than any personal faith or belief. All Japanese thought of patriotism as involving the worship of Shinto deities through household Shinto. Japan became a family state.

Traditionally the individual existed mainly to ensure the preservation, continuity, and good name of the family. Though physically a separate entity, the individual Japanese was looked upon as an extension of the larger group. This attitude often worked great hardship upon the Japanese individual. In school, boys and girls studied with the stern eyes of their families fixed upon them. Failure to pass injured the reputation of the entire family. The family, not just the boy and girl, had been discredited. In all relations with outsiders, the individual child bore the full weight of family responsibility. The accelerating tempo of modern life in Japan increased the anxiety of individuals by introducing greater competition among them and thus providing them with many more opportunities for failing their families. Individuals were reminded over and over again that they were an inseparable part of the family; whoever laughed at them laughed at the family, and this was a most shameful matter.

It was within the family system that the Japanese learned how to live in Japanese society. Within it a Japanese found the whole social pattern of Japanese society. Boys and girls learned early from their elders the proper ceremonials before the domestic shrines; the stern precepts of unquestioning obedience which governed relations between children and parents, husband and wife, and young and old; and the external forms of family etiquette demanded by Japanese society. The head of the family possessed all authority, assumed full responsibility for the status and continuity of the family, and was given the complete respect and obedience of all members. The young owed respect to the old, and the women owed loyalty and service to the males. Wives were subordinate to their husbands, younger brothers to older brothers, and servants to the masters of the household. Ultimately the entire Japanese nation was regarded as one large national family whose formal head was the emperor, and the whole Japanese people owed him the same loyalty, respect, and obedience which they owed to their personal family and household head.

Structure and Economy of the Family

The traditional family included the head and his wife, the eldest son either by birth or adoption, his wife and children, and any unmarried children. This family might also include a retired head of the house and his spouse, that is to say, the surviving grandparents. Thus, there are two and sometimes three American-style families in each basic Japanese family. The household might also include uncles, aunts, cousins, and nephews; in well-to-do families servants also lived under the same roof. In all these cases, those living under the same roof were considered as belonging to one household.

The household was the basic social unit of Japanese society. The size of a community was often computed in terms of households. The household head represented the members at important community meetings and activities, and to him all official documents and messages sent to the household were addressed. He was responsible for the acts of the members of his household and, at times, was even arrested when a criminal from his household could not be apprehended. A member of the household represented it at all the occasions in which it had an obligation to participate, such as weddings, funerals, and religious ceremonies.

A series of households of the same kin-group comprised the extended Japanese family. It consisted of the main family house called a *honke,* and the branch family house or houses called *bunkes.* In the *honke* or main house the eldest son stayed with his family and parents. The *bunke* or branch house was founded by the younger brother, for instance, when he left his parents' house, married, and raised a family of his own. The extended family also often included all the brothers and sisters of all male members of the house and children of the family head who may have married or been adopted out.

The Japanese family was primarily an economic unit. It had a common budget and held property in common. The family head, who acted as the trustee for the property and not as the owner, controlled and was responsible for all the finances of the household, doling out the money as members needed it and carefully scrutinizing all expenditures. In many Japanese households the family head deputized his wife to supervise the daily household expenses. Often he consulted with other prominent members of his family before he made major and sometimes minor financial decisions. In this way he shared his financial responsibilities with other members of his family, and if the decision turned out badly he could not be blamed alone.

The Japanese family, particularly the rural family, frequently played an important role in spreading scarce resources and in cushioning its members against economic shock. Owing to the delicate balance that existed between the Japanese people and their resources, if there were no mutual aid on the part of the family members many persons would have starved. Since the Japanese are somewhat averse and unaccustomed to receiving charity from the state, they depended upon their families to tide them over critical periods. During the depression of the 1930s, Japanese living in the cities hastened by the thousands back to their ancestral homes in the country where they shared the food of their families. After World War II, returning soldiers and repatriates also went to the countryside because there was little for them in the cities. In both cases the Japanese government was spared the trouble and expense of providing food, shelter, and clothing for millions of its people.

In the rural areas occupations were often traditional. The families in the country were tied to the soil, and the planting of wet rice or other grains was their main occupation. Generally, the eldest son carried on his father's occupation, whether it was farming, fishing, artisan work, or a combination of all three. Both in the cities and in the rural areas numerous manufacturing processes, retail marketing, and other economic activities were carried on in family households. In many cases the hired workers were regarded as members of the family.

Marriages

Marriages were arranged between families, not between individuals. Usually they tried to pick someone from the same social and economic level. A family friend undertook the job of go-between for each family; these persons met together to discuss such delicate matters as the character of the family, police records, social and economic status of the families involved, health of the intended mate, and other touchy questions that it might be impossible to speak about in face-to-face conversations between the two families.

When the preliminary arrangements had been negotiated to the satisfaction of both families, a date was set for the wedding. It was often chosen by astrologers who recommended a lucky day. The bride's family prepared various articles, such as a chest of drawers, trunks, clothes, and toilet articles, which the bride might need. The quantity and quality of the gifts the bride received depended, of course, upon the wealth of her family. Some wealthy brides had very elaborate wedding gifts costing a great deal of money.

Wedding ceremonies consisted in part of a formal exchange of cups of *sake,* a rice wine, between the go-betweens, the immediate relatives, and the bride and groom. There was usually a wedding banquet at which the relatives of the bride and the groom were introduced to each other. Also, at some time during the first few days of her marriage, the bride was introduced to the village and to the leading members of the community.

Sometimes the marriage was not officially registered immediately. If the marriage did not work out well, the bride could be sent home more easily if there were no official record of the marriage. Of course, when a child was expected, the marriage was registered immediately in order to legitimize the child. The birth of a child strengthened the marriage and secured the position of the wife in her new home.

Children and Adoption

Children were wanted and loved in Japan. Above all the Japanese couple wanted a male child, because the family line was continued through the males. If there were no sons born, they could ensure the continuation of the family by adopting a son.

A couple might adopt the younger son of the brother of the family head. If this was not possible, then a child of one of their other relatives was adopted. Occasionally, when a couple had a daughter but no son, they adopted a boy who then married their daughter and assumed their surname. He thereby became their son, and he inherited their property when they died. Adoption was sometimes carried to great extremes in Japan. There were cases of families adopting a niece and then adopting a son to marry her. Elder brothers have adopted younger brothers as sons, especially when there was great disparity between their ages. Some of Japan's great business firms were headed by men who were adopted into the family when other sons were lacking or when the natural son showed no desire to carry on the business.

Because the continuity, preservation, and reputation of the family depended largely upon these adopted sons, they were usually chosen very carefully. Their character, health, attitude, and other pertinent characteristics were investigated thoroughly before they were officially adopted.

Adoptions were legalized when they were recorded in the *koseki,* or family register, which was kept in the police station of the village to which the family was attached. This all-important family register indicated the legal and social status of the family members. It was necessary for identification, and a man without a *koseki* was regarded with suspicion. Legal marriage in Japan consisted in the formal transfer of the bride's registration by her father to the *koseki* of the groom's family. Both adoptions and marriages could be dissolved when they turned out to be undesirable.

Family Relationships

Parents and Children

The Japanese attached more importance to the relationship between parents and children than to the relationship between husband and wife. Theoretically, Japanese parents had almost unlimited power over their children, but, practically speaking, they were restrained by custom, society, relatives, and the law. The Japanese in general were usually sensitive to the dictates of public opinion, and most parents were careful not to exert their powers too harshly. On the other hand, children were subject to these same pressures, which required them to be obedient and respectful in all cases to their parents. Filial piety was regarded by the Japanese as the foundation of all virtues, and indeed it was the fundamental virtue upon which the Japanese have built their social patterns. The worst statement to make about a child is to say that he or she was unfilial. Parents had definite duties to perform in connection with their children. They had to teach them the difference between right and wrong, punishing them when they did wrong and commending them when they did right. They provided their children with some academic as well as a moral education. They were obliged to find mates for their sons and daughters, and to support their children and provide them with the necessities of life. They were required to instruct the children in the duties and ceremonies that they would later perform as adults. Girls were taught to assist in offering sacrifices at the domestic shrines and in the care of the household. Boys were taught whatever occupation they were expected to undertake, whether it was farming, business, artisan work, or a professional career.

Traditionally, the loyalties of the husband were directed toward his parents and blood-relatives rather than his wife. His kin came first and his wife second. If necessary, the dutiful Japanese son would give up his wife if his father or mother disapproved of her. It was the wife's duty to prove her worth to the husband's parents. Most Japanese marriages took place for the benefit of the man's house. It was in the man's house that the wife lived and worked, and it was to the success of his family that she devoted all her energies. He generally controlled the family property, and he was thought to be mentally and physically superior to the woman. The traditional attitude toward the married woman is expressed in the *Great Learning for Women* written during Tokugawa (1603 to 1868) times by Kaibara Ekken (1631 to 1714).

> When a woman is divorced after once marrying, she is disgraced all her life, even if she is married again to a rich husband, for it is against the way of women. . . . A woman has no master but her husband whom she should serve with respect and humility, never with a light attitude and disrespect. In a word, the way of woman is obedience. To her husband she should be submissive and harmonious, serving him with gentle and humble expression of the face and speech. Never should she be impatient and willful, proud and impertinent. This is her first duty. She should absolutely follow the husband's teaching and wait for his direction in everything of which she is not sure. If the husband gets angry and acts accordingly, she should fear and be ruled by him; never contradict him. The husband is Heaven to the wife. Disobeying Heaven only incurs righteous punishment. . . .[1]

Baroness Shidzue Ishimoto stated in her autobiography that there was no privacy in the Japanese house, "for the rooms are not locked and usually the sliding doors which separate the rooms are kept open even on cold winter days. So my husband and I behaved like strangers to each other while we lived in the midst of watching eyes. It was a life in which individuality was completely killed in order to create harmony for the family."

The Family Council

Rich and noble families possessed family codes which governed the behavior and activities of the family members. Of more practical importance was the family council which made decisions on all matters which the family head considered important enough to bring to the council's attention. Such matters were marriages, adoptions, investments, the education of family members (espe-

---

[1] Baroness Shidzue Ishimoto, *Facing Two Ways: The Story of My Life* (New York: Holt, Rinehart and Winston, 1935). Used with permission.

cially beyond the compulsory levels), funerals, and other weighty occasions. The family head usually determined whether or not a subject was important enough to be considered by the council. But since responsibility lay so heavily upon him, he tended to use the council when in doubt.

The membership of the family council varied from family to family. Usually it included the older family heads of the chief and branch families, and sometimes even the widows of the dead family heads, especially if they were competent. Paternal relatives, however, predominated.

Each household had a family council. Members of one family council might belong to other family councils at the same time, and thus many households were tied together by the members of the family councils. In these overlapping kinship groups members intimately related to one family might be peripheral to another. Because of this web of interconnected councils staffed by blood relatives, it can be said with some truth that the Japanese were tied together in one large family.

Family councils were solicitous about the good name of the families they watched over. (Formerly, only samurai and nobles had family names, but now everyone has a family name of which he is proud.) The name was not to be tarnished in any way. One of the common ways for a family to acquire a bad name was to have some black deed recorded against it on the official register. The family council was careful lest this occur, because the living, the dead, and the still unborn were all affected by such an act.

Family councils had functions besides those of decision-making with regard to important family matters. These councils provided the kinsmen with mutual support, even though members might be scattered throughout the countryside and in the cities. Branch houses were tied to the main houses, and scattered blood-relatives to each other. This system tended to preserve the older forms of Japanese social life and slow up the process of change which was being felt throughout Japanese society. Members of the family council were generally conservative and reluctant to modify the established patterns of social life.

Modernization and Change

There are still traditional families and traditional familial attitudes among the Japanese, for the cultural past and present are inextricably tied together. But there have also been changes in the structure and patterns of family life. And these changes are becoming more and more obvious in a largely industrialized and urbanized Japan.

Modernization has affected the size of Japanese families. The contemporary Japanese family commonly found in the cities and, with increasing frequency in the countryside, consists of husband, wife, and unmarried children. This is generally termed a nuclear family, and is the type of family familiar to most Westerners.

Urbanization has certainly contributed to the nuclear family system now prevalent in Japan. The majority of the Japanese now live in cities. For some years there has been a discernible shift in the population from the rural areas to the cities and towns. And today, Japan's cities rival those of the great cities of the world in terms of population. Tokyo, the capital, has over nine million people; Osaka, over three million; Yokohama, over two million; Nagoya, around two million; Kyoto about a million and a half; and Kobe, a million and a quarter. (There are still other cities, not mentioned here, with large populations.) Hundreds of thousands of people continue to pour into these and other cities daily. The Japanese scene, at least along Japan's Pacific coastline, is one continuous urban sprawl. Many of the former small independent villages which characterized the Japanese countryside have grown, merged, and developed into towns of considerable size. This growth of cities and towns has resulted in a congestion of people and a lack of space to house them. Most Japanese are lucky to find adequate space for their nuclear families; it is only the more affluent few who possess quarters commodious enough to house the larger traditional extended family.

Japan is the one Asian country which has taken effective action to meet the problem of overpopulation. There has been a real decline in the birth rate. Because of excellent medical services, adequate diet, improving health education, and other reasons, the population continues to increase, but a projection of present trends suggests that the population may actually start to decline after the 1990s.

In 1948, the Japanese Diet passed a law which provided for the dissemination of information about contraceptives, and the government has stated that its aim is to make available one person trained in family planning for every five hundred families. Japanese law also permits abortion when the health of the woman "may be affected seriously by continuation of pregnancy or by delivery, from the physical or economic point of view." It is estimated that more than a million abortions are performed each year in Japan. As a result of these official laws and governmental activities, together with continuously rising expectations and a phenomenal growth in education for both sexes, growing numbers of Japanese women have become convinced that fewer children may result in better health for the mothers, better education for the children, a higher standard of living, and fewer financial worries.

Both in the cities and in the rural areas of today's Japan there are still numerous small manufacturing processes, retail stores, and other small businesses which are carried on in family households. And in many of these instances the employees, who may not be kinfolk, are regarded as members of the family. But here, too, change is occurring. Whereas cooperative family enterprises were once the rule, today the breakdown of the extended family has led to other forms of economic association. Industrial and agricultural cooperatives and voluntary organizations composed of people who do not belong to the same family, either immediate or extended, are becoming more and more prevalent. Many modern Japanese in both the countryside and urban areas must find their security within their small immediate family, and rely upon their own efforts rather than upon the former traditional cooperative kinship endeavors. In many instances they have transferred their family patterns and kinship values to other larger institutions and organizations.

Increasing numbers of daughters and sons are leaving the family homes and going to work for business firms, industrial plants, and other organizations. They look upon these organizations as great families within which the relationships are similar to those within the immediate family. The heads of these great organizations frequently view themselves as heads of a household and act toward their employees in a paternalistic manner. Therein exists the same hierarchical pattern which was found in the traditional Japanese family. Toward his party members, the political leader, for instance, often acts as the family head or elder brother of the traditional household. Labor leaders, too, are frequently regarded as fathers of the laborers or as heads of large union families. A man's social status is now often judged by the prestige and standing of the organization he works for, much like traditional Japanese judged a man by the social status of his family. The old, prized values of loyalty, devotion, and obedience are still valued today, but in a different family context.

Although traditional attitudes toward the relationship between parents and children still pervade Japanese thought and practice, modern forces sweeping Japan tend to make children more independent of their parents. After they reach their late teens they do not always accept their parents' interpretation of what is right and wrong. The conflict between traditional and modern concepts of life, and the new knowledge to which they are exposed in the schools, weakens the power of the parents. Young sons and daughters who are forced to leave the family and go elsewhere in search of a living become indifferent to the influence of their parents. Even the young bride who comes to live in her husband's family home will now often vocally resent and sometimes rebel against the harsh words and discipline of a strong mother-in-law. Such traditional mothers-in-law are sometimes termed "feudal persons." Many contemporary young wives refuse to live with the husband's parents.

Traditionally, the husband's kin came first and his wife second, but this attitude is also being modified in modern Japan. Smaller families, greater independence, separation from the family home, and the absence of parents in the household have all helped to create the kind of an environment in which the young wife has greater freedom and greater influence in the home. The orientation of the husband in these circumstances is toward the wife rather than toward blood relatives who do not live with them. Under these conditions also, there is more companionship between husband and wife, greater emphasis upon the advice of the wife, and more freedom of association and intimacy.

Certain laws, some of them made under the pressure of the American occupation command, have also placed the wife in a more independent position. The new civil code, which went into force in January 1948, states expressly that "husband and wife shall live together, and shall cooperate and aid each other." It also states that "any property in regard to which it is uncertain whether it belongs to the husband or the wife, is presumed to be property in their co-ownership." The code states further that "husband and wife may effect divorce by agreement."

In contemporary Japan more and more young men and women are insisting on picking their own mates. And even when their parents choose young men or women for their consideration as possible mates, their consent is usually needed before the marriage plans can go forward. It is also true, however, that in the cases where they have independently chosen their wife or husband, the families still negotiate the marriage contract and make the necessary preliminary arrangements. And for most Japanese, families still play a major role in selecting the prospective mate.

34

The Japanese Woman

What is the use of developing the mind of a woman or of training the power of her judgment when her life is to be guided at every step by a man? Yet, it is highly important that she should be morally trained, so that she be always gentle and chaste, never giving way to passion inconvenient to others, nor questioning the authority of her elders.

—The Great Learning for Women

Japanese women are best in the home either as housewives or daughters. I came to realize this during my sojourn abroad. The cream of our womanhood is to be

Passage from *The Great Learning for Women* reprinted from *Year of the Wild Boar* by Helen Mears, Published by J. B. Lippincott Company, copyright 1942.

found in the country and the modern girls who go about wearing Western clothes in the city are the worst examples of our fair sex.

—Fumiko Hayashi in 1936

Art. 14. All of the people are equal under the law and there shall be no discrimination in political, economic, or social relations because of race, creed, sex, social status or family origin.

Art. 24. Marriage shall be based on the mutual consent of both sexes and it shall be maintained through mutual cooperation with the equal rights of husband and wife as a basis.

With regard to choice of spouse, property rights, inheritance, choice of domicile, divorce, and other matters pertaining to marriage and the family, laws shall be enacted from the standpoint of individual dignity and the essential equality of the sexes.

—The Constitution of Japan (1947)

For over a thousand years Japanese women have been taught that they exist to serve men faithfully and well. They have been carefully indoctrinated with the idea that women are subordinate to men. The traditional ideal woman of Japan is one who unquestioningly and dutifully follows the old Japanese rule of "obedience to a father when yet unmarried, to a husband when married, and to a son when widowed."

This subordination of woman is expressed in many social attitudes and practices. Boys are valued more than girls, and the birth of a male is hailed with greater joy than the birth of a female. Boys are rarely disciplined and often outrageously spoiled; while girls are treated with affection, but firmly disciplined in preparation for their future role of service in the household. Brothers rank ahead of sisters in the family hierarchy. Good wives are meek and subservient in the house, deferring always to the desires of their husbands. Traditionally, a well-trained wife walked several paces behind her husband on public streets, and she frequently carried the packages. The modern Japanese woman now walks alongside her husband. She generally does not share in his social evenings out, nor should she reprove him no matter what the provocation.

The following two stories illustrate the traditional attitude toward women. Lafcadio Hearn tells in one of his stories about a Japanese wife who served her husband with unflagging energy and dedicated her life to making him happy and contented. She was obedient in all things and completely loyal. After some years of happy married life, the husband fell under the spell of a lovely geisha girl. (Geishas are highly trained in the art of pleasing men. They sing, play musical instruments, recite poetry, and are capable of conversing on a great variety of subjects with intelligence and wit. The Japanese man often finds in the geishas the companionship that he misses in the faithful but stiff and proper wife at home.) The woman's husband began to come home later and later at night, but, as a dutiful and thoughtful wife, she was always waiting up to greet him when he came in and to serve him tea and perform any other service he might require. Some nights he did not come home at all, and on those nights the wife got very little sleep.

She wondered why her husband stayed out so many nights, but she dared not ask him. Eventually, her servants told her about the husband's affair with the geisha. Though deeply wounded by a loved one to whom she had dedicated her life, she could not express her grief; such action would be un-Japanese. Lafcadio Hearn describes her in the early morning hours, sleepless but still awaiting the return of her erring husband.

> She waited through all the morning hours, fearing for him, fearing for herself also; conscious at last of the wrong by which a woman's heart can be most deeply wounded. Her faithful servants had told her something; the rest she could guess. She was very ill, and did not know it. She knew only that she was angry—selfishly angry, because of the pain given her—cruel, probing, sickening pain. Midday came as she sat thinking how she could say least selfishly what it was not her duty to say—the first words of reproach that would ever have passed her lips.[1]

Helen Mears relates the story of Akiko, the modern young Japanese girl who had given up her family and her prospective adopted parents in order to marry a man of her own choice. She served him loyally both as a working companion and as a wife. Then, he too became involved with another woman. One night the police came to their house and arrested him on suspicion of Communism. Akiko was arrested at the same time on the theory that the wife must necessarily derive her opinions from the husband. After she was questioned, it became clear that she was not a Communist, and she was released. The husband was kept in jail.

---

[1] *The Selected Writings of Lafcadio Hearn*, edited by Henry Goodman (New York: The Citadel Press, 1949). Used with permission.

Although he had caused her great unhappiness by his affair with another woman and his radical activities, Akiko remained loyal. She visited him every two weeks, bringing him her small earnings. The trip to the jail was long and tiring. The wait in a dirty anteroom where she was confronted with an atmosphere of fear, suspicion, and dejection was an experience she dreaded.

Then one day she reached the prison just as her husband's mistress was leaving. She was shocked and hurt at learning that even in prison her husband was faithless. That day Akiko was told she must wait in the prison anteroom until evening visiting hours because the prisoners were allowed only one visitor each afternoon. Finally, after much persuasion the prison officials permitted her to see her husband. Somehow she found the courage to question him in un-Japanese fashion about this other woman. He admitted that the other woman came to see him frequently and brought him presents and implied that he enjoyed these visits.

Angry and upset, Akiko returned home and poured out her troubles and complaints to the two Western women, one American and the other English, with whom she lived and worked. The American woman described the scene. "The pressure of Akiko's tension seemed to fill the room with an oppressive weight. She leaned forward to us. 'You,' she said, 'you are Western women. Give me advice then. Do you think I am justified in taking him by the kimono collar and shaking him just a little?' "[2]

From Companion to Servant

The Japanese woman has not always occupied such a low position in Japanese society. In the very early period of Japan's history she was the man's equal, his companion and not his servant. The *Manyoshu,* written in the seventh and eighth centuries, the oldest Japanese anthology of ancient poems, speaks of young men and women dancing and singing together in the springtime. They married in those days by mutual agreement, and they did not need the services of a go-betweens. The woman was the equal of man, and she fought, governed, and led armies to war. A famous empress, Jingo, about 200 A.D., led a powerful army into Korea. Women then were judged, as were men, on the basis of merit, since they

[2] Adapted from *Year of the Wild Boar* by Helen Mears, published by J. B. Lippincott Company, copyright 1942. Used with permission.

were regarded as individuals with the same rights and privileges as men had.

Circumstances began to change about the sixth century A.D. At that time Buddhism and Confucianism, bearers of Chinese and Indian ways of life, carried other ideas, attitudes, and customs to the Japanese people. As the cultural influences from the mainland came to dominate the Japanese social scene and as Japanese social patterns evolved, woman's intelligence was questioned and her talents were ignored. She began to be considered a follower rather than a leader, and a servant rather than an equal, with a place only in the home. It was no longer possible for her to dance with men in the warm light of spring without being considered an immoral woman, nor could she lead armies or govern the country. She finally was transformed into the woman who thought it an extreme act of defiance to think of taking an erring husband by the kimono collar and "shaking him just a little."

Training of the Ideal Woman

The training of the traditional type of Japanese woman began in childhood. She learned early in life that obedience, devotion to duty, patience, good nature, self-sacrifice, and submissiveness were the virtues expected of her and that her goal in life was to become an acceptable wife and a respected mother. She was also given practical training. She was taught to be an efficient housewife. She learned to sew, clean mats, wash clothes and woodwork, cook and serve meals, and performed all other household chores.

Certain variations in her training depended upon the social level that she occupied. The farm girl learned to help in the planting and harvesting of rice and other crops and to work at other tasks required by a farming family. The daughter of a higher-class family was taught ritual etiquette—the proper way to open and close doors, to enter and leave a room, to greet superiors and inferiors, to speak to relatives and friends, and to perform a thousand other formalities accumulated over a period of fifteen hundred years. Many were also taught the elaborate conventions that governed the serving of tea and the making of flower arrangements and trained to play some musical instrument.

The restrictions placed upon upper- and middle-class women were more onerous and more strictly enforced than those placed upon women of the farming and laboring groups. The latter, particularly if they were married, were much freer in their associations; they frequently smoked and drank together with the men of the house. Women on the upper levels rarely acted so freely, even with men who were close relatives. There were a number of reasons why this situation arose. The attitude regarding women that originated in the sixth century A.D. had less effect on lower levels of society. Women who worked on farms and at other physical tasks were much more important economically to farming and laboring families than the women of the upper classes were to their more wealthy families. It was more difficult for the poorer families to subsist without the help of their women. Men on this level could not afford to pay for the ouside companionship provided by the geishas and other women, and looked toward the home for the informality and relaxation to be found in mixed company. Wealthier men, on the other hand, could find companionship with the geishas and at the same time impose strict limitations upon the behavior of their wives at home.

Gradual Emancipation of the Japanese Woman

With the opening of Japan to Western penetration in the nineteenth century, the status of the Japanese woman slowly improved. She gradually began to regain the equality she had lost centuries before.

At first her progress was almost imperceptible. After the Meiji Restoration in 1868, the new rulers of Japan wanted a new political order and a new economic system, but not a new social system. They kept the Japanese woman out of politics by refusing her the right to vote and the opportunity to occupy political office. Girls were permitted a small amount of formal education, but this schooling remained an extension of their home training. They were taught that the Japanese people were one family, that their fathers and husbands were the representatives of the emperor, and that to disobey them was to disobey him. They were taught that the purpose of their education was only to make them better Japanese wives and mothers. However, the fact that they received six years of compulsory education widened their horizons and exposed them to influences which encouraged their efforts to resist an inferior status.

Although the new rulers were successful in keeping Japanese women out of politics, it was impossible to keep them out of the new economic system. They were needed to provide the cheap and efficient labor that Japan required to maintain a competitive position in world markets and to fill the many jobs that mushroomed in a rapidly industrializing nation. By 1936, Japanese women were engaged in all kinds of economic activities. Dressed in either Western or Japanese clothes they operated the telephone exchanges and served as conductresses on the motor buses. They worked as stenographers and typists in large business firms. They worked as "gasoline girls" in the service stations, clerked in large department stores, and waited on customers in tea shops and restaurants.

In all these cases, the new rulers made a determined effort to utilize the services of women without exposing them to dangerous thoughts of equality or to the social ways of Western women. The treatment of textile workers is a good example of how women were employed in a useful occupation and yet shielded from alien influences. Made to dress in a uniform consisting of a white middy blouse and black skirt, they worked in large textile factories surrounded by high walls which kept them penned in until their contracts expired. Sometimes these contracts ran for three years or more. The workers were usually recruited from the farms where their indoctrination in womanly obedience and submission was already almost complete. When the textile management contracted with the head of the household for their services and wages were agreed upon, the girls were ordered by their fathers or the heads of their households to enter the plant. The management then assumed responsibility for them. It was supposed to continue their education along traditional lines. In the better factories, classes were conducted in sewing, flower arrangement, reading, writing, and arithmetic. The girls were encouraged to use their spare time in making trousseaus and in preparing themselves for their future married life. Most of their wages were either taken for their support within the factory walls or sent home to their family heads. They were rarely permitted outside the walls. Some never went outside until their contracts had expired and they returned home to be married.

Still, the Japanese leaders were not successful in isolating Japanese women completely from the social currents sweeping in from the West. Once they had experienced the adventure of reading and the satisfaction of receiving a wage, women began to function independently and to enjoy the fruits of self-reliance.

The most obvious and superficial break with tradition was in makeup and dress. Narrow eyes, a small mouth, demure lips with very faint artificial coloring, natural eyebrows, a willowy frame, and delicate curving lines were the traditional marks of a beautiful Japanese woman. A high and well-shaped nose was considered a woman's most important facial feature. She "enhanced" this beauty by applying a dead-white makeup and painting her teeth black.

This traditional conception of beauty was modified by the impact of styles from France, England, and the United States. Although, traditionally, curly hair was regarded as unnatural, permanent waves became the fashion. Large and deep-set eyes enhanced by mascara became the most striking facial feature. Former dead-white cheeks were now enlivened with pink rouge. Lipstick followed the contour of the lips, and teeth came to be polished white instead of blackened. Many Japanese women adopted Western dress. They wore hats, dresses, suits, and sometimes Western-style shoes and silk and nylon stockings. The latest fashions from abroad were displayed in large department stores.

However, the Japanese woman could not throw off the traditions and attitudes of centuries as easily as she changed her makeup style. In fact, she never completely gave up her Japanese dress. Even though she liked and wore Western-style clothes, she also retained a Japanese wardrobe. Kimono manners and kimono customs continued to persist though she dressed in Western clothes and used Western makeup.

With the coming of World War II and the occupation of Japan by American forces, the Japanese woman made significant gains in raising her status and increasing her freedom of action. The war speeded up the hiring of women in industry. More and more women were required to man the machines and take over the jobs that had formerly been performed by men. Women became essential for the full and efficient operation of the Japanese economy. They started to realize their importance to the war effort and to the economy of the nation, and their self-respect grew with this realization. Many Japanese women were now ready for the reforms and legal freedoms which the Occupation and the new Constitution granted to the woman of Japan.

In October 1945, the Japanese woman was given the right to vote and to hold political office. The new Constitution, which became effective May 3, 1947, guaranteed these rights and gave women legal equality with men. A Japanese woman can now vote, pursue a career, run for office, and become the legal guardian of her children. Legally, divorce is no more difficult for her to obtain than it is for her husband. In addition, the Civil Code was revised to grant women full civic rights, and a law was passed extending compulsory education from six to nine years and establishing co-education in secondary schools and universities. Labor laws were enacted which promulgated the principle of equal pay for equal work and provided for special maternity benefits.

In many instances the Japanese women have made good use of these rights. In the first three general elections after they acquired the vote, six women were elected to the Diet. When the Peace Treaty was signed in 1951, twelve women were in the Lower House and twelve in the House of Councillors. There were 961 women in various local assemblies, and five held the office of village chief. Women's organizations multiplied; membership in these organizations is estimated to be over six million today. Large-scale educational programs in political and social matters are being sponsored and undertaken by the Y.W.C.A., Japan's League of Women Voters, and the League of Democratic Women. The government has established a Women's and Minor's Bureau in the Labor Ministry to promote the interests of women and children. In 1960, a woman was appointed Welfare Minister. She was the first woman to hold a cabinet post, and served for four months. In 1969, there were seven women in the 486-member lower house, and thirteen in the 250-member upper house.

Expanding urbanization, as well as laws and better education, is also contributing to the liberation of the Japanese woman from the restraints of the past. Lured by beckoning opportunities, expanded freedoms, and material advantages, the youth of Japan, married and unmarried, are migrating from the rural areas to the cities, and staying there. The majority of Japanese now live in cities. Removed from the more conservative pressures of the countryside and influenced by the more liberal attitudes and practices of the city, young men and women are adopting customs and engaging in activities which are more like the modern West than the traditional Japanese. For instance, it has been estimated that almost 50 percent of the urban women workers are married (80 percent of the rural women workers are married, but this is a traditional Japanese practice). Traditionally, it was considered shameful for a husband to have his wife work outside the home. Encouraged by the example of others, and spurred by the desire to buy the better life—television sets, radios, stereos, apartments, houses, washing machines—growing numbers of wives as well as husbands are working at a variety of jobs outside the home. The forests of antennas that rise above suburban roofs, the car-packed streets, the now commonplace refrigerator and washing machine, are but a few witnesses of the rising income of Japanese families. And the working wife has contributed substantially to the purchasing power of this modern Japanese family.

Education, new laws, exposure to the city and the world, rising expectations, and economic necessity, have all contributed to the enlarging independence and equality of the Japanese woman. But Japan is still largely a man's country. The father still remains the head of the household, and sons are yet more welcome than daughters in many families. All-male nightly parties serviced by female entertainers in restaurant and night club are customary and socially acceptable in Japanese society, and tolerated, publicly, at least, by Japanese wives, and there are very few Japanese women holding important positions in government, commercial and other large organizations.

Many Japanese women remain traditional in their attitudes, customs, and dress. This is especially true of the decreasing numbers of rural women. Although she has felt some of the alien currents brought in by the Westerners, especially the Americans, and the sweeping winds of modernization, she has not always felt them deeply or applied them to her daily life. Her marriage is still arranged for her, her modesty and obedience still praised, and her more traditional female role stressed. Nor are arranged marriages confined to rural women. The husbands of Emperor Hirohito's two daughters were picked by the emperor's mother, the Dowager Empress Teimei. At the request of the emperor the court officials chose an eligible wife for the Crown Prince.

The impact of more liberal attitudes was felt first by the women of the upper and middle classes who lived mostly in the cities. They had been traditionally the most restricted and therefore the most eager to escape. These women were educated, exposed, and susceptible to those ideas and attitudes which promised them more freedom and independence. And the women of the cities are among the most progressive women of modern Japan.

35

Politics in Japan

Art. I The Empire of Japan shall be reigned over and governed by a line of Emperors unbroken for ages eternal. . . .

Art. III The Emperor is sacred and inviolable.

Art. IV The Emperor is the head of the Empire, combining in Himself the rights of sovereignty, and exercises them, according to the provisions of the present Constitution.

—The Constitution of the Empire of Japan (1889)

Art. I The Emperor shall be the symbol of the State and of the unity of the people, deriving his position from the will of the people with whom resides sovereign power. . . .

Art. III The advice and approval of the Cabinet shall be required for all acts of the Emperor in matters of state, and the Cabinet shall be responsible therefor.

Art. IV The Emperor shall perform only such acts in matters of state as are provided for in this Constitution and he shall not have powers related to government.

—The Constitution of Japan (1947)

Politics in Japan are being pulled in many directions by forces of the past and the present. In the short period of eighty years, Japan was torn from centuries of isolation, forced to put on the institutional trappings of Western democracies, and transformed from a semifeudal association of lords into a centralized modern nation.

During this period, aided by modern technology, Japan expanded into one of the greatest empires on earth. It defeated China in 1895, routed Russia in 1905, shared in the victory of World War I as an allied power in 1918, and annexed Manchuria in the 1939s. Her widespread empire disintegrated with terrible suddenness at the conclusion of World War II, and her own homeland was occupied and governed by American troops. The Americans launched a determined effort to change the political system of Japan into one patterned after Western models.

To have all this happen within the short space of eight decades to a country which had long been isolated from world events left most Japanese mentally and emotionally gasping. If permitted, the Japanese would probably have tried to retire from the world for a time to meditate on their recent history and to make plans for a slower pace in the future. But they were soon caught up again in the vortex of domestic and world crises. They have had little time or opportunity to plan their political evolution in a leisurely way, and they have been forced to search for suitable political institutions that will enable them to face the future with some degree of security and stability while at the same time coping with the daily complexities of government.

Whatever the outward appearance of their evolving political system, it will be permeated with a spirit that comes from deep in Japan's past. The Japan of tomorrow will be a product of the Japan of yesterday, and there will be no understanding of it until there is some understanding of old Japan's political life.

The Rise of the Imperial System

The Clan of Yamato

The early political life of the Japanese was organized around a clan system. About the beginning of the Christian era there were a number of clans in central and western Japan, each presided over by a high priest or priestess. One of these clans lived in the Yamato Plain just south of the present-day city of Kyoto in central Honshu and was called the Yamato clan. Loosely speaking, a clan is a division of a tribe which traces its descent from a common ancestor and the members of which bear the same surname. In China and in Japan a feeling of brotherhood and a spirit of cooperation characterized the clan institution.

The Yamato clan prospered and expanded until, by about the third or fourth century A.D., it was the dominant clan in central and western Japan. The high priest of the Yamato clan assumed first place among the clan chiefs, and worship of the sun goddess—the divine ancestress of the Yamato clan—became an integral part of the worship of the other clans. The descendant of the high priest of the Yamato clan reigns today as Hirohito, Emperor of Japan, and the sun goddess for many is still the primary deity of the Japanese nation.

The Emperor

The emperor system in Japan is remarkable for its age. For over fifteen hundred years the ancestors of the present emperor have reigned in Japan. Few families of royal blood today can claim such a history of unbroken reign reaching far back into the early centuries of the Christian era. It is true that, during most of this time, the royal family of Japan possessed little actual power, but the emperor as an embodied institution of divine descent has long commanded the reverence and honor of the Japanese people. The regime of Hirohito is a living witness to the tenacity and ability with which the Japanese have preserved a cherished heritage through all the vicissitudes of time.

This same tenacity and ability are manifested in the worship of the sun goddess. The transfer of her worship from a family to a national cult was completed by the sixth century A.D. From that time to the present this worship has been enshrined in the hearts of the Japanese people and constantly reinforces the right of the imperial family to reign. Just as the sun goddess is first among the gods of Japan, so must her descendant, the emperor, be first among the people of Japan.

Japan Borrows from China

From late in the sixth century until early in the ninth century, Japan borrowed heavily from the magnificent civilization of its neighbor, China. Buddhism was instrumental in calling the attention of the Japanese to the wonderful cultural achievements of the Chinese. Its priests carried samples of this culture from Korea to Japan. Gradually, the Japanese awareness of Chinese civilization turned into a desire to imitate, especially since this was the period when the T'ang Dynasty ruled in China. It was one of the finest periods in China's history, and the Japanese were impressed. Convinced that an adaptation of many of the administrative features and political institutions of this dynasty would strengthen the Yamato government, the Japanese leaders began a systematic and purposeful borrowing from China.

At that time Japanese clans possessed a large measure of autonomy. The chiefs of the Yamato or imperial clan ruled more by reason of prestige and by balancing and mediating struggles between clans than because of their own economic and military strength. Prince Shotoku, one of the earliest of those leaders who wanted to establish a strong central government headed by the imperial clan, stated the substance of their desire when he said: "The Sovereign is the master of the people of the whole country; the officials to whom he gives control are his vassals." These Yamato clan leaders controlled the Japanese sovereign; they schemed to increase his power in order to extend their own control over the autonomous clans.

In pursuit of this aim the Yamato state was reconstructed by its supporters to resemble the Chinese empire. The chief of the Yamato clan was installed as an emperor holding all secular power as well as functioning as the high priest of the country. Under a theoretically all-powerful emperor there was established a complex administration which, with some exceptions, was similar to that of the T'ang government in China. The country was divided into prefectures, approximately like states, and subprefectures, somewhat like counties. The emperor appointed officials to govern these prefectures in his name. This measure, of course, brought the clans under the closer supervision of the central government. The government bureaucracy was financed by taxing each adult who possessed land. The central government was housed in the new capital of Nara, which was especially built for this purpose and modeled after Ch'ang-an, the capital of the T'ang Dynasty. Thus, in the interests of centralization, a new system of local government, of land tenure, and of taxation was imposed upon the Japanese.

Although outwardly and on paper these imposed institutions gave the Japanese government a striking resemblance to the Chinese administration, they were in spirit and in content very Japanese. Adaptation and modification were inevitable, for while the Japanese could borrow the external forms of the Chinese system, they could not borrow the long centuries of evolution that had gone into the making of this system. The Chinese political system flowered from philosophical roots which had first been planted over a thousand years before in feudal China. Even in China it had not succeeded immediately. Not for many centuries did the key figures of the Chinese administration, the examination-tested civil servants, come to occupy the positions formerly held by hereditary rulers. A tradition of loyalty and public service had to be built up over the years; it did not come overnight.

In Japan, family and heredity determined one's position on the social scale. The aristocrat by blood ranked highest. Accordingly, appointment to top positions in the new Japanese bureaucracy was based on heredity and family connections rather than learning. Most of the provincial posts fell into the hands of the local aristocrats. At the capital the hereditary nobles occupied the important positions. The autonomy of the clans continued, though in theory they received their power to govern from the emperor. Instead of developing an administrative system which was staffed by an educated personnel loyal to the central government, as in China, the Japanese devised a system which confirmed the value of heredity and clan loyalties by confining official positions to aristocrats.

Another instance of the Japanizing of Chinese institutions and concepts is found in the emperor system. The Chinese emperor was checked in his use of absolute power by the right of the people to revolt if he should rule badly. This idea was alien to the Japanese because a divine emperor could do no wrong. Therefore, revolt against the emperor has never been condoned in Japan. The result was that the centralization of secular authority, borrowed from the Chinese system, conferred more power on the chief priest of the Yamato clan than had been enjoyed by the Chinese emperors.

Emperor's Power Flows into Other Hands

From the ninth to the twelfth century the emperor's power declined until he became almost a puppet in the hands of his court nobles and their allied provincial aristocrats. During this period most provincial posts were filled by local aristocrats, and at the capital hereditary nobles occupied the most influential positions. The ministerial offices of the central administration became hereditary—another example of the Japanese modification of China's administrative system—and the lands of the great court families and monasteries were exempted from taxation. One of the principal reasons for the decline of the emperor's power was the increase of these independent tax-free estates called *shoen,* or manors. As the amount of tax-free land increased, larger taxes were imposed upon the remaining taxable land. This additional tax forced the owners of the taxable land to cede their land to holders of tax-free estates. The holders of these lands would then give them back in return for a share in the produce. The increased wealth and power that came from the possession of tax-free land strengthened the great court families and the monasteries.

The Fujiwara were the greatest of these families. They held power in Japan by ruling through the emperor and using him as a figurehead. Kamatari, the founder of the Fujiwara family, began to rule Japan in this manner as early as 645 A.D. It was Kamatari who championed the introduction of a Chinese type of administration in order to centralize imperial government control. His son ruled behind six emperors during the period 659 to 720 A.D. The Fujiwara family maintained control of the emperor by marrying him to a Fujiwara girl and then forcing him to abdicate after he had fathered offspring old enough to carry out the ceremonies required of his office. The head of the Fujiwara family would then assume the office of regent who ruled during the minority of the emperor. In the ninth century the Fujiwara family transformed the regency into the office of civil dictator, which enabled a Fujiwara to rule openly even after the emperor had reached his majority. In effect, this was a dual monarchy, for the Fujiwara could also appoint the highest officers in the land and thus operate an independent and separate government.

In time, the offices and appointing power became hereditary in the Fujiwara family who continued to monopolize them until the nineteenth century. By that time, however, these offices and privileges had become merely nominal. Political power passed from the Fujiwara to the feudal military class. But just as the Fujiwara did not usurp the throne of the emperor, the new feudal leaders did not usurp the offices that had become hereditary in the Fujiwara family. This preservation of an office or institution even after the power it originally held has been lost exemplifies the tendency in Japan for offices to become hereditary and pointedly illustrates the respect the Japanese hold for tradition.

After the Fujiwara family declined in power, other family clans like the Taira, Minamoto, Ashikaga, and Tokugawa established feudal military governments which ruled the country. However, they continued to maintain the institutions of emperor, civil dictator, and regency and all the other apparatus of imperial government in Kyoto, the capital of the country. The latest example of dual government in Japan was the military government of the American occupation forces. This military government held all the real power in Japan, but the emperor and his civil government continued to reign by the side of the military government.

The Feudal Period of Japan

The period from the twelfth to the nineteenth century in Japan was the Feudal Period. The three main periods of Japanese feudalism were: 1) the Kamakura shogunate (1185 to 1333), which was founded by the Minamoto clan; 2) the Ashikaga shogunate (1333 to 1568); and 3) the Tokugawa shogunate (1600 to 1868).

Prior to the Kamakura shogunate there arose in Japan a military class which was supported by tax-free manorial estates. Territorial holdings, the most important source of wealth in Japan, could be retained and expanded only by the use of force. Under these circumstances the military class became the most important class, and in the twelfth century two associations of knights headed by the Taira and Minamoto clans respectively emerged as the strongest military forces in the country. The military association headed by the Minamoto clan was ultimately victorious and a military government, called the Kamakura shogunate, was set up at the city of Kamakura. The tax-free manors of the Taira clan were confiscated and given as grants to the loyal vassals of the Minamoto clan. Its chief, Yoritomo, was given the title of *shogun*, or "Barbarian-Subduing General," which gave him command of all the military forces in Japan. Thus began a feudalistic type of government in Japan which characterized Japanese government from this time until the entrance of Japan into the modern world system in 1868. It is frequently called *bakufu*, or "tent government."

Another example of the Japanese political custom of ruling through a figurehead is to be found in the early years of this shogunate. The Hojo family was a member of the Taira clan, but Tokimasa, its head, early joined the association of knights headed by the Minamoto clan. After Yoritomo's death, he became regent for Yoritomo's second son and thereby established a rule by Hojo regents who continued to use the shoguns as figureheads for over a hundred years.

Obviously, things are not always what they seem in Japanese politics. A noted modern authority on Japan, Mr. Edwin O. Reischauer, observed in his book *Japan Past and Present:*

Thus, one finds in the 13th century Japan an emperor who was a mere puppet in the hands of a retired emperor and of a great court family, the Fujiwara, who together controlled a government which was in fact merely a sham government, completely dominated by the private government of the Shogun—who in turn was a puppet in the hands of a Hojo regent. The man behind the throne had become a series of men, each one in turn controlled by the man behind himself.[1]

The Kamakura shogunate started a feudal type of military government which was uniquely Japanese in character. The military generalissimos called shoguns were aided in their rule of Japan by a number of powerful lords who held their land as grants from them. Though vassals of the shoguns, they were supreme within their own domains. This was feudalism in the sense that the right to govern was conceived of as a property right which belonged to anyone who possessed a manor or fief. The reciprocal relations of a military, social, and political nature which existed between the lords and the shogun, and between the lords and those who peopled their domains, were also feudal. The lords owed the shogun loyal and obedient service in return for the granting of their fiefs or domains. Those who lived in the lords' domains owed them also loyal and obedient service in return for their protection and livelihood. Thus Japan, alone among Asian countries, developed something very like European feudalism. The first British ambassador, Sir John Alcock, after seeing the daimyo with their armed retainers, remarked that it seemed like England in the time of the War of the Roses.

The period of the Ashikaga shogunate was marked by more fighting among the military men in the provinces, by the emergence of the peasant as a foot-soldier succeeding the knight on horseback, and by the rise of the great feudal lords called *daimyo*. These daimyo divided all of Japan among themselves, leaving nothing to the emperor or to the court nobles. Their well-defined territories were the foundation of the political system from about the fourteenth century to the Meiji Restoration of 1868.

These powerful daimyo were ultimately subdued and united

---

[1] Edwin O. Reischauer, *Japan: Past and Present,* ed. 2 (New York: Alfred A. Knopf, 1953). Used with permission.

by the efforts of three very famous men—Oda Nobunaga, Toyotomi Hideyoshi, and Tokugawa Ieyasu. The last founded the famous Tokugawa shogunate which continued until the nineteenth century and was Japan's ultimate feudal government prior to its emergence as a modern state.

The Tokugawa Shogunate

The basic political objective of Tokugawa Ieyasu, the founder of the Tokugawa shogunate, and his successors was to preserve the political power of their house forever. To this end Tokugawa established a political system which might be described as a centralized feudalism. It was feudal in that the basic political unit of the country was the daimyo's sharply outlined territory which he held as a grant from the shogun. The daimyo, within certain limits imposed by the shogun, was the absolute ruler of his land, and the office of daimyo was hereditary. The granting of these domains by the daimyo gave rise to the reciprocal obligations characteristic of feudalism.

The Tokugawa shogunate was centralized in that a strong central government was set up at Edo, the present Tokyo. It carefully scrutinized the words and actions of the daimyo and limited drastically their power and scope of action. Rigid controls were imposed upon these great lords, such as requiring them to keep their families in Edo as hostages, discouraging visits from one daimyo to another, and surrounding the domains of less loyal daimyo with those persons more loyal to the Tokugawa family. The Tokugawa government even produced a crop of spies who reported daily to the shogunate about the various activities of the daimyo and their supporters. Furthermore, visits of the daimyo or their supporters to the emperor in Kyoto were forbidden except with the express consent of the central government, because the Tokugawas did not want anyone else to control the imperial government at Kyoto. Change of any sort was frowned upon and the social structure of society, with the warrior class at the top and the merchants and artisans at the bottom, was frozen. Finally, to prevent any possible threat from outside the country, Japan was sealed off from the world and no one, Japanese or foreigner, was permitted to enter or leave the country. The only exceptions were the crew of a Dutch ship once a year and a few Chinese traders.

This centralized feudalistic system of government worked well for the Tokugawa shogunate, and for more than two centuries the Tokugawa family remained in power. It was only after a long evolution of economic and social forces, which exploded shortly after the forcible penetration of Japan by the West in the nineteenth century, that the Tokugawa shogunate fell. It was succeeded by a type of government more Western in form, but similar to the Tokugawa government in spirit and attitude.

Military Dominance in Japan

The spirit and attitude which characterized the Tokugawa shogunate are revealed in the continued dominance of the military class of Japan. Out of the stress and uncertainty of war in feudal Japan the military emerged as the dominant group with a special code of behavior and morality. First came the knight with his armor, horse, and sword, who introduced the ideals of mental and physical conditioning. He was succeeded by the *samurai*, or "one who serves," who carried on the military ideals and held a prominent place in Japanese political life well into the twentieth century. The code of the samurai warrior is called *bushido*, or "Way of the Warrior," which values loyalty to the overlord above all else and teaches that bravery and obedience are the fundamental qualities of the good Japanese soldier. For over seven hundred years these ideals were glorified. Personal loyalty, reciprocal obligations, mental and physical discipline, courage, and obedience were the criteria by which the Japanese judged themselves and others. Since it was the military class which best exemplified these virtues, the Japanese, even in modern times, have generally looked up to it. The military set the pattern by which the people lived. Their words were to be listened to with respect; their commands carried out without question.

It is not surprising that the modern political life of the Japanese has been greatly dominated by military leaders. It was a group of young samurai who started the revolution against the Tokugawas and replaced feudalism with a modern centralized state.

Encroachment by Western powers set the stage. In 1853 and 1854 Commodore Matthew C. Perry, an American, forced the closed gates of Japan by means of his black warships. In 1863 the English bombarded the southern city of Kagoshima in revenge for the murder of an Englishman. In the following year a fleet of allied Western warships fired on Shimonoseki, a city in southwest Japan, in retaliation for an attack on some Western merchant ships. In each case the Japanese were powerless to reply. This was a military lesson they never forgot, and from that time onward a small group of samurai leaders determined to make Japan as strong as possible.

They worked toward a strong state in two directions: they strengthened the central government by domestic reforms, and they started a systematic and intensive study of Western nations for the purpose of borrowing those qualities of Western culture which made Western nations strong.

Domestic Reforms

In 1868 the Tokugawa shogunate was removed and a government bestowed upon the people which, at least theoretically, centered around the emperor. He was brought from the obscurity of the old capital of Kyoto and installed as the head of the state in the new capital of Tokyo. The divinity of his ancestors and his absolute right to rule Japan were emphasized. The shogun was now pictured as a usurper of the emperor's power. Ancient Japanese mythology was revived in order to give further support to his divine authority. The sun goddess, ancestress of the imperial family, was honored as the primary deity of Japan. The emperor was made the main prop of the new Japanese government, and all religious and secular power was concentrated in his person.

There was precedence for this restoration, for the new leaders were utilizing the emperor in much the same way that the Fujiwara family and the shoguns had used him—as a front for their rule. As in old Japan, the emperor reigned but he did not rule.

Government was centralized even more than formerly. In a few short years, the daimyo were persuaded to deed their land over to the central government in exchange for money and privileges. These feudal domains were then made into prefectures governed by officials appointed by the central government. The samurai or warrior class was stripped of many feudal privileges. Universal military conscription was introduced, which brought all classes of young men into military service instead of only a priviliged few. Of course, the military ideals and spirit were retained, but the military was directly responsible to the central authority in Tokyo and not to some feudal daimyo.

Selections from the West

At the same time these vigorous samurai leaders initiated a study of Western institutions and technology that was far more systematic and extensive than the earlier study of Chinese culture. Students were carefully picked. They were then sent to various great nations to learn all they could about the special features for which each nation was famous. Naval students were usually sent to England, army and medical students to Germany, law and education students to France, and business and education students to the United States. One group, headed by Prince Ito Hirobumi, traveled all over the world searching for the Western constitution that would be most suitable for Japan's particular needs. Such a constitution was finally found in Germany.

Within a short time the political and economic face of Japan was radically changed. A constitution was adopted which provided for a cabinet and a parliamentary body consisting of two houses whose members were elected. The courts and law codes were reformed and patterned after those of France. A Western type of civil service was organized to administer the government. The tax system was broadened and standardized. A banking system was set up modeled after that of the West. Japan very soon resembled Western nations in many ways, but the resemblance was only surface deep, for Japan still retained her old ways of thought and action.

Control by a Small Group

The small group of men who governed the country in the name of the emperor numbered less than one hundred. From the restoration of the emperor in 1868 until 1918, this small band came mostly from the samurai class. But as time went on, they were joined by others who had amassed wealth in business and controlled great portions of Japan's economy. These men, too, were frequently samurai who had entered business when samurai privileges were removed. This economic clique, which worked closely with the militarists and bureaucrats in making Japan an industrialized and trading nation, is commonly referred to as the *zaibatsu*, which means "money faction." Led by four big business interests which overshadowed the others, the zaibatsu controlled the Japanese economy until the end of World War II. Large business groupings again dominate the economy today.

This oligarchy of military, economic, and bureaucratic cliques decided that universal education was required if the country was to make any substantial progress as a modern industrial state. The Japanese leaders soon learned that Japan could not industrialize, nor could her soldiers learn quickly the techniques of modern warfare, unless the Japanese were taught to read and write. Accordingly, universal education was instituted, and education for a minimum number of years—at that time six—became compulsory. It should be noted, however, that there already were many schools in Japan and many literate Japanese at this time. This education was not intended primarily to improve the individual's future standard of living or to meet individual needs, but rather to serve as a means of training and conditioning the people to be useful and submissive servants of the state. The goal was not to improve the individual but to improve the position of the nation on the international scene.

Although political parties arose during the twentieth century, which on the surface were democratic, they possessed a feudal structure and spirit which were peculiarly Japanese. Japan's political parties were headed by a leader or leaders who were regarded in much the same light by their members as the feudal lord of earlier days was regarded by his retainers. The same obedience was demanded, the same mutual relationship of responsibility and service was expected, and personal relations continued to be more important than law and principle. Here, as in the many other Western institutions borrowed by Japan prior to World War II the form was of the West but the spirit and heart were of old Japan.

In 1868 the Japanese were much more successful in establishing a centralized government than when they borrowed from China back in the seventh and eighth centuries. It was a much more efficient and systematic adoption and took place more rapidly. But in each instance, the new concepts and institutions brought in from the outside were imposed upon the country by a small band of leaders.

The Postwar Period

After Japan's defeat in World War II, a third purposive borrowing took place. Emperor Hirohito was persuaded to renounce his divinity and to become a symbol rather than a god to the Japanese people. Religion was divorced from politics, and church and state became separate as in the United States. The rights of the people and the worth of the individual were emphasized in order to offset and counteract the conception that the individual had value and meaning only as a member of a community. Equality of opportunity and equality before the law were stressed. Government by law was made fundamental in the new Japan, in contradistinction to the former concept that law was a guide for the ruler rather than a protector of the rights of the individual. All these innovations were incorporated into a new Constitution granted to the people of Japan by the occupying American authorities. A no-war clause was also incorporated into this new Constitution. This Constitution continues to serve as the basic legal authority and foundation for the present Japanese government although some of its underlying principles are now being reevaluated by Japanese lawmakers.

During most of the postwar period, Japan has been governed by a coalition of major business interests and bureaucrats. The party which they have led and supported is known as the Liberal Democratic Party. This party has also had the support of the rural people in Japan. The party leaders gave special attention to those living and working in the countryside while at the same time favoring the great economic interests of Japan at home and abroad. Their policies led to a fantastic economic boom in Japan, and ultimately to a ranking as the third economic power in the world. The United States and the Soviet Union rank one and two as economic giants in the world.

Real growth rates for the period between 1958 and 1963 averaged around 13 percent, and in 1968 it was around 12 percent. Since 1960, Japan's gross national product surged from forty-five billion dollars to over two hundred billion dollars. It has continued to move up but at a slower pace in recent years. Japan is the world's largest builder of ships. They are especially noted for their construction of super tankers and bulk carriers of more than three hundred thousand tons. Japan ranks behind the United States in the production of cars, trucks, and buses. It is one of the largest producers of steel, and its production of TV sets, radios, synthetic textiles, chemicals, plastics, and electronic equipment, among others, is very well known throughout the world.

Japan's trade and investments now span the world, ranging, for example, from auto assembling in Thailand, South Africa, and Mexico, to a pulp mill in Alaska, iron sheet fabrication in Ethiopia, iron mining in Brazil, and marketing and manufacturing in the United States. Resourceful engineers and business entrepreneurs are to be found in even the remotest parts of the world exploring for the natural resources Japan needs and arranging for the exploitation of these resources in partnership with Japan. The Japanese became so single-minded in their economic endeavors that their country became known to many as Japan, Inc.

It was, and is, necessary for the Japanese to import most of the raw materials they require to maintain and sustain their industrial machine. The land of Japan has few natural resources. This heavy dependence upon outside sources to preserve their economic way of life has resulted, at times, in a rethinking and, sometimes, changes in their domestic and foreign policies. In 1973, for example, the Arab leaders demanded that Japan take a more pro-Arab stand against Israel if the Japanese were to continue to receive oil from the Arab-producing states. The Japanese panicked. They are very dependent upon oil as an energy source. Their foreign policy shifted to a more pro-Arab one. They began placating the Arabs with promises of grants and technological aid. The Japanese continued to receive Arab oil, but at much higher prices.

These higher prices contributed to the soaring inflation which struck Japan and other countries in the world in recent years. Japan began to experience increasing unrest on the part of wage earners in many areas of their economic life. Strikes and demonstrations for higher wages became more common in Japan. The majority party, the Liberal Democratic Party, was blamed for not giving enough attention to the basic needs of the people, especially for those living in urban areas. The great majority of Japanese now live in urban areas. The Japanese began to vote in greater numbers for the Socialist and Communist Parties who promised to better the lives of the ordinary Japanese. These parties and the Komeito Party make up the main opposition parties in Japan. The Komeito Party, which has real if informal ties to the Buddhist sect known as Soka Gakkai, holds a significant, if minority, position in the Japanese Diet.

Japanese leaders are also grappling with the problem of Japan's future role in Asia and the world. During the postwar period Japan has been protected by a security treaty with the United States which provided the Japanese with a nuclear umbrella and sanctioned the presence of U.S. military forces on Japanese territory. This protection, plus the fact that the United States is Japan's main trading partner, has kept the Japanese closely tied to the United States. Japan has a very small defense force, and has been spending only about 1 percent of its gross national product on defense. Some authorities both inside and outside Japan have urged the Japanese to increase their spending on defense. However, most Japanese have been opposed to any policy which might lead to the militarism of the past. A number of Japanese, mostly leftist in attitude, have even demonstrated against the presence of American military forces in Japan. They, and other Japanese, believe that the presence of American forces would place Japan in a most dangerous situation if there was a confrontation between the United States and other great powers such as the Soviet Union and China. They argue that a peaceful and neutral policy stance will be most beneficial to the Japanese in the long run.

The Japanese leaders have taken certain diplomatic actions to improve their relations with their neighboring countries in East Asia. In 1972, Japan and the People's Republic of China agreed to establish formal diplomatic relations. They severed their formal diplomatic relations with Taiwan, although they continued to maintain economic relations between the two countries. At the request of the Soviet Union, the Japanese considered the possibility of cooperating with the Soviet Union in exploiting the resources of Siberia. Due to the intense Sino-Soviet antagonism, the Chinese did not look favorably upon such a cooperative arrangement with the Soviet Union. And there is the problem of Korea, an area of great concern to the Japanese. They have a large and increasing investment in South Korea, and there is always the possibility that the North Koreans might attempt once again to reunify Korea by force. Such a conflict would force some painful decisions upon the Japanese leaders. There is the continuing suspicion on the part of many Asians, especially the Chinese and Southeast Asians, about the present and future intentions of the Japanese. They have not forgotten the invasions of their soil by the Japanese prior to and during World War II. A number of Southeast Asian leaders have stated that the Japanese are now trying to get through economic penetration what they could not get formerly through military force. These and other factors are influencing the Japanese leaders as they formulate policies for their future role in Asia and the world.

The occupation troops have long left Japan, but for the most part the institutions they set up continue in force. There are many indications, however, that the innovations are now being modified to harmonize with the Japanese patterns of life. Rarely, if ever, is it possible to make an individual into one's own image and likeness; it is even less possible to remake a country to fit one's political convictions. The American leaders of the occupation tried with vigor and imagination to reform Japan's political and economic attitudes and institutions, but were only partially successful. Much that was done remains, but centuries-old political and social traditions bear much weight on the Japanese scene. Although domestic and outside pressures are forcing changes in the lives of the Japanese, they are made within the context of accustomed modes of thought and practice. The outcome is always something uniquely Japanese.

36

Southeast Asia

Up to this point, it would appear that the countries of South and East Asia have been over-emphasized. This would be true only if the ideological, economic, social, and political thought and institutions of these countries had no similarity to, or influence upon, the patterns of life and thought in other Asian countries. But this is not true, for many of the traditional beliefs and practices of the people of South and East Asia are embedded deeply in the traditions of all Asian countries. Selected aspects of the life of the people in the larger countries of South and East Asia were stressed in order to provide the reader with a basic knowledge of the life of *all* Asians. An understanding of the thought and life

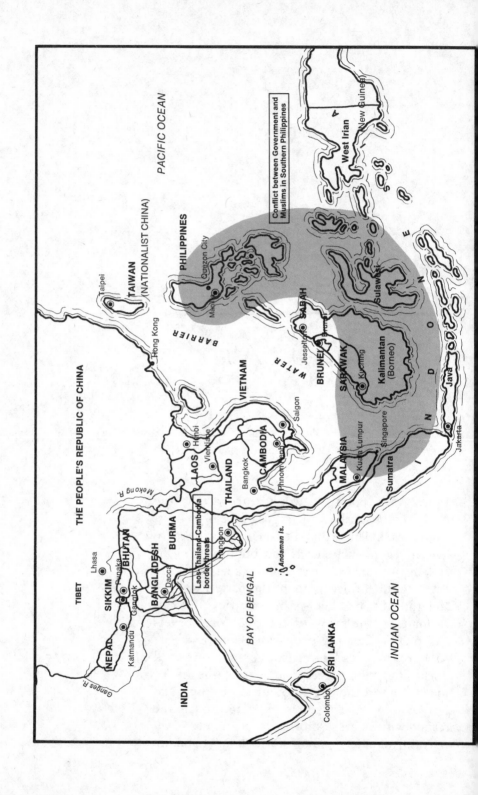

of the people of South and East Asia will bring with it a greater comprehension of all Asians and will serve as a firm foundation for more detailed readings on other individual countries and peoples, such as those of Southeast Asia.

Southeast Asia consists mainly of two regions—the Indochina peninsula on the mainland of Asia, and the two island groups of Indonesia and the Philippines. On the northern part of the island of Borneo are the Protectorate of Brunei and two parts of Malaysia—Sarawak and Sabah which together form East Malaysia. Vietnam, Laos, Cambodia, Thailand, Burma, West Malaysia, and Singapore are located on the Indochina peninsula.

Similarities to Other Regions of Asia

In terms of topography and climate, there is a great similarity between all of the Southeast Asian countries. Mountains are a prominent feature in every part of this region, and the cones of active volcanoes are a common sight in the Philippines as well as in Indonesia. The climate is either equatorial monsoon, with rain most of the year, or tropical monsoon, with periodic rains and a wet and dry season. In either case, rainfall is abundant. The similarity of topography and climate results in similar ways of living.

The general description, given in the early chapters of this book, of where and how most Asians make a living also embraces the people of Southeast Asia. Most of the Asians in this area, like Asians elsewhere, are farmers who depend upon human and animal labor rather than on the machine; water buffaloes and oxen are as intimately related to the people and the landscape as they are in other Asian countries. Like most Asians, the people of Southeast Asia look upon rice, vegetables, and, to some extent, wheat, as staple foods. The cultivation of wet rice creates long vistas of reflecting pools of paddies which are so many mirrors of rural scenes throughout Asia. Here, too, the villages house the majority of the people. Except for any striking differences in physical structure and facial characteristics, the Southeast Asian might find it very difficult to determine that an unidentified picture of a man stripped to the waist and cultivating his rice fields in another

Conflicts among and within the countries of Southeast Asia have sometimes involved non-Asian powers in modern times.

region of Asia was not a faithful portrayal of a typical Southeast Asian scene. But the bonds that tie them to other Asians are not merely physical; they are also spiritual.

Religion has played a key role in shaping the cultural heritage of the Asian people. Asians have long believed in the divinity of nature, and offerings to the spirits of the mountains, lakes, and forests are still a common practice. The great religions of Buddhism, Hinduism, and Islam have influenced all Asian cultures. Buddhism influences the life and thought of millions of Asians everywhere and is deeply rooted in the soil of a number of Southeast Asian countries. Hinduism did not have the missionary force that drove Buddhism outside the borders of India, but Hindu teaching and practice did penetrate Indonesia and other parts of Southeast Asia, Bangladesh, Pakistan and Indonesia are the largest Muslim nations in the world, and China, Philippines, and India all possess large minorities of Muslims. Confucianism and Taoism, products of Chinese thought, have influenced the religious and philosophical thought of some Southeast Asian countries for centuries.

Similar social customs connect the people of Asia. The people of Southeast Asia are familiar with the joint or large family system which is found throughout the entire region of Asia. Under this system father, mother, unmarried children, and married sons with their wives and children live together under one roof and generally have a common budget. There are variations of this family system from country to country, but the Thai, Burmese, Malayan, Vietnamese, and Indonesian people would immediately recognize and accept this system wherever they found it. They would know, too, that, with increasing urbanization and industrialization, this system is breaking down and that in Tokyo, Bombay, Osaka, and other large cities they will find increasing numbers of small Western-style families, because the same social change is evident in Jakarta, Saigon, Bangkok, Rangoon, and other large cities of Southeast Asia.

The women of Southeast Asia appreciate the attitudes and problems of women in other parts of Asia. Trudging home from the paddies at dusk, the women of Vietnam feel the same fatigue that grips their sisters who must labor in the fields of Japan. The traditional woman of Indonesia would find nothing strange in the attitude of the Indian woman who places the male before herself and grows old before her time in her constant and untiring efforts for the husband and the family. The modern woman of Malaysia and the Philippines sympathizes with her counterparts in China and Japan who are straining to raise their social status and, when necessary, fights with the same determination and spirit for her rights.

The young men and women who study and work in Southeast Asia share the eagerness of the youth in China, India, Pakistan, and Japan to change some of the traditional customs of their countries. It is still a common practice in Asia for marriage contracts to be negotiated and concluded between families, rather than solely between the individuals concerned. The prospective bride and bridegroom are frequently consulted and asked if they have any serious objection to the boy or girl under consideration, but the final decision is a family decision. The young Southeast Asian has the same longing as his peers elsewhere to be free to choose his own mate. However, even when he has this freedom, the wishes of the family are taken seriously, and their approval of the match is usually sought.

The young people of Southeast Asia, like their contemporaries in other countries of Asia, are impatient with the slow pace of their country's evolution into a modern nation-state. They blame their leaders for rigidity in holding to the ways of the past. They blame the peasants for their bovine attitude and for their resignation when natural and other calamities befall them. They blame the entire social system of the country for not affording them an opportunity to participate actively in the country's affairs, and they become frustrated. Their frustration, like that of their peers throughout Asia, leaves them receptive to suggestions to work actively in change-overnight schemes presented them by authoritarian dogmatists. They may, or may not, become dogmatic revolutionaries, but the conditions and processes that led them to the brink of acceptance are as familiar to them as they are to the youth of Laos and Vietnam.

The teachers of Southeast Asia have traditionally been held in the same respect as those of China, India, and Japan. Teaching was, and is, a most honored occupation. But all teachers, no matter where they live in Asia, realize that they are faced with a multitude of common problems. With few exceptions, they are confronted with the massive problem of illiteracy. Nowhere, with the possible exception of the Philippines, are there enough teachers for the classrooms. The vast majority of teachers are overworked and underpaid. Honor cannot pay the rent, the food bills, the clothing bills, and the many other bills a position of honor entails. Their social status is declining, their working conditions are deteriorating, their morale is dropping, and their future is rather bleak. But the typical Asian teachers recognize their responsibility and willingly endure frustration and hardship in order that their country may have the educated people that are essential to any progress. The teachers of Southeast Asia, like their confreres in other Asian countries, are a most dedicated band of men and women.

Similarities between the region of Southeast Asia and other Asian areas could be multiplied many times. The cities of this region are expanding at an extremely rapid rate and becoming the centers of political and economic control. The leaders are exerting every effort to industrialize in order to shore up their economic base and raise the standard of living of their people. Life expectancy does not generally go beyond forty years of age, and modern medical facilities are limited. Nationalism is rampant everywhere in Asia. In all of Asia, love of country is moving the people to act. Everywhere people are trying to reconcile this spirit with their traditional loyalties to the family, the clan, the caste, and the class. Everywhere the conflicts between old and new values are tearing the hearts and souls of the Asian people. The birth of nations in Asia has brought instability, uncertainty, fear, insecurity, pain, chaos, pride, and hope. The bonds of similar ways of life and thought that tie all Asians together, bonds that have been forged over the centuries, are now being reinforced by the rising expectations of all for a better life and by the advent of independence and nationalism.

Distinctive Character of Southeast Asia

Although there is much in the mode and view of life of Southeast Asians that is similar to that in one, or more, or all of the Asian countries outside this region, there is also diversity, sometimes great diversity. Many differences in thought and practice between Pakistan, Bangladesh, India, China, Korea, and Japan have already been shown. The Laotians, Cambodians, Burmese, and Thai from Southeast Asia and the East Asian Chinese, Koreans and Japanese all name themselves Buddhists but the Southeast Asian's interpretation of Buddhism differs significantly from that of the Chinese, Koreans, and Japanese. The vast majority of Indonesians, Pakistanis, and the Bengalis of Bangladesh profess Islam and adhere to the same basic doctrines, but the Indonesians have colored Islam to blend with their special environment and supplemented it with treasured indigenous usages of ancient origin. The social life of the Southeast Asians is differentiated from that of some other Asians by qualities that are derived from their own special heritage. There is a basic theme that runs throughout the social life of Asia, but there are variations of emphasis and stress, modifications, and additions which give to the social life of each country its individual character. The political posture and problems of the Southeast Asian countries demarcate them from other countries and, on occasion, from each other.

The accessibility of the area from the sea permitted long-continued Chinese and Indian cultural penetration and, more recently, the introduction of Japanese, European, and American influences. This mixture of Chinese, Indian, Japanese, Western, and indigenous cultures resulted in a special orientation to life. Southeast Asia has a distinctive character which sets it apart from the neighboring regions of Asia.

In recent years, the region of Southeast Asia has become important to the world of man. Three of the world's greatest powers —the United States, the Soviet Union, and the People's Republic of China—are vying there for power and influence; when violence flares up, this rivalry sometimes threatens world peace. In the past, names of countries and cities there—Cambodia, Laos, Vietnam, Phnom Penh, Vientiane, Hanoi, Saigon—were rarely mentioned and generally unknown. Today, newspaper, radio, and television mention these names frequently and, sometimes, daily. Competing ideologies, great power rivalries, erupting nationalism, frustrated expectations, traumatic transitions, have all coincidentally come together in Southeast Asia at this moment of history and made the solution of the problems they pose vital to the stability and peaceful future of all people.

37

Religion in Southeast Asia

Religion has had a profound impact upon the people of Southeast Asia. Their conception of the good life, their customs, their art, and their literature all witness to the influence of religion in the daily lives of the people. The profusion of temples, pagodas, monasteries, shrines, and mosques reveals to the most casual observer that religion has found a permanent home in this land. The humble shrine housing an unadorned village guardian and the majestic temple enshrining an array of breathtaking Buddhas have a revered meaning and function for the people. Wherever one walks in Southeast Asia, there one will find the spirit and evidence of religion.

Followers of all the world's religions are to be found in Southeast Asia today, but the beliefs and practices of the vast majority of the people stem either from animism, Hinduism, Buddhism, or Islam or from a combination of two or more of these religions. Buddhism, in the form called Theravada, is dominant in Burma, Thailand, Cambodia, and Laos. Islam is the prevailing religion in Indonesia and Malaysia, and has followers in all of the other countries. The religion of Vietnam is a blend of Mahayana Buddhism, Confucianism, Taoism, and animism. The majority of the Filipinos are Christian. But regardless of which imported religion predominates, certain beliefs and practices indigenous to the various countries of Southeast Asia remain an integral part of the religious life of the people. This is particularly true of animism, which was the original religion of almost all the people of Southeast Asia.

Animism is the belief that all objects, including trees, rivers, volcanoes, and other natural objects, possess a conscious life or are endowed with indwelling souls. In Laos, the people believe that certain spirits, or *phi*, possess great power over human destinies and are to be found throughout the material universe. Evil spirits, or *phi*, may cause disease or other troubles, and exorcists must be called in to drive them out of the body. Sometimes a Buddhist priest, who has this special knowledge, may be called upon to perform the ceremony of exorcism. In Thailand, the two religions of animism and Buddhism are intermingled. In almost every Thai village there is a tutelary guardian as well as a Buddhist *wat*, or compound. In many parts of Burma, the villagers still make their offerings to the *nat*, or spirit, who dwells in some natural object and whose favor is important to them and their community. It is an ancient spirit, for it was born in the legendary past of Burma, but it retains its vigor despite the passage of time. In Indonesia the people are careful to propitiate the spirits that inhabit their land, and offerings are faithfully laid before the powerful spirits of certain trees or presented to the spirits of the sea, the rivers, and the volcanoes. The spirit world of animism is still close to the people of Southeast Asia, and neither the imposition of another religion nor the introduction of an irreligious philosophy has been able to exorcise these spirits completely from the land and the people. But religions from India and China did enter Southeast Asia and gradually superseded or assimilated most of the original religious beliefs.

Buddhism in Burma, Thailand, Laos, and Cambodia

Through the instrumentality of Indian traders, priests, adventurers, and travelers, the culture and religious ideas of India were brought to much of Southeast Asia. Indian culture is strikingly evident in the literature, art, architecture, and dances of many countries in this area. The great Indian epic, the *Ramayana,* is well known in Burma, Thailand, Laos, and Cambodia, and although it has been modified to fit its new setting—Thailand has four versions of it—the general outline still remains. The *Mahabharata,* another great Indian story, has been so completely absorbed into Indonesian literature that the Indonesians think of themselves as the descendants of the characters in the tale.

Theravada Buddhism

The religion of the vast majority of people in the countries of Burma, Cambodia, and Laos is Buddhism in the form called Theravada, "the Path of the Elders." From India and the neighboring island of Ceylon, Theravada Buddhism spread eastward to these countries. It will be recalled that Buddhism eventually split into two major schools of thought known as Theravada or Hinayana ("Lesser Vehicle") and Mahayana ("Greater Vehicle"). Mahayana Buddhism, described earlier in this book, is followed in China, Korea, Japan, Tibet, and Vietnam. The Theravada school of Buddhism teaches the more austere and simple way of life. It is a more literal interpretation of Buddha's teachings and adheres rather closely to his original doctrines. It is more demanding upon the individual than Mahayana Buddhism. To carry out fully the Buddha's requirements, it is necessary to renounce the world completely and enter a monastery.

A person who follows these prescriptions literally and diligently will become an *arhat,* "worthy person," one ready to enter Nirvana. Individuals must do this themselves; they can expect no help from other humans or gods. It is self-purification, salvation through individual effort, not through grace.

In their interpretation of Buddhism, many of the people of Southeast Asia differ from the Chinese, Koreans, and Japanese—Zen Buddhism excepted—for generally these Asians do not emphasize the principle of self-help, but rather rely upon the redeeming merit of saintly ones who have refused Nirvana in order to help others achieve it. Mahayana Buddhism is a compassionate religion in that it is more concerned with helping others, and its highest ideal is that person who forgoes entrance into Nirvana until all have attained it. A story is told of four men who were climbing a mountain. One by one they approached the top of the mountain. The first man to reach the summit stood up, looked, and then with a great shout threw himself out of sight on the other side. The second and third man did likewise. When the fourth man reached the top and looked, he gasped in astonishment and awe, for there awaiting him was a paradise of beauty and eternal life. He had found his Shangri-la. But instead of jumping into it immediately as the others had done, he returned down the mountain and spent the rest of his life showing others the path to this earthly paradise. The first three men were followers of Theravada; the last one, a follower of Mahayana Buddhism.

In Theravada Buddhism, Gautama Buddha is not an object of worship but is regarded as the embodiment of a principle of enlightenment. He is merely an outstanding example of an eternal concept which has been made concrete in Buddhas before Gautama Buddha and will continue to be known in earthly form throughout time. The images of Buddha, which portray an idealized symbol rather than a real human being, are the result of this conception.

Since Nirvana could be achieved only by the unaided efforts of the individual, the gaining of merit became a fulltime preoccupation of the followers of Theravada. It became a monk-oriented religion. Theravada holds that adult males should become priests or monks—sometimes called *bonzes*—and many males put on the robes of a monk for a temporary period prior to marriage. The individual is free to remain a monk as long as he wishes. Even a short period as a monk is meritorious for the individual and an honor to his family. Yellow-robed monks alone, in pairs, or in groups are expected and accepted participants in the daily activities of the countries that practice Theravada, and as they sally forth in the early hours of the morning to seek food in the name of Lord Buddha, they are a constant reminder to the people of their Buddhist heritage and duties.

The Buddhist Wat

Unlike their colleagues in China, Korea, and Japan, who perform only limited functions of a religious nature, the Buddhist priests in Burma, Cambodia, Laos, and Thailand perform services that make them indispensable to the secular as well as religious life of the community. They officiate at religious festivals and ceremonies and pray over the sick. They are invited to birthdays or weddings to pray and speak and are required for funeral ceremonies and the naming of infants. In many rural areas they are the only teachers available, and their compounds the only schools in the neighborhood. They are necessary for almost every important family and community affair. In almost every village of these countries there is a Buddhist wat, or compound—wats are sometimes referred to as pagodas—which serves as the educational and social center of the community. Some of the larger cities have many wats. A wat consists of a group of buildings surrounded by a wall or fence. Within the wat there are halls or temples for both laity and monks, a library, dormitories, shrines, and sometimes bath houses. There may also be a crematorium, for the Buddhists cremate their dead. Almost every wat contains a school, either for the monks or the children of the community, or both. It is estimated that one-half of the primary schools of Thailand are located in wats. The villagers come to these wats to seek the advice of the monks, to relay local news and gossip, to leave their valuables for safekeeping, to rest, and to attend to a host of other secular matters in addition to making merit and undertaking other spiritual duties. Festivals also are often held within the wat, and during these periods it resounds with gaiety and joy. A most highly esteemed member of the village community, the abbot, presides over the wat. Monks of all grades are respected by the people, even by the foremost officials of the country. The abbot's counsel is often sought by the people, especially in matters of some importance to the family or the community, and in many instances his advice is preferred to that of the secular authorities. He mingles daily with the people, giving guidance, information, and assistance.

The people voluntarily support the wat and the monks, for it is the way of merit to Nirvana. It is estimated that in some countries the people spend from 5 to 10 percent of their income in supporting the wat, not including food and volunteer labor. Their wats and their monks are essential to their life.

Social and Political Aspects

Most of the Buddhists feel that their harmonious relationships within the family and the community are the result of Buddhist teachings and practices. The training of the mind to curb passions, anger, and greed makes them more forgiving and more tolerant. The Thais say that no good Buddhist will despise a person who has different views from his own. They point to the fact that even at their football and boxing matches there are rarely public displays

of temper and that at public gatherings of all kinds they are orderly and quiet. The Burmese claim that the teachings of Buddha on
the relationship that should exist between husband and wife,
parent and child, teacher and student, employer and employee,
friend and friend has been a major factor in the preservation of
harmonious relationships among the Burmese. Buddhists can be
violent, like all people, but Buddhism has mitigated this aggres-
siveness.

The imprint of Buddhism is vividly marked in the festivals of
the people in the Theravada countries. Many of these festivals
have flowered from the seed of Buddhism. In Laos, during the full
moon of the month of May, a festival is celebrated in memory of
the birth, enlightenment, and death of Buddha. Dances, proces-
sions, and puppet shows create an atmosphere of earthly gaiety,
but the religious significance of the festival is also present in the
blessing of children and expectant mothers and in the offerings
made to the priests. Each month of the Burmese calendar has its
special festival, as have the wats at various times of the year. In
Thailand, the annual Festival of the Great Pagoda, which is held in
the middle of the twelfth lunar month, draws throngs of people
from all over the country. They come primarily to pay homage
to the relics of Buddha housed there, but they stay to enjoy the
amusements and the many varieties of food and sweets available in
the fairground that surrounds the compound of the Great Pagoda.

Buddhism is not divorced from the political life of these countries. The Burmese have repeatedly stated that Buddhism is the
unifying and stabilizing force that welds them into one nation.
During periods of chaos, and domination by others, Buddhism has
played a major role in preserving them from disunity and despair.
The Burmese monks were in the forefront of the campaign for
independence from England. In Laos, all nobles were required to
take a yearly oath of allegiance to their king in the Temple of
Sisaket in the capital. After being defeated by the Thais, the oath
to the Thai ruler was taken in the same temple, and the French
continued the custom when they assumed power. In Thailand, the
Supreme Patriarch of the Buddhists is chosen by the king from
the nominations presented him by an ecclesiastical council. Although the monks of Thailand have refrained from political activities, the religious and secular authorities are closely linked.

The only word that properly describes the role of Buddhism in
the countries of Burma, Cambodia, Laos, and Thailand is *pervasive.*

There is no aspect of a person's life in these countries which is not affected by Buddhism. Monks are used to disseminate modern concepts of health and hygiene and other Western learning. Stories on Buddha's life and teachings have motivated and inspired numerous poets and writers, and even the more modern and secular literature has religious nuances. The sometimes overwhelming beauty of the architecture and statues is the result of a passionate impulse to bring divinity to stone, wood, and bronze. Buddhism is of the heart and mind of the people of Cambodia, Burma, Laos, and Thailand.

Cambodia and Laos are now ruled by leaders who profess to follow a Communist philosophy. The new Khmer Rouge leaders and followers of Cambodia have called the Buddhist monks "lazy people," "parasites," and other derogatory names. They have also used Buddhist pagodas as storage places for rice and turned some into pig farms. Statues of Buddha have been smashed. It is too soon, however, to adequately evaluate the effect their leadership will have upon the Buddhist beliefs and practices of the people they govern. The history of many people has shown, however, that long-cherished beliefs and practices are not easily eliminated from the hearts and minds of people.

Islam in Indonesia

Indians carried Hinduism and Buddhism to Indonesia. They, together with the Arabs, brought Islam to Malaysia and Indonesia. There they found an indigenous body of beliefs and practices which substantially stemmed from animism. It was around the first century A.D. that Hinduism and Buddhism began to become known in Indonesia. Indian priests, traders, and warriors introduced the Indonesians to the Sanskrit language, sacred texts, rituals, temples, and Indian literature. These two religions mingled with the original animism, and in the process of acceptance they were adapted by the Indonesians to fit their needs and setting. Hinduism and Buddhism—Mahayana Buddhism—vied for supremacy in Indonesia, and slowly Hinduism prevailed but not completely, for the resulting religious pattern was a combination of Hinduism, Buddhism and animism plus some other customary beliefs and practices. This fusion of Hinduism, Mahayana Buddhism, and animism endured until Islam became the dominant religion of Indonesia around the beginning of the sixteenth century. The fusion still endures in Bali, but its structure and content is Balinese, not Indian.

Islam started to spread in Indonesia about the thirteenth century, and within two hundred years was the religion of the majority. The process of conversion was a slow but peaceful one. Islam was not forced upon the people at sword point; the Indonesians responded to the attractiveness of the doctrine as described by the persuasive tongues of Indian traders from the west coast of India. These merchants established themselves in the main ports of Indonesia, and Islam radiated out from their headquarters. These Indian Muslims, on the surface at least, bore many similarities to the Indians who had preached Hinduism and Buddhism and, therefore, were not regarded as totally alien to the Indonesian scene. Further, there was much in Islam that appealed to the religious spirit of the Indonesians, and they were inclined to accept it. But again, as in the case of Hinduism and Buddhism, in the process of acceptance they contrived to make it uniquely Indonesian.

Because of the danger of idolatry, Islam frowns upon portrayals of living beings. It does not, however, forbid pictures of natural objects such as flowers, trees, or leaves. Since the Indonesian artists desired to portray living beings as well as lifeless objects, they invented a new form of art by making portraits of animals out of leaf and flower designs. Close up, the drawings appear to be merely leaf designs, but from a distance the image of an animal is clearly discernible. The walls of some mosques in Indonesia are decorated with these leaf designs.

Because shadow-plays were intimately connected with animism, and to a certain extent with Hinduism and Buddhism, Islam prohibited the exhibition of them. But the Indonesians knew that Islam encouraged decorations composed of Arabic passages from the Koran, and they began to use artistic Arabic characters in their compositions. Close up, they are finely written Arabic characters, but from a distance they have the figure of a *wayang* puppet. To make shadow-plays acceptable to all, the puppets were fabricated from tree stems rather than leather, and revered figures from Arabic and Muslim literature replaced the more ancient characters.

The architecture of the mosques is more Indonesian than traditional Islamic; it is square rather than circular and often lacks the usual dome for a roof. Mosques and Islamic cemeteries are sometimes entered through a Hindu-style gate, and names of Muslims are often of Hindu origin. Muslim girls are frequently named after the wife of Muhammed, but many are also named after Queen Sita, the heroine of the Indian epic the *Ramayana*. The amalgam of religious practices is illustrated in the celebrations that are held on important occasions such as the birth of a child and the initiation of community projects. Although a Muslim official might preside on these occasions, some relics of Hindu practices are preserved, and the custom of celebrating these events had its origin in the ancient animistic past of Indonesia.

The Indonesians have the knack of blurring the sharp lines which ordinarily divide religions in other parts of the world. They are, for the most part, Muslims, and they will not easily change their religion—Christianity has had little success in converting Muslims to its faith—but they are also Indonesians with a strong tendency toward harmonizing natural and supernatural forces. They are a tolerant people willing to accommodate rivaling points of view. They have succeeded in shaping animism, Hinduism, Buddhism, and Islam to fit their unique personality and environment.

Mahayana Buddhism in Vietnam

The Vietnamese, like the Indonesians, were open-minded and tolerant with regard to new religious ideas. What they liked, they accepted and blended with other beliefs and ways which they had previously adopted. Both Chinese and Indians introduced Buddhism to the Vietnamese, but the Chinese influence was predominant, and they preached the Mahayana Buddhism that flowered and flourished in China. For centuries Buddhism was patronized and encouraged by the Vietnamese rulers and became firmly rooted in Vietnam. However, the Chinese also introduced Taoism and Confucianism to the Vietnamese, and Taoistic practices have their own special role in the religious life of the people. Confucianism, since it is not really concerned with the afterlife, was confined to the more scholarly and to the officials of the country, although it was proclaimed as the official ideology of the state. The majority of the Vietnamese are regarded as followers of Mahayana Buddhism, but their original animism, and various forms of Taoism imported from China, are also vital elements in their religious life.

Christianity in the Philippines

Although there are large numbers of Muslims in Mindanao and Sulu, the great majority of the Filipinos are Christians. The Spanish governed the Philippines for almost four hundred years, and since one of their principal aims was the propagation of Catholicism, they made a special effort to convert the Filipinos. They were successful, and today most of the Filipinos are baptized Catholics. Almost every town of any size has a church which often dominates the community physically and socially. Most of the festivals—and there are many of them, for the Filipinos are a gay people—are held to honor some patron saint or to commemorate a religious feast day. Their religious rituals and practices often convey a sense of the dramatic which is characteristic of the Spanish approach to religion. With the assumption of power by the Americans in the late nineteenth century, many Protestant missionaries started to proselytize in the Philippines with some success, but their converts are still far outnumbered by the Catholics.

The people of Southeast Asia have welcomed many religions. Animism, Buddhism, Hinduism, Islam, Taoism, Confucianism, and Christianity have been received with tolerance, listened to with respect, and frequently adopted—if not entirely, at least in part. They have adapted them to fit their own environment and personality, for to most Southeast Asians the cultivation of the spirit is of the essence of life.

38

Social Life in Southeast Asia

Most of the people of Southeast Asia live in village-centered communities whose members are closely knit by ties of blood and marriage and by a communal spirit of cooperation. Except for certain areas, their land is relatively underpopulated, well watered, and generous in its response to those who cultivate it with even a little care. Fish and rice can be had by all who apply themselves, and the disruptive evils of near starvation and famine do not persistently disturb the relationships between the members of the community. Their lives are not dominated by the intense and insistent pressure to expend their total energies in the search for food as so many must do in

China, India, Korea, Pakistan, and other countries of South and East Asia. Their daily routine is slower and more tranquil, and they have the time and the inclination to meditate, to rest, to visit, and to play.

Characteristically, they regard their fellows as allies, rather than competitors, in the quest for happiness, and their relations with one another are frequently distinguished by mutual assistance and a spirit of helpfulness. They try to resolve conflicts as expeditiously and justly as possible. They base their social relations on the principle that harm to another is to be avoided even at the price of sacrificing one's own interests, and they believe that if all are imbued with the same charitable spirit the community will be at peace.

The distinctive trait of mutual assistance is most marked in the family and the village, but it also extends to the nation and beyond. It is magnificently illustrated by the dikes that contain the waters of the Red River of Vietnam. These dikes are estimated to run for a distance of sixteen hundred miles, and measure as much as sixty feet wide at the base and twenty feet at the top. The beginning of these dikes is unknown because it lies deep in the vague past of Vietnam, but for thousands of years the Vietnamese have continued to rebuild and maintain these monumental barriers against floods. The construction and maintenance of the dikes was a communal activity that included all within the area nourished by the river's waters; it still is today. When an alarm sounds warning of a breach in the dike, the neighborhood swarms to the danger spot to prevent an onslaught of flooding waters over the land. A striking example of self-help, this custom also indicates the venerable character and the lasting strength of the cooperative attitude that distinguishes many people in Southeast Asia.

This quality of mutual assistance circumfuses the daily life of the village and the family. Villagers join together in building schools, dams, dikes, roads, and secular and religious community buildings. They assist each other in constructing a house, in planting and harvesting the crops, in healing the sick and burying the dead, in securing husbands for the spinsters and brides for the bachelors, in celebrating the birth of children, and in all other matters where the hands and minds of many are needed. The Indonesians considered this practice of cooperation important enough to be formally prescribed as a part of the customary law, called *adat*, which regulates their social relations. To most Southeast

Asians, however, mutual help is a natural law, for it is neither debated nor forced but naturally and instinctively given.

The Family

The families of Southeast Asia have a tolerant flexibility with regard to the number of members included. In the Philippines, in Laos, and in the Southeast Asian cities, the family may sometimes be comparable in size to those of Western countries, but it is always prepared to expand and receive aunts, uncles, cousins, in-laws, even remote relatives, and friends, if they need its security. It is common to find within the family married daughters and sons, their children, and other relatives or friends, in addition to the parents and their unmarried children. There is always room for one more and, indeed, "the more the merrier" is a phrase that aptly describes the attitude of many families in this region, an attitude which renders orphanages and homes for the aged largely unnecessary.

There are certain practical advantages in having many members in the agriculture-focused families of Southeast Asia. Whoever is regarded as a member of the family is expected to do his or her share in providing for its support. At an early age the child starts carrying water, watching the water-buffalo and feeding the other animals, taking care of the babies, and handling other small but necessary chores. The aged help with the lighter field work and do much of the baby-sitting and cooking, sometimes freeing the mother and father for gainful labor outside the home and the fields. Over a long period of time the people have worked on the premise that the greater the number of persons supporting the family, the greater the income in food and kind.

Practical advantages or not, the group living of large families would be unbearable without a degree of concord among the members. The daily living together of large families is made possible by the rather well-defined roles and functions of the members. The roles may be defined differently from family to family because many Southeast Asian countries have large minority groups whose customs are of ancient indigenous origin or were born in alien soil and carried there by immigrants, but there are some general principles which are looked upon by many as basic to their family and communal living.

The young are subordinate to their elders and owe them respect, obedience, and devotion. Youth is a period for acquiring knowledge and learning social roles, for gathering the wisdom, know-how, and experience of the preceding generations. The prevailing theory is that a person cannot teach what has not been learned, or practice what has not been imbibed from childhood. Discord arises within the family and the community only from those who have not been well taught or well disposed to receive the instructions of their teachers. The word "teacher" is esteemed throughout Southeast Asia, for it signifies that most important function of preparing the youth for a future role in the family, community, and nation. If the older members of the family fulfill this role with distinction, their kin will be honored, and the reputation of their family enhanced. If they perform it badly, they shame their kin and dishonor their family. The responsibility to prepare the youth adequately for life weighs heavily upon the elders; for in a very real sense, the youth's future is their future.

Generally the child is receptive to what he or she is taught because it is accompanied by love. Children are wanted and welcomed, and they know it. They are the continuation of the family and the hope of the community. They are individuals destined eventually for the desirelessness of Nirvana or the complete satisfaction of all desires with God. Children are loved to the point where they are almost overindulged, but neither they nor the elders ever forget their subordinate place in the family.

The aged too must live up to their respected roles in the family. Their function is to advise, since the wisdom accumulated over the long course of their years must be shared with the family and the community. They participate in the deliberations of village and local councils because, since community projects require the efforts of all, all should be involved in the basic decisions that pertain to these projects. The degree to which decisions are arrived at through free discussions on the village level would amaze most Westerners, and the grass-roots feeling for democracy would call forth the envy of many Western political leaders. The aged are wanted, needed, and made secure, and there is not the onus on them, as in the West, of being expected to make a new life for themselves apart from the family they helped to found and preserve.

Men and women have their special roles in the family. The man is formally the head of the household, and his authority is buttressed by the long-held assumptions of tradition and religion which teach the inherent superiority of the male. The woman's placid acceptance of her lower rank further bolsters the male's status in the family and in the community where he represents the family in council deliberations and decisions. It is his duty to perform the more arduous work of the family, such as preparing the fields for cultivation, doing carpentry and masonry work, and carrying heavy materials. There are certain religious duties that only a male may perform and, in the Buddhist areas, he often assumes the robes of a monk for a short or long period depending upon his inclinations.

The woman is primarily responsible for the good ordering of the house, and all the domestic tasks that accompany housekeeping. She cooks, washes, sews, cleans, and, if she is the wife of a village farmer, she helps to care for the livestock, carries water, cultivates a garden, and lends a helping hand to her husband in the fields at planting, harvesting, and weeding time. In the care of her children she often has the assistance of older children and old people who cannot work in the fields. Like any mother, she is expected to be always ready to cope with the great and small emergencies that from time to time visit any household.

Although she is formally subordinate to the male, her counsel is sought and frequently followed in making marriage arrangements, planning family celebrations, managing the household, and other important family matters. She has always worked side by side with the husband on the farm and in business ventures, and is commonly seen alone selling her wares by the roadside and in the markets. Now she is even to be found in the professions, and there are growing numbers of women doctors, educators, lawyers, playwrights, authors, radio announcers, and business entrepreneurs. She does not compete with the male, and she has no desire to usurp his established role in the family. She knows her complementary role is essential to the smooth meshing of social relations within the family and the community.

Social Change

These understood roles are fulfilled today by most of Southeast Asian people, and they continue to contribute substantially to the agreeable nature of social life in this region, but forces are at work which are altering these roles, often imperceptibly and sometimes significantly. Modern education is conveying novel ideas to the people which are often accepted as better than traditional ones. In some parts of Southeast Asia polygamy was, and is, permitted, but there is increasing pressure from influential segments of the society to curtail and prohibit it. Even where it is legal, many refrain from practicing it because of possible social censure. In much, but not all, of Southeast Asia women have always had inheritance rights in the family property. Now new concepts of women's rights to inheritance are bringing this privilege to women in all areas. Unlike those in other parts of Asia, many women of Southeast Asia have had for centuries the right to secure divorces. This freedom, too, is now being extended to women in the few territories where it was unknown before.

The youth, intoxicated by the unaccustomed wine of social freedom he is obtaining from books, magazines, and movies is beginning to struggle against the restraints of a subordinate position. He is convinced that his new knowledge is far superior to that of his elders, and he prefers to supplant his usual passive role with a more free and active one. The hint of juvenile delinquency now found in the cities could grow into a major social problem if not properly handled.

The accelerating urbanization process is conditioning the social life of the people. The size of the family is being directly affected by this trend. Since cities are being inundated by people, urban land is becoming scarce and expensive and many families are forced to live in restricted quarters. The limitations of space have a direct physical bearing on the number of family members who can be accommodated. Moreover, unlike village-based families whose economy is founded upon an agricultural system that favors many workers, the city-based families rely upon other means of support which do not require the cooperation of many hands. But the traditional welcoming attitude toward those who want to be a part of them still persists in many families who migrate to the cities, and they try to make room for all who come. They may all have to be packed tightly in cramped quarters, but they feel that the spiritual and emotional warmth that results from their close association outweighs their sacrifice of special freedom.

The political chaos prevailing in some countries of Southeast Asia is expediting the breakdown of traditional values. Alien forces on this troubled scene have contributed to the sabotage of the old mores. Vietnam, one of these disturbed areas, vividly illustrates this threat to traditional social values. The prolonged war in

Vietnam caused a major upheaval in the social system of that area. This war created conditions which placed child against parent, brother against brother, and friend against friend. It sundered families and wrecked old friendships, with the result that traditional virtues regulating these relationships came to be regarded as of secondary importance. It is also reported that the new leaders of Cambodia, which are referred to as kampuchea, are attempting to radically restructure the social life and attitudes of their people.

To a greater or lesser degree these new influences are altering the social life of the people in all Southeast Asian countries. In some countries, such as Vietnam, Cambodia, and Laos, forces for change were abetted by violence and the implements of war. In other countries social change is occurring more peacefully and gradually, as a result of education, urbanization, industrialization, and other evolutionary factors. The problems created by nationalism and by intermittent political crises of regional or international scope are also drastically reshaping the social life of the Southeast Asian people.

39

Politics in Southeast Asia

Southeast Asia is at present a politically unsettled region. Serious problems of both internal and external origin are perplexing the political leaders of this area. They lack sufficient knowledge of, and experience in, the theory and practice of constitutional democracy; they still lean toward authoritarian leadership and tend to rely upon people rather than laws. The clash of minority groups and the confusing conflict of differing ideological doctrines add to their difficulties. Their external political problems originate in their relationships with their regional neighbors, in the proximity of China, and in the recurring crises that result from the moves of antagonists in the deadly drama of Great Power politics.

Inexperience in Democracy

Southeast Asian countries have a long history of authoritarian government at the national level, but a very brief history of the Western-style constitutional system of government. From the beginning of their history, the people have been accustomed to the idea of a ruler who neither sought nor wanted their advice, but demanded their obedience and support. Although at the village level decisions on matters which concerned the community were usually made only after long discussion and the consent of the family representatives, this democratic method was not practiced on the national level. Nor did the villagers want the ruler to be overly interested in their daily affairs—they felt prying officials would be annoying. All they generally asked from their rulers was a minimum of local interference, and few taxes.

Within the past few decades, most of the peoples of this region have been presented with constitutional democracies by their idealistic, revolutionary, educated élite. They were told that this was a new era, that they were now the real rulers of the country, and that their elected representatives would act on their behalf on the national and local levels. Parties were formed and candidates offered to the people for their consideration. In most cases, the people returned to power those who had previously ruled them or the revolutionary leaders who had gained national independence for them.

In the ensuing years, some progress has been made in educating the people to a better appreciation of democracy. Many of the people are now aware of the external trappings of democracy, but many have not yet grasped its spirit and philosophical basis. This is due in part to the lack of native roots for democracy—it is a recent import of Western origin—and in part to the little time people have had to adjust to it, and it to them. People cannot be expected to attune themselves overnight to political conceptions which grew and matured within a different environment and tradition. The basic principles of democracy are suitable for all persons, but the manner in which they are worked out in action varies with the character and traditions of the people. Moreover, time and peace are needed for the proper development of democracy, and the people of Southeast Asia have had neither adequate time nor a truly peaceful atmosphere in which to cultivate their new democracies.

Unfortunately, many believed that the establishment of a constitutional system of government would be an immediate panacea for their economic, social, and political problems. When it failed to provide a swift and effective remedy for their ills, some became impatient and turned for quick action to the time-tested, well-known pattern of government by a dictator. As a consequence there have been a number of coups and attempted coups in some countries of this region. In some cases, these sudden takeovers have disturbed the stability of the country, but in other instances, they have not. The latter has been true whenever the assumption of power by force is not alien to the political tradition of the region and, indeed, is more familiar to the people than constitutional democracy. The people merely request again of their new leaders that interference with their daily activities be minimized and their economic burdens lightened.

Except in territories controlled by the more radical socialist or communist leaders, life in Asia generally goes on just as it had before the transference of power, because the change is of men rather than policies. The number of men who have the capacity and opportunity to wield power in the country is limited. Consequently, the governing potential is a small group, consisting of those who have had similar economic and educational backgrounds and more or less follow the same policies in administering the affairs of government. The basic policy of most leaders is to preserve what is best in the culture and tradition of the people and at the same time advance along certain economic and social lines. A too radical change in the customary usages of the people might bring upon the government the wrath of the conservative peasant and military, and therefore the new leaders feel it is more expedient to channel their energies along accepted lines of action than to endanger their policies and positions by pushing the people impetuously into unfamiliar economic and social worlds. But too great an emphasis upon the preservation of the status quo may lead to stagnation and deterioration. Since it is necessary to conserve and advance at the same time, shifts in government are reflected more in the changing personalities of the leaders than in deviations in aims.

Nepotism

Under these circumstances, the character and orientation of the people in power become much more significant than constitutional provisions. It is more essential to know the views of the leader or leaders in a given situation than to understand the literal constitutional requirement. It is frequently better to be on the side of the right person than to be on the right side of the law. The ruler is prone to value loyalty and trustworthiness in his subordinates more than intelligence and competence. The former two qualities are indispensable; the latter are certainly useful but may prove harmful if loyalty is lacking. For this reason many leaders select their own relatives for government positions.

The families of this region have a strong tradition of mutual assistance. If a person is fortunate enough to become politically powerful or rich, that person's family and relatives naturally assume that they will share in the success. Because their fortunes are tied to his, they are his best source of trusted assistants. There are few sources from which the leaders of a particular country can recruit trained personnel for the administrative posts of government. These leaders are very conscious of this deficiency and are spending much of their countries' resources in their efforts to increase the number of educated men and women. In the meantime, they are compelled by circumstances to rely upon a small coterie which includes their families, friends, and political colleagues.

The assumption of power by the friends and relatives of the leader sometimes results in their obtaining material rewards far beyond their salaries. They feel, and tradition often supports them, that a substantial reward for their loyal services is not an unreasonable expectation. Their new positions often have attached to them indirect benefits, which have been there for a long time and thus have become customary and accepted, though not legal. The more common sources of additional income are: favored treatment for certain business enterprises, the granting of import and export licenses (these are very lucrative in countries where such licenses are difficult to obtain), manipulation of currencies, awarding of government contracts, and, in some instances, smuggling. The use of these avenues of income is condoned or overlooked if the bounds of propriety are not exceeded. If carried too far, however, these illegal practices may precipitate another coup or endanger the country's economy.

Some of the Southeast Asian leaders, mindful of the injurious consequences of this custom, have tried to inject a new attitude into their administrations. The late President Ramón Magsaysay of the Philippines was known and loved for his attention to the plight of the poor and for the absence of greed in his character.

Powerful Minorities

Most of the nations of Southeast Asia are troubled by sizable minority groups who demand special rights and at times carry on disruptive activities. The activities of these minorities, who are sometimes of indigenous origin and sometimes of foreign extraction, frequently agitate the domestic political scene. In the early days of Burma's independence the Karens, the largest tribal group in Burma, fought fiercely for a separate state of their own. They were defeated, but the rebellion retarded Burma's economic and political progress. The people of Sumatra, Celebes, and other Indonesian islands have caused that government much mental anguish and material loss by their uprisings. The Chinese in Malaysia are trying to maintain the integrity of their schools and culture in the face of a determined government effort to bring about greater national unity through a more Malayan-oriented education. Every country in Southeast Asia has its minority problems which, if not properly handled, could erupt in sudden bloodshed. Witness the recent uprisings of the minority Muslims in the Southern part of the Philippines against the government. These groups are also susceptible to the blandishments of those who seek to align them in a front against the established government.

The Indians and the Chinese are the two most influential groups of foreign lineage living in Southeast Asia. Both nationalities have been in the area for a long time, and stories about these lands passed on by Indian and Chinese visitors and merchants are often the only eyewitness accounts of events that occurred in the ancient past of Southeast Asian countries. It was, however, under the favored treatment of the Western colonial regimes that these two foreign groups made extraordinary commercial gains in this region. After achieving independence, many countries promulgated laws to curtail the commercial holdings of these people and to limit their enormous landholdings, but they still dominate much of the economic life of the region either in their own names or in the names of citizens used as fronts.

Of these two minority concentrations, the Chinese are by far the larger and the more influential. They are found in every country of Southeast Asia, and their number has been estimated at about twelve million. This figure is subject to further scrutiny because the Chinese are loath to report the exact number of their group. There probably are many Chinese residing in these countries illegally who, if exposed by a census, would be deported. Most Southeast Asian citizens display a degree of antipathy toward these two minorities, which arises in part from their foreign origin and separateness from the community and in part from the sway they hold over the economic life of the country.

The leaders of Southeast Asian countries are suspicious of the Chinese living among them because their numbers and their strategic economic position, coupled with a strong attachment for their original homeland make them a potentially dangerous fifth column in each country. The Chinese abroad generally think of themselves as part of the total Chinese community centered in China from whom they are temporarily separated by space but permanently linked by blood and culture. The Chinese adapt easily to any environment, but they are rarely assimilated. They cleave to their culture wherever they may be and make great sacrifice to perpetuate it in their children. There is a tenacious quality in the Chinese character which enables them to carry on their characteristic way of life despite an alien land and culture.

The Chinese in Southeast Asia have traditionally looked to their embassy for support and guidance in maintaining themselves on this foreign soil. The embassies have responded by assisting them in any way possible and have requested their assistance from time to time on projects of interest to the Chinese government. Thus the economic and political power of the Chinese group in each country is often at the disposal of the Chinese government to be utilized by it for such purposes as are deemed necessary and desirable.

This attitude on the part of powerful minorities poses grave problems for the governments of Southeast Asia. One of their primary aims is a unifed nation-state which has the full allegiance of all who live within its borders. They need the loyal support of all their people if they are to achieve this goal, but some minority groups are not responding. For this reason, the Southeast Asian governments have promulgated laws on citizenship, land ownership, business enterprises, government employment, and even permissible living areas, all designed to reduce the economic power of these groups, to impel them into a closer relationship with their country of residence, and to mitigate any future harm to the country resulting from their activities. The Indonesians rounded up all the Chinese residing in the rural areas of the country and concentrated them in the cities.

In fairness to the Chinese in Southeast Asia, it must be emphasized that many of them have intermarried with the inhabitants, entered into the life of the community, and merged their efforts with the majority to help build a viable state. The majority of them are more interested in making money than in advancing a political ideology, but threats of economic and political retribution may compel them to support ideological and propaganda activities. It is also true that many of them are more interested in building up the economic power of their own families and groups than in contributing to the economy of the country itself. Obviously, this preference is not in the national interest of their adopted country.

Ideological and Interregional Conflict

There is a conflict of political and economic theories in this region which is causing the leaders and the people a certain confusion in their approach to the development of their country. A great many of the modern Southeast Asian leaders are attracted to the philosophy of socialism. They generally favor models of socialism which will permit a combination of a planned society and the preservation of treasured traditions. They also are impressed with the rapid progress of China and the Soviet Union, and they want to emulate this advance in their own countries. They believe that the philosophy of these states has contributed to their successes, and thus Marxian teachings are rather popular in the thinking of many Southeast Asian leaders. But at the same time some are not inclined to impose the Communist system on their people. They prefer a more moderate Socialist approach. Furthermore, some of them remember attempted Communist coups of the past, for instance in Indonesia and Malaysia, and the bloody excesses that followed; they are fearful lest it happen again. On the one hand these Southeast Asian leaders are attracted by the idea of a planned economy; on the other they are repelled by the more extreme Socialists who seek to remove them from power and threaten the unity of the country.

The political problems of Southeast Asian countries also arise from external sources. Although the nations of this region are tied together by common religions, similar social customs, and in some instances a common ethnic origin, they are divided politically. A long history of invasions, seizures of territory, and rapine has left a residue of skepticism and animosity which still colors their relations with one another. The Cambodians abhor the Vietnamese, and view Thai activities with cynicism. On one occasion they stopped all commercial air communication with South Vietnam over a fancied affront, and once they gave political asylum to a South Vietnamese airman who bombed the presidential palace in Vietnam, killing some of its guards and residents. And Vietnamese troops fighting in Cambodia treated Cambodians harshly. The North Vietnamese fought a savage war in South Vietnam in an attempt to unify the area politically and ideologically, and they were abetted in this effort by a number of sympathetic Laotians. The Thais are skeptical of Cambodian intentions and fearful of a strong Vietnam. Thailand and Burma have not forgotten past wars between them which have ravaged their lands on a number of occasions. Malaysia, established only after World War II, has had less time to build up memories of hate and rancor, but it was torn for years by a struggle with Communist guerrillas, mostly of Chinese origin.

In May 1969, racial violence broke out in Kuala Lumpur and in other parts of Malaysia between the Malays and the Chinese (Chinese make up over 40 percent of the mainland Malaysian population) and many were injured and killed. Incidents like this aggravate the already suspicious relationship between Singapore on the south where the Chinese are a large majority, and Malaysia. In the past there have been periods of strained relations between the Philippines and Indonesia, and between Indonesia and Malaysia. The Philippines and Malaysia have been quarreling for some time over Sabah, located in the area formerly called North Borneo. Sabah is now an integral part of the state of Malaysia; the Philippines, however, claim legal sovereignty over it. The proximity of suspicious neighbors requires the constant attention of the Southeast Asian statesmen and further adds to their general political condition of suspense and uncertainty.

The Constant Presence of Powerful China

Finally, there is one powerful nation, which by reason of geography will always be of concern to Southeast Asians—China. China looms over the people of Southeast Asia, an ever present factor in their political policies and activities. For several thousand years China has played a role in the external affairs of these countries, sometimes threatening, sometimes benevolent, sometimes imperialistic, but always important. Historically, many of the Southeast

Asian countries have been influenced by the Chinese. The Chinese governed Vietnam for more than a thousand years, and the Vietnamese language and culture reflect the deep penetration of Chinese thought and practice during this long rule. Former Chinese political dominance in Burma is reflected today in the ethnic origins and spoken language of the Burmese people. Even after colonization by Great Britain, Burma acknowledged the overlordship of China by sending decennial tribute missions to Peking. The Thais and Laotians originated in South China and have long been susceptible to political and cultural currents flowing in from China. In their expansionist periods, the Chinese ventured as far as Indonesia where they forced some kingdoms to acknowledge the sovereignty of China. They have long been in Malaysia and make up the great majority of the population of Singapore. The location of Luzon, the northern province of the Philippines, close as it is to South China has resulted in trade and cultural interchange between the two areas. There is no country of Southeast Asia where the existence of China is not watchfully considered and thoroughly appraised.

Modern Chinese leaders continue to be vitally concerned with Southeast Asia, especially the mainland countries of this region. This fundamental interest along with China's proximity and military might make China a major concern of Southeast Asian leaders. A further complication is the continuing presence and influence of the United States and the Soviet Union in the area. The Soviet Union is intensifying her efforts to influence the people of this region; as a result, the Chinese are becoming even more suspicious of Soviet intentions towards them. With the withdrawal of U.S. combat troops from Vietnam and the normalization of Sino-U.S. relations, the Chinese regard American activities in Southeast Asia with less suspicion than previously. However, it is not easy for Southeast Asian leaders to maneuver safely amidst the competing interests of great powers.

The Vietnamese

The People and the Land

Some centuries before the beginning of the Christian era, the ancestors of the Vietnamese wandered from China to the land around the Red River known as Tongking. This region is now the heartland of northern Vietnam. Gradually, the Vietnamese moved southward along the coast, and by about the fifteenth century A.D. they had occupied the delta of the Mekong River in the far south of the country. This area is the great rice producing region of Vietnam and was the scene of many skirmishes during the recent conflict in Vietnam.

From around the third century B.C. until the tenth century A.D., the Chinese governed the Vietnamese. During a thousand years or more of close association it was inevitable that the Vietnamese should adopt many of the political, social, and cultural ideas and practices of the Chinese. Since the tenth century, the Vietnamese have been generally free of Chinese domination, but from time to time in the past the Chinese claimed sovereignty over Vietnam. The desire of the Chinese to play a role in the affairs of the Vietnamese has a historical foundation. The Vietnamese, however, do not relish the thought of Chinese influence, and they have sought to maintain their independence of policy and action.

The Vietnamese have had their share of war and civil struggle during their long history. They conquered their way southward; they have fought with the Cambodians, the Laotians, and the Thais; and they have made themselves feared in their region. In 1884, a French protectorate was established over the country, and in 1940 the Japanese occupied the land. During the Japanese occupation, nationalist forces grouped under the leadership of Ho Chih Minh, a veteran Communist leader, and fought against the Japanese. Later, they continued the fight against the French, who tried to reassert their rule over the country at the conclusion of World War II in 1945. The French were eventually forced to withdraw from the struggle, and a settlement was reached at Geneva on July 21, 1954. Soon thereafter war again raged in Vietnam.

The land is long and narrow, about one thousand miles in length and from thirty to three hundred miles in width. It has frequently been described as resembling a pole from the ends of which dangle two baskets of rice—slim in the middle and bulging at the extremities. The mountains sometimes run down to the sea itself, and endless pools of ricefields reflect the glare of a burning sun. There are jungles and gloomy rain forests. The population is about forty-four million. Some reside in large cities such as Hanoi and Saigon. But many more live in the farming villages of the countryside where comforts are few, the struggle to survive unrelenting, and knowledge of the world beyond the community very limited. The Vietnamese of the north and the Vietnamese of the center frequently show their scorn of the people who live in the southern portion, formerly called Cochin-China; and the southerners reciprocate with resentment and distrust.

Origins of the Recent Conflict

Under the terms of the Geneva agreement of 1954, many thousands of Ho Chih Minh's supporters were repatriated from South to North Vietnam, but some thousands also stayed in South Vietnam. The Geneva agreement also provided for free elections in both halves of the country for the purpose of uniting the country under one government by 1956. The President of South Vietnam, Ngo Dinh Diem, refused to hold elections on the grounds that no free election was possible in North Vietnam and that South Vietnam had not signed the agreement anyway. Ho Chih Minh had expected to win these elections; but when President Diem refused to hold them, Ho called upon his supporters in the South to act. A revolt started in South Vietnam.

With persuasion and with force, the antigovernment guerrillas gradually extended their control over the countryside. Many non-Communists joined the "Front for the Liberation of South Vietnam," the formal name of the group which opposed the Saigon government, because they believed Diem's government was corrupt, unmindful of the needs of the people, undemocratic, and lacking social consciousness. Those who fought against the Saigon government were called Viet Cong, or "Vietnamese Communists."

By 1960, there was little doubt that the Viet Cong were winning the war in South Vietnam and that the statement of North Vietnam's defense minister, General Giap, "Thousands of small victories accumulate into a great success," was being proven true. The people of South Vietnam lived in the midst of chaos and terror. The Saigon government ruled by day in the cities and wherever it had soldiers; the Viet Cong covered the countryside by night. Nowhere was there safety; no one felt secure. It was dangerous to travel the roads by day without an armed escort. Ambushes, the burning of buses and automobiles, the mining of roads, and the murder of travelers were common occurrences. Every day the newspapers reported incidents ranging from pitched battles between large government and Viet-Cong forces to the kidnapping of individuals. The social, economic, and political life of South Vietnam was being slowly strangled. By 1961, it was apparent that the government of South Vietnam was near defeat. The United States became extremely concerned, and President Kennedy sent General Maxwell Taylor to the battle scene to investigate and recommend action.

U.S. Participation in the War

The Americans had been concerned with the Vietnamese war long before this time. In 1950, the United States started to support the French financially in their struggle against the Vietnamese, and it is estimated that a total of 1.2 billion dollars was given by the Americans to the French in their attempt to reassert their dominance over the Vietnamese. When the French were on the edge of defeat in 1954, some American officials urged a military intervention in the war, but it is reported that the idea was vetoed by President Eisenhower. After the partition of Vietnam, the United States sent six hundred military advisers to South Vietnam, and by 1957, this number had risen to eight hundred. After General Taylor returned to Washington with his recommendations, the number of American military advisers in South Vietnam increased to eleven thousand. At that time, the Americans also started to fly the Vietnamese into battle and to construct airfields, port facilities, and other military installations. But the political and military situation continued to worsen. In November 1963, the Diem government was overthrown and Diem himself was killed. The Viet Cong continued to grow stronger, and the number of American forces continued to grow to thwart them.

Why Were the Americans in Vietnam?

On April 7, 1965, President Johnson gave the official reasons why the United States was in Vietnam. "We are there," he said,

> because we have a promise to keep. Since 1954 every American President has offered support to the people of South Vietnam. . . . Thus over many years, we have made a national pledge to help South Vietnam defend its independence . . . To dishonor that pledge, to abandon this small and brave nation to its enemy —and to the terror that must follow—would be an unforgivable wrong. . . . We are also there to strengthen world order. Around the globe—from Berlin to Thailand—are people whose well-being rests, in part, on the belief they can count on us if they are attacked. To leave Vietnam to its fate would shake the confidence of all these people in the value of American commitment. The result would be increased unrest and instability, or even war. . . . We are there because there are great stakes in the balance. Let no one think that retreat from Vietnam would bring an end to conflict. The battle would be renewed in one country and then another.

The central lesson of our time is that the appetite of aggression is never satisfied. To withdraw from one battlefield means only to prepare for the next. We must say in Southeast Asia—as we did in Europe—in the words of the Bible: "Hitherto shalt thou come, but no further."

U.S. Objectives in Vietnam

President Johnson in this same speech also stated the official objective of the United States in Vietnam. "Our objective is the independence of South Vietnam, and its freedom from attack. We want nothing for ouselves—only that the people of South Vietnam be allowed to guide their own country in their own way." He stated that we have increased our military support of the South Vietnamese government "in order to slow down aggression. We do this to increase the confidence of the brave people of South Vietnam . . . and we do this to convince the leaders of North Vietnam —and all who seek to share their conquest—of a simple fact: We will not be defeated. We will not grow tired. We will not withdraw, either openly or under the cloak of a meaningless agreement."

President Richard Nixon inherited the burdens and responsibilities of the Vietnam war, and stated what American objectives were and were not in a television speech on May 14, 1969.

We seek no bases in Vietnam. We insist on no military ties. We are willing to agree to neutrality if this is what the South Vietnamese people freely choose. We believe there should be an opportunity for full participation in the political life of South Vietnam by all political elements that are prepared to do so without the use of force or intimidation. We are prepared to accept any government in South Vietnam that results from the free choice of the South Vietnamese people themselves. We have no intention of imposing any form of government upon the people of South Vietnam, nor will we be a party to such coercion. We have no objection to reunification, if that turns out to be what the people of South Vietnam and North Vietnam want; we ask only that the decision reflect the free choice of the people concerned.

Criticism and Peace Proposals

At home and abroad, criticism of the American policy and activities in Vietnam grew and intensified. This criticism reflected a wide diversity of attitudes and reasons; moral, ideological, political, economic, fear of nuclear war, and other views swayed and shook the American public and the American leaders. In 1968, President Johnson halted the bombing of North Vietnam and called for peace negotiations. After 1968, the participants in the war met in

Paris. In his speech of May 1969, President Nixon also presented a formula for withdrawal of non-Vietnamese forces from South Vietnam.

> Over a period of 12 months ... the major portions of all U.S., allied, and other non-South Vietnamese forces would be withdrawn. At the end of this 12-month period, ... remaining U.S., allied and other non-South Vietnamese forces would move into designated base areas and ... not engage in combat operations. The remaining U.S. and allied forces would move to complete their withdrawals as the remaining North Vietnamese forces were withdrawn and returned to North Vietnam. An international supervisory body ... would be created for the purpose of verifying withdrawals, and for ... other purposes agreed upon. ... This international body would begin operating in accordance with an agreed timetable and would participate in arranging supervised cease fires. ... After the international body was functioning, elections would be held under agreed procedures and under the supervision of the international body. ... All parties would agree to observe the Geneva Accords of 1954 regarding Vietnam and Cambodia, and the Laos Accords of 1962.

In 1972, President Nixon reduced these conditions asking only for an internationally supervised cease fire and the release of American prisoners of war. If these conditions were met he promised complete withdrawal from Vietnam in a few months. He also resumed the heavy bombing of North Vietnam and blockaded the harbors.

Finally, in January 1973, the United States, North Vietnam, South Vietnam, and the Viet Cong signed a nine chapter agreement in Paris which formally brought an end to hostilities in Vietnam. The agreement provided for a cease-fire; the release of all prisoners of war on both sides; the withdrawal of all American and foreign combat personnel; various joint bodies to supervise the truce; the independence, unity, and territorial integrity of Vietnam as recognized by the 1954 Geneva Agreements; and the right of South Vietnamese people to self-determination among other provisions. American prisoners of war were returned to the United States, and American combat personnel were withdrawn from Vietnam. Finally, in 1975, the Saigon government collapsed under strong military pressure from the North Vietnamese armies. All of Vietnam then came under the direction of leaders who professed the same political philosophy of Communism.

During the Vietnamese struggle, the North Vietnamese constructed supply routes to southern Vietnam through the adjacent territory of Laos. They also helped to organize and support the Pathet Lao, a Communist-led force, which now governs Laos. Many believe that the ultimate authorities of the Pathet Lao are Vietnamese leaders who rule from behind the scene. There are those, too, who think that the goal of the Vietnamese is to eventually control the entire Indochina peninsula which includes the countries of Vietnam, Laos, and Cambodia. The Thais have complained that the Vietnamese are engaging in subversive activities in the northeastern portion of their country. Whatever the future intentions of the Vietnamese, there is no doubt that they will play an increasingly important role on mainland Southeast Asia.

External Political Problems

In addition to their fear of internal subversion and civil strife, the Southeast Asians have an abhorrence of colonialism in any form. Since most of them were under the colonial regimes of Western powers for some years, the deep suspicion they developed of the intentions of the Western powers in Asia has not yet been completely dissolved. Anti-imperialism and anticolonialism are still rousing and fighting terms for most Asians. Until settled in 1962, the West Irian (formerly West New Guinea) question was capable of firing the Indonesians into a high emotional flame. The Indians supported Nehru wholeheartedly in his forceful seizure of Portuguese-controlled Goa. The Indonesians readily supported their government in the 1976 annexation of Portuguese Timor. And many Asians view the American military presence in Asia as the concrete expression of a persisting imperialist attitude. Further, a number of Asians feel that a new kind of colonialism, neocolonialism, is threatening their independence of action through economic power. The colonial regimes left a tainted heritage in Asia which still conditions the feelings and attitudes of many Asians toward Westerners.

The Southeast Asian countries are caught up in the great power politics of the Soviet Union, China, and the United States. International issues are constantly arising on which their moral support is sought, and votes wooed in the United Nations. It is sometimes extremely difficult for some of these small nations to take a stand, for they will be "damned if they do and damned if they don't." At times they are requested by one of the great powers to take positive physical actions in their region which might bring them into conflict with another great power. Again they are faced with an agonizing decision which they do not want to make. Most of them are afraid of offending one of these great powers because such action might bring them immediate or future harassment and retribution.

In their search for the safest path between these mighty outside forces some of them have adopted a policy of neutrality or nonalignment. They believe that holding themselves somewhat aloof and impartial with regard to the great power issues plaguing them and the world is the best way to ward off danger and to preserve the independent existence of their nations. For some this policy has been somewhat successful; for others, it has not worked.

Neutralist Cambodia became a battleground of warring South Vietnamese, North Vietnamese, and Cambodian forces. Laos, formally neutral, became a highway for the movement of North Vietnamese supplies to the south, a target for American bombs, and a battlefield for Laotians, Vietnamese, and Americans. Indonesia turned sharply toward the West when, in 1965, the Communists almost succeeded in capturing the government there. Even strictly neutralist Burma has been having problems with groups sometimes armed and encouraged from the outside.

The leaders of these and other Southeast Asian countries are no doubt reassessing the advantages and disadvantages of neutrality or nonalignment. The foremost advocate of nonalignment for itself and nonalignment or neutrality for Southeast Asian nations, until the clash with China in 1962, was India. The Southeast Asians have noted that India no longer maintains a strictly nonaligned position as heretofore. Since 1965, the Soviet Union has been supplying India with much, if not most, of its military equipment. More recently, in August 1971, India and the Soviet Union signed a treaty of peace, friendship, and cooperation. The Soviet Union also supported the invasion of East Pakistan by Indian armies which resulted in the establishment of Bangladesh, the weakening of Pakistan, an increase in Soviet influence in that region, and in India becoming the dominant power in South Asia. In the eyes of the Southeast Asian leaders alignment, even a temporary or weak one, sometimes has its advantages.

Other Southeast Asian countries have chosen to line up with one power or the other in the pursuit of security for their war-threatened region. Thailand and the Philippines, for instance, became tied to the United States by treaties. North Vietnam was supported by both China and the Soviet Union, but walked a tightrope between the conflicting interests of these two giants.

Malaysia is trying to have the best of both worlds. In 1970, its prime minister, Tun Abdul Razak, called for the neutralization of Southeast Asia and a great power guarantee for such neutralization. And since this time a more cordial relationship has developed between China and Malaysia. But in April 1971, a defense agreement was signed by Malaysia, Singapore, Australia, New Zealand, and Great Britain. Among its provisions were an air defense system, the stationing of Australian, New Zealand, and British forces in Singapore and Malaysia, and a meeting of the signers in case of an external attack on Singapore or Malaysia. Malaysia claims that it is merely an interim agreement prior to the great power guaranteed neutralization of Southeast Asia. Officially, Indonesia has continued its policy of nonalignment, but much of its military equipment comes from the United States.

The political problems of Southeast Asia are many and pressing. Even the peaceful heritage of Buddhism, with its traditional stress on the more positive virtues of humans, does not appear capable of resolving the passionate hostilities that threaten this region. Freedom, independence, economic security, time-honored religions, traditions, and cultures, even existence itself, are in danger of being destroyed in Southeast Asia by war, the poisons of ideological suspicions, and the deadly erosion of the competing interests of great powers. It will require all the intelligence, courage, sacrifice, and dedication that can be mustered by the positively oriented people of Southeast Asia to check the negative, destructive forces that are besieging their land and people.

40

Asians Are
People With a Destiny

Now numbering over half the human race, the
Asians of today have finally begun to assert their
human right to determine their own destiny. Refusing to continue as the playthings of fate,
absolute monarchs, and other nations, they are
resolved to shape their own destiny to suit their
own needs, their own wants, and their own
ideals.

Asians are destined to eat better. Famine,
for thousands of years a familiar guest in their
homes, is no longer considered the decree of
sadistic spirits and gods, or the inevitable response of a violated earth, to be passively accepted; it is now regarded as a community
problem which can be understood in social and

economic terms and solved by the joint efforts of human minds and human hands. Hunger, a state in which many Asians continually live, is no longer regarded as a natural condition, but a cause for active dissatisfaction, and Asians are resolved to remove it from their destiny.

Asians are destined to be better informed. Education and literacy have been idealized by countless generations of Asian people. The scholar stood at the apex of Chinese society, and only he could administer the affairs of state. The educated Brahmins were of the highest status in India. The Japanese hierarchy was dominated by the soldier-aristocrat, but tradition required that he be able to read and write. In Korea, Indochina, Burma, Thailand, Indonesia, the Philippines, elsewhere in Asia, the educated person, who could read and write was respected. Today in Asia there is a tremendous drive toward the goal of universal literacy. Through literacy, Asians expect to gain access to the accumulated knowledge of mankind and thus build for themselves better and happier lives. Asian leaders are determined to industrialize their countries as fully and rapidly as possible; since modern industry requires workers who can read and write, these leaders are actively promoting mass education. Schools and village reading classes are springing up all over Asia.

Asians are destined to collectivize. Their leaders believe that they do not have the time to build up their industrial establishments in the same leisurely manner as did the great industrialized countries of the West such as Great Britain and the United States. They maintain that the quickening tempo of world events, the economic and political security of their countries, and the insistent demands of their people for a better standard of living require that they industrialize their countries at a breakneck speed, and they believe that this goal cannot be achieved without the collective organization of all the people and massive infusions of state aid.

Asians are destined to participate more in domestic politics. In Asia people are becoming actively involved in the political life of their countries. The leaders think and speak of themselves as the elected leaders of the people, whether they are or not. Asian people are told that it is *their* government and *their* will that the government expresses. Elections are held in a number of countries, and although the choice of candidates has usually been quite limited, many people do get a chance to express an opinion in a formal way. This is a new experience for them but one they have taken to with ease and enthusiasm. In Japan, India, Indonesia, the Philippines, Malaysia, and other countries, the candidates have gone out among the people to woo votes and detail their platforms, and there have been enthusiastic turnouts at elections.

Never before in the history of Asia have the ordinary people been given the impression that they are important in the political life of the country. Never before have so many Asians had the experience of expressing a preference, though a limited one, for a political leader. Most leaders in the past came with the sword, and they did not seek the permission of the people to rule. That permission is now formally sought by many Asian politicians, and in some countries it has been refused.

Nehru was an excellent example of a leading politician who spent much of his time with his people. It was not uncommon for him to speak to a hundred thousand or more at one time, and it is reported that, on one occasion, he took a six-day motor tour in which he traveled over two hundred miles and made twenty speeches a day. He tried very hard to give his people a feeling of participation in government.

Asians are destined to be more respected. Perhaps nothing has been more resented by the Asian than the conception of him as inferior by the white Westerner, whether colonizer, missionary, businessman or tourist. Clubs for white people only, in Bombay, Calcutta, Singapore, Hong Kong, Shanghai, Tokyo, Manila, and elsewhere, were and are hated symbols of white arrogance. City parks forbidden to natives by the British during their rule in Asia are painfully and bitterly remembered. A sense of elation spread throughout Asia, sometimes hidden, sometimes displayed, when the Japanese Asians defeated the whites in the early days of World War II.

Asians are determined to be respected. They feel that they are the equal of any other human group and the superior of many. Many of them are ready to forfeit law, order, and their own lives in order to obtain this respect.

The urge in most Asian countries to build up economic, political, and military power is in part motivated by the desire of these nations to be treated as equals of the Western nations. The reluc-

Tension and violence have characterized Indian-Pakistani relations since 1947. Sino-Soviet antagonism is reflected here in the Soviet Union support of India and the Chinese support of Pakistan.

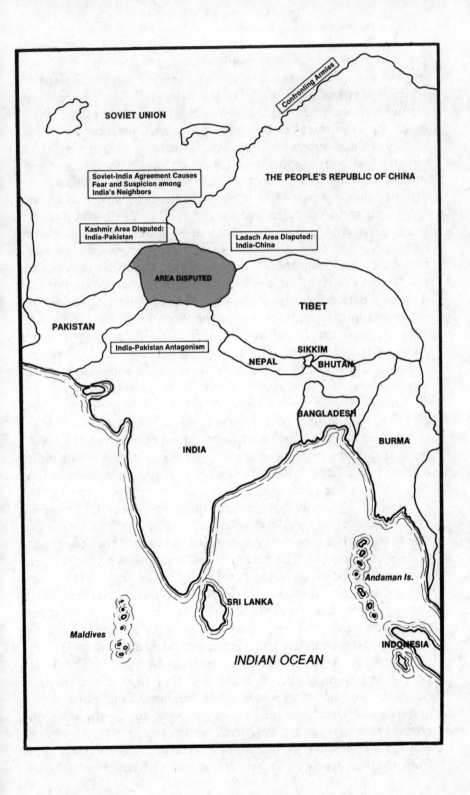

tance to employ foreign personnel, the extreme sensitivity to any implied slur by white foreigners, the sometimes harsh treatment of white Westerners living in Asian countries, the desperate, defiant attitude shown when logic is sometimes on the side of the Westerner, the resentment at being forced by circumstances to accept charity from Western nations, the insistence on running their countries without support from foreigners, especially if it has been offered with any hint of foreign superiority, are all in response to offenses given by past and present generations of white foreigners.

Asians are destined to become more nationalistic. Nationalism is a creative emotional factor today in Asia. Westerners taught the Asian people to forge the bonds of a new loyalty—loyalty to a nation-state. Previously the Asian people gave their first loyalties to the family, the clan, the caste, the class, or to individuals, but seldom to a national entity. Patriotism, love of country, was not an important motivation as it was in the West. When the Westerners came to Asia, they brought the spirit of nationalism with them. Asians sharing the same territory and possessing characteristics in common which distinguished them from neighboring Asians, such as a common language, race, tradition, history, and religion, began to think of themselves as a separate and special body of people—as a nation. The leaders of the various Asian countries in order to foster internal unity, deliberately promoted this feeling of belonging to a special group. Japan is an outstanding example of a people deliberately infused with a feeling of national pride, centered in this case in an emperor alleged to be divine. Asians, following the example of Westerners, attempted, quite successfully, to express this cultural unity in the establishment of independent nations. Today patriotism is emerging as a strong motivation for the actions of the Asian people. The nation is replacing the family, the clan, the caste, the emperor, as the first loyalty of the people. The political and intellectual leaders of the Asian countries are using every device to bring about a more intense and devoted love of the nation-state. Asians are becoming like Western nationals in their response to a waving flag and a stirring national anthem.

Asians are destined to resist colonialism everywhere. The Asian people detest colonialism so much that they fight it not only on their own soil, but wherever it exists. Indonesia fought bitterly to liquidate the Dutch colonial regime in New Guinea—Indonesians refer to this territory as West Irian—and replace the Dutch regime with an Indonesian government. She succeeded. India wrested Goa from the Portuguese. The broader attitude of Asian hostility to colonialism was expressed before in the United Nations General Assembly by Dr. Ide Agung, Indonesia's foreign minister, when he said: "The problems of colonialism are, of course, of particular interest to us and to the peoples of Asia and Africa, in general."

Asians are destined to resist external oppression. They have had their fill of foreign invaders who have lived off their land and dictated laws for them. Since the most recent oppressors in the long history of the Asian people were Westerners, Asian statesmen are particularly vigilant lest the great Western powers attempt to repeat their former successful invasions. The cry of "imperialism!" is still a familiar cry in Asia, and it conjures up vivid memories of Western administrators, Western soldiers, Western economic practices, Western exploitation, and Western arrogance. Imperialism is not a dead issue in Asia, but a vital one able to arouse the Asian people to intense and dedicated defiance.

But Asians are destined to engage in internecine conflict. The juxtaposition of major powers in Asia—India, China, Japan, and the Soviet Union—with a number of less powerful nations has already resulted in incidents, fears, border tensions, and conflicting spheres of influence. Nowhere are these problems more vividly illustrated than in the *White Papers* issued by the government of Pakistan entitled *India's War Propaganda Against Pakistan.* These documents charge that the Indian leaders have:

> never really reconciled themselves to the Partition of the Indo-Pakistan sub-continent and the creation of Pakistan. They hoped that it would prove a temporary phase and that Pakistan would soon be absorbed by India.
>
> The number of books and pamphlets which have been issued since the Partition in various Indian languages and advocating absorption of Pakistan into India must be running into hundreds.
>
> A study of the Indian press leaves no doubt that this absorption of Pakistan into India is to be brought about by means of force. In pursuance of this aim Indian leaders and Indian press have not only been urging the absorption of Pakistan by India but have seized every opportunity to preach war against Pakistan.

The invasion of Bangladesh by Indian armies was a contemporary expression of their antagonism. The feeling and spirit that pervade these official words of the government of Pakistan are reflected in the words of many of the other Asian nations with reference to their neighbors. The Nationalist Chinese government on Taiwan conveys in even stronger language its hatred and suspicion of the Communist Chinese government on the mainland. South Korean spokesmen have used very strong language when they speak of North Korean officials. Laos and Cambodia are extremely wary of the activities of the Vietnamese. Thailand, Burma, Malaysia, are all fearful of the colossus of China on their northern borders and frequently suspicious of each other. Some of the countries of Asia are suspicious of the intentions of the Japanese. The Philippines is at odds with Malaysia over Sabah and Malaysia has often regarded Indonesia and Singapore with suspicion.

There is a new, dynamic spirit abroad in Asia. No longer the slow-moving, nonchanging Asia of storybook and movie, it is now a militant, demanding, searching Asia, prepared to fight for its future. The people of Asia now know that there is hope for themselves and their families. They have learned from Westerners, from Asians educated in the West, from Asians educated in their own schools, and from their leaders and neighbors, that they have the power and capacity to wrest a better living from the earth. The exciting idea that man is not fated to live desolate and insecure has aroused them to action and transformed them into crusaders marching toward a better world. The new revelation that poverty can be abolished, that man is under no cosmic necessity to suffer starvation at regular intervals, that living ill-housed and ill-clothed is not the decree of some incomprehensible fate, that freedom and good government are not only desirable but possible, has stimulated them to try to eliminate forever the shadows of political and economic uncertainty under which they have lived for thousands of years.

The Asians are dreaming of a future when they will have enough to eat, comfortable homes, education for their children, medical services and medicine for their sick, respect for themselves as individuals, freedom, peace, and political stability and security. They want these dreams realized, preferably within their lifetime. They place continuous and unyielding pressure upon their leaders to secure for them more and better opportunities for happiness. They champion those who earnestly seek the fulfillment of their dreams; they are sullen and threatening toward those who are obstructing their destiny, and their protest is sometimes written in their blood.

The goading challenge facing the Asians and the world is how to realize their impelling visions of a better life. Frustration, turmoil, and chaos will result from an unrealized destiny, for if they must to make their dreams come true, the Asians are destined to sacrifice themselves—and others.

selected references

It is not possible to list all the writings on Asia that can be read with pleasure and profit. The following books will lead the interested reader to other authors who can provide additional valuable and interesting information on the Asian people.

Asia

Anderson, George L., ed. *The Genius of the Oriental Theater.* New York: New American Library, 1966. Interesting selection of Asian plays.

———, ed. *Masterpieces of the Orient.* New York: W. W. Norton, 1961. Asian literature in translation.

Asia Society. *An Introductory Reading Guide to Asia.* Annotated list of books for the general reader.

Association for Asian Studies. *Bibliography of Asian Studies.* Annual. Exhaustive list of books and articles on Asia that appear during the year.

Brecher, Michael. *The New States of Asia.* New York: Oxford University Press, 1966. Excellent political analysis.

Brown, Sidney Devere, ed. *Studies on Asia.* vol. 8. Lincoln: University of Nebraska Press, 1967. Selected essays dealing with a wide range of subjects.

Burch, Betty B., and Cole, Alan B., eds. *Asian Political Systems.* New York: Van Nostrand-Reinhold Books, 1968. Readings by Asians on China, Japan, India, and Pakistan.

Buss, Claude A. *The Arc of Crisis: Nationalism and Neutralism in Asia Today.* New York: Doubleday, 1961. Focuses on two important aspects of modern Asia.

Chan, Wing-tsit; Isma il Ragi al Faruqi; Kitagawa, Joseph M.; and Raju, P. T., eds. *The Great Asian Religions: An Anthology.* New York: Macmillan, 1969. Good samplings of religious writings in India, Japan, China, and of Islam.

Crossby-Holland, Peter. *Non-Western Music.* vol. 1. Edited by A. Robertson and D. Stevens. Baltimore: Penguin Books, 1960. Pelican history of music.

Dean, Vera, et al. *The Nature of the Non-Western World.* New York: Mentor Books, 1957. The significance of nationalism and social change in Asia.

361

De Bary, ed. *Sources of Indian Tradition*. New York: Columbia University Press, 1958; *Sources of Chinese Tradition*. New York: Columbia University Press, 1960; and *Sources of Japanese Tradition*. New York: Columbia University Press, 1958. Three indispensable reference books on Asian thought.

Ginsburg, Norton, ed. *The Patterns of Asia*. Englewood Cliffs, N.J.: Prentice-Hall, 1958. Geographic look at Asia.

Hinton, Harold C. *Three and a Half Powers*. Bloomington: Indiana University Press, 1975. Focuses on the new balance of power emerging in Asia involving the countries of China, the Soviet Union, Japan, and the United States.

Iriye, Akira. *The Cold War in Asia*. Englewood Cliffs, N.J.: Prentice-Hall, 1974. A good background study of modern international politics in Asia.

Jukes, Geoffrey. *The Soviet Union in Asia*. Berkeley: University of California Press, 1973. The Soviet Union continues to play an important role in the politics of Asian countries.

Kennedy, J. *Asian Nationalism in the Twentieth Century*. New York: St. Martin's Press, 1968. A rounded discussion of an extremely important subject.

Lach, Donald F. *Asia in the Making of Europe*. vol. 1, books 1 and 2, vol. II, books 1 and 2. Chicago: University of Chicago Press, 1965ff. This is a series of books detailing Asia's many contributions to European civilization. The latest volume was published in 1976.

Lach, Donald F., and Flaumenhaft, Carol, eds. *Asia on the Eve of Europe's Expansion*. Englewood Cliffs, N.J.: Prentice-Hall, 1965. Interesting accounts by European travelers and Asians in the fourteenth, fifteenth, and sixteenth centuries.

Lach, Donald F., and Wehrle, Edmund. *International Relations in East Asia since World War II*. New York: Praeger, 1975. Concentrates on nations of China, Japan, Korea, and Vietnam, and their developing international policies. Attention is also given to the roles of such superpowers as the United States and the Soviet Union in the area.

Levenson, Joseph R., ed. *European Expansion and the Counter-Example of Asia*. Englewood Cliffs, N.J.: Prentice-Hall, 1967. Discusses the period between 1300 and 1600 and focuses on the question why European expansion and technological advances and not Asian.

McLane, Charles B. *Soviet-Asian Relations*. New York: Columbia University Press, 1973. Useful study of Soviet policies in Asia.

Malm, William P. *Music Cultures of the Pacific Near East and Asia*. Englewood Cliffs, N.J.: Prentice-Hall, 1967. Broad introduction to Asian music and musical instruments.

Metraux, Guy S., and Crouset, Francois, eds. *The New Asia*. New York: New American Library, 1965. Asian writers discuss the last two centuries of change in various Asian countries.

Myrdal, Gunnar. *Asian Drama: An Inquiry into the Poverty of Nations*. New York: Pantheon Books, 1968. Three volumes of general and detailed information. Special stress on South Asia.

Pannikar, K. M. *Asia and Western Dominance: A Survey of the Vasco De Gama Epoch of Asian History, 1498–1945*. New York: Hillary House, 1959. A survey of the Vasco De Gama epoch of Asian History, 1498 to 1945, through the eyes and generalizations of an Asian.

Peterson, A. D. C. *The Far East: A Social Geography*. 2nd ed. London: Duckworth, 1951.

Reischauer, Edwin O. *Beyond Vietnam: The United States and Asia*. New York: Alfred A. Knopf, 1967. The author discusses past and present policies in Asia and suggests alternative policies for America in the future.

Ritter, Helen, and Spector, Stanley, eds. *Our Oriental Americans*. New York: McGraw-Hill, 1965. The origins and the development of Asians in America.

Sakai, Robert K., ed. *Studies on Asia*. vol. 7. Lincoln: University of Nebraska Press,

1966. Essays on many subjects including such topics as nineteenth century gunboat diplomacy, and the Sokagakkai movement in Japan.

Scalapino, Robert A. *The Communist Revolution in Asia: Tactics, Goals and Achievements.* 2nd ed. Englewood Cliffs, N.J.: Prentice-Hall, 1969. Comprehensive survey of communist governments, movements, and parties throughout Asia.

Smith, Huston. *The Religions of Man.* New York: Mentor Books, 1958. A readable paperback with clean and concise accounts of the Asian religions.

Visser, H. F. E. *Art Treasures from the East.* Amsterdam: Die Spieghel, 1954.

Ward, Barbara. *The Interplay of East and West.* New York: W. W. Norton, 1957. Deals with the problem of mutual understanding.

Wilcox, Wayne Ayres. *Asia and United States Policy.* Englewood Cliffs, N.J.: Prentice-Hall, 1967. An excellent writer and scholar deals with American policies toward the various Asian nations and relates their responses to these policies.

Wilcox, Wayne Ayres; Rose, Leo; and Boyd, R. Gavin, eds. *Asia and the International System.* Cambridge: Winthrop Publishers, 1972. A number of specialists deal with the foreign policies of the larger and smaller Asian States, the interaction of the United States and the Soviet Union in Asia, and other matters such as security and defense.

Wint, Guy, ed. *Asia: A Handbook.* rev. ed. Baltimore: Penguin Books, 1970. Wide selection of articles covering many topics and most of Asia. Good reference work.

Yohannan, John, ed. *A Treasury of Asian Literature.* New York: John Day, 1956. An introduction to the literature of Asia.

India

Appadorai, A. *Essays on Indian Politics and Foreign Policy.* Delhi, India: Vikas Publications, 1971. The domestic and foreign politics of India are very important to the world today.

Baig, M. R. A. *Muslim Dilemma in India.* Delhi, India: Vikas Publications, 1974. Since the British took over the leadership in India, the Muslims have been torn and pulled in many directions.

Barnds, William J. *India, Pakistan, and the Great Powers.* New York: Praeger, 1972. The interaction of India and Pakistan is a sensitive matter for all the great powers.

Basham, A. L. *The Wonder That Was India.* London: Sidwick & Jackson, 1954. An excellent introduction to traditional India.

Brown, D. MacKenzie. *The White Umbrella: Indian Political Thought from Manu to Gandhi.* Berkeley: University of California Press, 1953.

Burlingame, Eugene W. *Buddhist Parables.* New Haven: Yale University Press, 1922.

Chandrasekhar, S. "The Family in India." *Marriage and Family Living* 16 (Nov., 1954): 336–42. A succinct account of the Indian family.

Chaudhuri, Nirad. *The Continent of Circe.* New York: Oxford University Press, 1966. Provides a special insight into Indian attitudes, values, procedures, and general orientation toward life.

Chen, Kuan-I, and Uppal, J. S., eds. *India and China: Studies in Comparative Development.* New York: The Free Press, 1971. A variety of readings on the comparison of Asia's two giant nations.

Collins, Larry, and Lapierre, Dominique. *Freedom at Midnight.* New York: Simon & Schuster, 1975. An excellent description of the immediate events leading to the independence and partition of India and Pakistan. Graphic portrayal of the atrocities that accompanied partition. Also gives in much detail Lord Mountbatten's role in India during this period.

Dube, S. C. *Indian Village*. Ithaca: Cornell University Press, 1955. A good introduction to the village scene in India.

Dutt, Ashok K. *India: Resources, Potentialities and Planning*. Dubuque, Iowa: Kendall/Hunt, 1972. The development of India's economy has been rather sporadic.

Dutt, G. S. *A Woman of Bengal, Being the Life of Saroj Nalini*. London: Hogarth Press, 1929. Gives valuable insight into the attitudes of the Indian woman.

Emerson, Gertrude. *Voiceless India*. New York: John Day, 1944. A warm and engrossing book that sparkles with revealing descriptions of India's rural and social scene.

Fairservis, Walter A., Jr. *The Roots of Ancient India: The Archeology of Early Indian Civilization*. New York: Macmillan, 1971. A renowned scholar discusses India's origins.

Franda, Marcus F. *Radical Politics in West Bengal*. Cambridge, Mass.: M.I.T. Press, 1971. India, too, has been trying to cope with revolutionary and radical movements among the Bengalis.

Frankel, Francine R. *India's Green Revolution: Economic Gains and Political Costs*. Princeton N.J.: Princeton University Press, 1971. India certainly needs an abundance of agriculture, but what are the consequent costs?

Gandhi, Mohandas K. *An Autobiography or The Story of My Experiments with Truth*. Ahmedabad, India: Navajivan Publishing House, 1945. A candid account of himself and his times by a man whose name is synonymous with India's modern history and development.

Gates, Katherine, ed. and trans. *Ramabai Ranade, Himself: The Autobiography of a Hindu Lady*. New York: David McKay, 1938. Illuminates the attitudes of the Indian woman.

Ghose, Sankar. *Socialism and Communism in India*. Bombay, India: Allied Publishers, 1971. Socialism and communism are influential ideologies among large segments of India's people.

Gordon, Leonard A., and Miller, Barbara Stoler. *A Syllabus of Indian Civilization*. New York: Columbia University Press, 1971. For those who seek guidelines in dealing with Indian civilization.

Gosvami, O. *The Story of Indian Music*. New York: Taplinger Publishing, 1957.

Griffiths, Sir Percival. *The British Impact on India*. London: MacDonald, 1952. Gives a good picture of modern India's political institutions and ideas.

Grousset, Rene. *In the Footsteps of the Buddha*. London: Routledge and Kegan Paul, 1932.

Haigh, Sir Henry. *Some Leading Ideas of Hinduism*. London: Charles J. Kelley, 1903. Contains illuminating statements on this religion.

Hamilton, Clarence H., ed. *Buddhism: A Religion of Infinite Compassion*. New York: The Liberal Arts Press, 1952.

Hardgrave, Robert L., Jr. *India: Government and Politics in a Developing Nation*. New York: Harcourt Brace Jovanovich, 1970. Excellent treatment of the problems of political development in India.

Kapur, Promilla. *Marriage and the Working Woman in India*. Delhi, India: Vikas Publications, 1970. A pioneering work which looks at the sociology of Indian women.

——. *Love, Marriage and Sex*. Delhi, India: Vikas Publications, 1972. Broad inquiry on the attitudes toward sex, love, and marriage of educated working women in India.

Lamb, Beatrice Pitney. *India: A World in Transition*. rev. ed. New York: Praeger, 1975. A useful and readable introduction to the land and people of India.

McLane, John R. *The Political Awakening in India*. Englewood Cliffs, N.J.: Prentice-Hall, 1970. From nineteenth century political foundation to the independence of India.

Mason, Philip. *Matter of Honour—An Account of the Indian Army—Its Officers and Men*. Jonathan Cape, 1974. A subject that needs more attention in this modern period.

Maxwell, Neville. *India's China War*. New York: Doubleday, 1972. Using Indian documents, interviews, and other research, he concludes that India was more responsible for this war than China.

Mehta, Ved. *Portrait of India*. Baltimore: Penguin Books, 1973. A keen observer looks at modern India.

Menon, K. P. S. *The Indo-Soviet Treaty: Setting and Meaning*. Delhi, India: Vikas Publications, 1972. An extremely important treaty for both Asians and the world.

Morgan, Kenneth W. *The Religion of the Hindus*. New York: Ronald Press, 1953. A good introduction.

Nair, Kusum. *Blossoms in the Dust: The Human Factor in Indian Development*. New York: Praeger, 1962. The human factor is often neglected in state planning.

Nehru, Jawaharlal. *The Discovery of India*. Calcutta, India: Signet Press, 1946. *An Autobiography*. New Delhi, India: Allied Publishers, 1962. Strongly recommended as a basic book by India's first Prime Minister.

Orenstein, Henry. *Gaon: Conflict and Cohesion in an Indian Village*. Princeton, N.J.: Princeton University Press, 1965. The village is still basic to Indian life.

Overstreet, Gene D., and Windmiller, Marshall. *Communism in India*. Berkeley: University of California Press, 1959.

Palmer, Norman D. *The Indian Political System*. 2nd ed. New York: Houghton Mifflin Co., 1971. Good brief survey of structure and nature of Indian politics.

Park, Richard L. *Change and the Persistence of Tradition in India*. Ann Arbor: University of Michigan Center for South and Southeast Asian Studies, 1971. A series of five lectures focusing on the mixture of the old and the new.

———. *India's Political System*. Englewood Cliffs, N.J.: Prentice-Hall, 1968. Provides good understanding of India's political system.

Rudolph, L. I., and Rudolph, S. H. *The Modernity of Tradition: Political Development in India*. Chicago: University of Chicago Press, 1968.

Santokh Singh Anant. *The Changing Concept of Caste in India*. Delhi, India: Vikas Publications, 1972. An old institution in India is undergoing some change.

Singh, Khushwant. *The Sikhs Today*. Bombay, India: Orient Longmans, 1967. A people who have made a great impact upon the past and present of India.

Smith, Donald E., ed. *South Asian Politics and Religion*. Princeton, N.J.: Princeton University Press, 1966. Various authors discuss religion and politics in the various countries of South Asia.

Spear, Percival. *India: A Modern History*. Ann Arbor: The University of Michigan Press, 1961. Solid, well organized, and well written.

Wiser, William, and Wiser, Charlotte. *Behind Mud Walls, 1930–1960*. Berkeley: University of California Press, 1967. A gripping account of the way of life of the people in a village of India.

Zinkin, Taya. *India Changes!* New York: Oxford University Press, 1958. Points up the transitional social problems of modern India.

Pakistan and Bangladesh

Anwar, Muhammad. *Jinnah Quaid-e-Azam, A Selected Biography*. Karachi, Pakistan: National Publishing House, 1970. Very few biographies of the founder of modern Pakistan have been published in English.

Ayoob, Mohammed, et al., eds. *Bangla Desh: A Struggle for Nationhood*. Delhi, India: Vikas Publications, 1971. Selection of documents dealing with the Bengalis' development toward an independent nation.

Ayub Khan, Mohammed. *Friends Not Masters*. New York: Oxford University Press, 1967. Autobiography of former president, stressing political factors.

Banerjee, D. N. *East Pakistan: A Case Study in Muslim Politics.* Delhi, India: Vikas Publications, 1969. Former East Pakistan from the days of the East India Company to the rule of General Yahya Khan (late President of Pakistan) from the viewpoint of an Indian specialist.

Bolitho, Hector, *Jinnah: Creator of Pakistan.* New York: Macmillan, 1955. One of the few biographies about the "Father of Pakistan," who should be better known in the West.

Bhutto, Z. A. *Myth of Independence.* London: Oxford University Press, 1969. The President of Pakistan writes about foreign policy and relations among nations.

Caroe, Sir Olaf. *The Pathans: Five Hundred B.C. to A.D. Nineteen Hundred Fifty-Seven.* New York: St. Martin's Press, 1958. A history of the Pathans from the Parthian Wars of Alexander to twentieth century Pakistan.

Chaudhri, Muhammad Ali. *The Emergence of Pakistan.* New York: Columbia University Press, 1967. Informative study.

Choudhury, G. W. *Pakistan's Relations With India 1947-1966.* New York: Praeger, 1968. From the very beginning of their independence the relations between these two countries have generally been tense.

Crescent and Green. London: Cassell & Co., 1955. Contains a number of solid essays by various authors on the life and culture of Pakistan.

Eglar, Zekige. *A Punjabi Village in Pakistan.* New York: Columbia University Press, 1960. Pakistan, like most other Asian countries, is a land of villages.

Feldman, Herbert. *Revolution in Pakistan: A Study of the Martial Law Administration.* London: Oxford University Press, 1967. This is a study of the forty-four months from October 1958 to June 1962 when Pakistan was governed under martial law.

The Holy Qu'ran. 2 vols. Translation and commentary by Abdullah Yusuf Ali. Darien, Conn.: Hafner, 1946. Copiously documented with commentaries and notes.

Ikram, S. M., and Spear, Percival, eds. *The Cultural Heritage of Pakistan.* New York: Oxford University Press, 1955. An informed treatment of the cultural background of the Pakistanis.

Iqbal, Sir Muhammad. *Poems from Iqbal.* Translated by V. G. Kiernan. London: John Murray, 1955. *The Secrets of the Self.* Translated by Reynold A. Nicholson. Lahore, Pakistan: Muhammad Ashraf, 1955. The spirit of Islam and Pakistan glows in the lyrical verses of Sir Muhammad Iqbal.

Khan, Akhbar. *Raiders in Kashmir—Story of the Kashmir War 1947-48.* Karachi, Pakistan: Pakistan Publishers, 1970. The violent beginning of a continuing dispute between Pakistan and India.

Lamb, Alastair. *The Kashmir Problem.* New York: Praeger, 1967. An aching problem for both Pakistan and India.

Moraes, Dom. *The Tempest Within: An Account of East Pakistan.* Delhi, India: Vikas Publications, 1971. The author discusses the natural and human-made problems of Bangladesh, formerly East Pakistan.

Pickthall, Muhammad Marmaduke, trans. *The Meaning of the Glorious Koran.* New York: Mentor Books. 1953. An inexpensive paperback translation.

Sayeed, Khalid B. *The Political System of Pakistan.* Boston: Houghton Mifflin, 1967. A political experiment was tried in Pakistan.

Stephens, Ian. *Pakistan.* New York: Praeger, 1970. Useful work.

Wilcox, Wayne A. *The Consolidation of a Nation.* New York: Columbia University Press, 1963. An understanding analysis.

Ziring, Lawrence. *The Ayub Khan Era; Politics in Pakistan.* New York: Syracuse University Press, 1971. An important era in Pakistan's history which ended on a negative note.

Afghanistan, Sri Lanka (Ceylon), Himalayan States

Bailey, Sydney D. *Ceylon*. London: Hutchinson's University Library, 1952. A good introduction.

Husain, Asad. *British India's Relations with the Kingdom of Nepal*. London: George Allen and Unwin. 1970. A diplomatic history of Nepal from 1857 to 1947. Uses original documents and confidential papers to highlight this period.

Karan, Pradyumna P., and Jenkins, William M. Jr. *The Himalayan Kingdoms: Bhutan, Sikkim and Nepal*. New York: Van Nostrand-Reinhold Books, 1963. Bhutan, Sikkim, and Nepal are examined from various points of view.

——. *Nepal: A Cultural and Physical Geography*. Lexington: University of Kentucky Press, 1960. Contains a bibliographical list of over 200 items.

Karunatilake, H. N. S. *Economic Development in Ceylon*. New York: Praeger, 1971. A comprehensive look at the economy of Ceylon.

Kearney, Robert N. *Trade Unions and Politics in Ceylon*. Berkeley: University of California Press, 1972. Trade unions have played a role in the politics of Ceylon.

Newell, Richard S. *The Politics of Afghanistan*. Ithaca: Cornell University Press, 1972. A modern work on the political system of a little-known country.

Rahul, Ram. *Modern Bhutan*. Delhi, India: Vikas Publications, 1971. Contemporary look at one of the Himalayan States.

Tresidder, Argus J. *Ceylon: An Introduction to the Resplendent Land*. New York: Van Nostrand-Reinhold Books, 1960. An introduction to the land and people.

East Asia

Clyde, Paul H., and Beers, Burton F. *The Far East: A History of the Western Impact and the Eastern Response*. 5th ed. Englewood Cliffs, N.J.: Prentice-Hall, 1971. A good standard historical treatment of this area of Asia.

Kim, Young Hum. *East Asia's Turbulent Century*. New York: Appleton-Century-Crofts, 1966. Excellent selection of American diplomatic documents as well as interpretation of modern happenings in East Asia.

McNelly, Theodore, ed. *Sources in Modern East Asian History and Politics*. New York: Appleton-Century-Crofts, 1967. Readings are well selected.

Reischauer, Edwin O., and Fairbank, John K. *East Asia: The Great Tradition*. Boston: Houghton Mifflin, 1960. History of China, Korea, and Japan from early times to nineteenth century.

Reischauer, Edwin O.; Fairbank, John K.; and Craig, Albert M. *East Asia: The Modern Transformation*. Boston: Houghton Mifflin, 1965. History of China, Korea, and Japan from nineteenth century to present.

China

Barnett, A. Doak. *China After Mao: Selected Documents*. Princeton, N.J.: Princeton University Press, 1967. Key documents and projections into the future of Communist China.

——. *Uncertain Passage: China's Transition to the Post-Mao Era*. Brookings Institution, 1974. Many scholars are thinking about the future of China after Chairman Mao dies.

Barnstone, Willis, trans. In collaboration with Ko Ching-po. *The Poems Of Mao Tse-tung*. New York: Harper & Row, 1972. These poems reveal the Mao who loves the great literature and poetry of traditional China.

Bloodworth, Dennis. *The Chinese Looking Glass.* New York: Farrar, Straus, & Giroux, 1967. An interesting, informative, and provocative series of observations about the Chinese by a fine writer.

Bonsall, B. S. *Confucianism and Taoism.* London: The Epworth Press, 1934. A helpful work on Chinese ideology.

Buck, Pearl S. *The Good Earth.* New York: John Day, 1949. A classic description of peasant life in China which can be read at one sitting.

Bulletin of Atomic Scientists. *China after the Cultural Revolution.* New York: Random House, Vintage Books, 1970. Twelve articles on the causes and consequences of the Cultural Revolution. They deal with many aspects of modern thought and practice in China.

Chai, Ch'u, and Chai, Winberg. *The Changing Society of China.* New York: Mentor Books, 1962. An excellent introduction.

Chai, Winberg. *The New Politics of Communist China: Modernization Process of a Developing Nation.* Pacific Palisades, Calif.: Goodyear, 1972. Tells the story of the modernization process in China. Contains a number of useful appendices.

Chesneaux, Jean. *Secret Societies in China: In the Nineteenth and Twentieth Centuries.* Ann Arbor: University of Michigan Press, 1972. Secret societies have often played major roles in the social, economic, and political life of the Chinese.

Chiang Kai-shek. *China's Destiny.* Translated by Wang Chung-hui. New York: Macmillan, 1947. The thoughts of the former leader of Nationalist China.

Chinese Art, by many authors. London: B. T. Batsford, 1952.

Creel, Herrlee G. *Chinese Thought from Confucius to Mao Tse-tung.* Chicago: University of Chicago Press, 1953. A good introduction to Chinese ideology.

Cressey, George B. *Land of the Five Hundred Million: A Geography of China.* New York: McGraw-Hill, 1955. Standard work.

Croizier, Ralph C., ed. *China's Cultural Legacy and Communism.* New York: Praeger, 1970. One of the few books which focuses on the continuity of China's cultural past to the present.

de Grazia, Sebastian, ed. *Masters of Chinese Political Thought.* New York: Viking Press, 1973. A collection of the writings of classical Chinese philosophers.

Durdin, Tillman; Reston, James; and Topping, Seymour. *New York Times Report From Red China.* Chicago: Quadrangle Books, 1971. (New York: Avon Books, 1972.) Life inside the People's Republic of China as described by three distinguished journalists.

Duyvendak, J. J. L., trans. *The Book of Lord Shang.* London: Arthur Probsthain, 1928. A helpful presentation of Legalism.

Editors of Horizon Magazine. *Arts of China.* New York: American Heritage, 1969.

Fairbank, John K. *The United States and China.* 3rd ed. Cambridge: Harvard University Press, 1971.

Fitzgerald, C. P., and Editors of Horizon Magazine. *The Horizon History of China.* New York: American Heritage, 1969.

Gasster, Michael. *China's Struggle to Modernize.* New York: Alfred A. Knopf, 1972. A brief introduction of the Chinese efforts to modernize from the beginning of the twentieth century to the present.

Giles, Herbert A. *A History of Chinese Literature.* New York: Grove Press, 1958.

Grandqvist, Hans. *The Red Guard.* Translated by Erik J. Fries. New York: Praeger, 1967. A Swedish observer looks closely at the Cultural Revolution in Communist China.

Hinton, Harold C. *An Introduction to Chinese Politics.* New York: Praeger, 1973. A helpful and clearly written book.

———. *China's Turbulent Quest: An Analysis of China's Foreign Relations Since 1949.* rev. ed. Bloomington: Indiana University Press, 1972. A subject of growing importance to Asia and the world.

Hinton, William. *Fanshen*. New York: Random House, Vintage Books, 1966. This is a case study of the restructuring of the social, economic, and political life of a poor Chinese village by early Communist cadres.

Ho, Ping-ti, and Tsou, Tang, eds. *China in Crisis*. vol. 1, books 1 and 2. Chicago: University of Chicago Press, 1968. A comprehensive look at Communist China and the events leading up to the Communist victory there.

Hous, Franklin W. *A Short History of Chinese Communism*. Englewood Cliffs, N.J.: Prentice-Hall, 1967. Good summary of the emergence and history of Chinese Communism to 1967.

Hsiao, Gene T., ed. *Sino-American Detente and Its Policy Implications*. New York: Praeger, 1974. The growing understanding between China and the United States is a matter of importance to the makers of foreign policies in Asia and the world.

Hsien Chin-hu. *The Common Descent Group in China and Its Functions*. New York: The Viking Fund, 1948. A comprehensive work on the clan in China.

Hsu, Francis. *Americans and Chinese*. New York: Abelard-Schuman, 1953. A provocative interpretation.

Hsu, Immanuel C. Y. *The Rise of Modern China*. New York: Oxford University Press, 1970. Solid comprehensive history of modern China.

Hsu, Kai-Yu. *Chou En-Lai*. New York: Doubleday, 1968. Biography of one of the more important Chinese Communist leaders.

Karnow, Stanley. *Mao and China*. New York: Viking Press, 1973. An excellent account of the Communist revolution in China with special attention paid to the Cultural Revolution which took place in the last half of the 1960s.

King, Frank H. H. *A Concise Economic History of Modern China*. New York: Praeger, 1969. Traces the economic history of China from 1840 to 1961. One of the few books of its kind.

Lee Shao-Chang. *Popular Buddhism in China*. Shanghai: The Commercial Press, 1939.

Legg, James, trans. *Four Books, Chinese Classics,* and *Hsiao Ching*. London: Oxford, 1893–1895. These classic translations of Chinese philosophers are most helpful sources of classical Chinese philosophies.

Levis, John H. *Foundations of Chinese Musical Art*. 2nd ed. New York: Paragon Book Reprint Corporation, 1963.

Levy, Marion. *The Family Revolution in Modern China*. Cambridge: Harvard University Press, 1949. Aspects of Chinese rural and social life.

Li, Dun J. *The Ageless Chinese: A History*. New York: Charles Scribner's Sons, 1965. Good one-volume history of China.

——, ed. The Essence of Chinese Civilization. New York: Van Nostrand-Reinhold Books, 1967. Traditional China as seen through translations of Chinese writings. Good paperback.

Liao, W. K., trans. *The Complete Works of Han Fei-tsu*. London: Arthur Probsthain, 1939.

MacInnis, Donald E. *Religious Policy and Practice in Communist China*. New York: Macmillan, 1972. A good treatment of the subject.

Mao Tse-tung. *Quotations From Chairman Mao*. Peking: Foreign Languages Press, 1966. The quotations of Chairman Mao best known to the Chinese people.

Melby, John F. *The Mandate of Heaven: Record of a Civil War, China 1945–49*. Toronto, Canada: University of Toronto Press, 1968. Interesting account of Civil War Period in China by an observer who was there.

Mote, Frederick W. *Intellectual Foundations of China*. New York: Alfred A. Knopf, 1971. A concise and clear account of the early thinking and philosophies of the Chinese.

Myrdal, Jan, and Kessle, Gun. *China: The Revolution Continued*. New York: Random

House, Vintage Books, 1972. The authors revisit a village they had studied and reported on in 1962.

Needham, Joseph. *Science and Civilization in China.* vols. 1,2,3,4. New York: Cambridge University Press.

Richman, Barry M. *Industrial Society In Communist China.* New York: Random House, Vintage Books, 1969. An in-depth study of an important sector of Chinese life today.

Ridley, Charles P.; Godwin, Paul H. B.; and Doolin, Dennis J. *The Making of a Model Citizen in Communist China.* Stanford, Calif.: Hoover Institution Press, 1971. The ultimate goal is to make the "New Communist Person."

Salisbury, Harrison E. *War Between Russia and China.* New York: W. W. Norton, 1969. The author is rather pessimistic about future harmonious relations between Russia and China, but he presents a graphic description of the Russian attitudes toward the Chinese.

Schram, Stuart. *Mao Tse-tung.* New York: Simon & Schuster, 1966. Critical and scholarly biography of Communist leader of China.

Schurmann, Franz, and Schell, Orville, eds. *The China Reader.* 3 vols. *Imperial China, Republican China, Communist China.* New York: Random House, Vintage Books, 1967. Fine overview of past and present of China through well-selected readings.

Snow, Edgar. *Red Star Over China.* New York: Random House, 1938. Classic about Mao and the Communists in Yennan. A revised edition was put out in paper back in 1968, by Grove Press, New York.

Sun Yat-sen. *Three Principles of the People.* Translated by Frank Price. London: Routledge and Kegan Paul, 1928. Gives valuable insight into the political thought of China.

Terril, Ross. *Eight Hundred Million: The Real China.* New York: Dell, 1972. Interesting and informative book on life of people in modern China.

Tsou, Tang, ed. *China in Crisis: China's Policies in Asia and America's Alternatives.* Chicago: University of Chicago Press, 1968. The book deals mostly with China's foreign policy.

Tuckman, Barbara W. *Stillwell and the American Experience in China.* New York: Bantam Books, 1972. Well-written book which provides a picture of China prior to and during World War II.

Tu Fu, China's Greatest Poet. Translation and commentary by William Hung. Cambridge: Harvard University Press, 1952. Poems by one of the world's greatest poets.

United States Senate, Committee on Government Operations (86th Congress, 1st session). *National Policy Machinery in Communist China.* Washington, D.C.: U.S. Government Printing Office, 1959.

Varg, Paul A. *The Making of a Myth: The United States and China 1897-1912.* East Lansing: Michigan State University Press, 1968. From around the turn of the century to modern times, the author believes that American foreign policy toward China was founded on "myths." Interesting book.

Vogel, Ezra. *Canton Under Communism: Programs and Politics in a Provincial Capital, 1949-1968.* Cambridge: Harvard University Press, 1969. The author discusses the communist programs and politics in Canton from 1949 to 1968. He stresses the organizational ability of the Chinese, and sees in this ability the success of the Communist leaders in bringing the masses into the political life of the country.

Waley, Arthur. *Three Ways of Thought in Ancient China.* London: George Allen and Unwin, 1936. A fine writer on Chinese philosophy.

Waller, Derek J. *The Government and Politics of Communist China.* New York: Doubleday, 1971. A concise and clear account of the contemporary structure and philosophy of government in China.

✗ Wang, C. C., trans. *Dream of the Red Chamber.* New York: Doubleday, 1929. A good translation of a classic Chinese novel which graphically portrays social life in traditional China.

Wilmott, W. E. *Economic Organization in Chinese Society.* Stanford, Calif.: Stanford University Press, 1972. A good work on this subject.

Wilson, Dick. *Anatomy of China. An Introduction to One Quarter of Mankind.* 2nd ed. New York: Mentor Books, 1969. A well-written survey of the People's Republic of China.

Wolf, Margery. *The House of Lim: A Study of a Chinese Farm Family.* New York: Appleton-Century-Crofts, 1968. An absorbing study of a Chinese farm family on Taiwan.

Korea

Brandt, Vincent S. R. *A Korean Village: Between Farm and Sea.* Cambridge, Mass.: Harvard University Press, 1972. To understand Korea, one must also understand Korean villages.

Chung, Kyung-Cho. *New Korea: New Land of the Morning Calm.* New York: Macmillan 1962. A Korean looks at this land.

Guttman, Allen, ed. *Korea and the Theory of Limited War.* Lexington, Mass.: D. C. Heath, 1967. Focuses on the issues raised by the Korean War.

Hen, Woo-keun. *The History of Korea.* Translated by Kyung-shik Lee. Edited by Grafton K. Mintz. Honolulu: East-West Center Press, 1972. Good solid work.

Kim Il-sung. *Revolution and Socialist Construction in Korea: Selected Writings of Kim Il-sung.* New York: International Publishers, 1971. Selected writings by the leader of North Korea.

Kim, Se-jin. *The Politics of Military Revolution in Korea.* Chapel Hill: University of North Carolina Press, 1971. Provides an understanding of the politics of the dominant force in Korean politics for many years.

Kim, Young C., ed. *Major Powers and Korea.* Silver Springs, Md.: Research Institute on Korean Affairs, 1973. Korea has long been influenced by major powers both near and far who have sought to influence the country's policies.

Kyung, Cho Chung. *Korea: The Third Republic.* New York: Macmillan, 1971.

McCune, Shannon. *Korea.* New York: Van Nostrand-Reinhold Books, 1966. Concise and clear introduction to the land and people of Korea.

Scalapino, Robert A., and Lee, Chong-sik. *Communism in Korea.* 2 vols. Berkeley: University of California Press, 1972. An extensive study of a subject of continuing importance to Korea and interested countries.

Japan

Beasley, W. G. *The Modern History of Japan.* New York: Praeger, 1963. History of Japan from the early nineteenth century to the early 1960s.

Befu, Harumi. *Japan: An Anthropological Introduction.* San Francisco: Chandler, 1971. A detailed analysis of Japan's cultural and social development.

Brzezinski, Zbigniew. *The Fragile Blossom: Crisis and Change in Japan.* New York: Harper & Row, 1972. Their rush to economic greatness has also rushed the Japanese to crises and changes.

Cole, Robert. *Japanese Blue Collar: The Changing Tradition.* Berkeley: University of California Press, 1971. Japan's industrialization and modernization is changing the environment and the attitudes and behavior of the people.

Dore, R. P. *City Life in Japan.* Berkeley: University of California Press, 1958. Japan is urbanizing rapidly. This is a study of a Tokyo ward.

Earhart, H. Byron. *Japanese Religion: Unity and Diversity.* Belmont, Calif.: Dickenson, 1969. A brief but excellent treatment of Japanese religions.

Embree, John. *Suye Mura: A Japanese Village.* Chicago: University of Chicago Press, 1939. An introduction to a traditional Japanese village.

Emmerson, John K. *Arms, Yen and Power: The Japanese Dilemma.* New York: Dunellen, 1971. Economic power is closely related to political power. The rise of the Japanese to great economic power raises vital questions about their future role in Asia, about an expanded military system, and other questions.

Gibney, Frank. *Five Gentlemen of Japan: The Portrait of a Nation's Character.* New York: Farrar, Straus & Giroux, 1953. An excellent general introduction.

Guillain, Robert. *The Japanese Challenge: Race to the Year Two Thousand.* Philadelphia: J. B. Lippincott, 1970. A perceptive French observer writes about the new powerful Japan and its future.

Hall, John Whitney, and Beardsley, Richard K. *Twelve Doors to Japan.* New York: McGraw-Hill, 1965. Introduction to Japanese culture and society.

Hane, Misako. *Japan: A Historical Survey.* New York: Charles Scribner's Sons, 1972. The title is descriptive.

Hearn, Lafcadio. *The Selected Writings of Lafcadio Hearn.* Edited by Henry Goodman. New York: The Citadel Press, 1949. Contains appealing descriptions of the Japanese people by a man who labored for many years to catch and convey their spirit and who loved them deeply.

Hellman, Donald C. *Japan and East Asia: The New International Order.* New York: Praeger, 1972. Discusses the various possibilities that confront Japanese policymakers in view of the contemporary political changes in East Asia.

Ishimoto, Baroness Shidzue. *Facing Two Ways: The Story of My Life.* New York: Farrar & Rinehart, 1935. Yields insight into the domestic life of the Japanese and the attitudes of the women of Japan.

Kajima, Morinosuke. *A Brief Diplomatic History of Modern Japan.* Rutland, Vt.: Charles E. Tuttle, 1965. A concise comprehensive account of Japan's foreign affairs from around 1868 to 1965.

Keene, Donald, ed. *The Anthology of Japanese Literature.* New York: Grove Press, 1955.

Langdon, Frank. *Politics in Japan.* Boston: Little, Brown, 1967. Emphasis on behavior of those performing political roles, what they do, rather than what they are supposed to do.

Langer, Paul F. *Communism in Japan.* Stanford, Calif.: Hoover Institution Press, 1972. A Comprehensive look at Communism in Japan.

MacArthur, Douglas. *Reminiscences.* New York: McGraw-Hill, 1964. The autobiography of a general who ruled Japan during the American occupation of Japan.

Malm, William P. *Japanese Music and Musical Instruments.* Rutland, Vt.: Charles E. Tuttle, 1959. An introduction to the music of Japan.

Mears, Helen. *Year of the Wild Boar.* Philadelphia: J. B. Lippincott, 1942. Warm glimpses of the family and daily life of Japan and of the Japanese woman.

Meyer, Milton W. *Japan: A Concise History.* Boston: Allyn & Bacon, 1966. Brief and clear presentation in 226 pages.

Michener, James A. *The Floating World.* New York: Random House, 1954. An interesting treatment of Japanese prints.

Morley, James William. *Forecast for Japan: Security in the 1970s.* Princeton, N.J.: Princeton University Press, 1972. A selection of readings looking toward Japan's future in this decade.

Reischauer, Edwin O. *Japan: The Story of a Nation.* rev. ed. New York: Alfred A. Knopf, 1970. An excellent general introduction to the history and people of Japan.

Sansom, G. B. *Japan: A Short Cultural History.* rev. ed. New York: Appleton-Century-Crofts, 1962. Excellent one-volume study.

Seidensticker, Edward, and the Editors of *Life. Japan.* New York Times, 1961. A beautifully illustrated and sensitively written introduction to Japan.

Statler, Oliver. *Japanese Inn.* New York: Pyramid Books, 1961. An unusual look at the people and life of the Japanese through the history of an inn.

Tsuneishi, Warren M. *Japanese Political Style.* New York: Harper & Row, 1966. Introduction to government and politics of modern Japan.

Yoshino, M. Y. *Japan's Managerial System: Tradition and Innovation.* Cambridge, Mass.: M.I.T. Press, 1971. Provides a good insight into a subject which is receiving more attention by both Japanese and foreign observers.

Southeast Asia

Allen, Richard. *A Short Introduction to the History and Politics of Southeast Asia.* New York: Oxford University Press, 1970. A clear overall introduction to the region.

Bain, Chester A. *Vietnam: Roots of Conflict.* Englewood Cliffs, N.J.: Prentice-Hall, 1967. Good brief survey of history of Vietnam.

Benda, Harry J., and Larkin, John A. *The World of Southeast Asia.* New York: Harper & Row, 1967. The authors use historical readings to present the reader with graphic and discerning descriptions of the past and present of Southeast Asia.

Benitez, Conrado. *History of the Philippines: Economic, Social, Cultural, Political.* rev. ed. New York: Ginn & Co., 1954. General introduction to the Philippines.

Bloodworth, Dennis. *An Eye for the Dragon: Southeast Asia Observed.* New York: Lancer Books, 1970. Southeast Asia through the eyes and experiences of an excellent journalist.

Brachman, Arnold C. *The Communist Collapse in Indonesia.* New York: W. W. Norton, 1969. Discussion of a turning point in modern Indonesian history.

Burling, Robbins. *Hill Farms and Padi Fields: Life in Mainland Southeast Asia.* Englewood Cliffs, N.J.: Prentice-Hall, 1965. An anthropologist writes about the cultures, societies, and peoples of mainland Southeast Asia.

Busch, Noel. *Thailand: An Introduction to Modern Siam.* New York: Van Nostrand-Reinhold Books, 1959. Brief survey of the land and people.

Cady, John F. *A History of Modern Burma.* Ithaca: Cornell University Press, 1958. An informed author.

———. *Southeast Asia: Its Historical Development.* New York: McGraw-Hill, 1964. Detailed and solid historical study of the region from early times.

Champassak, Sisouk. *Storm Over Laos: A Contemporary History.* New York: Praeger, 1961.

Coedès, G. *The Making of Southeast Asia.* Translated by H. M. Wright. Berkeley: University of California Press, 1966. An excellent presentation of the early cultural life and history of the mainland Southeast Asians.

DuBois, Cora. *Social Forces in South-East Asia.* Cambridge, Mass.: Harvard University Press, 1959. Social life and social change in Southeast Asia.

Fall, Bernard B., ed. *Ho Chi Minh On Revolution.* New York: Praeger, 1967. Selected writings of most famous modern Vietnamese leader from 1920 to 1966.

Fall, Dorothy, ed. *Last Reflections on a War: Bernard B. Fall on Vietnam.* New York: Schocken Books, 1972. The late Bernard Fall was regarded as one of the foremost authorities on the Vietnam War.

Fenichel, A. H., and Huff, W. G. *The Impact of Colonialism on Burmese Economic Development.* Montreal: McGill University, Center for Developing-Area Studies, 1972. Very brief survey.

Fifield, Russell J. *The Diplomacy of South-East Asia: 1945-1958.* New York: Harper & Row, 1958.

Golay, Frank H., *et al. Underdevelopment and Economic Nationalism in Southeast Asia.* Ithaca: Cornell University Press, 1970. Discusses the real economic problems of the region.

Gordon, Bernard K. *The Dimensions of Conflict in Southeast Asia.* Englewood, N.J.: Prentice-Hall, 1966. The author discusses the broad range of conflicting interests among the nations of Southeast Asia, and the prospects for stability there.

Hall, E. G. B. *A History of South-East Asia.* New York: St. Martin's Press, 1955. A good general history.

Herz, Martin F. *A Short History of Cambodia.* New York: Praeger, 1958. A brief introduction to this country.

Hicks, George L., and McNicoll, G. *Trade and Growth in the Philippines: An Open Dual Economy.* Ithaca: Cornell University Press, 1971.

Holt, Claire. *Art in Indonesia: Continuities and Change.* Ithaca: Cornell University Press, 1967. The past and the present in Indonesian art.

Hughes, John. *Indonesian Upheaval.* New York: David McKay, 1967. Excellent account of events between October, 1965 and March, 1966, resulting in decimation of Communist Party, fall of Sukarno, and dominance of military in Indonesia.

Ingram, James C. *Economic Change in Thailand, 1850-1970.* Stanford, Calif.: Stanford University Press, 1971. A look at over a century of change in the economic life of the people.

Jacobs, Norman. *Modernization Without Development: Thailand as an Asian Case Study.* New York: Praeger, 1971. Many of his findings could be applied to other Southeast Asian countries.

Koentjaraningrat, ed. *Village Communities in Contemporary Indonesia.* New York: Paragon, 1966. Villages remain a most important part of Indonesia.

Lacouture, Jean. *Vietnam Between Two Truces.* New York: Random House, Vintage Books, 1966. A perceptive French observer writes about Vietnam.

McAlister, John T., and Mus, Paul. *The Vietnamese and Their Revolution.* New York: Harper & Row, Torchbooks, 1970. A perceptive look at the origins and development of the Vietnamese revolution.

Milne, R. S. *Government and Politics in Malaysia.* Boston: Houghton Mifflin, 1967. Good political treatment.

Moerman, Michael. *Agricultural Change and Peasant Choice in a Thai Village.* Berkeley: University of California Press, 1968. One cannot discuss agriculture in a practical way in Asia without discussing the attitudes and values of the peasants.

Morgan, Theodore, and Spoelstra, Nyle, eds. *Economic Interdependence in Southeast Asia.* Madison: University of Wisconsin Press, 1969. Many are proposing a Common Market for Southeast Asia as one of the solutions to their economic problems.

Nitisastro, Widjojo. *Population Trends in Indonesia.* Ithaca: Cornell University Press, 1970. An important topic for most Asian nations.

Pearson, Harold F. *A History of Singapore.* London: University of London Press, 1956. A quick but useful look at Singapore.

The Pentagon Papers. New York: Bantam Books, 1971. Government documents covering U.S. involvement in Vietnam from around the middle 1950s to around the middle 1960s.

Pike, Douglas. *Viet Cong: The Organization and Techniques of the National Liberation Front of South Vietnam.* Cambridge, Mass.: M.I.T. Press, 1966. The classic work on this subject.

Purcell, Victor. *The Chinese in Malaya.* London: Oxford University Press., 1948. The great bulk of Malaya's population is divided between the Malays and the Chinese. *See* Winstedt below.

Pye, Lucian W. *Southeast Asia's Political Systems.* rev. ed. Englewood Cliffs, N.J.: Prentice-Hall, 1974. Fine treatment of the political organization in various countries.

Raskin, Marcus G., and Fall, Bernard B., eds. *The Vietnam Reader.* New York: Random House, Vintage Books, 1965. Large selection of articles and documents on American foreign policy and the Vietnam crisis.

Ravenholt, Albert. *The Philippines: A Young Republic on the Move.* New York: Van Nostrand-Reinhold Books, 1962. A brief introduction to the land and people.

Shaplen, Robert. *Revolution and Reaction in Southeast Asia.* New York: Harper & Row, 1969. Good contemporary historical overview of entire area.

Simon, Sheldon W. *War and Politics in Cambodia.* Durham, N.C.: Duke University Press, 1974. One of the few books on this subject.

Skinner, G. William. *Leadership and Power in the Chinese Community of Thailand.* Ithaca: Cornell University Press, 1967. An important minority in Thailand who have long controlled directly or indirectly the economy of the country.

Steinberg, David Joel, ed. *In Search of Southeast Asia: A Modern History.* New York: Praeger, 1971. A selection of readings focusing mostly on the contemporary history of the region.

Thompson, Virginia. *Thailand: The New Siam.* New York: Macmillan, 1941. An older work on the prewar period in Thailand which is still useful.

Tilman, Robert O., ed. *Man, State, and Society in Contemporary Southeast Asia.* New York: Praeger, 1969. The selected articles cover a broad range of topics: geography, tradition, change, education, politics, ideology, economics, and national and international policies, among others.

Vandenbosch, Amry, and Butwell, Richard. *The Changing Face of Southeast Asia.* Lexington: University of Kentucky Press, 1967. An overview of the changing character of Southeast Asia.

Vasil, R. K. *Politics in a Plural Society: A Study of Non-Communal Political Parties in West Malaysia.* London: Oxford University Press, 1971.

Vlekke, Bernard H. M. *Nusantara: A History of Indonesia.* rev. ed. Chicago: Quadrangle Books, 1960. A solid history of this country.

Vo-Nguyen Giap. *People's War People's Army.* New York: Praeger, 1962. The Minister of Defense and Commander in Chief of North Vietnam's army presents his techniques for insurrections.

Wilson, David A. *The United States and the Future of Thailand.* New York: Praeger, 1970. A noted authority treats a question requiring continuous evaluation of both countries.

Windstedt, Sir Richard. *The Malays: A Cultural History.* rev. ed. London: Routledge and Kegan Paul, 1950. For the Chinese in Malay, see Purcell above.

Wit, Daniel. *Thailand: Another Vietnam?* New York: Charles Scribner's Sons, 1968. Stresses political heritage and system in Thailand.

Woodman, Dorothy. *The Making of Burma.* London: Cresset Press, 1962. A fine survey of Burma.

———. *The Republic of Indonesia.* New York: Philosophical Library, 1955. A comprehensive work on this country.

Wright, L. R. *The Origins of British Borneo.* London: Oxford University Press, 1971. A good history of a little-known part of Southeast Asia.

Zacher, Mark W., and Milne, R. Stephen, eds. *Conflict and Stability in Southeast Asia.* New York: Doubleday, Anchor Books, 1974. An informative work which concentrates on the primary political problems of the Southeast Asians.

Periodicals (Selected List)

American Universities Field Staff
Asia
Asian Studies
Asian Survey
China Quarterly
Current History
Far Eastern Economic Review
Foreign Affairs
India Quarterly
International Affairs (London)
Journal of Asian Studies
Journal of Southeast Asian History
Journal of the American Oriental Society (New Haven, Conn.)
Journal of the Royal Asiatic Society
Journal of the Royal Asiatic Society, Malayan Branch (Singapore)

index

Abraham, 139, 140, 143, 145, 147, 149, 151
acupuncture, 35
adat, 331
agriculture, 27-32, 153, 187; castes, 91; cattle, 29-30, 315; crops, 32, 45, 136, 315; problems, 29; tools, 45, 48
Agung, Ide, 359
Akbar, 126, 133
Alcock, John, 303
Ali, Rahmat, 134
Amaterasu, 259, 262-263
Americans and Chinese (HSU), 168
Amitabha Buddha, 80, 162, 192-193
Analects, 165, 171
ancestor worship: China, 164, 211-213, 214-215, 216; India, 103
animism, 321, 326
Arab oil embargo, 310
architecture: China, 194; Japan, 11, 156; Muslim, 61, 132-133, 327-328; village, 41-43
arhat, 322
Arnold, Edwin, 72
artisans, 41, 45; and caste system, 44, 96-97; in China, 188, 201
Aryans, 89-90, 119-120
Ashikaga family, 301, 302
Asoka, Emperor, 67, 84, 123-124
asramas, 75
astrology, 105
Atharvaveda, 69
Atman, 71

Australia, 353
Avalokitesvara, 193
Awami League, 137

Babur, 126
Bahrain, 119
bakufu, 302
Bali, 25-26, 326
Baluchis, 136
Bandaranaike, Mrs. Sirimavo, 60
Bangkok, 37, 316
Bangladesh, 131, 132, 135-136, 352, 359; birth rate, 27; formation, 137; religion, 54, 84, 316
Bengalis, 136, 137
Bhagavad-Gita, 69
Bhutto, Zulfikar Ali, 137
Bodhisattva, 191-192, 193
Bombay, 35, 37
Bombay Divorce Act of 1947, 106
Book of Changes, 164-165
Book of Documents, 164, 165
Book of Lord Shang, 183
Book of Poetry, 164, 165
Book of Rites, 165
Brahamas, 69
Brahma, 70
Brahman, 71, 72
Brahmaputra River, 25, 135-136
Brahmins, 66, 74, 90, 91, 95, 97, 121, 123, 335
Brahmo Samaj, 127-128

British Commonwealth of Nations, 60, 127
Brunei, 315
Buddha, Gautama, 78–79, 81, 83–84, 122, 192
Buddhism, 3, 132; and China, 54, 61, 84, 157, 161–174, 190–197; and Confucianism, 194; doctrine, 81–85; and Hinduism, 79, 83, 84; and India, 65, 67, 78–85; and Japan, 84, 259–260, 270–273, 298–299; literature, 80, 194; and politics, 310, 325; and Shintoism, 267, 272–273; in Southeast Asia, 4, 316, 318–319, 322–326; spread of, 67, 84–85; and Taoism, 182, 193–194; in West, 11; *see also* Mahayana Buddhism; Theravada Buddhism; Zen Buddhism
Burma, 25, 30, 341, 344, 352, 360; birth rate, 27; life expectancy, 33; religion, 80, 84, 321, 322–326
Bushido, 258–260, 305

Calcutta, 37, 136
California gold strikes, 16
Cambodia, 25, 343–344, 346, 352, 360; life expectancy, 33; religion, 321, 322–326
Canton, 37, 41
caste system, 66, 87, 89–100, 133; councils, 98–99; and eating, 94–96; and education, 97–98; and family, 101–102; and Hinduism, 74–75, 89; laws, 98–99; and marriage, 92–94, 98, 104, 105, 115; and occupation, 44, 96–98; in villages, 44
Celebes, 341
Ceylon: *see* Sri Lanka
Ch'an Buddhism, 271
Chandragupta Maurya, 122–123
Chandragupta II, 125
Chandrasekhar, S., 113
Ch'ang-an, 231, 299
Charles Martel, 145
Chiang Kai-shek, 157, 215, 233, 235, 248
Chi'in Dynasty, 161, 164, 184, 188–189, 230
Child Marriage Acts, 104
children, 220; adoption, 278–279; health, 33–34, 219; in India, 106–107, 119; in Japan, 278–280, 284, 294; in Southeast Asia, 333
China, 3; agriculture, 30, 32, 153, 239, 246–247; area, 25, 155; art, 156, 194; cities, 199–200, 201–202; clans, 209–216; education, 172, 199, 213, 220, 231; emperor, 157, 161, 170, 171, 184–185, 203, 204, 230, 235; family, 171–173, 175, 217–227; gentry, 198–200,

(China, *cont.*)
202–204, 206–207, 220; and India, 157; and Islam, 316; and Japan, 2–3, 155–156, 266–267, 297, 298–300, 311; and Korea, 4, 155–156; land reform, 239, 241; marriage, 196, 203, 221–222, 224–226; medicine, 35; peasants, 200–202, 205–306, 207–208, 220–221, 242; philosophy, 158–161, 162, 229, *see also* Confucianism, Legalism, Taoism; politics, 202–206, 228–249; population, 25, 37, 153, 155; religion, 54, 61, 84–85, 138, 157, 161–162, 190–197, *see also* Buddhism; Republic, 157, 164, 199, 215, 229, 233, 249; rivers, 25; science and technology, 156–157; and Southeast Asia, 328, 341, 345, 346; and US, 16, 248–249; and West, 5, 17, 157, 232–234, 237; women, 196, 221–223; *see also* People's Republic of China
Ch'ing-Meng festival, 213
Cho-son: *see* Korea
Chou Dynasty, 159, 165, 229, 230
Chou En-lai, 224, 249
Christianity, 84, 127, 132, 328–329; and Islam, 139–140, 147, 328
"'Chronicles of Japan," 261
Chu Hsi, 173, 174, 212
Chuang Tzu, 176, 177, 181, 182
Ch'un Ch'iu, 165
Chung Yung, 165–166
Circles, Doctrine of, 124–125
cities, 37–38, 195–196; ancient, 119; China, 199–200, 201–202; India, 37, 87, 88, 119; Japan, 37, 294–295; population, 37; Southeast Asia, 316, 332, 325
civil disobedience, 123
clans, 209–216, 252, 259–260, 297–298, 318
Classic of Songs, 164
clothing, 45, 48, 156, 226, 292–293
Cochin-China, 347
"Collection of a Myriad Leaves," 261
colonialism, 4, 5, 61, 127–128, 351, 358–359
concubinage, 93
Confucianism, 3, 54, 158, 161, 163–175; and Buddhism 194; and ceremony, 169–171; doctrine, 166–173, 188, 234, 235; and family, 171–173, 175, 218; and Japan, 155–156, 259, 260, 272; literature, 164–166; and politics, 230, 231–232; and Southeast Asia, 316, 321, 328; and Taoism, 164, 169, 174, 212; and US, 14–15
congee, 30
Congress Party (India), 60, 129–130, 134

Cousins, Norman, 7
Cressey, George B., 21

Dacca, 136
daimyo, 303–304, 306
debt, 29, 47, 201
Delhi, 126
Democratic People's Republic of Korea:
    see North Korea
Dhammapada, 80
dharma, 75–76, 124
Diem, Ngo Dinh, 347
divorce, 55, 106, 141, 225–226, 293–294,
    335
Doctrine of the Mean, 165–166
dowries, 104, 105, 221–222
Dravidians, 120
Dutt, G.S., 108

East Pakistan, 59, 132; *see also* Bangladesh
Edo, 304
education, 36–37, 355; and caste system,
    97–98; in China, 172, 199, 213, 220,
    231; and democracy, 338; in India, 88,
    125, 128; in Japan, 36, 279, 294, 307–
    308; and women 55, 88, 110–111, 114,
    115–116, 290–291; *see also* teachers
Eisenhower, Dwight D., 348
Ekken, Kaibara, 280
elections, 56, 238, 298, 355–356
Emerson, Gertrude, 42
Engishiki, 261
environmental pollution, 37

Fa-Hsien, 125, 194
family, 40, 55; in China, 171–173, 175,
    217–227; in India, 87, 101–107, 111–
    113, 116; in Japan, 274–275; and mod-
    ernization, 116, 223–227; in Southeast
    Asia, 316, 332–334; *see also* joint family
    system
famine, 10, 29, 33, 219, 330, 354
feng shui, 212
festivals, 31, 201, 207, 213, 258, 265,
    267, 323, 325, 329
feudalism, 159–160, 229–230, 301–305
Five Classics, 164–165
Five Gentlemen of Japan (Gibney), 10
Floating World, The (Michener), 10
food, 27–32, 45; and religion, 94–95
Ford, Gerald, 249
Four Books, 164, 165–166
Four Noble Truths, 82–83
France, 5, 127, 325, 346, 348
Freedom Party (Sri Lanka), 60
Front for the Liberation of South Vietnam,
    347
Fujisama, 264

Fijiwara family, 301, 303
funerals, 29, 31, 47, 201, 207, 281, 323

Gandhi, Indira, 60, 116, 129–130
Gandi, Mahatma, 40, 66, 77, 87, 112, 114,
    118
Ganges River, 25, 59, 96, 119, 135
Germany, 5
Giap, General, 347
Gibney, Frank, 10
Goa, 351, 358
Great Britain, 5, 61, 348, 353; and India,
    58–59, 118, 121, 127, 128–129, 134
Great Learning, 165
Great Learning for Women, 280, 286
Great Proletarian Cultural Revolution,
    196, 247–248
Greco-Roman culture, 61–62
Greece, 15
Guptas, 122, 125–126
Gyogi, 267

Hagar, 143
Han Dynasty, 164, 172, 189, 230
Han Fei-Tzu, 183, 185
Han River, 251
Han Yu, 173
Hanoi, 346
Harappa, 118
Harsha, 125
Hayashi, Fumiko, 287
health problems, 29, 32–35, 219
Hearn, Lafcadio, 287–288
Hideyoshi, Toyotomi, 304
Hijra, 145
Hinayana Buddhism, 80; *see also*
    Theravada Buddhism
Hindu Code Bill, 106
Hinduism, 3, 68–77; art, 61; and Buddhism,
    79, 83, 84; doctrine, 70–71, 89, 94–96,
    120, 124; and India, 54, 66–67, 84,
    127–128, 131–132; and Indonesia, 316;
    literature, 69; and marriage, 105, 106;
    and Sri Lanka, 59; tolerance, 124
Hirohito, 295, 298, 308
Ho Chih Minh, 346, 347
Hojo family, 302, 303
Hokkaido, 153, 255
Holland, 5; colonies, 60, 127, 358
Hong Kong, 35, 37, 227
Honshu, 25, 255, 297
housing, 40–44
Hsien Chin Hu, 209
Hsu, Francis, L.K., 168
Hsuan-tsang, 194
Hunzas, 136
hypergamy, 93

I Ching, 164–165, 174
Ieyasu, Tokugawa, 301
India, 58, 61, 358; agriculture, 32; area, 25; art, 125, 132–133; birth rate, 27; castes, 44, 89–100; and Ceylon, 3; children, 106–107, 119; and China, 157; cities, 37, 87, 88, 119; culture, 65–67; diet, 33, 94–96; education, 88, 125, 128; family, 87, 101–107, 111–113, 116; government, 121–122, 123, 129–130; houses, 42, 43, 119; and Islam, 126–127, 131–134, 138–139, 147; law, 128; literacy, 36; marriage, 92–94, 98, 103–106, 111; nationalism, 99–100, 123, 128–129; and Pakistan, 2, 359; politics, 56, 117–130, 352; population, 25, 37; religion, 54, 66–67, 119, 123, 127–128, *see also* Buddhism, Hinduism, Islam; and Southeast Asia, 322, 341; and Soviet Union, 64, 248, 352; villages, 39, 42, 44, 46, 105, 121–122; women, 88, 108–116
India's War Propaganda Against Pakistan, 359
Indonesia, 315, 331, 352, 358; area, 25–26; birth rate, 27; religion, 54, 138, 321, 326–328
Indus Valley Civilization, 118–119
industrialization, 55, 355; and agriculture, 31; Japan, 32, 307–308; and social customs, 96; and women, 115–116
infant mortality, 34
Irrawaddy River Delta, 25
Isaac, 143
Isaiah, 139, 143
Ise, 264
Ishimoto, Shidzue, 280
Ishmael, 143, 145
Islam, 3, 54, 138–150; architecture, 61, 132–133, 327–328; doctrine, 146–151; five pillars of, 148–151; history, 143–145; in India, 126–127, 131–134, 138–139; in Indonesia, 319, 321, 326–328; and Pakistan, 3, 84, 127; tolerance, 139–140; women, 133, 140–141
Ito Hirobumi, 307
Izanagi, 262
Izanami, 262

Jainism, 66, 123
Jakarta, 25, 37, 316
Japan: area, 153, 255; art, 11; birth rate, 27; and China, 2–3, 155–156, 266–267, 297, 298–300, 311; cities, 37, 294–295; Constitution, 287, 293–294, 296, 307, 308–309; education, 36, 279, 294, 307–308; emperor, 258, 263, 268, 275, 295, 298, 304, 306; family, 274–275; industrialization, 32, 307–308; and

(Japan, *cont.*)
Korea, 4, 155, 251, 254, 289, 298–299, 311; life expectancy, 33, 34; literacy, 36; marriage, 277–278, 279, 280; medicine, 35; modernization, 281–285; nationalism, 358; Occupation, 15, 293, 297, 308–309, 311; politics, 56, 296–312; population, 37, 153; religion, 84, 85, 257–273, 290, 298, *see also* Buddhism, Shintoism; and Southeast Asia, 360; trade, 309–310; and West, 293, 306–307; women, 286–295
Japan Past and Present (Reischauer), 303
Japanese Americans, 19
Java, 25–26
jen, 166–167, 168, 185
Jesus, 139, 140, 143, 147
Jews, 139, 143, 147
jihad, 140
Jimmu Tenno, 263
Jingo, 289
Jinnah, Mohammad Ali, 131, 134
Johnson, Lyndon B., 348–349
joint family system, 55, 87–88, 102–103, 218–219, 316

Kaaba, 145, 151
kachchi food, 94–95
Kagoshima, 305
Kalidasa, 101
Kamakura shogunate, 302, 303
Kanarese, 120
Karachi, 25, 37, 118
Karens, 341
karma, 73, 74–75, 76, 81–82
Kennedy, John F., 348
Khadija, 142
Khan, Yahya, 137
Kim Il Sung, 253, 254
Kipling, Rudyard, 11
Kojiki, 261–263
kokai, 37
Komeito Party (Japan), 310
Koran, 139, 140, 141–142, 143–144, 145–146, 147, 148, 149
Korea, 250–254; agriculture, 153, 253; and China, 4, 155–156; industry, 253–254; and Japan, 4, 155, 251, 254, 289, 298–299, 311; population, 251, 253; religion, 190; and Soviet Union, 251, 252; *see also* North Korea, South Korea
Kshatriya caste, 74, 91
Kuala Lumpur, 344
Kuan Tzu, 183
Kuan-yin, 162, 192, 193
Kun Fu-tzu: *see* Confucius
Kuomintang, 205, 233, 238–239
Kwangtung, 41, 210, 214

Kyoto, 297, 302
Kyushu Island, 25, 255, 263, 304

labor unions, 60
Lahore, 37
Lao Tzu, 176–177, 182
Laos, 321, 322, 326, 332, 344, 345, 351, 352, 360
law: and caste system, 98–99, and marriage, 104, 105, 284; and women, 55
law of fishes, 120
Legalism, 159, 163–164, 168, 183–189; and Confucianism, 188; doctrine, 161, 181, 184–188, 230
li, 169–170
Li Chi, 165, 169–170
Liberal Democratic Party (Japan), 309, 310
life expectancy, 33, 318
Light of Asia, The (Arnold), 72
Lincoln, Abraham, 14, 15
literacy, 36–37, 355
Liu Shao-chi, 196
Lothal, 119
Lu, 165

Macao, 37
Madras, 37
Madura, 25–26
Magayasay, Ramón, 340
Mahabharatas, 69, 73, 117
Mahayana Buddhism, 80, 162, 191–193, 267, 271; in Southeast Asia, 321, 322–323, 326, 328
Maina Canon, 116
Malayalam, 120
Malaysia, 54, 56, 315, 341, 353, 360; Chinese in, 341, 344; religion, 84, 138, 321
Maldives, 58
Manchuria, 250–251, 297
Manchus, 234
Mandate of Heaven, 173, 229, 234
Manila, 35
Mantras, 69
Manu, Law of, 69, 89, 113
Manyoshu, 261, 289
Mao Tse-tung, 157, 196, 224, 226, 235–236, 249; quotations, 229, 240, 241–245
marriage: and caste system, 92–94, 98, 104, 105, 115; child, 104; in China, 196, 203, 221–222, 224–226; contracts, 55, 317; India, 103–106, 111; and Islam, 141–142; Japan, 277–278, 279, 280; laws, 104, 105, 113
Maurya Dynasty, 67, 121, 122–125
Mears, Helen, 274, 288

Mecca, 142, 143, 144–145, 149, 151
medicine, 34–35
Medina, 139, 145
Mekong River, 25, 346
Mencius, 165, 174, 198, 212, 217
Michener, James A., 10
military class, 74, 91, 124, 136; in Japan, 258–260, 272, 310–302, 305–306, 355
Minamoto family, 301, 302
Mindanao, 328
Ming Dynasty, 231
minority conflicts, 341–343
Mirza, Iskander, 135
Mohenjo-Daro, 118
moneylenders, 46–47, 91
Mongolian People's Republic, 153–155
Mongols, 5, 126, 153–155, 232
monsoons, 60, 61, 136, 315
Moraes, Frank, 17
moxa, 35
Mughal Empire, 126, 132–133, 136
Muhammed, 139, 142–146
Muslim League, 134
Muslims: see Islam

Nakatomi clan, 260
Nalanda University, 125
Nalini, Saroj, 110
Nara, 267, 299
nat, 321
nationalism, 4, 358; China, 208, 236–237; India, 99–100, 123, 128–129; and Southeast Asia, 318
Nationalist China, 197, 215, 233, 234, 242, 359
nationalization, 60, 239–240
Nehru, Jawaharlal, 14, 114, 129, 351, 356
Nehru, Madame Pandit, 14
Neo-Confucianism, 173–174
Nepal, 58
nepotism, 339–340
New Delhi, 25, 120
New Guinea, 358
New Zealand, 353
Nihon-shoki, 261–263
Ninigi-no-Mikoto, 263
Nippon, 255
Nirvana, 83, 191, 322, 324
Nixon, Richard M., 249, 349, 350
Noble Eightfold Path, 82, 83–84
Nobunaga, Oda, 304
nonalignment, 352
North Korea, 251, 253–254

Okinawa, 248, 249
O-mi-t'o: see Amitabha Buddha
"Origin of Rites," 261
Osaka, 37

Pakistan, 58, 131–137, 352; birth rate, 27; cities, 37; Constitution, 131, 135; history, 134–137; and India, 2, 359; population, 132; religion, 3, 84, 127, 131–132, 134–135, 316
pakki food, 95
Pali, 78, 80, 123
panchayat, 121, 122
pao chia system, 232, 234–235
Park, Chung Hee, 252–254
Parsis, 132
Pathans, 136
Pathet Lao, 351
Peking, 25, 35, 37
People's Liberation Army, 196
People's Republic of China, 31, 215–216, 229; agriculture, 32, 241, 246–247; and Buddhism, 85; family, 223–227, government, 245–249; industrialization, 31, 246; and Japan, 311; and Southeast Asia, 319; and Soviet Union, 247, 248; and US. 248–249
Perry, Mathew C., 305
Persian culture, 126, 132–133, 136
phi, 321
Philippines, 315, 332, 340, 344; birth rate, 27; education, 36; religion, 84, 138, 316, 341; and US, 14, 15, 248, 352
plantation system, 32
polygamy, 141–142
Pondicherry, 61
population, 25, 37, 153, 155
Portugal, 5; colonies, 60, 127, 351
Prajnaparamitas, 80
professional group, 199, 334
Punjabis, 136
Puranas, 69
purdah, 114, 115
Pyongyang, 251, 254

racial equality, 133, 143, 173, 356
Rahman, Sheikh Mujibur, 137
Rahula, 79
Rajputs, 91
Ramadan, 150–151
Ramayana, 69, 109, 327
Ranade, Ramabai, 109–110
Rangoon, 316
Razak, Tun Abdul, 353
"Record of Ancient Things," 261
Record of Rituals, 165
Red Guards, 196, 247–248
Red River, 331, 345
Reischauer, Edwin O., 303
religious toleration, 123–124, 135, 137, 324, 328, 329
Republic of Korea: see South Korea
Rhee, Syngman, 252

rice, 30, 61, 136, 315; shops, 200
Rigveda, 68, 69
Roosevelt, Franklin D., 14
Roy, Ram Mohan, 114, 127–128

Sabah, 315, 344, 360
Saddharmapundarika, 80
Saigo family, 259–260
Saigon, 316
Sakyas, 122
Samaveda, 69
Samiti, 120–121
samurai, 258–259, 281, 305
sannyasin, 75
Sanskrit, 80
Sarah, 143
Sarawak, 315
Satyavan, 109
Savitri, 109
scheduled castes, 44, 91
Seoul, 25, 254
Shang Dynasty, 159, 229
Shang Shu, 164
Shang Yang, 183
Shanghai, 35, 37
shih, 185, 186
Shih Ching, 164
Shikoku Island, 25, 255
Shimonoseki, 305
Shin-shu, 271
Shintoism, 85, 261–269; and Buddhism, 267, 272; doctrine, 258, 259, 263–267; literature, 261–263; shrines, 18, 264, 265, 267; state, 268–269
shoguns, 302–305
Shotoku Taishi, 84, 270–271, 272, 299
shu, 186–187
Shu Ching, 164
Sikhism, 66
Sindhis, 136
Singapore, 37, 315, 344, 353; literacy, 36; politics, 56
Singhalese, 59
Sisaket, 325
Sita, 109, 327
Siva, 70
skandhas, 81–82
Smriti, 69
Soga family, 270
Sokagakkai, 273
South Africa, 19
South Korea, 15, 248, 251, 252, 359–360
Southeast Asia, 3, 4, 313–353; and China, 328, 341, 345, 346; cities, 316, 332, 335; family, 316, 332–334; politics, 337–353; religion, 320–329; villages, 330–331
Soviet Union, 343; and China, 247, 248,

(Soviet Union, *cont.*)
254; and India, 64, 248, 352; and Japan, 311; and Korea, 251, 252, 254; and Mongolia, 155; and Southeast Asia, 319, 345, 351
Spain, 5, 328
Spring and Autumn Annals, 165
Sraddha, 103
Sri Lanka, 3, 37, 59–60; diet, 33; religion, 80, 84
Sruti, 69
stupas, 61, 67
Sudra caste, 74, 91
Sui Dynasty, 231
Sukhavativyuha, 80
Sulu, 328
Sumatra, 341
Sumerian civilization, 119
Sun Yat-sen, 157, 164, 214, 228, 233, 236–239
Sung Dynasty, 210, 231, 232
Sunyata, 80
Susa-na-wo, 262–263
suttee, 128

Ta Hsüch, 165
Tadong River, 251
Tagore, Rabindranath, 99–100, 110
Taira family, 301, 302
Taiwan, 157, 205, 227, 359; agriculture, 153; and Japan, 311; literacy, 36; and US, 218, 249
Tamerlaine, 126
Tamils, 59, 120
Tang Chu, 176, 177
T'ang Dynasty, 157, 162, 167, 218, 231
Tantrism, 84
Tao Te Ching, 176–177, 181
Taoism, 3, 54, 84, 158, 176–182; and Buddhism, 182, 193–194; and Confucianism, 164, 169, 174, 212; doctrine, 161, 177–181; and Japan, 258; popular, 181–182; and Southeast Asia, 316, 321, 328
taxes, 121, 232, 240, 299, 300–301
Taylor, Maxwell, 348
teachers, 36–37, 202–203, 317–318, 324, 333
Teimei, 295
Telugu, 120
Thailand, 27, 30, 32, 344, 345, 346, 351, 352, 360; religion, 80, 84, 321, 322–326; and US, 248, 352
Tharus, 42
Theravada Buddhism, 59, 80, 193; in Southeast Asia, 321, 322–323
Three Principles of the People, 236–240
Tibet, 84, 193

Tientsin, 37
Times of India, 17
Ti-ts'ang, 192
Tokimasa, 302
Tokugawa, 260, 271, 280, 301, 304–305, 306
Tokyo, 25, 37, 306
Tongking, 345
Tours, Battle of, 145
Tripitaka, 80
Ts'inling Mountains, 153
Tu Fu, 167
Turkey, 15

United Nations, 249, 252, 351, 359
United States: attitudes toward, 2, 13–20; and China, 16, 248–249; colonialism, 3; life expectancy, 33; and Southeast Asia, 319, 345; and Vietnam, 248, 249, 347–350
untouchables, 87, 90, 121
Upanishads, 69, 71, 79
urbanization, 55, 96, 316
Urdu, 136

Vaisaya caste, 74, 91
Vajracchedika, 80
Vedas, 69, 79
Vedic period, 119–121
Viet Cong, 347, 348
Vietnam, 25, 344, 345–351, 360; religion, 328; and US, 248, 249, 347–350; war, 16, 249, 335–336, 347–351
villages, 39–48; and India, 39, 42, 43, 44, 46, 105, 121–122; politics, 121–122; social system, 40, 44–46; in Southeast Asia, 315–316, 330–331
Vishnu, 70
Voiceless India (Emerson), 42

Warring States Period, 161, 184
wat, 323–324
weddings, 29, 31, 46–47, 104–105, 207, 323
West Irian, 351, 358
West River, 25
Western influence, 5–6, 356, 358; in China, 5, 17, 157, 232–234, 237; and Japan, 293, 306–307; in Southeast Asia, 316, 319
widows, 112–113
Wilson, Woodrow, 14
women: changing attitudes, 55, 109–110, 114–116; China, 196, 221–223; and education, 55, 88, 110–111, 114, 115–116, 290–291; in home, 110–113; in India, 88, 108–116; and Islam, 133, 140–141; in Japan, 286–295; in politics, 60; rights, 114, 141, 224–115; in South-

(women, *cont.*)
    east Asia, 316–317, 334, 335; in villages,
      39–40, 45, 46
Wu, Emperor, 189
Wuhan, 37

Yajurveda, 69
Yama, 109
Yamato clan, 259, 262, 263, 266–267,
    297–299

Yangtze River, 25, 30
Yellow River, 25
yin and yang, 266
Yoritomo, 302
Yuan Dynasty, 231, 232
Yuan Shih-k'ai, 233

zaibatsu, 307
Zen Buddhism, 18, 259, 270, 271–273